Education, Religion and Creativity

Modernization, Globalization and Social Transformation

Edited by: ISHWAR MODI

Titles in this series:

Volume 1	Modernization, Globalization and Social Transformation
Volume 2	Education, Religion and Creativity
Volume 3	Polity, Civil Society and Development
Volume 4	Gender, Identity and Multiple Marginalities

Modernization, Globalization and Social Transformation

Education, Religion and Creativity

Essays in Honour of Professor Yogendra Singh

Edited by
Ishwar Modi

RAWAT PUBLICATIONS
Jaipur • New Delhi • Bangalore • Hyderabad • Guwahati

ISBN 978-81-316-0571-4

Published by
Prem Rawat for **Rawat Publications**
Satyam Apts, Sector 3, Jawahar Nagar, Jaipur 302 004 (India)
Phone: 0141 265 1748/7006 Fax: 0141 265 1748
E-mail: info@rawatbooks.com
Website: www.rawatbooks.com

New Delhi Office
4858/24, Ansari Road, Daryaganj, New Delhi 110 002
Phone: 011 2326 3290

Also at *Bangalore, Hyderabad* and *Guwahati*

Typeset by Rawat Computers, Jaipur
Printed at Chaman Enterprises, New Delhi

Contents

Introduction vii

Contributors xix

Part I: Education

1 Higher Education in 'Global' India: The Need for Critical Sociology 3
Maitrayee Chaudhuri

2 The Decline of the University as a Public Institution in India 23
N. Jayaram

3 Globalization: Emerging Trends in Higher Education in India 41
Gattu Satyanarayana

4 Sociology of Textbooks: Conceptual Narrative 52
Rajiv Gupta

5 Trends of Youth Sexuality in Globalizing India: Challenge for Curriculum 70
Swati Shirwadkar

6 Society Caught Between 'Tradition' and 'Modernity': Is India Ready for Sex Education? 80
Niharika Tripathi and T.V. Sekher

7 Globalization and Civil-Military Relations: A Culture of Peace Process in Kashmir (Case Study of a School Near LOC) 97
Leena Parmar

Part II: Religion

8 Mobilizing Religion for Dignity and Development: Revisiting the Mahar Buddhists of Maharashtra 113
Surinder S. Jodhka

9 Kalpathy Heritage Village: Sacred and Modern 138
Susan Visvanathan

10 Jagannath Temple Organization: Symbiosis of Hindu Religiosity, Inter-Sect Understanding and Social Values 164
Ramanuj Ganguly

11 Hinduism: Exclusivist or Inclusivist? 184
Hetukar Jha

Part III: Creativity

12 Literature, Society and the Calling of Creative Public Spheres: Towards a New Art of Cross-Fertilization 193
Ananta Kumar Giri

13 Time and Creativity: Towards a Sociological Perspective 208
Indra Deva

14 The Art of Sharadchandra Chattopadhyay 228
M.S. Gore

15 Diversity, Diffusion and Social Transformation of Rabindra Sangeet under Globalization 261
Susmita Bhattacharyya

16 From Site to Terrestrial Television: Television in Everyday Life in Rural Rajasthan 27
Biswajit Das

17 Touristifying Himalayan Sikkim: Is the Commodification of its Nature and Culture Sustainable? 29
Vibha Arora

18 Tourism in the Era of Globalization 30
Neha Kala

Index 31

Introduction

Ishwar Modi

The first volume of the four-volume Festschrift for Professor Yogendra Singh outlined not only his academic journey and the worldview of his ideas on the relevance of Western scholars but also the major concerns and challenges before the sociologists in India, then as well as now, more so in the context of globalization. Besides this, several contributors to first volume also extensively and critically reflected on his academic contributions and also his personality. Taking into cognizance the thrust of that volume entitled *Modernization, Globalization and Social Transformation* almost all the contributors focused their attention not only on the conceptual dimensions of the concerned phenomenon and their interlinkages but also examined in detail the relationship of these phenomena with other contemporary social and sociological concerns such as marginalization, social movements, middle class, culture and consumer culture, technology, ethnicity, and even global society and risk society. Issues of modernity and post-modernity were also analysed in a wider context.

In continuation of the general title of the Festschrift, *Modernization, Globalization and Social Transformation,* this second volume has been brought out under the title *Education, Religion and Creativity* taking cognizance of the fact that a large number of papers by eminent colleagues have been contributed in the areas of their specialization broadly focusing on the themes of education, religion and creativity including such aspects of creativity as art, music and literature, as well as such creative and recreational dimensions of creativity as television, leisure and tourism. As such it was considered appropriate that these papers be put together in a volume having these themes.

While I am thankful to all the contributors of this second volume, I must pay my special gratitude and remembrance to late Professors M.S. Gore and Indra Deva who are no more with us now. They were kind enough to have provided their papers for the Festschrift. We wished this Festschrift and particularly this volume could have been brought out in their presence, but, alas, it could not become possible. I offer my special tribute to them both.

II

The first paper in the category of papers clubbed together under the sub-title of 'Education' in this volume "Higher Education in 'Global' India: The Need for Critical Sociology" is by Maitrayee Chaudhuri, presently the chairperson of the Centre for the Study of Social Systems, Jawaharlal Nehru University, which was founded by Yogendra Singh and where he is now Professor Emeritus. She begins by observing that 'global' universities form part of the buzzwords in current higher education discourses. It is indeed but one of the many buzzwords in circulation that seek to capture the massive and far-reaching changes underway in the higher education sector both globally and in India. This paper maps the broad global context within which higher education has entered the market as a viable and productive industry. India in this story has a key role to play, not only as a huge market of students willing to pay, but also as a growing economy in need of skilled human resource. The paper contends that in this period of global capitalism, even as we witness a rapid decline of critical social science we find an all-encompassing spread of management discourse with its practical recipes and platitudes emerging as the intellectual face of the regime. Even as policy makers announce new visions of 'global universities' and 'global curricula', western universities reach out to the rich and collective scholarship of Indian social science to internationalize their curricula. This is historically an important moment for Indian higher education, too significant to get lured by hollow catchwords. It is in this context that this paper proceeds to bring back into focus: (i) the importance of liberal education and the role of social science in promoting the spirit of critique; (ii) the deliberations within Indian academia, particularly in sociology on the role of social science; and (iii) the legacy of modern Indian social science and the threat that recent trends pose to it.

Taking up the same theme of higher education and the universities, N. Jayaram laments about the decline of the university as a public institution in India in his paper under the title, "The Decline of the University as a Public Institution in India". He points out that the university system in India was introduced by the British in 1857 as a public institution. Modelled after the University of London, the pioneer universities – established at Bombay, Calcutta and Madras – were largely affiliating and examining bodies with very little intellectual life of their own. Since independence, the implanted university system has expanded phenomenally, but has declined as a public institution. Discussing this decline, the essay is divided into four parts: part one outlines the historical background of the university system in India, part two elucidates the nature of university as a public institution, part three analyses the distortion of its objectives and deterioration of its quality, and part four examines the spatial aspects of the university and the erosion of its legitimacy.

Going a step further, Gattu Satyanarayana in his paper "Globalization: Emerging Trends in Higher Education in India" examines the impact of globalization on higher education. He is of the opinion that in the era of globalization Indian state and society have been facing a serious crisis in adopting global policies and programmes on the one side and to meet the needs and aspirations of the people within the framework of constitutional obligations, on the other. His study mainly aims to explain the implications of globalization for higher education in terms of policies and programmes within the framework of problems and prospects.

Continuing to debate education in the broader perspective of globalization, Rajiv Gupta examines the sociology of textbooks and has also tried to answer 'why textbooks?' in his paper on "Sociology of Textbooks: Conceptual Narrative". He observes that the personalities of readers relating to any book comprise (i) imaginary, (ii) symbolic, and (iii) real. The author has derived this perception from Lacan on the one hand and Safadar Hashmi and Gulzar on the other. Textbooks are one of the social productions of social unit known as 'author' by which 'centres' and 'peripheries' of (un)known universe are communicated to social categories known as 'readers'. Textbooks are structured with the help of languages which convert memories, observations, imagination, assumptions and possible outcome(s) into set of ideas, knowledge and sub-systems of information. The reading of textbooks is an attempt to establish the element of 'reliable'. Belief systems based on faith, religiosity, science and metaphysics are products of textbooks. The article is a sociological attempt to construct answer of the question 'why textbooks'?

Moving the debate from the textbooks to curriculum is a natural corollary. As such it is in the fitness of things that Swati Shirwadkar has focused her attention on the challenges for curriculum in the broader context of both youth sexuality and globalization in her paper "Trends of Youth Sexuality in Globalizing India: Challenge for Curriculum". Her paper contextualizes the issue of youth sexuality with emerging changes in the global market economy. She presents a short review of some studies on emerging trends of youth sexuality around the time of publication of the book on *Culture Change in India* by Professor Yogendra Singh in 2000. The relation of significant social factors in the process of globalization and cultural change that perhaps propelled the emerging trends in youth sexuality is brought out. She concludes with a plea that there is a need of capturing these changes in the curriculum of sociology for student's discursive learning. She hopes that this may help in exploring a meaningful balance between research and teaching, as suggested by Professor Singh.

How it is possible that we talk of youth sexuality and changes in curriculum but forget about the feasibility of sex education or that of family life education (FLE) in India. There are several dilemmas. Niharika Tripathi and T.V. Sekher in their joint paper on "Society Caught Between 'Tradition' and 'Modernity': Is India Ready for Sex Education?" discuss about these dilemmas and the controversies surrounding the issues of introducing sex education more so at the school level. They emphasize that FLE/sex education has been one of the most controversial issues in Indian society, illustrating the dilemma of a society caught between 'tradition' and 'modernity'. Due to increasing incidences of HIV/AIDS, RTIs/STIs and teenage pregnancies, there is a need to impart sex education among youth. However, introducing sex education at school level always received opposition from various segments of Indian society. An attempt has been made in this paper to understand the expectations and experiences of Indian youth regarding FLE. For this purpose, available evidence from two nationally representative surveys like District Level Household and Facility Survey (DLHS: 2007-08) and Youth Study in India (2006-07), undertaken by the International Institute for Population Sciences (IIPS), has been used. The authors found significant gap between the proportion of youth who perceived sex education to be important and those who actually received it. It was also found that women who received FLE were more aware about the reproductive health issues as compared to those who did not receive. The study further illustrates that an overwhelming majority of young men and women are in favour of introducing FLE at school level – from standard 8th onwards – and parents are the best resource persons to impart sex education. The findings emerging from the nation-wide surveys strongly support the acceptance and need for sex education among youth in India. The authors are of the opinion that challenge before educationists and administrators is to develop a scientific and culturally-sensitive sex education curriculum which is acceptable to all sections of our society.

How can a school become a ray of hope for an area/region ravaged by armed conflicts and militancy and also under constant threats of insecurity in spite of significant presence of military has been dealt with in the paper "Globalization and Civil-Military Relations: A Culture of Peace Process in Kashmir (Case Study of a School near LOC)" by Leena Parmar, who is an expert on Military Sociology and also the founder convener of the ISS Research Committee on Military Sociology/Armed Forces and Conflict Resolution. Her paper explores the impact of the post-Cold War era on the social structure of the armed forces in India, which is undergoing social transformation. It examines how armed forces are seeking to re-define their role and re-design their approaches in order to address the domestic challenges and also to achieve greater flexibility in their organizational structure. The conventional notion of security has been and remains state-centric with military as its major instrument, entrusted with the duty to defend the territorial integrity of the nation-state. However there are equally, if not more vital concerns and facets of security that are often ignored in the specialized security discourse of military strategists, where the concerned area is ravaged by militancy, hatred and innocent killings. Military security through arms and ammunition generally neglects the social structures, people's movements and non-state actors, thus making the entire process elitist, parochial and often insensitive.

The changing nature of civil-military relations in Asia has been the focus for any serious scholar of peace and security. This current research is also on the civil-military relations, and an army-corporate world initiative, which is aimed at bringing peace to the people of the Kashmir Valley. In this paper, the army-corporate world initiative has been illustrated by the example of a school, which is situated at the India-Pakistan border, near Line of Control (LOC) in Uri Sector of Jammu & Kashmir. The author focuses on how the school, which was opened just a couple of years ago, is transforming the people in that area. This effort is meant to be collaborative and interactive – entirely a partnership between a corporate house and the common people, who lived for years with fear and terrorism.

The paper also highlights people's aspirations and expectations. The common man/woman in the area is interested more in two times meal, poverty alleviation programmes, electrification in their homes, road and transport system and health clinics. Above all they want a secured future of their children and this school is a ray of hope for them. They want to live in a peaceful atmosphere, as they are tired of cross-border terrorism, militancy and uncertainty. The present structure of violence and aggression needs to be reconsidered from the vantage point of the people at the periphery.

III

The next section under the rubric 'Religion' begins with the scholarly paper of Surinder S. Jodhka on "Mobilizing Religion for Dignity and Development: Revisiting the Mahar Buddhists of Maharashtra". The author observes that the socially excluded and marginalized groups struggle not only for equity and entitlements but also for cultural and symbolic resources, of which religion is an important part. Even when they mobilize against dominant religious ideologies, such as the ex-untouchables questioning the practice of caste and untouchability in Hinduism, they do not reject religion *per se*. It remains an important component of their notion of well-being. Thus, instead of turning to 'secular modernity' or 'moving out of religion', they mobilize their communities for autonomous religious identities which offer them a dignified mode of self-representation, and a way out of, what they view as, a degrading and humiliating status within the dominant religious tradition.

Based on qualitative fieldwork, the paper looks at the movement for neo-Buddhist conversions among the Hindu Mahars of Maharashtra. The study explores their quest for dignified social existence and the struggle for material development and empowerment through religious mobilizations. Thanks to the religious movements, the Mahars of Maharashtra have evolved as a strong and autonomous community. The movement has helped them produce a galaxy of motivated leaders who have been working hard for the socio-economic development of their community members. Along with building autonomous symbolic or cultural resources for their fellow Dalits, such as ritual practices and sacred places, they have also been investing in laying down structures for the socio-economic development of their community. The movement has also significantly raised their awareness about the value of education. The newly developed community networks and resources give them a sense of confidence and pride about their identity. The investments they have made in developing educational institutions and other supporting systems makes it easier for them to move ahead economically and diversify into different activities for livelihood and well-being.

Susan Visvanathan, in her paper "Kalpathy Heritage Village: Sacred and Modern" has also dealt with the questions of development in and around a Kerala heritage village predominantly inhabitated by Palghat Iyer Brahmins in the broader context of globalization through the diary method of fieldwork conducted by the author under the title "Kalpathy Diaries" spanning several years from 2006 to 2011 and based in the town of Pallakad, Kerala. The chief concern in this paper is to look at the country-town nexus in the context of globalization. The Palghat Iyers are well known for their contribution to the political economy of modern India. In the 1920s it was the greatest recipient of money orders in British India, since Agraharam Brahmins made a living, working as administrative staff in colonial India in the presidency towns. With 'merger' during the time of Indian independence, Palghat came to Kerala from Madras presidency. This paper looks at contemporary questions of culture, identity, residence, occupation and caste within the framework of tourism and urban landscape, where the hinterland of the countryside is an important social fact. The conclusion, thus, looks at the way in which the Mallapuram dam provides both water and recreational sites for the local people on both sides of the ghats, since Tamil and Malayali groups converge to celebrate development which does not as yet create emotional turmoil. As a small town develops into a boom town, with industrialization, the question of the volume and density of population, questions of space, water, and energy potentialities as they exist will have to be re-evaluated.

The issue of the sacred and secular (which may as well be seen as modern) has been taken up by Ramanuj Ganguly in his paper "Jagannath Temple Organization: Symbiosis of Hindu Religiosity, Inter-Sect Understanding and Social Values" in the context of one of the most famous temples of India – the Jagannath Temple – while taking into cognizance the views of Professor Yogendra Singh. The author reiterates that Professor Singh is of the view that India has been exposed to cultural contacts with other civilizations since millennia. It has been continually making adaptive changes in the cultural styles, traits and forms as it encountered other cultures. It has a history of accommodating identities. The present article, following the argument, argues that how Jagannath Temple, as a unique local cultural tradition, so different from other Hindu religious organizations in India, represents a space where sacred and secular intersect without undercutting each other, rather complementing one another for the changing needs of the society as well as the organization. The temple has a continuous history of change, adaptation and survival, includes various sections of the society under one arch, and promotes exclusivism, inclusivism and pluralism at the same time.

The paper looks at the religious practices and religious institutions as an ever-evolving process that is less rigid than the way it is projected. Effort has been made to understand the dynamic interrelationship between a religious organization, its agent, and the communities of followers, who are involved in constantly producing codes and representations, thereby, analyse the nature and composition of social life around it. It is observed the religious practices emerge cybernetically, that is, the practices are often 'goal-corrected' with continual on-course adjustments while the public and private space overlap within the temple complex. The paper finally turns to explain how the dynamics of this tradition with its unique practices and values have absorbed and assimilated all those various tenets that divide the Indians at mundane level. The author observes that this spirit, promoted for more than nine centuries, imbibes religiosity but sobers it with the idea of progress, tolerance and openness.

Further subscribing to the arguments offered by Ganguly regarding symbiosis of Hindu religiosity and its liberal tradition in the broader context of Jagannath Temple, Hetukar Jha, in his paper "Hinduism: Exclusivist or Inclusivist?" also establishes that Hinduism is inclusivist as against the general view of its being exclusivist. The exclusivist view of Hinduism implies its ethos as being opposed to the forces of social change and development. However, according to Jha, the history of its existence since its origin in the medieval period does not subscribe to this view generated in the colonial period. The understanding of Hinduism based on its history indicates its prevalence as a broad liberal tradition affording space for any deviation or innovation.

IV

The third section on 'Creativity' encompasses such aspects of life and society as art, literature and creativity as well as such creative and recreational dimensions as music, television and tourism. Ananta Kumar Giri, in his paper "Literature, Society and the Calling of Creative Public Spheres: Towards a New Art of Cross-Fertilization" propounds that exploring and realizing creative relationship between literature and society is an adventure in co-realizations and transformations going beyond the logic of the fields of both literature and society. It also calls for understanding their manifold conceptualizations and realizations. Our conventional understanding of literature is that it is created by men of literature. It is not always realized that literature is part of life and society; when it is done so it is usually conceptualized and represented in a language of mirror and adaptation: literature is either a mirror of society or it adapts to the logic of society. But literature is not only a mirror of society but also a field of creative expressions and confrontations which breaks existing mirrors of society and creates new languages of self and social realizations and new landscapes of imaginations. Both literature and society are not only fields of adaptation but also fields of transcendence and transformations in which individuals and groups strive to go beyond adaptation and create new conditions of self-, co- and social realizations. These are the fields in which there is interrogation and confrontation of the existing logic of literature and society. Literature is thus not only a field of murmuring but of grumbling and also of contestation and confrontations of the existing grammar of society based upon a higher grumbling of self and awakened social groups and movements.

Giri holds that in exploring relationship between literature and society, the language of interdisciplinary transaction, as it happens in conventional academic corridors, is not enough. We need a new language and practice of transdisciplinary cultivation, beyond adaptation and meditative verbs of transformations. The author discusses some of these issues and also the calling of creative public spheres and a new art of cross-fertilization.

One of the former Presidents of the Indian Sociological Society and a long-time colleague of Professor Yogendra Singh at the University of Rajasthan at Jaipur, late Professor Indra Deva, in his extremely perceptive and creative paper on "Time and Creativity: Towards a Sociological Perspective" has examined the relationship between time and creativity in its various ramifications from a sociological perspective. Indra Deva begins his dialogue by observing that from a sociological angle, the categories both of time and creativity are social constructs. Since human experience and action occur in time, every human society tends to develop certain ways of perceiving and organizing time which are consistent with its cultural and structural pattern. Time is perceived through changes that occur in man and nature, and there are various systems of measuring it in terms of human and cosmic cycles. Apart from the varying conception of time as cyclical or linear, the perception of time involves certain concepts of sequence and duration which vary from society to society. Citing the Hindus' *rites de passage* or *samskaras*, Indra Deva points out that the accounting of time in different societies clearly has social and cultural concomitants. Besides this, each culture has, as a part of its world view, a pattern of attitudes towards past, present and future. However, the basic notions of time and space, which are implicit in each culture, are seldom made explicit.

Discussing about the notion of creativity itself, Indra Deva observes that the current notion of creativity seems clearly to be a product of the modern age and it appears to be bound by the culture to which it belongs. The prevailing concept of 'creativity' emerged in the West during the Renaissance and was first given formal expression by the philosophers of Enlightenment. It seems to be imbued with an exaggerated sense of individualism. On the other hand, when we consider the process and conception of creativity in a non-modern western culture, the traditional Indian culture for instance, the picture is strikingly different. Traditional Indian culture gives little importance to the individual in the process of creation.

Indra Deva further argues that as regards the folk stream of culture, the emphasis on individual creativity is conspicuous by its absence. The significance of this cannot be minimized: for the bearers of the folk tradition have constituted the bulk of the total population in countries like India, and indeed of all peasant civilizations, since the dawn of history. The fact is that even the ordinary language of the unlettered folk makes greater use of symbolism and imagery for expressing subtle feelings in a precise manner, and as such attaining significant levels of creativity.

The paper by distinguished scholar, literateur and sociologist late Professor M.S. Gore on "The Art of Sharadchandra Chattopadhyay" is a masterpiece in the realm of sociology of literature. In discussing Sharadbabu's works, Gore has not followed a chronological sequence of the publication of his works but has considered some of the work of his period of maturity. As such he begins his perceptive analysis of the life situations of the various characters of Sharadbabu's novels and the Bengali society, particularly the middle class as depicted in his novels – Pather Dabi (1926), Vipradas (1935) and Shesh Prashna (1931). He then moves on to Sharadbabu's other novels, namely, Gaon-Ganga (1916), Vijaya-Dutta (1917-19), Bhairavi (1923), Chhota Bhai (Ramer Sumati, 1914), Arakshneeya (1916), Virajbahu (1914), Charitraheen (1917), Shesher Parichaya (1943) and, of course, Shrikant, which is generally considered to be largely autobiographical.

Gore observes that in Sharadbabu's novels two types of issues are raised almost constantly – one relating to the poor and the deprived and the other relating to the status of women within the family and in society. As a novelist, he is not concerned with offering ready solutions to any of these problems but rather with depicting the situations in which his characters are placed, why they behave the way they do and how they cope with the situation in which they find themselves.

It is possible to say that there is a pan-Indian social reality at a certain level and in certain social contexts – particularly in the traditional middle class familial context and in the traditional context of caste hierarchy. In a very general way one could say that in a large part of the country the patrilineal and patriarchal three-generation joint family pattern prevailed through a good part of the late 19th and early 20th century. Even today the situation is not as changed as one might imagine though the subjective world of a woman has undergone a great deal of change in the middle classes. The joint family was based on the two facts of pre-industrial India with land as the base of the economy and joint family as the social unit among the landowning classes. The men belonged to the family, whereas the women were outsiders and had to be subjugated to conform and adjust to a new family and also to make for a clear pecking order within the house. Familial units never adhere strictly to the model but the model is clearly spelt out. And, even then there were systemic and idiosyncratic variations from one area of the country to another and between the mainstream caste society and the tribal societies in different parts of the country.

Sharadchandra wrote primarily about Bengali society in Bengal in the first half of the 20th century though some of his novels are located in Burma and one in Agra. But when you take the whole of his work you find that he has written about nearly every stratum of Bengali society though the point of vantage is that of a member of the middle class. The author did not suggest that Sharadbabu has sought to justify or idolize the middle class, but only that he was himself located in the urban middle class. But, he strides across the rural-urban, the rich-poor and religious-ideological divides. He wrote naturally about the society that he saw and experienced. But his life experience must have been so varied and so steeped in genuine humane values that he takes you into nooks and corners of Bengal society – the Bengal in the large metropolis of Kolkata, the Bengal of the zamindari villages, the Bengal of the district towns, the Bengal of the revolutionary movement, the Bengal of the Bhadralok, the Bengal of the village untouchables and the Bengal of the urban working class and he is able to project with sympathy the varied life styles and does so without imposing preconceived notions of morality.

Gore concludes that every creative artist is influenced by his times. This does not mean that all writers born in a particular milieu will respond to their environment in the same way. The influence of the times is mediated through the particular artist's life circumstances and by his personality. In Sharadbabu's writings his particular life circumstances and his sensibilities proved very important.

Deliberating on another dimension of creativity, i.e., music, Susmita Bhattacharyya, in her paper, "Diversity, Diffusion and Social Transformation of Rabindra Sangeet under Globalization", presents a cultural construct of Rabindra Sangeet of Bengal in the contemporary context both of social transformation and globalization. She posits that just as music is a cultural construct of a particular society, so is the Rabindra Sangeet of Bengal. The author observes that on the occasion of the 150 years of birth celebration of Tagore, the popularity of Rabindra Sangeet got clearly reflected in the music market of Bengal and elsewhere. She feels that a lot of listeners are associated with this genre all over the world. The phenomenal incidence of transformation of Rabindra Sangeet is dependent on media, market and listening community. TV channels and FM radio stations give a fillip to the spreading effect of Rabindra Sangeet. Professionalism and technicality are the associated parts of this genre. Noteworthy factors of transformation of Rabindra Sangeet are the impact of westernization and modernization with respect to cultural globalization, emergence of utilitarian orientation and the impact of technology. According to the structural approach, each listener should have a structured prototype of preference music while the socio-cultural approach focuses on particular social context. Functionalism revolves around unity-oriented aspects of Rabindra Sangeet and the Frankfurt school defined this situation with the notion of 'culture industry'. The bureaucratic configuration of Rabindra Sangeet industry is concentrating on rationalizing application of the debate between quantitative and qualitative aspects of this genre nonetheless parishioners of Rabindra Sangeet never ignore the artistic eternity.

As observed above, both the TV channels and FM radio stations give a fillip to the spreading effect of music, Biswajit Das has taken up the issue of the interface between television and its viewers in his paper "From Site to Terrestrial Television: Television in Everyday Life in Rural Rajasthan". His paper offers a qualitative and descriptive analysis of the ways in which viewers lived in a significant proportion, with wider ramifications, their everyday life with TV in rural Rajasthan. Das attempts to capture the viewer's relationship with the quasi-objects in the day-to-day interaction in everyday life as our everyday experience is embedded within cultural and institutional formations that are malleable but durable. He poses and answers such questions as: How do people relate themselves to the medium and the televised events in their day-to-day lives? In the sphere of everyday life, do people trust television? Do people believe what it says? And finally, do people believe what the people say in the television?

It is well accepted that creativity and leisure are intertwined and deeply related phenomena. Of late, tourism has appeared as one of the most cherished dimensions of leisure the world over. Besides acquiring the status of a major leisure activity, tourism is also being identified as an engine of economic growth and human development. But, at the same time, commodification of tourism is also seen as a factor of debasing local cultures. Vibha Arora, in her paper "Touristifying Himalayan Sikkim: Is the Commodification of its Nature and Culture Sustainable?", written on the basis of her field experiences and research in Sikkim, draws our attention to the interrelated issues of tourism, its commodification and sustainability. She observes that tourism has been identified as the engine of Sikkim's human development, economic growth, employment generator and poverty alleviator. Tourism is increasingly becoming the catalyst for the evolutionary selection and the framing of local culture(s) in Himalayan Sikkim. In colourfully illustrated and 'carefully' scripted pages of tourist brochures and booklets, and in periodically staged performances at various locales, the commercialization of nature and culture and the development transition of Sikkim is much evident. Some critical voices are questioning this spectacular transition of Sikkim into a tourist locale and tourism as a development necessity. To what extent are locals participating in this process of commodification of their culture and nature in Sikkim? Documenting mixed experiences, the author observes that local people have differing positions depending on their community, the how, where, and when aspects of their interaction with tourists. The Sikkim government has shifted from a strategy to promote mass tourism towards one of promoting sustainable and responsible eco-tourism and cultural tourism. Eco-tourism and village/rural tourism can preserve rural culture, heritage, generate employment and economically develop the hills and valleys without causing undue pressure on the eco-system and environment. She feels that sustainable tourism, especially eco-cultural tourism, requires a multi-stakeholder approach that integrates different sections of the economy and members of diverse groups living in a multi-ethnic setting and elicits high levels of community participation, which unfortunately is not evident in contemporary Sikkim.

Analysing the overarching impact of globalization on all walks of life, Neha Kala in her paper "Tourism in the Era of Globalization" examines the interface between tourism and globalization. She begins her paper by observing that the whole dynamics of the present era can be summed up in a single term called 'globalization' which is characterized by economic liberalization, privatization and proliferation of new information and communication technologies. Globalization has severe impacts on virtually all dimensions of society. Tourism remains no exception. Her paper not only analyses the interface between tourism and globalization but also discusses the implications of such interplay between these two phenomena. On one hand, globalization promotes tourism through de-territorialization and on the other hand, tourism promotes globalization through cross-border interaction. It is true that both the phenomena increase the interconnectedness of world. When tourism and globalization intersect, a compatible and positive relationship appears. However, when the issue of sustainability arises, the relationship appears to be incompatible.

On the whole, this second volume of the four-part Festschrift for Professor Yogendra Singh analyses the situation of higher education in a globalizing India and shows how the university as a public institution is on decline. It examines the trends of youth sexuality in the context of globalization and also the challenges for curriculum. Attention has also been given to sex education in the broader context of the debates and dilemmas between tradition and modernity. Sociology of textbooks has also been examined in detail. A case study of a school also raises the hope of peace near the India-Pakistan border in the overall context of civil-military relations. The second section of this volume, mainly focusing on religion, investigates how religion has been mobilized for dignity and development among the Mahar Buddhists of Maharashtra. This section also describes how a heritage village besides being a sacred place can also emerge as a modern place leading to the path of development and as a place of tourist attraction. Another paper shows that how Jagannath Temple, representing a space where sacred and secular intersect without undercutting each other, has a continuous history of change, adaptation and survival, includes various sections of the society under one arch, and promotes exclusivism, inclusivism and pluralism at the same time. Yet another paper argues out that Hinduism is inclusivist and not exclusivist. Moving on to the section on creativity, the papers examine not only the relationship between literature, society and the calling of creative public spheres but also between time and creativity from sociological perspective. A thorough sociological review of the art of Sharatchandra Chattopadhyay has also been undertaken enriching the sociology of literature. Likewise, diversity, diffusion and social transformation of Rabindra Sangeet has also been examined in the context of globalization. What part the terrestrial television is playing in everyday life in rural Rajasthan has also been examined empirically. Also, due attention has been paid to the creative and other dimensions of tourism in this section.

Contributors

Ananta Kumar Giri, Associate Professor, Madras Institute of Development Studies, Chennai.

Biswajit Das, Director, Centre for Culture, Media and Governance, Jamia Millia Islamia, New Delhi.

Gattu Satyanarayana, formerly Professor and Head, Department of Sociology, College of Arts and Social Sciences, Osmania University, Hyderabad.

Hetukar Jha, formerly Professor and Head, Department of Sociology, Patna University, Patna.

Indra Deva, formerly Professor of Sociology and Dean, Faculty of Social Sciences, Ravishankar University, Raipur. He was also the President of the Indian Sociological Society from 1995 to 1997.

Leena Parmar, formerly Professor and Head, Department of Sociology, University of Rajasthan, Jaipur.

M.S. Gore, a renowned social scientist, was awarded Padma Bhushan by the President of India in 1975. He worked as Principal, Delhi School of Social Work (1954–1962); Director, Tata Institute of Social Sciences (1962–1982); Vice-Chancellor, University of Bombay (1983–86); and Chancellor, Jawaharlal Nehru University, New Delhi. He was also the President of the Indian Sociological Society from 1981 to 1983.

Maitrayee Chaudhuri, Professor and Chairperson, Centre for the Study of Social Systems, School of Social Sciences, Jawaharlal Nehru University, New Delhi. She was also the Director, Women's Studies Programme, Jawaharlal Nehru University (2006–08), and Coordinator, Global Studies Programme (2004–05).

N. Jayaram, Professor and Head, Centre for Research Methodology, Tata Institute of Social Sciences, Mumbai. He has also been Director of the

Institute for Social and Economic Change, Bangalore. He is presently a Fellow at the Indian Institute of Advanced Study, Shimla and also the Managing Editor of *Sociological Bulletin.*

Neha Kala, Assistant Professor, Banaras Hindu University, Varanasi.

Niharika Tripathi, Doctoral Fellow, International Institute for Population Sciences, Mumbai.

Rajiv Gupta, Professor and Head, Department of Sociology and Social Work, University of Rajasthan, Jaipur.

Ramanuj Ganguly, Associate Professor and Head, Department of Sociology, West Bengal State University, Barasat, North 24 Parganas.

Surinder S. Jodhka, Professor of Sociology and formerly Chairperson, Centre for the Study of Social Systems, School of Social Sciences, Jawaharlal Nehru University, New Delhi and currently ICCR Visiting Professor, University of Lund, Lund, Sweden.

Susan Visvanathan, Professor of Sociology and formerly Chairperson, Centre for the Study of Social Systems, School of Social Sciences, Jawaharlal Nehru University, New Delhi.

Susmita Bhattacharyya, Assistant Professor and Head, Department of Sociology, Prasanta Chandra Mahalanobis Mahavidyalaya,West Bengal State University, Kolkata.

Swati Shirwadkar, Professor and Head, Department of Sociology, University of Pune, Pune.

T.V. Sekher, Associate Professor, International Institute for Population Sciences, Mumbai.

Vibha Arora, Assistant Professor, Indian Institute of Technology, New Delhi.

Part I

EDUCATION

1

Higher Education in 'Global' India

The Need for Critical Sociology

Maitrayee Chaudhuri

- 'Look no further for *global* education. Meet the world at Sharda University ...'
- 'Sharda University with the motto '*Global* Outlook ... Indian Values'
- '*Global* Curriculum, *Global* Faculty, *Global* Ambience, *Global* Community' Sharda University
- 'The *Global* Open University Nagaland'
- 'O.P. Jindal *Global* University (JGU)'
- 'Techno *Global* University, Shillong, Meghalaya'

The Context

Quite evidently 'global' is the buzzword in university education. It may appear a bit odd to begin an essay on the role of social science education in India with a set of advertisements. I do not know whether it may appear less odd if I mention that 'education' sector was the top sector in print advertising during 2010 (*AdEx News Letter*, 17 August 2010). The question of course is 'odd' for whom? I am probably thinking of academics brought up at a time when 'national' was the key word and education's role was seen in terms of 'nation building' in a wider sense than simply developing human resource. The 'market' then was not so central to education as the 'state' was. This however is not to simply reiterate a somehow fallacious story of the decline of the state and rise of the market but to point towards a reconfiguration of the state-market relation in contemporary India. Since the early 1990s we have seen both the rise of India as an economic power and a concerted attempt to redefine and legitimate a free play of 'market ideology' in public discourse (Chaudhuri, 2010a). It is against this context that the shift in contemporary educational discourse has to be located. Browsing the web I find innumerable sites on higher education that suggest how education is a big business. For our teachers, a generation that reached adulthood and entered university with India's independence, vision of education was centrally about core 'national/constitutional' values.[1] Social science in such a scheme was important. The scene has now dramatically changed in India and 'globally'. Some bare facts may illustrate the changed context better:

> With 400 million people under the age of 18 and a blistering economy that has readjusted aspirations across the country, higher education in India is a boom market. Indians already spend $7.5 billion annually earning degrees in other countries. On American campuses, their presence is bigger than that of any other nationality. As India looks to dramatically expand and improve higher education at home, the possibility of luring top-flight American schools is an intriguing one. (Hannon, 2010)

A review of a recent book published in the USA on the changing profile of universities captures this dramatic transformation:

> Universities are obsessed by the global marketplace for students and professors. They are trying to attract as many students from abroad as possible (not least because foreign students usually pay full fees). Nearly 3m students now spend some time studying in foreign countries, a number that has risen steeply in recent years. Universities are also setting up overseas. New York University has opened a branch in Abu Dhabi. Six American universities have created a higher-education supermarket in Qatar. Almost every university worth its name has formed an alliance with a leading Chinese institution.
>
> But globalisation is going deeper than just the competition for talent: a growing number of countries are trying to create an elite group of 'global universities' that are capable of competing with the best American institutions. China and India are focusing resources on a small group. The French and German governments are doing battle with academic egalitarians in an attempt to create European Ivy Leagues. Behind all this is the idea that world-class universities can make a disproportionate contribution to economic growth. (*The Economist*, 13 May 2010)

The fact is that higher education is a central site for competition in contemporary global capitalism. India herself is a significant player in this global scenario, even as India's own domestic concerns of tribe, caste and class inequity, inclusion, social justice play out its own dynamics in the higher education sector. This however is not our main concern here in this paper. The focus here is on the implications of a market-driven education industry for the idea of the university as a centre of intellectual ferment and the related conception of liberal education with which social sciences and critical sociology is so closely linked. My contention here is that there is somehow an inadequate appreciation of this in the present times. This I argue remains true despite the apparent flurry of action in the higher education sector, including the opening up of new universities and massive expansion plans.[2] In a world where management discourse is dominant,[3] where snappy one liner and acronyms are deployed to convey complex processes, it is sad that it is management discourse, which has captured the imagination of educational administrators.

My reference to *management discourse* is deliberate. It has two aspects to it: one, management literature is technical, composed of practical recipes for improving the productivity of organizations (here, educational institutions) as one improves the performance of a machine; and two, it simultaneously has a high moral tone, if only because it is a normative literature stating what should be the case, not what is the case. If one looks at any brochures of the new educational institutions today, one will encounter both a host of practical recipes and a flood of platitudes posturing as profound knowledge.

Take the example of Sharda University projection of '*Global* Curriculum, *Global* Faculty, *Global* Ambience, *Global* Community' Sharda University. Or of its Mission Statement:

- Creating a stimulating and flexible learning environment for its students as well as faculty
- Leveraging academic research to form strong industry linkages
- Developing a culture that strongly promotes innovation and continued betterment in all facets of life

While words such as 'flexible', 'leveraging' and 'innovative' abound, there is very little in terms of substantive vision. A cursory comparison with the vision statement of Jawaharlal Nehru University of 1966 would make the distinction I seek to make between buzzwords and management mantras from deliberated humanist values clear.

The First Schedule, The Jawaharlal Nehru University Act, 1966 states that:

> The University shall endeavour to promote the study of the principles for which Jawaharlal Nehru worked during his life-time, namely, national integration, social justice, secularism, democratic way of life, international understanding and scientific approach to the problems of society.

Towards this end, the University shall:

(i) foster the *composite culture* of India and establish such departments or institutions as may be required for the study and development of the language, arts and culture of India;

(ii) take special measures to facilitate students and teachers from all over India to join the University and participate in its academic programmes;

(iii) promote in the students and teachers an awareness and understanding of the *social needs of the country* and prepare them for fulfilling such needs;

(iv) make special provision for integrated courses in humanities, *science and technology* in the educational programmes of the University;

(v) take appropriate measures for promoting inter-disciplinary studies in the University;

(vi) establish such departments or institutions as may be necessary for the study of languages, literature and life of foreign countries with a view to *inculcating* in the students a world perspective and international understanding;

(vii) provide facilities for students and teachers from other countries to participate in the academic programmes and life of the University.'

The key terms like national integration, social justice, secularism, democratic way of life, international understanding, and scientific approach to the problems of society are derived from a worked out Nehruvian vision, part of India's long intellectual engagement with colonial rule as it sought to develop a distinctive modern but culturally rooted national identity. One need not dwell on the stark difference between such a vision and the catchwords that seem to be the defining mark of the host of new universities as they vend their visions on huge billboards that dot the new highways of Indian cities.

In this context, where distinctions between serious intellectual discourses and 'management mantras' disappear, it becomes an imperative need to emphasize the role of social science and critical sociology for a democratic and just society. There is a deep and significant difference between the two forms of knowledge. Social science is equipped to analyse deep structures, specific dynamics of historical contexts, social processes and the links this has with emergent products including knowledge forms. Management literature 'makes no claims to be exhaustive'. Their orientation is not constative, but prescriptive. 'In the manner of edifying books or manuals of moral instruction, they practice the *exemplum,* select the cases according to their demonstrative power – what is to be done as opposed to what is not to be done and take from reality only such aspects as confirm the orientation to which they wish to give some impetus' (Boltanski and Chapello, 2005: 58). For instance, if within this framework they have to look at higher education, they would suggest prescriptions for efficient and transparent functioning but not questions of the normative visions on which an institution rests. An example here would be in order. Responding to this massive expansion in higher education sector and rise of intense competition, a central fear expressed from an 'industry' and 'management' perspective would be the problem of malpractices and misrepresentation in advertisements.

> Competition is intensifying in higher education sector and many institutions in India are engaged in over-promising and misrepresenting. This happens in other consumer sector too, however here stakes for the consumers (students) are very high. A detergent company claiming whiteness of shirt has very different implications as compared to an educational institution claiming 100 per cent placement or a coaching institute claiming selection to top institution, when the reality is poor offering. The influence of unfulfilled claims is not only on the career and expectations of students but their families too. (Choudaha, 2010)

While the above comment reveals an acute understanding of the difference between a detergent company and an educational institution, it operates however with a model of education as industry and derived from that a model and ideas of fair practices. The critique is about 'unfulfilled claims' and not about the very nature of 'claims'. It falls short of (indeed it has to fall short of) either understanding or analysing the far-reaching implications of such a model of education for a good society, democratic and inclusive citizenship and the very spirit of critique, which social sciences and humanities embody. My contention is that we as social scientists and especially as sociologists have a vantage point to explicate conditions which propel this race in higher education as well offer a critique that puts forward an alternative idea of higher education before contemporary developments take us over.

As Yogendra Singh writes, 'the globalization and liberalization of the economy also creates new opportunities and demands for certain types of skills and education, which may pull away an increasing number of scholars and students from liberal and humanistic social sciences such as sociology'

(Singh, 1996: 11). He however fears that vocationalizing sociology would invariably disturb its core for '*sociological training* ...' which is to 'inculcate in them *the ability to critically comprehend the place of these forces in the scheme of social order* from a critical-historical perspective' (ibid.: 13). Since Yogendra Singh's perceptive observations in 1996, developments have been rapid. If we are not to be swamped by either a management discourse or by a discourse of sociology/social science, which is only about quantifying, organizing and evaluating techniques, we have to act quickly.

We have to understand the historical contexts, which promote a language of 'useful' and 'practical' and promote social science research, which is usually about corporations conducting 'pre-research', NGOs evaluations, or 'women employing statistical analysis to evaluate the effectiveness of USAID' (Hunter and Yates, 2002: 337). This not only provides the authority by which action is justified, but it also supplies an idiom by which 'the work' is accomplished on a day-to-day basis. The very 'practical' outcomes against which such research can be gauged makes such social science a more desirable knowledge practice in a world where 'doing' rather than 'thinking' is the mantra of present times. Since our universities have often been bane to a culture of 'doing nothing' or engaged in activities other than education, there is a readiness with which critique of 'liberal education' is accepted. The mantra is about 'results' and 'social science research' harnessed to corporations, NGO and international institutions. It is about offering tangible findings and solution to problems set by the concerned funding body. The state of many of our malfunctioning higher educational institutions make academics willing to accept any recommended change, any sense of accountability, any sense that some work is getting done.

It is against this backdrop that this paper proceeds to bring back into focus (i) the importance of liberal education, 'globalization', state and the role of social science in promoting the spirit of critique; (ii) the deliberations within Indian academia, particularly in sociology, on the role of social science; and (iii) the legacy of modern Indian social science and the threat that recent trends pose to it.

Whither Liberal Education: From the National to the Global Project

The buzzword 'global' is perhaps as frequent as the other buzzwords about 'industry tie-ups' and 'employable' human resource in the current discourse on education. My contention is that such one-sided emphasis would undermine the space and role of liberal education for which familiarity with social sciences is crucial. I quote from the stated objectives of one of those universities, the Global Open University (GOU), Nagaland to underscore its skewed approach. The GOU:

> ... revises its curriculum periodically as per the industry requirements and offers latest subjects and technologies empowering the students to get the latest skills to be employable. Learning Resource Provider also has industry tie ups with different Multinational Companies, Banks, Financial Institutions, Hotels and Restaurants, Hospitals, Clinics and other establishments to give hands-on industry exposure to the students.

Once the purpose of education is seen as only as catering to the needs of the industry, there would necessarily be a break from liberal education seen as a 'public good'. By liberal education I broadly refer to an education that promotes critical thinking, examination of life, encounters with difference, and free exchange of ideas.[4] At such a time as this where students are seen as customers, teachers as service providers, where the impact of education would be measured only in terms of direct tangibles such as employability, it is necessary to invoke another time, another spirit not for any purpose of nostalgia but for its persisting relevance. Humayun Kabir, one of India's most distinguished education ministers, himself a scholar of repute, observed way back in the 1950s:

> Higher education – as distinct from professional training – is abstract and often has no direct relation to the practical problems of life. *Its abstractness is however its saving virtue, for it gives to such education a universal aspect.* (Kabir, 1956: 186; emphasis mine)

This is not to argue against skill acquisition and education for employability. This is to challenge the idea that skill acquisition and abstract education have to be dichotomous. Or worse that employability should be the *sole* defining criterion for education. A point of contention that is invariably raised in India today about higher education and globalization is the question of privatization. This somehow suggests that state universities are necessarily national universities. The paradigm of the national university cannot simply be reduced to the state university or the question of funding by agencies of the state. Rather, it is more important to consider the national university in terms of its complete integration into the intellectual life of the nation. Put differently, the national model defines itself vis-à-vis a national public sphere, both in cultural and political terms. The students ought to be perceived as academic citizens whose education is related not only to the needs of the state (administration) but also to the needs of the civil society (Schelling, 1966). Martha Nussbaum's recent proposal to reinvigorate the American undergraduate curriculum invokes the idea of the education of citizens. Critical of older definitions of the national community for its cultural exclusiveness, she reconnects her project to the political nation defined in multicultural terms (Nussbaum, 1997: 90–91). In our own Indian context this implies that it is possible to be critical of the nationalist framework for its exclusiveness, yet argue for a democratic and inclusive political nation, a just world order without necessarily dropping the national, democratic project entirely.

My key contention is that what is taking place in contemporary India is a reframing of what constitutes the national project. This I argue is linked to the liberal concept of the public sphere, which has been so essential for the emergence of the modern national university (Habermas, 1989). The question that looms large in present-day India is what happens when 'the public sphere itself has openly transcended national borders and reflects global concerns?' (Hohendahl, 2005: 89). Or:

> ... Put differently, what happens to the university when it has to define its mission in transnational terms? I argue that this relatively new situation has changed the way the university looks at and assesses its resources as well as its

> achievements. *It can no longer be satisfied with the task of serving the nation. Instead, it develops a global map for its mission and negotiates its role within a broader international public sphere.* This transition entails not only new opportunities but also new and different responsibilities that could possibly conflict with the idea of a traditional, national university. (ibid.)

At one level 'global concerns' such as global peace or global ecology are indeed more desirable than narrow national concerns. The crux of the matter however lies in who defines 'global concerns'. An article in *The Hindu* titled 'Issues in University Education' reflects one influential view of 'global' concern. It is not irrelevant to mention that it is authored by Calestous Juma, a professor of the practice of international development at Harvard University's Kennedy School of Government. This particular piece is written in the context of Africa but the prescription for us would not be very different. I quote him at length to illustrate what exactly the key think tanks visualize as university education for the developing countries:

> Leaders of the industrialised world, who met at the G8 summit in Gleneagles, Scotland last week, have agreed to help develop professional skills through networks between higher education institutions and centres of excellence in science and technology. This is a big shift in aid policy from the current focus on primary education. ... But funding for such activities will have little impact *unless African countries reform their universities and research institutions to focus on solving local problems*. Many African universities were created to train civil servants, but *times have changed*. Today, Africa needs to stimulate economic growth so it can work its way out of poverty. *Universities must contribute to this task ... universities can also play role of social entrepreneurs ...* The *university* could use radio and other tools such as podcasting to extend its mission to the wider community. ... It is also crucial that emphasis is placed on bringing research, teaching and community outreach together ... Finally, *universities* should enjoy greater autonomy from state control so that they can adapt in a timely manner to a changing world. ... These reforms need to be made even if financial aid is not available because the times have changed. As philosopher Eric Fromm once observed, *in times of change only learners inherit the earth*. (Juma, 2005; emphasis mine)

Without commenting on what Fromm would have had to say on this unusual invocation, the direction that higher education ought to take could not be stated any clearer. Critical social science simply has no space in this vision, nor does liberal education which critical social science promotes.

Even if one were not to enter the terrain of liberal education, it is important to distinguish between professional and polytechnic training. Kiran Karnik, NASSCOM president, observed how 'the future of India is linked to the knowledge industries, and our success in these depends upon how well we nurture and grow our human resources'. But significantly warns that '*it is important not to convert professional education into polytechnic training*' (Karnik, 2005: 10). He argues how

> *the ability of learning how to learn is an essential part of good education* ... As we do more work of greater sophistication, the need for qualified researchers – those who have done a masters or a doctorate – is going to grow ... However, to do this, *teaching needs to be made, even a more attractive profession. Today, not only are*

> *teachers poorly paid, even their social status has suffered a decline* ... with privatisation, market forces will hopefully play a role in ensuring quality. *It may, however, be necessary to go beyond market forces. This may be one area where the state can set the highest standards, creating a benchmark for private institution'*... India also needs to foster innovation, an area in which we have a unique advantage ... *We need to inculcate the habit of questioning answers, rather than answering questions.* (ibid.)

International policy makers are forthright about what the role of universities in countries such as ours should be. One is less sure that our national policy makers have thought things through. At the ground level, one fall-out of the race to be 'global' has been a mindless explosion of memorandum of understandings (MOUs) with 'foreign' universities. Success of a university therefore tends to be assessed simply by the number of MOUs signed. I argue that what is presently taking place is an apparently unchallenged ascendancy of the corporate vision in defining both the 'national' and the global'. For Brand India is the new 'nationalist and global vision'. It is the dominant public discourse.[5] The national bourgeoise and the transnational capitalist class cannot possibly pursue the same agenda. My contention is that India is undergoing precisely this conflict and negotiation of very different visions of the nation and what it represents. Not surprisingly we have had a serious look at our state of higher education. The report of the Committee to Advise on Renovation and Rejuvenation of Higher Education (CARRHE) was submitted on 1 March 2009. It begins with an idea of the university, restating ideas not so different from the idea of freedom articulated by Hohendahl in the western context. I quote from the CARRHE:

> A university is a place where new ideas germinate, strike roots and grow tall and sturdy. It is a unique space, which covers the entire universe of knowledge. It is a place where creative minds converge, interact with each other and construct visions of new realities. Established notions of truth are challenged in the pursuit of knowledge. (CARRHE, 2009: 9)

This invocation that 'the university has also been regarded as the trustee of the humanist traditions of the world' (ibid.: 10) is accompanied by a quite contrary view that 'university education is no longer viewed as a good in itself, but also as the stepping-stone into a higher orbit of the job market, where the student expects a concrete monetary return, and consequently in this perception, the university of today is expected to be in tune with the emerging needs of the society'(ibid.: 9–10). The many global universities with whose marketing we began this paper with obviously have the job market as their sole objective and revenue generation as the criterion of viability and success. However, the report of CARRHE also mentions that university is no longer a place only for socially privileged students and therefore the matter of employability and skills become even more crucial. I have no quarrel with this stance. This formulation however seems to suggest that the humanist tradition of university education is essentially an elite project. Some of the most interesting conceptual challenges to mainstream Indian sociology in recent times however have come from the margins (Chaudhuri, 2010b). I would like to return to the CARRHE report to look more carefully at the term 'autonomy', one more of the current buzzwords in circulation. The CARRHE report argues that in order to bring back the humanist project of universities, 'universities have to be autonomous spaces' (CARRHE, 2009). It further states:

> Universities need the *autonomy* to operate in a healthy competitive setting. The leadership of the university must be driven by the objectives of the institution and draw on government only for macro policies. They need to set their own policies and thereby experiment with strategies on university governance. They need to be accountable to the various stakeholders – *the society, government, students, recruiters, alumini, etc.* (ibid.: 61; emphasis mine)

The question that arises is: autonomous from whom? In a society long used to government control 'autonomy' seems to suggest autonomy necessarily from the state. However, what are the mechanisms that would ensure 'autonomy' from corporations or other private funding organizations. In 2011 India we are more aware about not just state culpability but also the deep inroads that corporate India has made into public life and educational institutions, not to mention the state itself. The state itself is not what it used to be. I have also argued elsewhere how state censorship is far easier to discern than market censorship (Chaudhuri, 2005, 2010a). I think therefore a comparison with what has transformed in the Indian media with what is underway in the university would throw interesting light on the idea of 'autonomy'. One would also like to question the idea of accountability to the various stakeholders – the society, government, students, recruiters, alumini, etc. On the one hand, such a formulation appears to emphasize accountability and democratic participation in form. On the other hand, it erodes the very content of accountability by deflecting the point that these stakeholders are unequally poised and unequally able to influence the content and structure of higher education. Surely corporate recruiters would be in a better position to call the shots than students. Such a formulation I argue emanate from the all-pervasive management discourse, which I have discussed at some length earlier, and which threatens to take over the manner that social science is imagined and practised.

At this point one needs to reiterate that corporate heads today are not just feted for their achievements in the corporate sphere in India, but also seen as intellectual visionaries who would know what is best for education of the country. The corporate vision has become the legitimate national vision though a certain degree of unease may have started to be felt even within state and corporate structures. C.N.R. Rao, scientific advisor to Prime Minister Dr Manmohan Singh, commented that 'If you are worried about economic competitiveness and not worried about scientific competitiveness, then I think the future will be bleak' (*The Times of India*, 23 July 2006).

In this new world of pragmatism, theoretical and ideological debates are seen with some relief as remnants of a well-rid past. My contention here is that a concerted attempt has to be made by academics to bring back theoretical issues and ideological questions. For the commonsense of the current regime is deeply ideological even as its ideology is clothed in the garb of 'pragmatic deliverables'. Further, my contention is that in order to do so, we need to focus on the body of work that Indian social science has produced and also look back on the debate on relevance of social sciences.

Indian Social Science, Sociology and the Spirit of Critique

The contemporary context one has sought to show is abuzz with the possibilities of expansion of higher education and 'global' universities. A central point that I would like to make is that while Indian social science has a body of scholarship and a legacy of intellectual debates about modern education since the 19th century, the current discourse reflects nothing of this collective knowledge. Kapil Sibal, the present Union Minister for Education, remarked that the key problem is infrastructure and economic reforms.[6] The rest he stated would follow. This paper strongly argues otherwise. My contention has been that it is management discourse that has acquired hegemony. This is particularly unfortunate as India faces incredible opportunity and untold challenges to its social science. It is imperative that we re-engage with the past debates (Oommen and Mukherjee, 1988).

In these debates sociologists have had a major role to play – a part that needs highlighting today.[7] Sociologists have introspected often enough 'about the nature of the enterprise in which he is involved' (Jayaram, 1980: 18). Sociologists have also noted this penchant of theirs to '... air their disciplinary anxieties ...' (Uberoi, 2000: 14). 'What can be the reason for this?' The phenomenon ..., some suggested, was simply 'happenstance', the serendipitous conjunction of the editors' personal networks and particular moments in some individual sociologists' life histories. But, as Uberoi pertinently remarks 'of course, such circumstantial contextualizations do not explain why this happenstance should happen so often in the case of sociologists (say, at least once a decade for forty years), and not so much to other people' (ibid.)! I argue however that this penchant of sociology to reflect and critique emerges from its intellectual orientation – a product of the public enlightenment project. I return to this role of sociology in the concluding part of this paper in an effort to buttress my contention that a sociological perspective would be crucial for liberal education.

In Indian context, marked by a colonially mediate modernity, this search for 'public enlightenment' was compounded by its anti-colonial struggles, its nationalist visions and the struggles of groups outside the nationalist framework. The questions *why* social science and *what* kind of social science have been central to Indian social science discourse (Singh, 1986; Oommen, 2000)? 'In the late 1960s, the social sciences in India were astir in search of a direction and an identity. Phrases like 'science and swaraj' were in the air' (Saberwal, 1980: 10). J.P.S. Uberoi elaborates:

> Every swarajist should recognize what are the essential precondition, under this system, for the advancement of universal science in our environment. *Until we can concentrate on decolonization, learn to nationalize our problems and take our poverty seriously, we shall continue to be both colonial and unoriginal.* (Uberoi, 1968: 123; emphasis mine)

The international division of labour and power was taken as given. The view was strong that 'the problem or problems of science in a rich, technologically satiated society are different from, even opposed to, its problems in a society of poverty lately liberated from colonial bondage' (ibid.: 119). This changed over the next decade as did 'the scene in international politics'. 'Even though the social sciences in India have begun to be financed relatively well, the Young Turks of yesteryear discovered that greater insulation was not synonymous with better growth; that autonomy – personal and collective – could be stagnative as easily as creative' (Saberwal, 1980: 10).

Reading through the debates of the seventies one is struck by the fact that the entire issue of autonomy and freedom of social science research was primarily geared vis-a-vis state funding, and much less that of corporate funding. Sabyasachi Bhattacharya, writing in 1972, thus, observes that while the problems autonomy '... would also apply to *the situation of the social science consultant vis-à-vis the corporate sector. In fact, such possibilities are likely to be far greater and more pernicious. But links between social science work and the private sector have not yet been established in a big way*' (Bhattacharya, 1972: 39; emphasis mine)

At the turn of this century the scene had entirely changed.

> Forced to go where the funding is, the sociologists' research priorities and criteria of relevance are determined by the sponsoring agencies, whether government or, increasingly the big extra-and multinational funding agencies. Each has its attendant hazards, *but in either case the role of sociology as social engineering is likely to prevail*, for every project – if it is not to be deemed infructuous – is expected to yield a clear set of policy implications and recommendations. Cross-country comparative projects, though often lushly funded tend to be devised without consultation with the Indian partners who are merely expected to execute the Indian 'country study' according to a predetermined protocol! (Uberoi, 2000: 19; emphasis mine)

A key contention in the debates was about the very role of social sciences, i.e., whether they should be involved in social engineering. Can one frame the debate in the abstract set of choices between *social engineering* and that of the *critical understanding* (Beteille, 1972: 14)? Or is this very framing of the choice in these terms missing the colonial story that spelt different trajectories of modernity for the West and the rest. P.C. Joshi elaborates:

> In the first place, professionalisation has created and sustained the conception of a 'scientific man' possessing skills and tools and standing, as it were, outside and above social problems and conflicts ... underdeveloped countries have, however, inherited not the Renaissance conception of the social scientist as a *social critic* who was as much a participant in as an analyst of human affairs; they have inherited the contemporary conception of social scientist as a value neutral *technician* or a *specialist*. In this way, the very definition of a social scientist today puts a high premium on certain attributes which do not meet the basic needs of the underdeveloped countries. By sanctifying value-neutrality, non-activism and social rootlessness as the desirable attributes of a social scientist, *professionalisation promotes the alienation of social scientists from their own societies*. (Joshi, 1972: 25; emphasis mine)

While Joshi draws attention to how professionalism in our context can easily be reduced to social rootlessness, it is I think important not to necessarily conflate professional functioning with alienated one. It is enlightening to look at the way Satish Saberwal (1980: 14) seeks to explain how the colonial experience has shaped 'non-professional' mode of functioning even within the academia with the insight that historical sociology alone can provide.

Returning to the matter of *relevance*, Ashis Nandy comments that 'it is an artificial distinction designed to give prominence to relevance at the cost of quality. As if the inept could be relevant ...'. Nandy further says:

> We have had nothing but relevant research during the last two decades. Since the beginning of the nineteen fifties we have been producing with fanatic zeal hundreds of unreadable scientific profanities on the *panchayat raj system, agricultural extension, family planning, public administration and management. Few more hundreds of studies have done on social stratification in villages, inter-community perceptions, social distances and prejudices*. The number of village studies run into thousands. And now election studies and socio-economic surveys are being bred at a rate which will put to shame our population growth rate. Prima facie, all of them are relevant. Prima facie very few of them can be used by anyone, let alone the policy maker (if that happens to be, by any chance, your concept of relevance). (Nandy, 1972: 30; emphasis mine)

In 2011 we are once again bludgeoned by calls to be 'relevant'. We are flooded by research that 'few can use' to draw from Nandy's observations forty years ago. This author, commenting on research by women studies centre in 2005, once again makes the same point while she explicates what social science research ought to be:

> Women studies scholars are expected to move away from this narrow academic view. NGOs claim that they on the other hand constantly keep in view the subjects of their research. However, *women studies research is not for just locating immediate problems or seeking immediate solutions. It has a wider scope. It seeks to delve into history, to understand other disciplines by a careful reading of their theories attempting thereby to locate biases and shortcomings in mainstream disciplines in the way they articulate women's lives and hopefully, and thereby evolve new theories and methodologies.* While immediate problems are indeed necessary, these broader engagements are equally important as an intellectual enterprise for creating new knowledge, that form the basis for understanding issues and formulating action. Hence, all women studies research need not only be empirical research. Both theoretical and empirical work constantly complement each other. (Krishnaraj, 2005: 3008; emphasis mine)

The contemporary academic world is governed by certain markings of the current corporate culture. Like the advertisements around us society values quick and tangible success that demands high visibility. Social scientists cannot but be part of this, even if in the process of making smart sound bites in the electronic media, we end up either squashed by the anchor, a little lost or much more commonly plain superfluous, just one more ingredient in the programme director's menu. I think social scientists ought to engage in public discourse but to the extent possible, in their own terms. The deeper problem however rests on how this is seen within the academia. If we read Rajni Kothari's comments in 1972, it suggests that:

> The disease itself is deeper and is to be found in a field which does not really know what its role is, seeks shortcuts to success (e.g., the number of times you are summoned by the AIR), is not subject to rigorous professional demands ... *and measures competence by status instead of bestowing status on those who are competent.*

In a world dominated by electronic media and sound bites one can well imagine how deep and pervasive such 'short cuts' to fame would be. What do we do then? Turn away cynically? Resort to cryptic managerial solutions? Or carefully look at our collective strengths, cumulative social science knowledge and examine the current context both to analyse the problem and offer fruitful possibilities. This is a task I argue sociology is fully capable of.

The Call to do 'Useful' Social Science and Why We Need to be Cautious

This paper has recognized the often stagnant and sad state of our academia, which has created social conditions which make the call for 'useful' social science seem completely appropriate. I have already argued how this idiom of 'usefulness' captures the spirit of contemporary capitalism and how in turn management discourse encapsulates its very essence. Kothari's description of the academia in the 1970s will bring home the point why people are cynical and why there is widespread public opinion that academics do 'nothing'.

> It is a very different and very depressing world. Exchange of examinerships and nominations to selection committees, cooking up first classes and doctoral degrees for one's favourites and denying these certificates of greatness to others, getting on to committees of the UGC and the ICSSR, going to ministers to get professorships and waiting on foreign dignitaries for a trip abroad, 'putting up a fight' for a larger office or better furnishing – or an exclusive peon – as compared to one's colleagues, 'keeping in their place' younger and more competent members of the department (in case they managed to get in the first instance) and reporting to the Vice Chancellor or the more powerful Registrar on the misdeeds of others – these are the engaging activities of the grey and not so grey eminences of our university departments of the social sciences. (Kothari, 1972: 18)

UGC and ICSSR are no longer what they used to. Nor is the state what it used to be. My contention is however something else. My question is: 'Are other organizations like the now expanding non-governmental sector different?' While a trip abroad is no longer so infrequent, nor so rationed, does it mean that the petty everyday politics of institutions is over? (A good guess would be that the stakes are higher today.) Is the state alone responsible for this? And, most importantly, is this the prime crisis that higher education faces today?

Kothari identifies the undue interference of the state as entirely undesirable. His contention is that higher education and the academia is neither agriculture nor economics. It is in fact the duty of the state to exercise an element of self-abnegation and to facilitate both the expression of individualized creativity and dissent in this sphere. It is on this basis that a wide ranging debate on other goals leading to clear-cut policies will become possible, for it is in the latter that a sustained collective effort is called for. The growth of an autonomous state and society involves this combination of open discourse and sustained cooperation (Kothari, 1975: 30). This I think is the point to be taken.

If we are to go by the stated objectives of the new 'global' universities and the rationale on which they rest, can we justifiably claim that they would create conditions for 'open discourse'? What we require is a higher education, which provides the skills of critically examining the specificity of distinct historical junctures and the implications they have for the form and content of social science knowledge. Despite the sordid story of everyday functioning of the academia, the fact is that that we have indeed developed a body of rich social science literature. We have also engaged in debates on the nature and function of social science that may offer fresh and critical insights at this point in history.

This paper has argued at some length the changing contexts within which the race to be global and the rush to do 'useful social science' are taking place. It is crucial that we pause, think and reflect. Given that we have a tradition at hand, we need to engage with that. But first a careful consideration of why the rush to be 'useful' has its persuasive power, a point I mentioned earlier too. We witness the increasing presence of non-governmental organizations – national (NGOs) and international (INGOs); research projects funded and sponsored by diverse bodies; and increasing interest of corporate bodies on social matters. We also observe how scholars are completely caught up in a tight schedule of projects, field work, consultations and workshops. For anyone used to the laid back, lazy world that most institutions of higher learning are assumed to be (and sometimes are) this flurry of action is a welcome relief. Since many of these researches and workshops are directly geared to action or evaluation of projects in action the whole exercise seems to be a far more worthy and fruitful endeavour, than traditional academic pursuits.

Indeed, as Partha Chatterjee remarks, 'there are positive things that have also been said about this kind of sponsored research': (a) They are often more closely tied to urgent policy issues or social movements. (b) Since there is less baggage of traditional disciplinary rigour, researchers can afford to be more adventurous and innovative in their methods. (c) Their vision may be less clouded by the abstract concepts of academic social science theory; they may listen more carefully and sympathetically to the concrete knowledges actually accumulated by ordinary people in the course of their experiences and struggles. But, as Chatterjee himself warns:

> A more radical version of this argument in favour of sponsored research would go so far as to say that a country like India cannot afford the luxury of pure academic social science research. Researchers here must be able to demonstrate that their studies are of some direct use for those whose business it is to do things in society – for producers, managers, administrators, labourers, citizens, etc. Research that fails this test cannot legitimately claim any funding, whether state or non-state. (Chatterjee, 2002: 3610)

This, of course, immediately raises the issue of the division of intellectual labour. This apparently radical-sounding position on the social accountability of the social scientist, if adopted, would actually lead to a situation where fundamental theoretical research would be confined to the first world universities and the third world researchers would be sent out to the field only to do empirical policy-oriented research. In fact, this is actually the situation today in most third world countries.

Even as policy makers[8] at the helm of affairs remain oblivious of Indian scholarship, particularly in social sciences and humanities, the 'global' universities of the West are in a rush to internationalize their curriculum and appropriate Indian debates on issues ranging from culture, identity and multiculturalism to new approaches arising from gender and historical studies in India to mention just some areas.

At a time in history when India is poised to expand its higher education sector, grossly uninformed of its academic legacy, moving dangerously from one buzzword to another, it becomes extremely important to draw our attention today to the fact that:

> India is one of the very few exceptions where there exists an institutional network and a pool of trained social scientists capable of fully participating in the international field of social science discourse and contributing albeit in varying degrees, to the theoretical debates in the different social science disciplines. *These are institutional and intellectual assets that have been built over several generations and at some social cost. It would be foolish and irresponsible to throw them away*. (Chatterjee, 2002: 3610–11; emphasis mine)

As Chatterjee observes, 'even in the former socialist countries (including China), there appears to be no social science research today that has any original theoretical content; the younger and brighter social scientists there are desperately trying to catch up with the currently fashionable trends in the first world' (ibid.). Indian social scientists have to urgently ensure the space they have today is retained in the future. Unfortunately, we too are witness to trends that reflect a desperate attempt to be with the latest, to deploy theories as ornamentation and with a gross lack of historical perspective.

I mention this unfortunate gap between academics and policy makers for two reasons: one, that the contemporary period to my mind is a historical turning point in geo-political relations with deep implications for higher education generally and for India in particular; and two that social science in general and a sociological perspective in specific has much to offer in terms of both analysis and visions of a democratic and just society. This is particularly crucial at a time when the rhetoric of India's growth and global power threaten to obliterate more lasting and time-tested normative values such as peace and equity. And, when influential global policy makers suggest that a more productive way forward would be to gear our higher education either to solve 'local problems' or produce more efficient 'global human resource', it is in this scenario that sociology needs to put forward its 'critical' and 'public enlightenment' best foot forward rather than be a willing handmaiden of human resource education.

Why Sociology and What Links with Liberal Education?

A key contention that runs through this paper is that a social science, informed of critical sociology, is required at a time in history where we seem to be dangerously perched on the race to 'global'. I have also dwelt on the significance of liberal education and its close links to some basic tenets of sociology – a point that Peter Berger explicates:

> ... *the teaching of sociology is justified insofar as a liberal education is assumed to have a more than etymological connection with intellectual liberation*. Where this assumption does not exist, where education is understood as purely technical

> or professional terms, let sociology be eliminated from the curriculum. It will only interfere with the smooth operation of the latter, provided, of course, that sociology has not also been emasculated in accordance with the educational ethos prevailing in such situations. Where, however, the assumption still holds, *sociology is justified by the belief that it is better to be conscious than unconscious and that consciousness is a condition of freedom.* (Berger, 1966: 198; emphasis mine)

I also argue that the theoretical openness of sociology, seen as a lack especially versus a discipline like economics, is 'useful'.

> *One of the great advantages of sociology in the context of a democratic conversation is precisely its openness*. The self-reflexivity of individuals is also reflected in that of the discipline itself ... The crucial point about sociology is that by challenging such constructs it is not only alternative theories that may be advanced but other ways of seeing the world which in turn might lead to different policy prescriptions. This enables sociology to be part of a democratic conversation that is not dominated by one particular model of how we think and act, thereby confining debate within set parameters. (Lauder et al., 2004: 8)

In Kushal Deb's words sociology seemed to 'possess a strong subversive potential', an 'ability to unravel the relations of power and domination implicit in everyday life, and in social processes and institutions' (Deb, 2010). Going back to Bottomore I reiterate the two features of sociological thought that he thought justified speaking of an inherently radical orientation. In the first place, he emphasized 'as the principal legacy of the Enlightenment in sociological thought, and in Marxism as one of its forms, the critical outlook of science, rather than the idea of the domination of nature and its extension to social practice in the domination of men'. Bottomore further argued that it is one of the positive, and radical, features of sociology considered as a science that it 'involves a continuous criticism of all extant theories of society, including those everyday conceptions of the social world which shape practical life' . ... The second feature of sociology to which Bottomore drew attention to was the social consequences and how these are conceived within sociological thought. If the aim of sociology was taken to be the discovery of the hidden mechanism of social life, which is then communicated in the training of a small elite of 'social engineers', he asked whether this entails the production and reproduction of a form of domination. But if he asks, 'the aim is seen as the diffusion through society of an understanding of how social relationships are established, persist, or can be changed – as a kind of public enlightenment – then its effects can well be seen as liberating' (Bottomore, 1975: 15–16). As Robert Lynd once observed: 'Social science is not a scholarly arcanum, but an organized part of the culture which exists to help man in continually understanding and rebuilding his culture' (Lynd, 1939: ix).

However dismal parts of our academia are, we cannot turn away from liberal education and social science. More importantly, while stories of our dysfunctional institutions catch public attention, the cumulative body of social science scholarship, 'globally' recognized, remain invisible. Further, for what ails in higher education, and a great deal does, we cannot have one-shot solutions, plethora of buzzwords and smart sound bites touted as education policy. I end the paper with Rajni Kothari's words:

> No one can deny the importance of the social sciences in our time – both in regard to the advancement of knowledge itself and in regard to the relationship between knowledge and purpose in society. *We are at a stage in history when the social sciences constitute the new frontiers of science.* The physical sciences *per se* have come to a grinding halt in dealing with the most pressing problems of human evolution and are looking to the social sciences-to the new developments in psychology and anthropology, to political economy, to demography – for analysis and illumination. *The social science also constitute the new frontiers of philosophy and normative studies* ... There is little sensitivity, let alone sustained analysis, of the kind of world we are living in and the kind of future that is unfolding before us and the nature of challenges thrown up by these developments to us as citizens and as students of society. (Kothari, 1972: 17; emphasis mine)

Notes

1. I mention this early in the paper for Professor Yogendra Singh who has been my teacher and belongs to a period when his generation was actively engaged in higher education for nation-building. Nation-building itself was marked by some very clear ideas about what Indian nationalism stood for. He has written on this extensively and the story of the Centre for the Study of Social Systems, Jawaharlal Nehru University of which I am a product and now teaching, for more than two decades, bears an imprint of this vision (Unnithan et al., 1967; Singh, 1986; Chaudhuri, 2011).
2. T. Jayaraman, a theoretical physicist, commenting on recent policy statements writes: '... even *prima facie*, it seems that this round of proposals and announcements has a substantially *ad hoc* character leading one to doubt whether they indeed amount to a serious initiative to re-vitalize research in the basic sciences ...' (*The Hindu*, 9 August 2005: 10).
3. See Manish Thakur (2010).
4. The task force vision of a liberal education stresses cognitive skills on the one hand (e.g., the ability to think critically and distinguish between valid and invalid inferences), and breadth of knowledge on the other (e.g., some familiarity with the sciences, some knowledge of human achievements of the past and philosophical and religious concepts). Apart from the acquisition of the values of responsible and modern citizenship mentioned above, liberal education is to be valued because, if done right, it allows an understanding of the nature of learning itself. This is a necessary foundation for a lifetime of re-learning, a key attribute of survival in a knowledge-based economy (Abraham, 2000: 19).
5. I have argued earlier how advertisements since the 1990s have redefined Indian media and thereby public discourse. See Chaudhuri (2000, 2001, 2005). In recent years I see indications that the academia too may play a similar role.
6. This was at the *Mail Today Education Conclave*, 30 July 2011. www.1edupage.com/secondary-education

7. See D.P. Mukerji (1951).
8. My reference here is primarily to social science education. However, a recent remark made by a senior minister about the fame of IIT resting on its global standard students and not the faculty, in essence capture the disjunction between the academia and government. Likewise, the repeated invocation of Harvard University as a reference model by the minister-in-charge of education reflects a grossly inadequate appreciation of India's strength, distinction and visibility in social science academia.

References

Abraham, Itty (2000). 'International Trends', *Seminar*, 494, October, Special Issue on 'Higher Education in South Asia'.

Beteille, Andre (1972). 'The Problem,' *Seminar*, 157, September, pp. 10–14.

Berger, Peter L. (1966). *Invitation to Sociology: A Humanistic Perspective*. Harmondsworth: Penguin.

—— (2003). 'Newness in Sociological Enquiry', in Maitrayee Chaudhuri (ed.), *The Practice of Sociology*, New Delhi: Orient Longman, pp. 403–19.

Bhattacharya, Sabyasachi (1972). 'All the ifs', *Seminar*, 157, September, pp. 37–40.

Boltanski, Luc and Eve Chapello (2005). *A New Spirit of Capitalism*. London: Verso.

Bottomore, T.B. (1975). *Sociology as Social Criticism*. London: George Allen & Unwin.

CARRHE (2009). Report of 'The Committee to Advise on Renovation and Rejuvenation of Higher Education'.

Chatterjee, Partha (2002). 'Institutional Context of Social Science Research in South Asia', *Economic and Political Weekly*, 31 August, pp. 3604–12.

Chaudhuri, Maitrayee (2000). 'Feminism in Print Media', *Indian Journal of Gender Studies*, 7(2): 263–88.

—— (2001). 'Gender and Advertisements: The Rhetoric of Globalisation', *Women's Studies International Forum*, 24(3 and 4): 373–85. Reprinted in Joseph Turow and Matthew McAllister (2009). *The Advertising and Consumer Culture Reader*. Chapter 11, London: Routledge.

—— (ed.) (2003). *The Practice of Sociology*. New Delhi: Orient Longman.

—— (ed.) (2004). *Feminism in India*. New Delhi: Kali for Women and Woman Unlimited.

—— (2005). 'A Question of Choice: Advertisements, Media and Democracy', in Bernard Bel et al. (eds), *Media and Mediation: Communication Processes*, Vol. 1. New Delhi: Sage, pp. 199–226.

—— (2010a). 'Indian Media and its Transformed Public', *Contributions to Indian Sociology*, 44(1 and 2): 57–78.

—— (2010b). *Sociology in India: Intellectual and Institutional Practices*. Jaipur: Rawat Publications.

Choudaha, Rahul (2010). 'Advertising (mal)practices: Lack of Professional Standards'. www.dreducation.com/2010/…./education-advertising-malpractices. h ….18 October 2010. Accessed on 16 July 2011.

Deb, Kushal (2010). 'The Challenges in Teaching Sociology at IIT: Are 'Karl' and 'Marx' Relevant?', in Chaudhuri (2010b), op. cit., pp. 215–34.

'Global Universities, An Old Idea Refashioned, How to Create a Higher-education Supermarket', *The Economist*, 13 May 2010. www.economist.com/node/16103856. Accessed on 17 July 2011.

Habermas, Jurgen (1991). *The Structural Transformation of the Public Sphere: An Inquiry into a Category of Bourgeois Society*. The MIT Press.

Hannon, Elliot (2010). 'Learning Curve', *New Delhi Times* in Partnership with CNNN, 1 November. www.time.com/time/magazine/article/0,9171,2026887,00.html. Accessed on 16 July 2011.

Hohendahl, Peter Uwe (2005). 'The Transnational University and the Global Public Sphere', in Max Pensky (ed.), *Globalising Critical Theory*, Lanham: Rowman and Littlefield Publications, pp. 89–112.

Hunter, James Davison and Joshua Yates (2002). 'In the Vanguard of Globalization: The World of the American Globalizers', in Peter L. Berger and Samuel P. Huntington (eds), *Many Globalizations: Cultural Diversity in the Contemporary World*. Oxford: Oxford University Press.

Jayaram, N. (1980). 'The Social Reality', *Seminar*, 254, Special Issue on 'Studying Our Society', pp. 18–22.

Joshi, P.C. (1972). 'The Question of Relevance', *Seminar*, 157, September, pp. 24–29.

Juma, Calestous (2005). 'Issues in University Education', *The Hindu*, 15 July.

Kabir, Humayun (1956). *Education in New India*. Allen & Unwin.

Karnik (2005). *The Hindu*, 18 July.

Kothari, Rajni (1972). 'In Search of a Role', *Seminar*, 157, September, pp. 17–23.

—— (1975). 'Policy and Culture', in Satish Saberwal (ed.), *Towards a Cultural Policy*, Delhi: Vikas, pp. 25–31.

Krishnaraj, Maithreyi (2005). 'Research in Women Studies: Need for a Critical Appraisal', *Economic and Political Weekly*, 9 July, XL(28): 3008–17.

Lauder, H. et al. (2004). 'Sociology and Political Arithmetic: Some Principles of a New Policy Science', *The British Journal of Sociology*, March, 55(1): 3–22.

Lynd, Robert S. (1939). *Knowledge for What?* Princeton: Princeton University Press.

Mail Today Education Conclave (2011). www.1edupage.com/secondary-education. Accessed on 31 July 2011.

Maitrayee, Chaudhuri (2011). 'Looking Back: the Practice of Sociology at CSSS', in Sujata Patel (ed.) *Doing Sociology in India: Genealogies, Locations, and Practices*. Delhi: Oxford University Press, pp. 158–187.

Mukerji, D.P. (1952). 'Sociology in Independent India', *Sociological Bulletin*, 1(1).

Nandy, Ashis (1972). 'Conspiracy of Incompetence', *Seminar*, 157, September, pp. 30–32.

Narlikar, Jayant V. (2005). 'Reaching for the Stars', *The Times of India*, 30 July, p. 24.

Nussbaum, Martha C. (1997). *Cultivating Humanity: A Classical Defence of Reform in Liberal Education*. Cambridge, Mass.: Harvard University Press.

Oommen, T.K. (2000). 'Professionals without Professionalism', *Seminar*, 495, November, pp. 24–28.

Oommen, T.K. and Partha Mukherjee (eds) (1988). *Indian Sociology: Reflections and Introspections*. Bombay: Popular Prakashan.

Saberwal, Satish (1980). 'For Renewal', *Seminar*, 254, Special Issue on 'Studying Our Society', pp. 12–18.

Schelling, F.W.J. (1966). *On University Studies*. Ohio University Press.

Singh, Yogendra (1986). *Indian Sociology*. New Delhi: Vistaar.

—— (1996). 'Constraints, Contradictions and Interdisciplinary Orientations: The Indian Context', in Kanjiv Lochan (ed.), *JNU: The Years*, JNU Silver Memoir Committee, Mumbai: Popular Prakashan, pp. 56–65.

Thakur, Manish (2010). 'Of Mainstream and Margins: Sociology in Indian Institutes of Management (IIMs)', in Chaudhuri (2010a), op. cit.

Thapan, Meenakshi (1991). 'Sociology in India: A View from Within', *Economic and Political Weekly*, 11 May, 26(19): 1229–34.

'The Problem', *Seminar*, December, pp. 10–11.

Uberoi, J.P.S. (1968). 'Science and Swaraj', *Contributions to Indian Sociology*, (n.s.)2: 119–23.

Uberoi, Patricia (2000). *'Déjà vu'*, *Seminar*, 495, November, pp. 14–19.

Unnithan, T.K.N. et al. (eds) (1967). *Sociology for India.* New Delhi: Prentice-Hall.

Wildavasky, Ben (2010). *The Great Brain Race: How Global Universities are Reshaping the World*. Princeton: Princeton University Press.

2

The Decline of the University as a Public Institution in India*

N. Jayaram

The success of any large-scale democratic polity and its efforts at sustained economic development is contingent upon the effective functioning of its public institutions. In a democracy, public institutions such as schools and universities, hospitals and banks, legislatures and courts, the civil service and the army – as different from private institutions like families, extended kin groups, and religious communities – are expected to contribute to the common good, irrespective of caste, creed or religion. As such, in multi-religious and socio-culturally heterogeneous societies like India, public institutions have an even greater role to play.

Almost all the public institutions currently functioning in India were originally introduced there by the British rulers as part of the colonialist modernization project.[1] These institutions were modelled after their counterparts in Britain, and they were intended to serve the economic and political interests of the British and help them consolidate their rule in the country. All the same, both in their 'morphological forms' and in 'the values that (gave) them meaning and legitimacy' (Béteille, 2000: 154), these new institutions differed from those existent in the country. They were premised upon universal normative structures and legal-rational considerations.[2] So much confidence was reposed in the efficacy of these institutions that they were adopted, with little or no modification, by the state managers after India became independent.

*The is a revised version of a paper presented at the seminar on 'Public Institutions and Social Transformation in India and Sri Lanka', jointly organized by the India-Sri Lanka Foundation and Indian Council of Social Science Research, at Colombo on 18–20 October 2007. Given Professor Yogendra Singh's abiding interest in institutions, I deem it a privilege to present him this essay.

It is 65 years since India attained independence and 62 years since she adopted the republican form of government. But for the brief dark interregnum of the Emergency era (1975–77), its track record as a functioning democracy has been remarkable. Within the democratic framework it has been negotiating significant socio-economic changes and addressing a plethora of socio-political movements. Taking a long-term perspective of six decades, it is hard to deny that the India of today is significantly different from the India on the eve of its independence. In retrospect, one is tempted to ask: what has become of the British-implanted public institutions that India inherited and adopted at the time of independence? This question assumes greater sociological significance considering that these institutions did not have organic roots in the native society. In this paper an attempt has been made to answer this question with reference to one of these public institutions, namely, the university.[3]

The Historical Background

The foundation for the university as a public institution in India was laid by the British colonial regime in the mid-19th century (Ashby and Anderson, 1966: 54–146). The initial educational efforts of the Christian missionaries and the East India Company generated a protracted controversy between the 'Anglicists', commending a western course, and the 'Orientalists', favouring an indigenous direction. William Bentinck finally resolved this controversy in favour of the Anglicist orientation, barely a month after Thomas Babington Macaulay had penned his (in)famous *Minute* (on 2 February 1835). Charles Wood's *Despatch* (of 19 July 1854) reaffirmed his policy. Upon the recommendation of the committee appointed on 26 January 1855, the first three universities were established at Bombay (now Mumbai), Calcutta (now Kolkata) and Madras (now Chennai) in 1857.

Modelled after the University of London (established in 1836), these pioneer universities were largely affiliating and examining bodies with very little intellectual life of their own. They lacked, what André Béteille has called, 'corporate identity' (2000: 159). All the universities that were subsequently established, including those in the princely states of Mysore (1916) and Hyderabad (1919), developed in an isomorphic fashion set on the pattern of the original universities.

The British educational implantation in India, as noted earlier, was conceived to serve the economic, political and administrative interests of the British and, in particular, to consolidate and maintain their dominance in the country.[4] It emphasized English, which not only was taught as a language, but was also made the exclusive medium of instruction in higher education. The content was biased in favour of languages and the humanities, and against science and technology.

It is not as if the British rulers did not realize the problems associated with such an educational implantation or its adverse consequences for the colonized society. Yet, it was only during the early years of the 20th century, thanks to the initiative of Lord Curzon, the then Viceroy of India (1898–1905), that efforts were made to 'rescue the original concept of the university from its corrosive narrowness'.[5] Several inquiries were instituted during the last three decades of the colonial rule, but 'hardly any of their major recommendations were translated into university policy or practice' (Tickoo, 1980: 34).

Thus, the legacy of the university system inherited by India at the time of its independence was already crisis-ridden. As an integral element of colonial underdevelopment, it was 'anaemic, distorted and dysfunctional'. Low level of enrolment, 'liberal' nature of education, 'enclavization' of the institutes of higher learning, and spurious modernization were its festering features (see Raza et al., 1985: 100–09). While the obsolescence of the inherited university system, by and large, persisted, the system itself underwent such a phenomenal expansion as never before seen in the world. At the time of its independence in 1947, India had 20 universities and 496 colleges catering to 2,41,369 students. After a massive expansion of the university system during the next 62 years, by the end of 2009 it had 496 universities and university-level institutions and 29,951 colleges catering to almost 12 million students.

Thus, India today has the third largest university system in the world (after China and the United States of America). It is also noteworthy that this system has a history of 150 years. It has been producing graduates and doctorates in science and technology, arts and humanities, medicine and law, etc., in thousands every year, making India the second largest repository of university credential holders, and the fourth largest science and technology workforce in the world.

The University as a Public Institution

As a public institution, the university is ascribed to a purpose, and it carries a meaning, not only to those who directly participate in it, but also to those who are indirectly affected by it. Accordingly, every university sets for itself a vision and mission and draws up a roadmap to realize its vision and accomplish its mission. All universities, at the time of their establishment, have a statement to this effect. But as they grow and age, there develops a disjunction between their vision/mission statement and what they do and what happens in their precincts. And, in many a case, the university just begins to drift and go moribund.

While the strain towards such disjunction and drift is noticeable across the board, obviously, not all universities experience it uniformly or in the same fashion. This is because the universities vary widely on several parameters. The nature of the disjunction and drift experienced by any university, therefore, is a subject for empirical analysis. This paper does not undertake such an analysis. Rather, focusing on the strain towards such disjunction and drift, it seeks to discuss the decline of the university as a public institution in India generally. The discussion here will be substantiated by instances drawn from some specific universities.

As a public institution, a university is expected to (a) produce and refine knowledge and transmit it from one generation to the next, (b) train successive generations in the vast variety of skills required for the sustenance of the society, (c) certify the acquisition of knowledge and skills by those enrolled into the system, and (d) engage itself in a meaningful way with the community in which it exists. Thus, as the University Education Commission (1948–49) (the Radhakrishnan Commission) described, universities are 'the organs of civilization' and 'the homes of intellectual adventure' (cited in Raghavan, 1985: 240–41).

It is from the foregoing expectations that the university derives its legitimacy and fulfil them with requisite authority. As a public institution, it enjoys legal status and is subject to regulative authority. In India, universities are established either by an Act of Parliament and regulated directly by the Government of India's Ministry of Human Resource Development (MHRD) (the central universities) or by an Act of State Assemblies and regulated by the respective state governments (the state universities).

Besides the central and the state universities, a large number of institutions have been recognized as 'institutions deemed-to-be universities' under the University Grants Commission (UGC) Act, 1956[6] and several university-level institutions (including the Indian Institutes of Technology) have been conferred the status of 'institutions of national importance' by the Government of India. The deemed universities and the institutions of national importance are also empowered to award degrees which, according to the UGC Act, 1956, can be granted only by a university.[7]

Not only are the universities, institutions deemed-to-be universities, and institutions of national importance established following the due process of law or recognized under provisions of duly enacted laws, they are also substantially supported financially by the government. The central universities and several deemed universities get their funds from MHRD (through UGC), and the institutions of national importance, from the respective ministries under which they come. The state universities are financed by the respective governments, though they also get some funds from UGC.

Thus, it is important to emphasize that the university is essentially a public institution in India, and it is under state patronage that it has hitherto expanded. The concept of a purely private university (of the American type) is new in India. The bill to provide for the establishment of private universities, introduced in the Rajya Sabha (the upper house of Parliament) in August 1995, has since lapsed. Meanwhile, invoking the existing legal provisions (for example, the UGC Act, 1956), several private institutions of higher education have been given the 'deemed university' status, but without any financial assistance from the government.

Considering that higher education is a concurrent subject under the Constitution, some states (like Chhattisgarh) had enacted private university acts of their own, and private universities had begun to mushroom in these states. This has, no doubt, attracted the adverse attention of UGC, which only feels helpless. However, in its judgment of 11 February 2005, the Supreme Court of India has held certain clauses of the Chhattisgarh Private Sector University Act, 2002 'unconstitutional' and cancelled the registration of 112 private universities as void (see Thomas and Tiwari, 2005). The judicial pronouncement of the apex court of the land has endorsed the university's status as a public institution. In what follows let us see how the university system has functioned vis-à-vis the expectations from it as a public institution.

Distortion of Objectives and Deterioration of Quality

The Missing Research Orientation

It must be noted that research (i.e., production and refinement of knowledge), as an essential part of the university system, was not emphasized during the colonial era. The colonial legacy of universities as retailers of knowledge has persisted. As the former Director General of the Council of Scientific and Industrial Research (CSIR), R.A. Mashelkar notes, 'Despite the two-fold increase in the number of universities and rise in expenditure on research and development by 16 times during 1980–2000, the quantum of research has gone down' (cited in *The Navhind Times,* Panjim, 2 September 2002, p. 11). According to the report of The World Bank's Task Force on Higher Education and Society (2000: 124–25), the number of papers in sciences and social sciences from India increased only marginally from 13,623 in 1981 to 14,883 in 1995 (i.e., by 9.25% in 15 years). This is negligible compared to the phenomenal 784.38 per cent (from a meagre 1,293 to 11,435) increase registered by China during the same period.

Mashelkar also abstracted a report which records India's decline in the number of scientific papers abstracted in the International Science Citation Index from 15,000 to 12,000 during 1980–2000: whereas India slipped from 8th rank in the world in 1980 to 15th in 2000, China improved its position from 15th to 9th! In absolute terms, there was, no doubt, an increase in the number of citations of Indian scientific papers – from 56,464 in 1981–85 to 90,162 in 1993–97 (i.e., by 59.68%). But this increase appears to be minuscule compared to the stupendous increase in the number of citations of Chinese scientific papers for the corresponding period – from 8,517 to 77,841 (i.e., by 813.95%) (ibid.). Quoting a CSIR report, B. Vijayakumar notes that 'in the entire history of CSIR of India, only three out of over 20,000 papers published by the scientists have been cited 100 times against a world average of one in every 250'. He further adds that a paper with 'thousand citation counts' (i.e., a paper that has been cited 1,000 times) is either nil or extremely rare (2003: 4–5). No wonder, there has been a growing disquiet over the declining quality of science education and research in the country.

While the University Education Commission (1948–49) (also known as the Radhakrishnan Commission), appointed by the Government of India soon after independence, examined the growth of higher education and made proposals for its future expansion and improvement, and reflected on the philosophy of higher education and suggested measures for improving the standards of teaching, it had very little to say about how to reorient the university system towards research, excepting noting the teachers' obligation 'to engage in research' and 'to keep themselves up-to-date in their knowledge' (cited in Raghavan, 1985: 247).

It is in the report of the Education Commission (1964–66) (also known as the Kothari Commission)[8] that we find a well-articulated proposal for reorienting the university system towards research. Perhaps the most important reform that this Commission envisaged was the development of five or six 'major universities' where conditions may be provided, both as to staff and students as well as to the necessary equipment and atmosphere, to make first-class postgraduate work and research possible. The standards of these universities, it was emphasized, 'should be comparable to the best institutions of their type in any part of the world ...' The Commission was confident that, if given top priority, the idea of 'major universities' can be realized in ten years (Ministry of Education, GoI, 1971: 506–7).

Given the large capital expenditure involved and also the delay in the process of establishing such universities, the Commission recommended that UGC should select 'from amongst the existing universities, about six universities (including one of the IITs and one agricultural university) for development as major universities'. It spelt out guidelines for the recruitment of 'an intellectually distinguished group of teachers who will be able to provide the requisite training and make valuable research contributions' and for the enrolment of qualified students who can benefit from the superior training to be given, and recommended the provision of 'adequate facilities and satisfactory conditions of work' (ibid.: 510 ff).

As a supplement to its idea of 'major universities', the Education Commission recommended the expansion and strengthening of the UGC's Centres of Advanced Study (CAS) scheme. This, the Commission thought, could be undertaken as a preparation to the establishment of major universities, or as a consequence of their establishment. Ideally, 'clusters' of advanced centres could be established in select universities, as had been done in the University of Delhi. Such a cluster of advanced centres, the Commission hoped, would strengthen and enrich one another, and promote interdisciplinary research. Where such clusters are not possible, UGC could begin with the establishment of single centres of postgraduate teaching and research, especially in areas where such centres do not exist (ibid.: 512).

The Education Commission's eloquent proposal for the establishment of 'major universities' was, however, opposed from all quarters. It was summarily rejected by the Parliamentary Committee and the Vice-Chancellors' Conference. While scholars like Dr D.R. Gadgil,[9] who opposed elitism in all its forms, were extremely critical of the proposal, it did not find favour even with academics who generally favoured a selective approach to higher education (see Naik, 1982: 111–13). A rhetorical ground on which the proposal was opposed and rejected was that it was elitist and antithetical to the egalitarian ethos of a socialist-democratic polity. The Commission had anticipated such a criticism of the proposal, and it conceded that its proposal would, at that stage, involve a differentiation between universities. 'This', the Commission held, 'is not only inevitable in an economy of scarcity but is also the only sure and practicable way to benefit all ultimately in the shortest time possible.' It went on to argue that 'we must recognise that pursuit of excellence implies and requires a discriminatory approach; and that to provide equal resources to all irrespective of the quality of their performance and potentiality for growth merely promotes mediocrity' (Ministry of Education, GoI, 1971: 509).

Even those who accepted the principle of selective approach for qualitative improvement argued against the concept of major universities on the ground 'that a *department*, and not a university, should be taken as the unit, that *all* departments of *all* universities should be eligible for selection as Centres of Advanced Study ...' (see Naik, 1982: 113). They, however, accepted the idea of clustering a number of advanced centres into some selected universities where conditions were favourable. This idea was also endorsed by the Parliamentary Committee which reviewed the report. While the idea of 'major universities' was shelved, the idea of clustering of centres of advanced study found a place in the National Policy on Education (1968). However, as J.P. Naik, Member-Secretary of the Commission, observes, this 'was of no avail and no effective steps were taken to implement the proposal even in this modified form'. In March 1987, there were as many as 25 independent Centres for Advanced Study in science subjects, and 15 in humanities and social sciences. However, the 'prestige and glamour' that the idea of Centres of Advanced Study had in 1966 were lost (ibid.).

The neglect of university in science policy formulation has often been interpreted as a failure on the part of scientific leadership and management (see Dadhich, 2004: 2181). According to Jayant V. Narlikar, paradoxical as it may sound, 'the manner of establishment of institutes like the TIFR ... has been largely responsible for the present decline in the following of basic sciences amongst the students today' (2003: 8–9). TIFR was established in 1946 on the eve of India's independence, and the research institutes and laboratories established after independence were all based on this model: they enjoyed considerable autonomy and generous funds and facilities, and they were 'decoupled from universities so that teaching undergraduate or postgraduate students should not come 'in the way' of the researcher' (ibid.: 9). The catch in this was that the researcher was not only decoupled from university/college teaching, but also from students. 'So while research got progressively to the back seat in universities, teaching became noticeably absent from the research institutions' (ibid.).

Thus, while research got an enormous boost from the creation of such specialist institutes, facilities and laboratories, the fact that they were developed outside the university system undermined whatever little research potentialities that the universities had by contributing to an 'internal brain drain' of science talent from the universities to institutes and laboratories. One may recall, as Sushanta Dattagupta (2005: 19–20) does with reference to physics, that J.C. Bose worked in Presidency College, before he founded the Basu Vigyan Mandir (now under the Department of Science and Technology or DST), C.V. Raman was in Calcutta University and the IISc (Bangalore) before establishing the Raman Research Institute (also under DST), and M.N. Saha moved from Allahabad University to create the Saha Institute of Nuclear Physics (now under the aegis of the Department of Atomic Energy).

The divorcing of teaching from research by building research institutes outside the university system seems to have had adverse consequences for the former, too. The autonomous research institutions are finding it 'increasingly difficult to attract young talent, with the problem that a vacuum is slowly but steadily being created at the younger age of the spectrum. Since it is this young age group that eventually grows to take up higher responsibilities, scientific projects which proceed in a mission mode ... are experiencing serious humanpower shortages' (Narlikar, 2003: 11). With research getting progressively to the back seat in universities, 'the very lifeline of science graduates from universities that fed young scientists to (the research) institutions began to get more and more tenuous and is now close to becoming extinct' (ibid.). Thus, the divide between teaching and research has perhaps done the most damage to the universities as centres of creation of knowledge.[10]

Orienting Universities towards Research

In 1985, the new Congress government proposed to embark on the complex task of 'restructuring the system of education'. Towards this end, in August that year the Ministry of Education (since reorganized as the Ministry of Human Resource Development) presented to parliament a 119-page document titled *Challenge of Education: A Policy Perspective*. This document placed the utmost emphasis on higher education, and noted that because 'major national inputs have gone to laboratories outside the universities', there has been 'great deprivation in terms of facilities for frontline work' in the university system. It called for correcting this anomaly (Ministry of Education, GoI, 1985: 49), while at the same time, recommending a moratorium on the expansion of the conventional pattern of colleges and universities and the establishment of new centres of excellence.

The Programme of Action of the National Policy on Education (MHRD, 1986) was reviewed by the Acharya Ramamurti Committee (MHRD, 1991). The recommendations of the Central Advisory Board on Education that considered the review report were adopted by parliament in May 1992. The revised *Programme of Action – 1992* (see MHRD, 1992) laid emphasis on the need for strengthening research. The setting up of Inter-University Centres for providing common facilities for research in key areas of science, support to departments under the scheme of 'Strengthening of Infrastructure in Science and Technology', and the signing of a memorandum of understanding between UGC and CSIR in 1991 for providing scientists in universities access to research facilities in CSIR and vice versa were all the outcomes of the New Education Policy, 1986 (see ibid.: 66–67).

The revised *Programme of Action – 1992* also recommended the establishment of university-industry linkage on 'a priority basis in metropolitan areas, cities and regions with a concentration of industry', and 'inter-institutional links between universities in India and 'state of the art' research institutions abroad'. More important, it recommended the constitution of 'a high-powered committee', with representatives of Department of Science and Technology, CSIR, Indian Council of Social Science Research (ICSSR), Indian Council of Historical Research, etc., 'to assess the quality of research' in the universities. However, not all these recommendations have received the serious attention that they deserve.

Appreciating that teaching without research is sterile, on its part and in accordance with the changing educational policies, UGC has been undertaking several schemes to provide substantial support to universities and colleges to strengthen their teaching and research activities. Besides the Centres of Advanced Studies (CAS) referred to earlier, UGC gives financial support to select well-established departments under the Special Assistance Programme for undertaking academic programmes in specific fields. UGC also extends financial assistance to 'major' (long-term) and 'minor' (short-term) research projects undertaken by individual teachers or a group of teachers or by a department as a whole.

For research to go on and major breakthrough to come about, there should be a symbiotic relationship between research and teaching. As a follow-up of the New Education Policy's revised *Programme of Action – 1992*, as stated above, UGC has established specialized Inter-University Centres as world-class facilities which could be used by university teachers and students. The Inter-University Centre for Astronomy and Astrophysics (Pune), Nuclear Science Centre (New Delhi) and Inter-University Consortium for Department of Atomic Energy Facilities (Indore) are such common facilities. Modern computer-based information centres have been set up at IISc (Bangalore), SNDT Women's University (Mumbai) and M.S. University of Baroda. UGC's Inter-University Centre for Information and Library Network (Inflibnet), Ahmedabad is now providing access to current literature through e-subscription of journals. Such centres, of course, are no substitute to establishing 'research universities', but considering the general state of affairs in the universities, these and similar initiatives are welcome developments.

Perhaps the most significant effort of UGC in the direction of research-oriented universities – à la 'major universities' recommended by the Kothari Commission more than four decades before – is its heavily funded scheme of 'Universities with Potential for Excellence' (UGC, 2002–03: 127–28). Based on the proposals submitted by several universities and presentations made by their vice-chancellors on their achievements and promise, UGC has selected five universities – Jadavpur University, Jawaharlal Nehru University (New Delhi), University of Hyderabad, University of Madras (Chennai), and University of Pune – and given each a fabulous development grant of ₹ 300 million for five years.

Deterioration of Quality

How well is the university system performing the functions of knowledge transmission and training in skills? As is to be expected, rapid expansion of higher education in post-independence India has been at the cost of its quality.[11] The deterioration in quality is most glaring in the state universities in general, and at the undergraduate level in affiliated colleges in particular. This crisis now encompasses the conventional postgraduate courses offered in the university departments, too. These courses are now performing an extended 'baby-sitting' function. This is understandable considering the relatively low unit cost of running these courses, and that the students entering this stream pay absurdly little towards their education – far less than what students in the private sector primary schools pay. The unregulated expansion of this sector of education has been invariably identified as the main cause of its quality crisis.

What goes on in the name of higher education in many a state university and college is pathetic. In many institutions, the physical facilities are so deplorable and the library and laboratory facilities are so woefully inadequate that they have earned the sobriquet 'academic slums'. While lack of resources[12] – a general refrain heard in this context – is primarily responsible, we cannot blame it alone. What is serious is that even the prescriptions governing the minimum qualifications for the appointment and promotion of academic staff are violated, the minimum number of working days is not met, the calendar of academic activities, if at all, exists only on paper, and the administration has virtually collapsed. In most universities, student feedback and evaluation of teacher performance are either perfunctory or non-existent. All this has adversely affected the quality of education imparted in the universities. Naturally, there is very little in the university system to attract the best talent.[13]

Furthermore, the undue emphasis on certification rather than on teaching-learning process seems to have distorted the orientation of university education. André Béteille rightly draws attention to 'the constant threat to the institutional focus of the Indian university from the pressures of certification. Examinations are no doubt important, but when a university subordinates its other concerns to the concern for certification, there cannot but be a loss of institutional focus' (2000: 158). Perhaps there is a good case for transferring the conduct of examinations at the undergraduate level to a Board, as in the case of Secondary or Higher Secondary School Certificate examinations.

Unlike its British counterpart, UGC[14] in India has the responsibility of regulating the quality of education in universities and colleges.[15] However, considering the inordinate number of universities and colleges it is required to oversee, and being endowed with very little power, UGC has been virtually reduced to a fund-disbursing agency, incapable of enforcing its own recommendations. As a step in the direction of quality control in higher education, following the National Policy of Education (MHRD, 1986), in 1994, UGC set up an autonomous body called the National Assessment and Accreditation Council (NAAC) (see Stella and Gnanam, 2003). The scheme of assessment and accreditation as of now is voluntary, but the idea of an external institution doing this was not received well by universities and colleges. By September 2011, NAAC had assessed and accredited only 159 universities and 4,171 colleges (NAAC, 2010: 20). How far this will improve the state of affairs in the university system, even if indirectly, remains to be seen.

Spatial Aspects of the University

The Physical Space

The institutional life of the university needs to be located in physical space; there must be a congenial environment for scholarly interaction among students and teachers. Many universities in Europe and North America are as much known for their buildings and campuses as for their knowledge-generation and academic activities. Some of the European universities – Cambridge and Oxford in England, St Andrews in Scotland, Louvain/Leuven in Belgium and Heidelberg in Germany, for example – are educational towns. They are abuzz with intellectual and cultural activities. This is what Lord Curzon had in mind when he bemoaned the University of Calcutta lacking 'corporate existence' – 'it is not a collection of buildings, it is scarcely even a site' (quoted in Ministry of Education, GoI, 1971: 498). Universities that were established since Curzon's time, including the ones in Benares and Delhi, took into consideration the spatial dimension of the university as a public institution. 'The idea that every university must have its own campus has now come to be generally accepted' (Béteille, 2000: 158), though not all universities succeed in having a well-laid out campus of their own.

It must be noted, however, that physical space (campus), though necessary, does not by itself guarantee a vibrant academic and cultural life. Many a university campus is located far away from the city: Bangalore, Mangalore, Calicut and South Gujarat readily come to one's mind. Even after 35 years of its shifting to the new campus (Jnanabharathi), the Bangalore University busses its students, teachers and staff from and to the different parts of the city. Incidentally, for three decades it even ran a transport system for this (which has since been handed over to the Bangalore Metropolitan Transport Corporation)! It was first housed in the century-old Central College (a masterpiece of Gothic architecture) campus in the city centre, and was surrounded by many educational institutions – an arts-and-science college, a law college, an engineering college, a women's college, a commerce college and a polytechnic. Thanks to the powers that be, a great opportunity of developing a vibrant university campus in the heart of the city was lost.

Whatever may be the logistics for locating the university campus away from the city, unless it is a residential campus, it has invariably resulted in loss of academic vitality of the institution. Many of them become ghost campuses after the classes are over, and in some cases even as early as early afternoon. Even in Goa University, the campus is deserted in the afternoon, as students and teachers, who come from far-off places, are eager to get back home. Thus, interaction between teachers and students is confined to the classroom setting only, and no extra-curricular academic or cultural activity is possible. In most universities, even sports as a part of university life is non-existent.

Another facet about the physical dimension needs to be mentioned here. Even when universities put up their own buildings, some at huge cost, the maintenance of these buildings becomes very poor. 'Peeling walls, broken windows-panes, leaking taps, unswept corridors and filthy toilets meet the eye everywhere, and the sad thing is that teachers and students become so easily inured to the dirt and decay' (Béteille, 2000: 166). Financial constraint is the familiar refrain we hear from the university authorities. While financial crunch is certainly a problem, the way the universities expend their scarce resources makes one wonder whether cleanliness and upkeep of the precincts are missing as a cultural value in our universities. The slogans, graffiti and posters mercilessly defacing the university walls are a living proof of the woeful lack of civic culture in many universities.

The Social Space

In absolute terms, apparently, the opportunity for university education has expanded. Estimates of the participation rate vary from a conservative 7 (National Knowledge Commission, 2007) to a liberal 10 per cent (MHRD, 2007: 61; 2008: 16), and the Government of India itself has set a modest target of 30 per cent by 2020. If the rate of growth of enrolment during the last two decades is any indicator, even this modest target appears ambitious (see Parhar, 2002). That is, despite the phenomenal increase in enrolment, the vast majority of the youth in the age group 17–23 years not only remains outside the sphere of higher education, but will remain so for decades to come.

The limited participation rate notwithstanding, the social composition of the university has changed remarkably since independence. In 1950–51, the percentage of women in total enrolment in higher education was only 10, and this percentage has peaked at 40 in 2004, but there are significant regional variations in women's enrolment in higher education. Thanks to the policy of protective discrimination, there has been a slow but steady increase in the enrolment of Scheduled Caste (SC) and Scheduled Tribe (ST) students. In 2004, the SCs constituted 10.7 per cent of the enrolment in higher education, and the STs, 3.7 per cent (cited in Jayaram, 2010: 164). Several state governments have extended the reservation of seats for students belonging to backward castes and communities, too. Further, more and more students from the rural background are entering the university.

Thus, there is a noticeable broad-basing of the university as regards its student body is concerned. The teacher community too has been undergoing a similar change. An examination of the changing composition of university as a public institution is due. However, the dialectics of cosmopolitanism and parochialism is noticeable in the universities. On the one hand, the university is a forum where students and teachers belonging to different sexes, communities and socio-economic backgrounds can meet and interact. On the other hand, it is also a site for contestations of symbols and struggle for interests. If sectional interests succeed in influencing academic decisions, as it is noticed in several universities across the country, the university will be doomed as a public institution.

The Political Space

As a self-governing public institution, in a democracy, the university is naturally expected to provide space for some form of politics. The university campus is, in fact, the meeting place for divergent and often opposed views, opinions and interests. As the highest centres of learning, it was expected that the universities would play a significant role in fostering a political culture to gel with democratic institutions and procedures. Regrettably, they have failed in this, and as a consequence academic politics is today 'all politics and hardly academic' (Béteille, 2000: 169). As Béteille rightly observes, 'Leaders of teachers' unions have not enhanced their own dignity or the dignity of the university by becoming petty instruments' of political parties. 'And they could hardly protect the autonomy of the university by surrendering their own autonomy to their parties' (ibid.: 168–69).

That organization of teachers is engrossed only with securing better pay, career advancement and easy conditions of work, rather than with scholarship and professional issues, is now well known (Jayaram, 2003). What is not equally well known is the violent and abusive language used by the teachers in academic bodies. Based on his experience about the Academic Council of the University of Delhi and 'from hearsay about similar bodies in other universities', Béteille feels that the tone displayed by the teachers is 'now marked by a conspicuous, even deliberate, lack of civility' (2000: 167). What is pathetic, 'many scholars and scientists have begun to feel that it is no longer possible to participate in the decision-making bodies of the university and maintain their self-esteem' (ibid.).

The students emulate their teachers. In many universities student unions function as extensions of the national-or the state-level political parties. They fight elections for representative offices in the university on the financial and moral support from these parties. The party functionaries even address election meetings on the campuses. In campuses where the involvement of political parties is not open, candidates contesting elections get indirect support from politicians. Often, the politicization of the campus life results in violence, destruction of university property, and suspension of academic activities, particularly during elections.

The teachers and students alone are not responsible for the politicization of the campus. In most states the autonomy of the university as a public institution is eroded by the aggrandizement of the state. Almost all the states have now enacted legislations to bring the universities under their control. In most state universities, the vice-chancellor and other functionaries of the university are now appointed by the political bosses running the government. Their nominees also sit in the decision-making bodies of universities. No wonder, the New Education Policy (1985) contemplated, though unrealistically, the depoliticization of the academia.

The Loss of Legitimacy

Since independence the university system has expanded rapidly, and haphazardly, too. Contrary to the moratorium on the expansion of the conventional pattern of universities, as contemplated by the New Education Policy (1985), the National Knowledge Commission (NKC) is recommending the expansion of this system even more rapidly. With little thought being given to the institutional life of universities, many of the old universities are decaying, and the new ones too will follow suit. It is as if each university has a life-cycle: born with euphoria, seeing a phase of growth and then becoming stagnant and moribund.

As Béteille observes, 'An important aspect of the university as an institution is that its individual members – whether students or teachers – should have some sense of it as a whole. Not many persons can say confidently or honestly that they have such a sense about Delhi University today, and in that regard it is now different from what it was forty years ago and what the Jawaharlal Nehru University still is today' (2000: 157). If this is what a senior academic has to say about a university located in the nation's capital, one can well imagine what could be said of universities elsewhere!

Along with the growing loss of its identity as a public institution, there is also the erosion of the credibility and integrity of the university. The pervasive mistrust of the integrity of the academic selection process, with every selection invariably being questioned in courts of law; the umpteen scandals about university affairs reported in the media; the debilitating inbreeding in universities, resulting in mediocrity breeding more mediocrity; the shocking self-assured complacency among the academia; and, not the least, 'the demoralising effect of the irrelevance and purposelessness of most of what is being done' (Naik, 1982: 163) – all these have seriously violated the dignity of the university and undermined its legitimacy as a public institution.

Epilogue

It is hardly surprising that not even one Indian university or institute found a place in a recent academic ranking of top 100 universities and institutions of higher education in the world, and only two institutes and one university found listing under ranks below 200: IISc (Bangalore) (ranked in the bracket 202–301), IIT (Kharagpur) and University of Calcutta (Kolkata) (both ranked in the bracket 404–502) were the top three Indian institutions of higher education in that order.[16] Surely, the university as a public institution is now moribund.

There has been no dearth of suggestions for stemming the rot and improving the state of affairs. Several committees and commissions, including the Kothari Commission in the mid-1960s, have reviewed the situation and offered recommendations. Even in the best political climate, such proposals were rejected on grounds of elitism, and the government was content with tinkering with the system. Considering the economic and political cost of wholesale overhauling, and in view of the compulsions of coalition politics now, radical reform proposals are sure to remain on paper only.

Notes

1. If not on the same scale, similar institutions were implanted by the Portuguese and the French in those parts of India that they had colonized respectively.
2. This is not to imply that the administration of these institutions was not influenced by personal or sectional interests. After all, these were institutions of the 'rulers', and not that of the 'ruled'. However, the history of public institutions in colonial India would, by and large, vindicate the integrity with which they were administered. It is not surprising that streets/roads, residential areas and establishments in many Indian cities and towns are named after the great administrators of public institutions during the colonial era.
3. In writing this paper, I have drawn on (a) my earlier work on higher education in India (see Jayaram, 2003, 2004, 2006, 2007, 2010), (b) my experience of working in two universities (Bangalore University and Goa University), an institute deemed-to-be university (Tata Institute of Social Sciences, Mumbai), and a research institute (Institute for Social and Economic Change, Bengaluru) outside the university system, and (c) my formal interaction with faculty, students, and administrators in several universities during the last 35 years.
4. Higher education in India was intended to evolve a small class of English-educated Indians who may act, in Macaulay's words, as 'interpreters between us and millions whom we govern – a class of persons Indian in blood and colour, but English in tastes, in opinions, in morals and intellect' (in Sharp, 1965: 116). It was never their intention to spread modern education among the masses. The British rule gradually supplanted the pre-colonial indigenous system of education consisting of Buddhist *viharas*, Hindu *pathashalas* and *tols*, and Muslim *madrasahas* by stopping financial aid. The Indian urban elite, too, welcomed English education as it was viewed not only as an avenue to jobs but also an instrument for social and political regeneration of India (Basu, 2002: 168).
5. About the University of Calcutta, one of the three pioneer universities in the country, Lord Curzon observed: 'How different is India! Here, the university has no corporate existence … it is not a collection of buildings, it is scarcely even a site. It is a body that controls courses of study and sets examination papers to pupils of affiliated colleges' (Ministry of Education, GoI, 1971: 498).

6. These institutions either specialize in some area of knowledge or are heirs to a tradition. They are not expected to grow to be multidiscipline universities of the general type.
7. The Indian Institutes of Management, which are also national-level institutions, are not vested with the power to award degrees, though their 'fellowships' are treated on par with university degrees.
8. The Kothari Commission was the first commission in India's educational history to look comprehensively at almost all aspects of education and to evolve a blueprint for a 'national system of education' (see Ministry of Education, GoI, 1971). The Ministry of Education, which processed the report, obliterated it by treating in a piecemeal fashion selected aspects of what was conceived to be a package deal (Naik, 1982: 31–32).
9. In his Convocation Address to the University of Poona (1966), Dr Gadgil used the choicest epithets to describe the proposal: 'favours', 'elitism', 'grandiose', 'no relevance to an improvement of existing conditions in our universities and colleges' but will 'surely worsen these conditions', 'monstrous idea that I am prepared to risk the misunderstanding' (quoted in Naik, 1982: 111–13).
10. What is said about the disjunction between universities (teaching) and institutes (research) with reference to science would hold good for social sciences, too. This is confirmed by a report on the social science research capacity in South Asia commissioned by the Social Science Research Council, New York in 2001 (see Chatterjee, 2002).
11. Lacking any objective measurement of higher education standards over a period, it is, no doubt, difficult to determine precisely the nature and extent of deterioration. Nevertheless, there is no denying that India's standards compare unfavourably with the average standards in educationally advanced countries. The Education Commission had drawn attention to this as early as the mid-1960s (see Ministry of Education, GoI, 1971: 66). No wonder, then, that degrees awarded by Indian universities are not regarded by many foreign universities as equivalent to their degrees; employers in India, including the government agencies, are wary of these degrees; and the students are resorting to 'shadow education', or private tuition conducted through 'coaching classes'.
12. There has been a drastic cut in public expenditure on higher education between 1980–90 and 1994–95, the share of higher education in development (plan) expenditure decreased from 12.6 per cent to 6 per cent, whereas the same in maintenance (non-plan) expenditure declined from 14.2 per cent to 11 per cent (Tilak, 1996). Overall, the allocation for higher education, which had peaked at 28 per cent in the Fifth Five-Year Plan (1974–97), has steadily declined in the successive plans to just 8 per cent in the Tenth Five-Year Plan (2002–07), which is the same as the allocation in the First Five-Year Plan (1951–56). As a proportion of total government expenditure, the share of higher education declined from 1.57 per cent in 1990–91 to 1.33 per cent in 2001–02. Considering the trends in per student expenditure – from ` 7,676 in 1990–91 to ` 5,873 in 2001–02 (in 1993–94 prices) (by 23.49%) – the decline in public expenditure on higher education would appear even more drastic (Tilak, 2004: 2160–61).
13. The salary differentials between the state-supported university system and the private sector are so wide that teaching is now no more an attractive career option.

14. UGC (University Grants Commission) was established by an Act of Parliament in 1956 as a centralized authority vested with the power to provide funds and to set and coordinate standards of higher education (Singh, 2004). It was modelled after the British UGC (established after World War I, since abolished).
15. The standards of academic performance in professional education are coordinated and regulated by statutory bodies such as the Indian Medical Council, the All India Council of Technical Education, the Bar Council of India, the Dental Council of India, the Pharmacy Council of India, and the Nursing Council of India. The Indian Council of Agricultural Research looks after agricultural education. These bodies were created by different ministries of the central government, and the lack of coordination among them is a problem. The question of jurisdiction between these bodies created by acts of parliament and the universities established by acts of parliament or state legislative bodies has often been agitated before courts of law. The National Knowledge Commission (2007: 53) has recommended the abolition of these bodies and the establishment of an Independent Regulatory Authority for Higher Education.
16. This ranking was based on a study of 2,000 universities and institutions of higher education across the world undertaken by the Institute of Higher Education, Shanghai Jiao Tong University, Shanghai, China. On the methodology of ranking adopted by this study, see http://ed.sjtu.edu.cn/rank/2004/top500list.htm. As of now, there is no official ranking of institutions of higher education in India. Some news magazines have attempted such a rank of colleges, but their rankings are populist and lack methodological rigour.

References

Ashby, E. and M. Anderson (1966). *Universities: British, Indian, and African.* London: Weidenfeld and Nicolson.

Basu, A. (2002). 'Indian Higher Education: Colonialism and Beyond', in P.G. Altbach and V. Selvaratnam (eds), *From Dependence to Autonomy: The Development of Asian Universities*, Chestnut Hill, MA: Center for International Higher Education, Boston College, pp. 167–86.

Béteille, A. (2000). 'Universities as Institutions', in *Antinomies of Society: Essays on Ideologies and Institutions*, New Delhi: Oxford University Press, pp. 153–71.

Chatterjee, P. (in collaboration with N. Banerjee, A.K. Baruah, S. Deshpande, P.R. de Souza, K. Hachhethu, B.K. Jahangir, M.S.S. Pandian, N. Wikramasinghe, S.A. Zaidi and I. Abraham) (2002). *Social Science Research Capacity in South Asia: A Report.* SSRC Working Paper Series, Vol. 6, New York: Social Science Research Council.

Dadhich, N. (2004). 'Indian Science Experiment', *Economic and Political Weekly*, 39: 2181–84.

Dattagupta, S. (2005). 'The State of Physics', *Seminar*, 547: 19–22.

Jayaram, N. (2003). 'The Fall of the Guru: The Decline of the Academic Profession in India', in Philip G. Altbach (ed.), *The Decline of the Guru: The Academic Profession in Developing and Middle-Income Countries*, New York: Palgrave Macmillan, pp. 199–230.

—— (2004). 'Higher Education in India: Massification and Change', in P.G. Altbach and T. Umakoshi (eds), *Asian Universities: Historical Perspectives and Contemporary Challenges*, Baltimore, Maryland: The Johns Hopkins University Press, pp. 85–112.

—— (2006). 'India', in J.J.F. Forest and P.G. Altbach (eds), *International Handbook of Higher Education (Part Two: Regions and Countries)*, Dordrecht, The Netherlands: Springer, pp. 747–67.

—— (2007). 'Beyond Retailing Knowledge: Prospect of Research-Oriented Universities in India', in P.G. Altbach and J. Balán (eds), *World Class Worldwide: Transforming Research Universities in Asia and Latin America*, Baltimore: The Johns Hopkins University Press, pp. 70–94.

—— (2010). 'Disparities in Access to Higher Education in India: Persistent Issues and the Changing Context', in Fred Lazin, Matt Evans and N. Jayaram (eds), *Higher Education and Equality of Opportunities*, Lanham, Maryland: Lexington Books, pp. 161–81.

Ministry of Education, Government of India (1971). *Education and National Development (Report of the Education Commission, 1964–66).* New Delhi: National Council of Educational Research and Training (reprint edition).

—— (1985). *Challenge of Education: A Policy Perspective.* Delhi: The Controller of Publications.

Ministry of Human Resource Development (MHRD), Government of India (1986). *Programme of Action: National Policy on Education.* New Delhi: The Controller of Publications.

—— (1991). *Towards an Enlightened and Humane Society: Report of the Committee for Review of National Policy on Education – 1986.* New Delhi: The Controller of Publications.

—— (1992). *National Policy on Education – 1986: Programme of Action – 1992.* New Delhi: Publications Division.

—— (2007). *Selected Educational Statistics – 2004–05.* New Delhi: Statistics Division, Department of Higher Education.

—— (2008). 'Higher Education in India'. www.education.nic.in/stats0405.asp (accessed on 24 April 2008).

Naik, J.P. (1982). *The Education Commission and After.* New Delhi: Allied Publishers.

Narlikar, J.V. (2003). *How to Recapture the Thrill for Basic Sciences in Higher Education*. UGC Golden Jubilee Lecture Series, New Delhi: University Grants Commission.

National Assessment and Accreditation Council (2010). *NAAC News*, 10 (2).

National Knowledge Commission (2007). *Report to the Nation – 2006.* New Delhi: Government of India.

Parhar, M. (2002). 'Enrolment Projection in Higher Education', *University News*, 40 (27): 1–4.

Raza, M. et al. (1985). 'Higher Education in India: An Assessment', in J.V. Raghavan (ed.), *Higher Education in the Eighties*, New Delhi: Lancer International, pp. 95–173.

Sharp, H. (1965). *Selections from Educational Records – Part I: 1781–1839.* New Delhi: Published for the National Archives of India by the Manager of Publications, Government of India (reprint edition).

Singh, A. (2004). *Fifty Years of Higher Education in India: The Role of the University Grants Commission.* New Delhi: Sage.

Stella, A. and A. Gnanam (2003). *Foundations of External Quality Assurance in Indian Higher Education.* New Delhi: Concept Publishing Company.

The Task Force on Higher Education and Society (2000). *Higher Education in Developing Countries: Peril and Promise.* Washington, DC: The World Bank.

Thomas, Prince Mathews and Deepak Tiwari (2005). 'Two-Room University!', *The Week*, 23 (13): 36–37.

Tickoo, C. (1980). *Indian Universities.* Madras: Orient Longman.

Tilak, J.B.G. (1996). 'Higher Education under Structural Adjustment', *Journal of Indian School of Political Economy*, 8 (2): 266–93.

—— (2004). 'Absence of Policy and Perspective in Higher Education', *Economic and Political Weekly*, 39 (21): 2159–64.

University Education Commission (1948–49) (1985). 'Extracts', in J.V. Raghavan (ed.), *Higher Education in the Eighties* (Appendix I), New Delhi: Lancer International, pp. 240–47.

University Grants Commission (2002–2003). *Annual Report 2002–2003.* New Delhi: University Grants Commission.

Vijayakumar, B. (2003). 'Regeneration of Quality Research in Higher Education: Ways Ahead', *University News*, 41 (41): 3–7.

3

Globalization

Emerging Trends in Higher Education in India

Gattu Satyanarayana

Higher education has been gaining a lot of importance all over the world more so in India due to the impact of globalization and global policies on the one side and also changing needs and aspirations of the people of respective countries on the other. It is a well-known fact that the concept and purpose of education though the same for all categories of people and nationals all over the world but its process, system, curriculum development may vary depending on the unique socio-economic and cultural conditions of a given nation and its various sections. Sometimes the system of education may vary depending on the socio-economic cultural patterns of the various sections of the population within the nation. As such there are a variety of educational systems and processes at a given time all over the world at various stages of education. Though the western education systems and models have been highly appreciated for their scientific, practical orientation and utility but eastern educational systems particularly Indian education has been theoretical and oriented to integrated personality development despite its very high achievements in various fields of knowledge since ancient times. However, there are changes taking place in all systems of education such as general, technical and professional education of India at every stage in response to global policies of contemporary times. As such, Indian education has been experiencing a crisis in adopting the trends of the world and its consequent effects are very serious not only on the structure and function of education but also on various sections of population specially the weaker and deprived sections. Every nation has been orienting and revamping educational systems for its human resource development and marketing them in line with global policies and perspectives.

In view of the above situation, there are radical changes taking place in India in the structure, functions and curriculum of all courses of higher learning in line with globalized policies.

This paper aims at understanding globalization and its impact on higher education in India in terms of policy pursuits and structural changes. Further, it also deals with the problems and prospects of the emerging trends in higher education and their positive and negative impact on the various sections of the people specially the marginalized.

However, it is generally viewed that the education system in India specially higher education has been acquiring and adapting a system of western model which is commercial in nature and it is accessible only to those who can afford and are interested, and which is against the indigenous model of Indian educational system which is inclusive of various sections of the population who cannot afford, specially such as the Scheduled Castes, the Scheduled Tribes and backward castes and women. In the post-globalization era those who are marginalized sections would be further marginalized and it would be difficult for them to cope with the new system which is resulting in a lot of disparity and inequality in opportunities.

Evolution of Higher Education in India

The ancient history of India reveals that there were mainly two centres of higher learning, namely, Taxila and Nalanda. Western education was introduced during the British Raj. The modern education system in India falls under concurrent list, i.e., in the control of central and state governments. Besides these, there are institutions which are autonomous in nature. There are articles in the Indian Constitution which provide for education as a fundamental right and universities in India are run by state and central governments. Besides, there are some private universities and deemed universities. Historically private educational institutions have been contributing a lot. It is interesting to note that despite increasing investment in education, still 40 per cent of the population is illiterate and only 15 per cent of the students go to high school. It is estimated that as of 2008, India's post-secondary high schools offer only enough seats for 7 per cent of India's college age population, 25 per cent of teaching positions nationwide are vacant, and 57 per cent of college professors lack either a master's or Ph.D. degree ... . Further, by 2007, there were 1,522 degree granting engineering colleges in India with an annual student intake of 5,82,000 plus 1,244 polytechnics with an annual intake of 2,65,000. However, these institutions face shortage of faculty and concerns have been raised over the quality of education.[1]

In the context of achievement of institutional excellence in higher learning of various fields of knowledge in comparison with world universities, the following discussion reveals the status of higher education in India.

'Although, no Indian University made to the top 300 of the Chinese conducted Academic Ranking of World Universities in 2006, three Indian Universities were listed in the Times Higher Education list of the world's top 200 universities – Indian Institutes of Technology, Indian Institutes of Management, and Jawaharlal Nehru University in 2005 and 2006. Six Indian Institutes of Technology and the Birla Institute of Technology and Science, Pilani were listed among the top 20 science and technology schools in Asia by *Asia Week* while the National Institute of Information Technologies has been renowned as the largest provider of Information Technology training and education company in Asia and among the top 15 global heads of education. The Indian School of Business, situated in Hyderabad was ranked number 15 in global MBA rankings by the *Financial Times of London* in 2009, while the All India Institute of Medical Sciences has been recognized as a global leader in medical research and treatment.'[2]

G. Satyanarayana,[3] in his preface to *Globalization: Indian State and Educational Pursuits*, states that the 'contemporary Indian society has been facing a lot of crisis in the field of education. The problems and issues of educational pursuits, in terms of curriculum development, syllabus preparation, selection of students and teachers, teaching problems of the teachers and the overall environment of teaching and learning, problems relating to examinations, evaluations, medium of instruction, teaching aids and lastly the philosophy of education and its aims and objectives have all been raising anxious debates and large-scale experiments. The trends of changes which are taking place are as follows:

1. Ownership of education (state ownership is declining, private ownership is increasing).
2. Disparities are increasing in educational pursuits among various communities and sections within the communities such as tribal, rural and urban and also due to socio-economic and political background.
3. The problems of medium of instruction, curriculum development and syllabus framing are increasing.
4. Making the relevance of education in the changing socio-economic conditions of the students and the society needs serious attention.
5. The inaccessible trends of education for poorer and rural students, which is against the spirit of the nature of state and its declared policies such as universalization of education, uniform education and compulsory education are to be examined.

He further opines that 'the emerging trends of educational pursuits are not in line with Indian Constitution of universalisation and uniform policy of education and Indian philosophy of education such as Gandhiji's concept of education "earning while learning"; Rabindranath Tagore's aesthetic, creative and elitist education; Vivekananda's concept of education that "it is a process of manifestation of internal capacity of a person which already exists in one self"; and Mother Mirra Alpha's concept of education is that it is not gaining something or conquering somebody but it is a process of learning by which one should reach to the outmost perfectibility in life'.[4]

He further states that the contemporary trends in educational pursuits reflect the 'increasing expenditure on education and declining interest of the state, growing unemployment, declining importance to conventional courses, including the conventional engineering courses; capitalist kind of commercialization of education and as a consequence inability of the majority students to bear the expenditure. Further, the government is also increasingly withdrawing its role and responsibility from the management of education'. As a result, there are various changes taking place in the educational system and consequent implications are multidimensional. One may be curious to know the changes in terms of – 'What are the emerging trends in education? And what are the implications? And what is the present status of education among the various sections of the societies? What will happen to the earth-bound societies who are still out of the framework of educational process, living in the dark and ignorance and struggling to exist? What are the constitutional obligations of the state? Who have to own the educational responsibility of the poorer sections? What will be the implications of liberalization, globalization and privatization of higher education in India?[5]

Satyanarayana,[6] while quoting Jawaharlal Nehru's concept of capitalism, from *Glimpses of World History*, states that 'Capitalism is like a rock, however the long you may cook it, it would not yield you the food, only thing you can do with it is that you have to remove it altogether'. Further, the dominant discourse of the contemporary times reveals declining importance of social sciences and increasing importance of computer sciences. This will certainly and adversely affect the majority students in India who normally come from rural and deprived sections and who prefer to study non-technical and non-engineering courses which are affordable and understandable without much external aid and without much guidance from their families.

Satyanarayana,[7] while discussing the responses of academic community on globalization and its implications states:

> In response to the above policy trends there are seminars, symposiums, debates and discussions initiated all over the world by the intelligentsia concerned for the cause of marginalized nations and societies. One such international conference was organized by the World/Asian Social Forum from 2nd to 7th January 2003 at Hyderabad. It is a historical event. The chief guest of valedictory function was none other than the former President of India Sri K.R. Narayanan who is one of the intellectual giants of contemporary India. He has cautioned in his valedictory address that most of the nations of the world and more so the Indian nation and its states are going to be adversely affected by the process of globalization to the extent of uprooting identities. This effect will be more in the context of underdeveloped and developing societies and more so the indigenous earthbound poorer sections of the developing world. He concluded that 'unipolar systems are unnatural while multipolar systems are natural'. Hence, there is a need for unity of the developing societies to resist the developed world and their policy impositions. This is the only way to help the helpless people of developing world not to further marginalize those societies.

The following statement by Dr Manmohan Singh,[8] the Prime Minister of India, reflects the alarming situation of Indian higher education in the era of globalization:

> Our university system is, in many parts, in a state of disrepair ... . In almost half the districts in the country, higher education enrollments are abysmally low, almost two-thirds of our universities and 90 per cent of our colleges are rated as below average on quality parameters ... . I am concerned that in many states university appointments, including that of vice-chancellors, have been politicized and have become subject to caste and communal considerations, there are complaints of favouritism and corruption.

Globalization would further complicate the Indian education system in terms of its accessibility, affordability, nature, content, losing control of the state and its accountability. The following discussion reflects the existing status of Indian higher education:

India's higher education system is the third largest in the world, after China and the United States. The main governing body at the tertiary level is the University Grants Commission (India), which enforces its standards, advises the government, and helps coordination between the centre and the state. Accreditation for higher learning is overseen by 12 autonomous institutions established by the University Grants Commission.

As of 2009, India has 20 central universities, 215 state universities, 100 deemed universities, 5 institutions established and functioning under the State Act, and 13 institutes which are of national importance. Other institutions include 16,000 colleges, including 1,800 exclusive women's colleges, functioning under these universities and institutions. The emphasis in the tertiary level of education lies on science and technology. Indian educational institutions by 2004 consisted of a large number of technology institutes. Distance learning is also a feature of the Indian higher education system.

Some institutions of India, such as the Indian Institutes of Technology (IITs), have been globally acclaimed for their standard of education. The IITs enroll about 4,000 students annually and the alumni have contributed to both the growth of the private sector and the public sectors of India.

Besides top rated universities which are providing highly competitive world class education to their pupils, India is also home to many universities which have been founded with sole objective of making easy money. Regulatory authorities like UGC, AICTE have been trying very hard to extirpate the menace of private universities which are running courses without any affiliation or recognition. Students from rural and semi-urban background often fall prey to these institutes and colleges.[9]

The following discussion reveals the picture of the technical education of contemporary India. 'From the first Five Year Plan onwards India's emphasis was to develop a pool of scientifically inclined manpower. India's National Policy on Education (NPE) provisioned for an apex body for regulation and development of higher technical education, which came into being as the All India Council for Technical Education (AICTE) in 1987 through an act of the Indian parliament. At the level of the centre the Indian Institutes of Technology are deemed to be of national importance. The Indian Institutes of Management are also among the nation's premier education facilities. Several Regional Engineering Colleges (RECs) have been converted into National Institutes of Technology. The UGC has inter-university centres at a number of locations throughout India to promote common research, e.g., the Nuclear Science Centre at the Jawaharlal Nehru University, New Delhi'.[10]

Madhuri,[11] while explaining the importance and challenges of higher education in 21st century, elucidates various issues in context of India such as the significance of higher education, the skills required in the management of higher education, the requirement of sound regulatory mechanism to assess and accord accreditation by taking into account all the aspects of higher education, the need for evaluation and assessment of academic excellence, curriculum development with a balance between regional and national development, the need for the UGC to be empowered to provide an environment of teaching, training, development and participation, and colleges to empower in all respects and provide moral and material support. She also emphasizes the need for autonomous colleges with an objective of 'greater willingness on their part to accept the responsibility and accountability'. Interestingly, it is pointed out that there is not much enrolment in the undergraduate science educational courses. Further, it is also emphasized that the technical education system should promote industry-institutional interaction through apprenticeship opportunities, consultancies and sponsored research. There should be university-industry interface to raise resources from non-traditional sources such as industries and other commercial concerns and to make use of highly qualified and trained manpower produced by the institutions of higher education. It is also pointed out that open university system in the country is on lines parallel to the general university system without initiating any innovative courses ... it should be ensured that course material should be easily accessible to the common man. Library facilities and the access to books have been declining in proportion to the increase of demand and the requirement. The idea of networking libraries providing shared access to journals and books needs to be encouraged by providing necessary infrastructural support. Further, there is a lot of hue and cry of increasing fees of higher education which cannot be affordable to weaker sections of the society and there should be a rationale in the fees structure. The meritorious students of the weaker sections should be encouraged through the various systems of financial support such as scholarships. In the era of globalization it is natural that the foreign students are attracted to the higher education. The fees they pay will be a vital source of foreign exchange for the country. The examination reforms should be initiated with appropriate mode of testing student ability, aptitude, and performance without favour and corruption on the objective lines instead of issuing mere diplomas and degrees. As such, India can enormously emerge as a manpower resource centre and as an asset in the 21st century if human resource is properly trained and encouraged. Further research and development at university level should be in tune with the long-term goals of national development. The higher education institutions should be accessible to the people regardless of their class or caste. Opportunities should be made available to all the people. While concluding Madhuri states that, 'the old dogmas of higher education cannot face new challenges. Our national education has to get out of conventional degree-oriented education and get to grips with national demands of developments and global market needs. A synthesis of material and spiritual values instilled through our higher learning is our salvationist instrumentalities and tools of collective progress'.

Pankaj Das,[12] while explaining democratization of education, and issue of social exclusion in policy, depicts the actual picture in the context of Scheduled Castes' and Scheduled Tribes' education. Referring to K. Sujatha (2002), he states:

> In India, the Scheduled Castes and Scheduled Tribes have been socially underprivileged, educationally backward and economically deprived for centuries. Historically both the groups were denied social access to education. Scheduled Castes were systematically segregated from the village and were denied access to education. The exclusion of the Scheduled Tribes, on the

> other hand, was based on a different set of social and cultural factors. In one of the studies they were defined as the 'double disadvantaged group' owing to their socio-economic and spatial marginalisation.

Further, he states while quoting Jaffrelot (2003) that 'India is a case of political democracy without social democracy. The whole policy environment for inclusion in India reflects the fulfillment of political interest rather than the social interests; where equity is not a major agenda.'[13]

Anil G. Mudbidri,[14] while explaining the implications of globalization and privatization on reservation provisions of Indian Constitution, points out that 'Article 14 of the Indian Constitution states that education will be free and compulsory till the age of 14 years. Education is considered a fundamental right. Hence, it confers equal opportunity to all in the field of education. Privatization of education, it is feared, goes against the sprit of this article. Today, there is no application of "Reservation Policy" in privately managed business houses and industries and the same may come true in the field of education. The number of students enrolling for university education will come down drastically. Today, due to the encouragement given by the government, India has one of the highest number of students obtaining postgraduate education, but this may change with privatization.'

Mallesh Sankasala,[15] while discussing the impact of economic reforms on dalit population of India, states that the Constitution framers under the chairmanship of Dr Ambedkar envisaged that state would play an important role in the planning and socio-economic development of its citizens to establish egalitarian society. As such they provided certain safeguards such as social, educational, cultural, religious, economic and political in the Indian Constitution for 'dalits' and other weaker sections. But, 'the free market ethos unleashed by the reforms, conceptually can neither conform to the democratic sprit of the Indian Constitution of "one vote, one value", nor can it coexist with the system of positive discrimination embodied in these safeguards'. While discussing the impact of new economic policy, it states that it has very adversely affected the reservation policy of India in the public sector and also private sector. The new economic policy, which envisages privatization with increased high technology and its optimum use, has adversely affected the job market for all the sections, particularly vulnerable sections such as the 'dalits' who are mostly at the lower rung of organized sector jobs without technical skills. As such they lose not only their jobs but also their livelihoods which they cannot find in other fields because of demand of technical skills and intensive competition for the less available number of jobs as compared to the past.

National Policies and the Neo-liberal Agenda

Harihar Mishra,[16] in his unpublished article on 'Globalization and Education: National Policies and the Neo-liberal Agenda' critically examines globalization and its implications on the national policies of education in India. He states that 'the review report had made recommendations for significant changes in the National Policy on Education (1986) in consonance with the terms of reference which had directed the Committee to:

(a) make education an effective instrument for securing a status of equality for women, and persons belonging to the backward classes and minorities;
(b) give a work and employment orientation to education;

(c) exclude from (education) the elitist aberrations which have become the glaring characteristics of the education scene;
(d) lay special emphasis on struggle against (the) phenomenon of educational institutions ... increasingly being influenced by casteism, communalism and obscurantism; and
(e) move towards genuinely egalitarian and secular social order'.

He further argues that the political and economic framework for subjugation by global forces in the education sector emerged soon after the announcement of the New Economic Policy, when the Indian government was 'persuaded' by the IMF and the World Bank to accept the twin concepts of structural adjustment and a social safety net in planning and budgeting for social sectors. There was no choice, the government told the people, justifying its apparent 'helplessness', since these were the preconditions set by the Bretton Woods institutions for extending further loans. Plainly speaking, these twin concepts implied that the government would, as part of the structural adjustment programme, incrementally reduce public spending on social sectors such as health, education and social welfare. Recognizing that such a reduction could lead to severe socio-political tensions, the IMF and the World Bank 'offered' to create a social safety net by extending loans for the social sector on certain terms and conditions.

According to Harihar Mishra,[17] as was the case with the Macaulayian approach to education, globalization also aims at using education as a tool for building up various skills and capacities that are useful for the global economy. In the post-Jomtien framework, educational aims are being trivialized and curricular knowledge is either being reduced to mere literacy skills (for reading product labels and prices), or is fragmented into bits of information or competencies (for reading factory instructions, punching keys at the computer keyboard or accepting the dictates of the market uncritically). This amounts to rejection of a holistic approach to building up of an enlightened and humane society. In this paradigm, knowledge of the sciences, social sciences and humanities would need to be divested of its philosophical, historical, ethical, socio-cultural and aesthetic roots. Given the predominance of the market forces in the globalized world, it can be predicted that only those courses, research programmes or training activities would receive financial support which have saleable value in the global market. In this sense, there is a fundamental conflict of an epistemological nature between globalization and social development.

Alienation of knowledge from the social ethos is a logical outcome of globalization. Increasing preference for the internet as a source of 'knowledge' and its screening or filtration by corporate forces on the basis of marketability, will lead to uprooting of a substantial population of knowledge from its social ethos. Those communities, sections of society or nations that are denied equitable access to digital technology or English, the dominant language of information technology, will neither share the digitalized knowledge nor will be able to contribute their knowledge for human progress. Geo-cultural diversity will come to be largely ignored and eventually have little role to play in defining or qualifying knowledge. This trend will, over a period of time, establish the hegemony of only globally acceptable parameters of what is worth knowing in the age of globalization.

Similarly, globalization as Harihar Mishra[18] opined, 'it leads to fragmentation of knowledge. There is no place in the post-Jomtien view of curriculum for the world of work being pedagogically integrated with the world of knowledge. Similarly while defining child-centeredness, joyful learning or multi-grade teaching in DPEP literature no attempt is made to envisage knowledge in the content of the social ethos'.

National Knowledge Commission

The Prime Minister of India, Dr Manmohan Singh[19] constituted National Knowledge Commission (NKC) on 13 June 2005. 'The commission was to advise the Prime Minister's office on policy related to education, research institutes and reforms needed to make India competitive in the knowledge economy.

The terms of reference of Knowledge Commission are:

1. build excellence in the educational system to meet the knowledge challenges of the 21st century and increase India's competitive advantage in fields of education of knowledge;
2. promote creation of knowledge in science and technology laboratories;
3. improve the management of institutions engaged in intellectual property rights;
4. promote knowledge applications in agriculture and industry; and
5. promote the use of knowledge capabilities in making government an effective, transparent and accountable service provider to the citizen and promote widespread sharing of knowledge to maximize public benefit'.

Many of the recommendations of the NKC are already in the implementation stage. There are a number of controversies which have erupted since its inception, with regard to its recommendations of and their consequences on structure and functions of higher education and their implications on various sections of Indian society specially the deprived. 'The commission spoke out against the human resource development ministry's plans to increase quotas for backward castes in institutions such as IIT's .... Majority of the vice-chancellors had rejected the policy direction given in NKC report to nation's 2006 policy on the higher education .... However, some of the former and present vice-chancellors of various leading universities accept major directions like structural reform, augmentation of university number, freeing appointment of vice-chancellors from direct or indirect intervention on the part of the government, etc.'

As a backdrop of NKC, the Yashpal Committee (2009)[20] has been constituted to advise renovation of rejuvenation of higher education. It has recommended several things of which major is the setting up of a constitutional body 'The National Commission for Higher Education and Research'.

Uttam B. Bhoite[21] in his exhaustive review of higher education in India in its historical perspective aptly highlights the impact of globalization and its implications not only on various sections of Indian society but also on the emerging structural and functional orientation of higher education in India.

He also explains 'its pervasive impact on national policies, cultural systems, institutional structure, interpersonal relations, etc.'. He states that, it is prudent to examine the wider implications of globalization on a unique society like India. Since 'higher education is now being treated at the policy level as more for the individual good than public good. So, it does not deserve any special support from the government. Since it is more for the individual good, its beneficiaries have to bear its cost ... . The principle of cost recovery is a core part of this educational neo-liberalization. However, it would be prudent to examine carefully as to how far it would be wise to adopt it in a society like India which continues to be characterized by traditionally inherited acute inequalities based on class, caste, gender, ethnicity and religious affiliations and having larger sections of disadvantaged population to awaken to the notion of equality and aspiring for upward social mobility'. While concluding he states that 'It can also be reasonably predicted that unless India articulates a comprehensive policy with regard to higher education and unless the supervisory and monitoring agencies exercise their authority diligently and with reasonable strictness, the Indian higher education system is likely to plunge into deep chaos'.

Conclusion

In view of the above discussion the following conclusions may be drawn. The higher education is going to be steadily privatized and commercialized for which the state will readily provide policy, legislative, financial and technical support. Knowledge will be gradually trivialized, fragmented and alienated from its social ethos as well as its aim of social development. All deprived sections of society such as 'dalits', tribals, the majority of other backward classes, cultural and linguistic minorities and the physically and mentally disabled, two-thirds of each section being girls, will suffer from further discrimination and exclusion in the education system.

The national economy will not be reprioritized for the purpose of allocating adequate resources for education and social development. Instead, there will be increasing dependence on external aid to fulfill constitutional obligations by compromising under pressure from global market forces.

The Constitution and laws will be marginalized, amended and even tampered with in order to fulfill the combined dictates of globalization.

Thus, it may be concluded within the above limited spectrum, globalization and its impact on higher education has wider implications of privatization, commercialization and consequent structural and functional changes experienced in the field of education which obviously enable the rich and enlightened sections to enjoy the educational facilities. The consequent grabbing of the socio-economic and political power and other advantages more at the cost of those who have not yet benefited even after 65 years of independent India's policies of uniform education for all, accessible and affordable education system would be a distant dream. In my imagination it will never come true. As a consequence of this trend, the marginalized sections will be further marginalized and the state will have no role to play which will be the natural justice that is 'survival of the fittest' and the sufferers will suffer due to their birth in disadvantageous socio-economic and political conditions and they should be prepared to suffer consequent futureless life for generations.

Notes

1. http://en.wikipedia.org/wiki/Education_in_India (p. 1 dated 9 November 2009).
2. Ibid.
3. G. Satyanarayana (2006). 'Preface', in Satyanarayana et al. (eds), *Globalization: Indian State and Educational Pursuits*, Hyderabad: Department of Sociology, Osmania University, pp. v–vi.
4. Ibid., 'Introduction', p. vi.
5. Ibid.
6. Ibid., pp. vi–viii.
7. Ibid., pp. xi–xii.
8. http://en.wikipedia.org/wiki/Education_in_India (p. 4 dated 9 November 2009).
9. Ibid., pp. 4–5.
10. Ibid., p. 5.
11. N.V. Madhuri (2006). 'Higher Education System in 21st Century India: Some Reflections', in G. Satyanarayana et al. (eds), op. cit., pp. 45–56.
12. Pankaj Das (2009). 'Democratization of Education: Issues of Exclusion and Inclusion in Policy', *Social Action*, 59 (2): 182.
13. Ibid., p. 187.
14. Anil G. Mudbidri (2006). 'Higher Education in India: Challenges and Implications of Globalization and Privatization', in G. Satyanarayana et al. (eds), op. cit., p. 38.
15. Mallesh Sankasala (2006). 'Globalization-Economic Reforms and its Impact on Dalits: Reservation in Private Sector', in G. Satyanarayana et al. (eds), op. cit., pp. 258–59.
16. Harihar Mishra (2009). 'National Policies and Neo-liberal Agenda', unpublished paper.
17. Ibid.
18. Ibid.
19. http://en.wikipedia.org/wiki/'National_Knowledge_Commission' (dated 9 November 2009), pp. 1–2.
20. http://en.wikipedia.org/wiki/Bachelor_of_Science_in_Agriculture.
21. Uttam B. Bhoite (2001). 'Higher Education in India: A System on the Verge of Chaos', *Sociological Bulletin*, 58 (2): 157, 164 and 177.

4

Sociology of Textbooks

Conceptual Narrative

Rajiv Gupta

One of the indicators of development of a discipline (subject) is related with evolution of various branches which depict appearances of development of concepts, conceptual categories, methodological refinement, specialized thoughts and 'super specialization'. Such 'super specializations' make related discipline diverse and multi-paradigmatic intellectual enterprise. These processes of advancement also express those directions by which a society moves toward 'knowledge society'. Sociology of textbooks, in authors' opinion, can be accepted as that branch within sociology which scientifically and rationally provides space to understand 'what textbook is'? Generally, no one gives attention to understand and think about the nature, character and scope of textbooks. The content structure of knowledge in general and (super) specialized knowledge in particular is communicated to the reader(s) through books. Thus, a 'book' can be elaborated as that organized stock of ideas, relating to an issue or set of issues, constructed with the logic of description, elaboration, analysis, evaluation, imagination, comparison and criticism by author or a group of authors, in the form of writing (in form of publication after industrial revolution) which is distributed to the readers for enhancing their understanding about the issue(s). Thus, book is the 'communicator of knowledge' which provides space to the readers: (i) to know the knowable, (ii) to know the knowable more, (iii) to know the knowable comparatively, (iv) to unknow the knowable, and (b) to replace the 'false' knowable by appropriate alternative knowable. In one sense, each book is a set of written traditions so that oral traditions could get continuity because oral traditions are converted by authors into text in the textbooks nowadays. The (imaginative) experiences of men about the entire environment or universe become philosophical roots

The author is highly thankful to University Grants Commission which gave him research award on 'Sociology of Textbooks: Culture and Knowledge as Perspective'. This article is based upon those constructions which the author made during the course of the research award.

to construct a book. Books also make survival of history possible. In other words, 'books' can be used as a criterion to classify society into 'preliterate' and 'literate'.

Information-Knowledge Interface in Books

The creation of knowledge and dissemination of knowledge are basic objectives of educational establishments in modern societies. Books are those medium by which creation and dissemination of knowledge systems are institutionalized. Child at early stage, with the help of textbooks and classroom interaction, internalizes the existing systems of knowledge so that (s)he could create new dimensions of knowledge at later stage. Textbooks also contribute toward dissemination of information. In this context, we can find two types of books: (i) research-based books which are used as sources of knowledge and of new information by students as well as by academic intellectuals, and (ii) knowledge and information-based books which are used by students and academia as sources for (further) research because knowledge and information are arranged in such a way that insights become natural outcome. In this sense, books are 'direct' as well as 'indirect' teachers for the students, while continuous publication of these books makes teachers the 'student of the said discipline'. Teacher is always a student because (s)he always makes 'live' interaction with (good) books failing which it becomes difficult for her/him to keep pace with dissemination of knowledge. Students as consumers of knowledge, information and education are bound to enter in the 'world of books'. Such 'world of books' appears in academic institutes as the 'library'. Students also purchase books from market on the basis of the suggestions of the teachers and senior students as well as on the basis of their own choices, wisdom and likings. These books encourage students to enter in the 'space of learning' deeply and acquire the statuses of 'remarkable/best books'. Such books are products of composite skill of the author(s). The composite skill of an author comprises of: (i) command over language(s), (ii) analytical understanding of history, (iii) inter-disciplinary perceptions, (iv) a vast knowledge and information of historical and empirical evidences, (v) ability to frame sentences, (vi) ability to narrate experiences as examples to readers according to their age, taste and abilities, and (vii) understanding of nature of readers so that explanatory framework in the book are constructed accordingly. For the continuous advancement of knowledge, it is necessary that author in the book, to an extent, challenges the prevailing viewpoints so that 'dialectics' as process could find place in the structure of the book. In this context, it can be said that enlightened readers always expect that a book never means a presentation of neutral value/objective document or parochial/sectarian views based on cluster of thoughts. Readers, to a certain extent, can accept a book with little or less knowledge of the subject but they always reject a book where false knowledge with stylish presentation is produced along with attractive designs. Books are always true and reliable friends because they contribute in shaping the mindset of (creative) productive nature but at the same time books also act as worst enemies when they legitimize and rationalize the deviance against the values of humanity and make readers destructive. The aim of books should be 'to encourage the readers for becoming the part of process of change and transformation rather than resisting it.' The author of this article firmly believes that books, the products of 'existing set of discourses', always produce 'new set of discourses' in any society. But in any case, no book should be written in a way that suppresses academic and cultural debates. Denial of authentic states of mind makes any book that product which leads to tendency of alienation amongst readers.

Sociologically, textbook is also a product of author's experience. These sets of experiences, in the field of knowledge and in the spheres of action, are communicated to readers through structures of sentences constructed by using language. If these sets of experiences of author/authors are felt by readers, then book becomes valuable and authentic. Through such kind of books, knowledge becomes power and writing a book becomes a powerful act for socio-cultural transformations.

These interpretations, now, can be used for constructing the concept of books and its forms. (Text) books have always been an indivisible organ of knowledge system in general and education system in particular. Now, at this stage, the concept of book can be framed. Books, in sociological sense, can be defined as 'structured narratives of ideas and information on set of identified issues prepared by author(s) and produced for the readers by publication industry'. These books can be categorized as: (i) reference books, (ii) textbooks, (iii) fictions, (iv) non-fictions, (v) biographies, (vi) autobiographies, and (vii) books for competitive examination/personality development and linguistic/professional skills which make readers conscious and rational. Books make men encyclopedic and confident because knowledge systems as content structures direct readers to modify their life experiences. Since books stimulate readers to assess and reassess the ideas or views which they have, books act as means of (de) and (re)socialization processes. In formal educational sectors (primary education, secondary, senior secondary, higher education of professional and non-professional nature and related allied sectors) several kinds of books particularly reference books and textbooks (prescribed, suggested and related/available) play instrumental roles in improving knowledge, enhancing, understanding and shaping classroom interaction between teachers (teachers–teachers), pupils (between students) and between teacher and pupil. At this stage, books become effective tools for acquiring success in examination(s) which make textbooks publication a 'competing industry' – a part of 'culture industry'. 'The art of acquiring success in examination' now shapes the nature of textbooks particularly. The qualitative presentation of content structure in the textbooks, 'to a larger extent' is replaced by success, strategy based content structure. From academic viewpoint, this phenomenon in school system as well as in education system raises the questions like: (i) What are the attributes of a good teacher and a good student? (ii) Why teach the pupil with academic sincerity when books as tools for attaining sure success as higher/highest marks are available in the market? (iii) Who are the students? (iv) What is the pattern of examination and its relation with the textbooks? (v) Who is the paper setter and the evaluator of the 'examination content' produced by examinee – the teacher teaching in the schools or the author(s) of the textbooks? These questions also construct an important issue of 'who determines/shapes what? Does book determine the nature of examination or examination determines the nature of book? This structural and processual nexus between author(s) of textbooks, market of education and examination system has contributed to the decline of education system particularly the quality content of education. Because of this nexus, students do not search for reference books as well as standard textbooks in the market. Teacher's advice about selection of books becomes important for students also. The advice of the teachers about suggested readings is by and large determined by market forces and examination-centric approach.

This 'organized-strategic-utilitarian' development in the field of education has made education a major area of dispute. Curriculum, books, their authors and knowledge-information content in the book, as a result, are now issues of close scrutiny. The socialization of children and students on the basis of these books is one of the most important issues of 'sociology of textbooks'. Selective 'public spheres as knowledge-information content' are placed by the author(s) in these textbooks in such a way that socialization process, slowly and gradually, converts into the process of indoctrination. The process of globalization in each nation-state has formed a complex structure known as 'diasporic public sphere' which is dominantly presented on visual and electronic media. The victim of this change is the 'world of textbooks'. People, to a certain extent, are delinked from the capacity to read and write. The written words in book forms are facing 'decline of popularity'. Thus, there is a need of introducing certain changes in process of book writings so that the features of attraction and interest could continue in the (text) books. The task of the author(s) of a book is to preserve realities in form of written words, i.e., one of the parts of maternal culture so that they could continue with future generation as their memories. In this way, the writing of a book by authors/intellectuals of the respective academic fields and its publication by particular (private or public) publishing agency/agencies is a part of 'cultural politics'. Each book may also be projected as 'biography/autobiography of civilization'. An author by writing a book also tries to enhance her/his own personal identity. Unfortunately, market forces have developed relationship of varying nature with the author(s) of the book. A book from conceptual perspective can be projected as an organ of sociology of scientific knowledge. The presentation of content structure in the book should be based on 'Philosophy of Edinburgh School'. This school gives primacy to the principle of symmetry. 'Scientific truth needed to be explained socially in the same manner as scientific error' can be accepted as logic for writing a book. In Indian society, suddenly 'education-society interface' has taken an important turn. Every child between 6–14 years of age is now entitled to free and compulsory primary or elementary education. Since bill relating to right to free and compulsory education provides priority to mother tongue as medium for instruction at elementary stage, it becomes responsibility of the author(s) to write such books which communicate 'local heritage' and 'struggled life' of the people to the students with a sense of history. Books should be prepared in such a way that child studies the content with deep interest and eagerness. This aspect is a prerequisite to identifying the quality of textbooks. These quality textbooks contribute significantly in making India a 'literate society'. With the active help of these quality textbooks, children/pupil can know 'own self' and the 'other'. This understanding of the 'self' and the 'other' makes pupil's knowledge comparative and critical. But, at the same time, the comparison between the 'self' and the 'other' in textbooks acquires legitimacy by using all forms of stereotypes. As a result, the pupil develops a sense of hostility, systems of prejudices and feeling of pride. These aspects of understanding can never be accepted in the field of education in general and social sciences and humanities in particular. The textbooks relating to social sciences and humanities should be impartial. In such writings, 'self-restraint' must be an attribute of authors' personality. Stigma based narratives constructed by the author(s) in such textbooks lead to ethnocentric attitudes amongst pupil resulting into socio-cultural divisiveness. The ideas formulated by Krishna Kumar provide us with a valuable insight about roles of textbooks and related social concerns of the intelligentsia.

Every society worries about how the young will think about the past because knowledge of the past has so much to do with attitudes and beliefs that are important for a society's survival. As nation-states, modern societies place a heavy responsibility on the historian who writes for the young. I feel that these ideas constitute 'application based proposition' in all the fields of social sciences and humanities. How the textbooks treat: (i) literary traditions, (ii) specific culture systems, (iii) gender relations, (iv) religious minorities, (v) political parties, (vi) private space-public space debate, and (vii) social issues including use of language and symbols, are those questions by which pupil construct images about their own society and other societies. Since school textbooks transmit knowledge to the pupil, the language content, text-content interface, questions, size of the content, evidences, ethical propositions and symbolic presentations should be formed by the author(s) in accordance with the age set of the pupil. The purpose of any textbook should be smooth socialization with natural interactionism. The logic of 'compressed age' of pupil cannot be accepted in relation to textbooks otherwise textbooks act as that weapons (like TV, computer and movies) which destroy the childhood.

In Indian society the hierarchies of schools also make impact on content structure, style and publishing patterns of textbooks. The textbooks published by National Council of Educational Research and Training (NCERT) and used by several private/elite schools along with central schools/Jawahar Navodaya Vidyalaya/Sainik Schools are qualitatively better to the books published by state government controlled and operated educational boards and used by state government schools/affiliated schools. There are some schools in each state of India affiliated to the Indian Council of Secondary Education (ICSE). These schools use books published by private publishers. The textbooks developed by state boards of primary and secondary education fail to attract the pupil because of inferiority in all aspects. These textbooks reveal detachment with 'real-life' education. Such textbooks cannot be identified as 'knowledge/literary landscapes'. Textbooks published by state boards are neither representatives of power of language nor power of knowledge. If production of knowledge does not appear through these textbooks, then pupils/students can never establish functional familiarity with cultural enlightenment. Poverty of ideas and poverty of linguistic skill are related consequences of such textbooks. Understanding of such textbooks creates hurdles in continuance of those efforts by which success in receiving appropriate employment opportunities become possible. Such textbooks do not reveal the cultural and economic profiles of Asia and different states of India. In various states of India such as Rajasthan and Madhya Pradesh, textbooks of various classes/standards (from first standard to tenth standard particularly) are distributed free amongst the poor students. The quality of textbooks has always been kept low intentionally so that students studying in the schools controlled by state governments could not find any possibility to compete with the students of private schools, public schools, central schools, Jawahar Navodaya Vidyalaya and Sainik Schools. In state government schools, the most important objective of teachers is 'completing the syllabus'. But, it never happens because teachers in the state government schools as employees are engaged with non-academic activities assigned to them by state governments. These administrative roles compel teachers to teach students with the tools of descriptive pedagogy. Low quality textbooks are taught to the students with descriptive pedagogy. As a result, unquestionable mindset and sectarian attitude become a part of students' personality. These textbooks, in authors' opinion have failed to change the behaviour of students in favour of law, constitutional ideals and formal-rational institutions. As a result, the questions like 'why am I?' and 'who am I?' are answered by the students in terms of theo-religious principles rather than on the basis of scientific principles or logic. Students socialized by these textbooks find difficulties in construction of interplay between 'what then?', 'what now?' and 'what next?'. Thus, textbooks are leading to intellectual underdevelopment in the space of 'culture of students' and space of 'knowledge of students'. Consciousness amongst students has been constructed as 'prepackaged ideas' due to these textbooks. In other words, these textbooks are instrumental in perpetuating 'organized intellectual poverty' amongst different categories of students. In this context one can point out the possible 'hidden objectives' of these textbooks. These textbooks negate 'joyful learning' and perpetuate 'fragmented knowledge and sectarian cultures'. Thus, a school is converted into an unsuccessful school. According to Nash, selectivity in textbooks is a reality in so many nations. He gives the examples of history books taught in junior schools in Britain. There were thousands of slaves in South Africa during the 17th, 18th and 19th centuries, but children taught from these texts would never know about it. Even where proper mention is made, it is usually in emotionally neutral terms, as if making slaves of people were a quite acceptable and normal way of treating them. For example, to help them in their work they used slaves who were Negroes brought from other parts of Africa and poor people from Asia (Nash, 1972). This comment of Nash expresses the fact that authors of the textbooks construct those narratives in the text by which the ideas of the authority in 'trusted forms' are communicated to the society through 'pupils'. The course of study with a specific design is presented in the textbooks by those authors who have been selected by the authorities.

Sociologically, it is a fact that the writing patterns of books vary from class standard to class standard. The style of presentation of text for the pupils of first standard or eighth standard will be different from the style of the text prepared for class tenth and twelfth. Similarly, the nature, character and style of school textbooks will be different from the textbooks constructed for college and university students. This classification of textbooks stimulates the students of 'sociology of education' and 'sociology of textbooks' to examine the relationship between language and education. The basic socio-economic and politico-cultural dilemmas that have confronted humanity since its social inception, in any case, should be included with different styles in all the textbooks so that pupil understand the meaning and importance of two kinds of dialectics, i.e., between nature and man and between man and man. These evolutionary frames to understand human society and its multifaceted development through textbooks at various 'class standards' give rise to cultural perceptions (culture perspective) and knowledge perceptions (knowledge perspective). The communities with which students/pupils confront in day-to-day life can also be understood deeply when sets of interaction between teachers and pupils in 'classroom situation' or 'classroom-like situation' take place. Students by discussing several examples can develop certain views about 'conflict of interest of opposing social groups operating in their respective localities'. These narratives are essentialities of a textbook in a nation-state like India where young people of age between fifteen to thirty five are in large number and now fundamental right of free and compulsory education is given to children of age between six to fourteen. If students, right from the formative phase, are exposed to multiple realities of Indian society through textbooks, then people-interest centric models of development can become the issues of public discourse. It needs preparation of textbooks on the basis of organized research supported by documents and evidences of proven character. Storytelling to the pupils is one of the prerequisites to textbooks but such stories should not be of biased nature. To avoid such biases, author(s) should select words and composition of sentences carefully. A comprehensive introduction of the topic with the attribute of applicability makes textbook an interesting reading. The conversational style makes textbook familiar to students and in return students develop the skill of exploration in their personalities. The author(s) of such textbooks can be identified as 'transformative intellectuals' because these author(s) through their textbooks encourage teachers in their classroom interaction to produce critical voice. But, at the same time, the textbooks relating to early classes particularly up to fifth class standard should be written or compiled in such a way that the culture of childhood is not denied. In school-age children the denial of childhood leads to aggression, frustration and structural/processual tension between children in terms of play, culture, education and development. The denial of childhood through textbooks and classroom interaction particularly becomes one of the causes of indoctrination. It also gives rise to concept of 'compressed age'. At the level of schooling, textbooks can also be identified as the sources of communication by which teachers stimulate the pupils. Textbooks introduce learning material before the pupils. With the active help of the textbooks and classroom interaction of pupils with teachers, students are able to write, record, describe and reproduce information and knowledge about those issues/topics which have been introduced to him/her through related textbooks. Thus, students in the school appear as 'demonstrators of knowledge and understanding'. In the field of 'sociology of textbooks' a book comprises 'oral-written-oral' exercise of presentation of knowledge and information. The delivery of knowledge and information to students makes them enlightened and sometimes pro-active. Thus, textbooks in all societies have become one of the vital organs of 'super-structure'. Olson and Torrance (2001), in their edited book *The Making of Literate Societies,* define literate society as that structure in which a majority of people know how to read and write along with as a cluster of those systems in which important aspects of social life such as economics, law, science and government are organized around texts and documents to form what we may call 'textual institutions'. These 'textual institutions' place the significance of social literacy. Social literacy fosters social networking, makes the rule of law feasible, complex economics viable, and formal education useful and worthwhile. For perpetuating social literacy in different spaces of society, there is need of textbooks having local, national and international contexts elaborated in 'known languages'. Since textbooks prescribed by appropriate authorities express legitimate knowledge, the students and enlightened citizens use these textbooks for development of systems of specialized knowledge and appropriate action(s). Such textbooks may produce accountable citizens who successfully rationalize the phenomenon of traditionalism-modernity dilemma. The roles of the textbooks in Indian society can be evaluated with certain specificities also. There is cultural acceptability of 'guru-shishya parampara' in contemporary school systems operative mainly in 'rural spaces'. Since the author(s) of textbooks are teachers, their sets of arguments and information are accepted by the students without raising any question or doubt. Thus, textbooks are 'sacred objects' and subjects of worshipping on several religio-cultural ceremonies. Unfortunately, author(s) of several textbooks have incorporated those systems of knowledge and information in their textbooks which cannot be accepted due to divisive nature. Such textbooks may be 'religiously-sacred' objects but not 'secular-sacred' objects. The roles of such textbooks in empowering children in schools become highly questionable. It is one of the responsibilities of educators, parents, education planners, thinkers, action social scientists, language experts and folk intellectuals to examine and evaluate the textbooks so that depiction of societies/communities through textbooks could be 'updated'. This regular evaluation of textbooks contributes to the formation of enduring and functional learning. The lack/absence of evaluation of these textbooks makes pupils 'under-achievers'.

Since literacy rate in rural and tribal world is low, it is essential that the content and style of presentation in textbooks should be different from the textbooks available in urban world/space. Books in rural and tribal world must appear with that vision which establishes the importance of development. People in rural world also have a vision of development which will benefit them and it should also be incorporated in the textbooks.

According to 2001 census of India, 61 per cent of the workforce live on agricultural and allied activities but the way of life of these people has found only marginal presence in the textbooks. In other words, textbooks do not depict 'real-life situations of marginalized sections of Indian society'. Such state of affair regarding textbooks is present in India, Pakistan and Bangladesh. The presence of 97 per cent illiterates out of four hundred million illiterates of South Asian region is an evidence of such paradoxical character of the textbooks. In our opinion the system(s) of social inclusion and social exclusion can be used for analysing 'how textbooks work amongst pupil'. Since textbooks are not written with these frames, their inferior quality/qualities have been a global and national concern. This aspect of quality can be viewed in terms of ideological perceptions. In fact, textbooks act as ideological tools on 'academic/educational landscape'. 'People are also ruled by ideas' is the logic by which authors develop contents of the textbooks. Sometimes this logic acquires the nomenclature of 'value free' presentation of the realities along with innovative and imaginative constructions. In textbooks, these constructions, as content structures, are framed in such a manner that neither parents nor children can realize the intentions of the author(s) who knowingly or unknowingly act as allies/agent of ruling class. In societies like India, these textbooks prove that the ideas of the ruling class are in every epoch the ruling ideas. Since these set of ideas raised in the textbooks do not address the issues linked with marginalized sections of societies, textbooks contribute in creating distance between students and teachers. Classroom interaction lacks 'liveness' making 'formal education' at formative phases a highly debatable exercise. Students 'read' these books for the sake of reading and use these textbooks as instruments of 'rote learning' so that they could get success in the examinations.

Sociology of textbooks becomes an important branch of enquiry when an analysis between the relation of education and globalization is made. The process of globalization has perpetuated the phenomenon of 'identity politics' because of 'economic insecurity'. The processes of liberalization and privatization provide logic to 'culture of openness' because it supports the dominance of market as well as consumerism thesis. Thus prosperity, possession of material assets, life styles depicting use of multinational brands and successive successes due to individual efforts construct identities in the society. These processes, however, on the other hand, institutionalize social exclusion and do not approve the idea of success of a person based on contribution of 'collective'. As a result, these process 'silently' legitimize authoritarian action, dictatorial attitudes and functionality of traditional institutions. In other words, feudalism based interaction and neo-liberal patterns of interaction are tolerant spheres in the age of globalization. These dialogical frames of reference as knowledge systems can be viewed in the textbooks. Textbooks become the part of public sphere of education due to these frames of reference. In sociology of textbooks, there is necessity to examine the social world of author(s) in relation of processes of secularization, modernization and democratization, so that it is known that up to what extent texts of the textbooks are close to the world of science, logic, rationality and reality. In

India, these presentations in textbooks are prerequisites to 'constitutional morality'. Textbooks of this nature make students responsible and accountable citizens (of future). In the textbooks of social sciences particularly the narratives must be free from biases and parochialism. But, it has not happened. The textbooks fail to establish the 'logic of science' because inadequate and one-sided propositions are generally found in textbooks making pedagogical practices specific and non-scientific. There is another dimension also. In all developed and developing countries the secular-rational character of the public sphere is almost undermined in pedagogy. Such status in societies like India makes education unscientific and biased in which teachers as social category play important roles. The theo-religious spheres are part of textbooks in such a way that the relation between education in general and textbooks in particular and modernization process can be questioned at several places. The close and conscious watch of several cities reveals the fact that there is sharp rise in the number of religious complexes in every city if comparison is made with the presence of academic establishments and health centres. It leads to deficit in social and cultural capital which perpetuates poverty of culture and meaningful relations. Education in developing societies, as a result, does not generate democratic personality, equality directed aspiration and secular conscience amongst students successfully. To a certain extent, legitimacy to political feudalism in India and militarization of educational activities in schools is given by present patterns of education subscribed effectively by respective textbooks. The 'culture of intolerance' is also a product of classroom interaction taking place between students and teachers through textbooks. Sometimes it appears that author(s) of textbooks select and narrate text without application of academic and scientific mind. These textbooks make child 'aggressive in action' and 'alienated about social issues'. Since textbooks do not make much contribution to the process of empowerment, sociology of (new) education emerges as a critique of such state of apathy.

Sociologically, textbooks, to a certain extent, exhibit moral ambiguities and do not encourage the accumulation of trust – an element associated with social capital. These textbooks through texts (selected or constructed by author(s)) lead to varieties of suspicion making series of doubts about institutional practices. These series of doubts construct a peculiar kind of understanding amongst students. What teachers say in the classroom and what has been presented in the text by (textbooks) author(s) are 'only' correlated propositions (beyond challenge) because these propositions become instrumental in achievement/success through examination process. It can also be argued that we live in a literate society, i.e., we are surrounded everywhere by 'book space'. Child as part of a literate society finds own self, in the school(s) particularly, as user of the books without knowing the producers, authors and distributors or circulators of the books. In any school, very rarely, children find opportunities to have interface between author(s) of the books, concerned teachers and parents, producers of the books and related categories of the students. In this sense, textbooks are alien objects. Teachers 'interpret' the text of the textbook and students understand or rather 'use' the text of the textbooks. The text of the textbooks is always outside the concerned teacher (interpreter) because (s)he is not the producer/creator of the text. Thus, in the world of the school/classroom the interplay between books (through author(s)), students and concerned teachers is the interplay between 'unknown' or 'impersonals'. It makes textbook a social fact with the attributes of exteriority, constraint and generality. This system of interplay in classroom raises the issues of perception, experience, operationality and understanding on the one hand and attitude, interest and intentionality on the other. In 'sociology of textbooks' these dimensions must be given significance whenever texts of the textbooks are examined. The roles of the textbooks in enhancing the world of understanding and levels of success in examination sometimes appear as contradictory to each other. Generally, during popular discourse students state that they could secure higher percentage because they read textbooks with examination specific strategy while one category of students securing percentage of marks below the expectations argue that they studied all chapters of the textbooks with equal importance (ignoring the suggestions of teachers to have examination specific preparation) but could not achieve desired results. This dilemma as inclusive efforts versus expectation linked achievement reveals that textbooks are not effectively communicated to the students by teachers in the classroom because teachers treat examination more importantly to the advancement of knowledge into students' personality. The pathological consequences of this dilemma contribute to relate sociology of textbooks with inequality of educational opportunities. 'Segregations within segregation', thus, becomes the feature of schools. In fact, these sub-systems of segregations can also be found apparently or hidden in the textbooks. In other words, inequalities are taught to the students by teachers with the active help of textbooks. These inequalities are perpetuated further due to regular use of parallel study material (other than prescribed textbooks) by students, suggested by teachers (due to marketization of educational success) and senior/fellow students (due to imitative behavioural patterns). Pedagogy also perpetuates such patterns of inequalities. The continuance of these patterns of inequalities in successive classroom interaction constructs identities amongst students. Sociologically, it can be argued that these patterns of understanding and communication do not convert teacher(s) into critical educator(s) because teachers while communicating text or content do not use language of analysis or language of criticism. The text communicated to students lacks 'experiential knowledge' and 'ground realities'.

The process of globalization has made meaningful impact on performance of students of various social categories. The different and diverse kinds of books, the world of information and knowledge available on computer, the interaction of 'elite schools' with the schools of various countries under exchange programmes, privatization, marketization and commercialization of education and stress on professional education for constructing knowledge societies are some of the products or by products of globalization which have altered education policies, selection process, admission processes in schools, preferences to subjects and interface between students, teachers and parents. But, these technology-dominated or directed educational developments have assaulted on humanities, social sciences, liberal disciplines (such as art) and pure sciences. Globalization process along with technological revolution establishes the logic that the managerial skill is now indispensable for career development. Thus, disciplines linked with engineering education (particularly computer and information technology) and the degree of management construct the hierarchy of preferences in education. These factors have divided education. The marginalized sections of society along with working class are, to a large extent, unable to send their children in those academic establishments or schools which produce 'competent children' – a notion constructed by the institution of market and associated market forces. Private schools and schools operated under private-public partnership have found central place in 'academic market place'. It has made unprecedented impact on publishing industry. The textbooks, in terms of printing, are now completely changed. These books attract the children. Books from different parts of western/developed world are easily available in the market attracting the children of prosperous sections of society. In elite schools these books have been used by students as 'parallel books' which contribute in advancing the multifaceted aspects of knowledge and information. It has been found that students of elite schools get comparatively more success in 'National Talent Search Examination' in comparison of the students of non-elite schools. This success has been achieved because of more and more engagement of these students with foreign books. Surprisingly the success rate of these students at tenth and twelfth level engaged with private schools is comparatively low if the result of central schools is taken in consideration. Such parallel reading material also leads to proficiency in English language making these students able to enter in global economic competitiveness. Thus knowledge, power, culture and dominant identities undergo the process of socialization of students in schools where textbooks, parallel reading material and material available on computer together construct the personality of students and make them rich in terms of academic and culture capital. It is interesting, sociologically, to examine the socio-cultural and socio-economic background of the students with nature of schooling who that have entered into elite centre of higher learning and have got employment opportunities in multinational or trans-national organizations. Students of such background have now entered into politics and civil services because of economic recession. This trend of Indian society raises several issues, vital for the understanding of complexities of sociology of education, sociology of new education and textbooks. It appears, in the era of globalization, that textbooks are not intellectual products or products leading to the phenomenon of intellectualism. Textbooks are, rather, 'consumeristic products' in which students are allowed to act as 'voluntaristic consumers' who select only those texts for study (with the help of teachers) which play instrumental role in achieving success in examination.

The interplay between academic establishments (schools, colleges, universities, research/professional institutes, etc.), students and books have entered into the areas of stress and tensions due to neo-liberal roles of the state. Restrictions on regular appointment of teachers and overemphasis on recruitment of contractual knowledge workers are important causes of these systems of tension appearing in academic establishments. Political leadership, bureaucracies, defense forces and judiciaries in the era of globalization have become controversial institutions due to their alleged involvement in non-institutional practices. But, still a large part of academic intellectuals (academia) can never be hired. Unfortunately, the services associated with social sectors in general and health and education in particular are being converted into 'hired services' or 'contractual services' giving rise to the state of 'organized anarchy'. This neo-liberal role of state provides legitimacy to marketization of education and health, dominated/controlled by private players. Hired or contractual knowledge workers (teachers) cannot enter into classroom with a sense of security. Students cannot pay them desired regards because interaction of students with contractual faculty is not enduring. In our opinion, contractual faculty is 'institutional drop out' of teachers. These teachers cannot generate 'interest-specific' connectedness with the textbooks. Such lack of interest makes teachers 'non-critique' of textbooks because any reaction from these teachers about textbooks can be harmful to their contractual or hired job. These situations have perpetuated 'culture of militarization' in classroom interaction in general and 'academic establishments' in particular. In schools, nobody tolerates, encourages and celebrates the minimum spirit of humour. Thus, cultural and interactional distance of students with schools, teachers and textbooks become a fact of educational life. Schools, teachers, students, parents and textbooks (along with their authors) are, in fact, alien to each other. Schools are not those places which can approve or even accept 'logic of laughter'. In textbooks' writings author(s) do not incorporate that content, having humour, even if that is considered as one of the best reading materials to understand the related phenomenon. Humour-based narratives can be the alternative way of learning as having fast pace is not the organ of mindset and writing skill of the author(s) of the textbooks. This absence of the text of humour in textbooks makes students distant from fearless conversation and joking interaction which is necessary for the continuance of 'culture of childhood'. Sometimes it appears that textbooks act as enemies of child because child is forced to dissociate own self from 'what child is' or 'what child should be'? In fact, there is growth of the 'adversary culture' constructed by textbooks (to a certain extent) around the 'life-world' of the child. We can frame this deterministic statement because textbooks neither expand nor deepen the values of democracy, secularism, liberty, equality and justice. But, there are no alternatives to textbooks also, thus, there is sociological need to transform the world of textbooks. Democratization of content structure incorporated in the textbooks is must for initiating reforms in education. In segmented societies, secularization of content structure of textbooks is the necessity so that diversity of social life could become the pattern of social life of the students. These aspects with normative-scientific framework make sociology of textbooks an important sub-discipline within sociology.

We have already pointed out the fact that academic establishments of all kind are organically linked with the sub-systems of (rational) choices and (desired or appropriate) opportunities. The textbooks should be prepared with the understanding of these sub-systems. There is thus need of following stages before preparing the textbooks as well as during preparation of textbooks:

(a) Pre-preparation Stages

(i) Discussion between author(s) or members of textbooks development committee about nature of curriculum and syllabus.

(ii) The exchange of ideas between authors about possible socio-cultural, economic, linguistic and regional background of the related students so that appropriate content covering the topics could be identified.

(iii) The exchange of ideas between the students, the parents, the teachers and the authors about collecting and understanding local knowledge and 'language of use' and 'language in use'. These discussions encourage children to reveal those perceptions which they have about the topics/issues, i.e., the organs of syllabus.

(iv) Collection of the reading material with evidences, if necessary, by the author(s) and selection of the material on the basis of (collective) wisdom of the author or authors. The selection of material must be child or student friendly (along with local examples).

(b) Preparation Stages

(i) Collection of reading material in such a way that local, regional, national (multi-regional) and global systems of knowledge appear before the students in chronological and systematic order.

(ii) Examples, folk knowledge, photographs, media reports, views of known personalities, humour based narratives, family-society interface and arguments constructed by author(s) should be placed in such a way that appropriate world of knowledge and information in accordance with relevant age groups is exposed in an interesting way along with inbuilt questions so that child could start questioning not only before peer group and teachers, but before family members also. Such content is bound to generate questionable mindset amongst students. Classroom interaction becomes 'live' and also acts as source of communication of knowledge and culture.

(iii) The reading material should be examined closely by the author(s), concerned teachers, parents and enlightened citizens regularly so that 'ethnicization of culture' does not become the part of students' conscience. Contradictions of knowledge, place, context and belongings can be incorporated in the textbooks with this strong perception that any thing associated with violation of human rights and negation of the constitutional norms with values of universalism are never there or logically disapproved. There is always a need of updating the reading material so that students are in latest touch with knowledge and information.

(iv) Textbooks should be published by the state or its agency so that quality publication is available to the students at low cost. Book writing and its outcome in the form of responses produced by various sections should be published in the related editions of the book at last.

(v) It is also desirable that along with textbook, a book incorporating reference material should also be published for the teachers. Such books should be published with the involvement of the same author(s), so that these books could produce transformative changes in the nature of pedagogy.

All these stages are workable propositions and in no way is an attempt to intervene the autonomy of the author(s). But, in our opinion, all these stages make book writing process a social product in which various kind of 'collective' actively but indirectly play significant roles relating to 'providers' of knowledge and information or pointing out those sources by which relevant material relating to proposed textbooks can be drawn. In one sense textbook writing appears as a 'collective responsibility' used by author(s). In real sense, 'books are the best friends which take the student wherever his/her mind commands'. Textbooks at early stages should incorporate content with the world of play, drama, mysteries, folklores, folk songs, folk stories having localized inputs and adventures' narratives so that learning could emerge with sustainability. To a certain extent the textbooks of such kind can be treated as best friends for the students.

Social education, world over, is based upon textbooks because the regular interplay of students with textbooks at elementary, secondary and senior secondary levels construct mindset, attitude, behavioural skills, values, ethical standards and moralities by which students act as knowledgeable social units with possible qualities of cultural reproduction in future. These three systems (along with sub-systems) of school education give rise to higher education system and related sub-systems (generally linked with professional education). It is also a fact that school education system(s) in any society act as those organs which make inclusive society and inclusive development possible. The question arises at this stage, 'are textbooks at the levels of school education systems supportive to the ideas of inclusive society/development?'. If such support is not there in the textbooks, then there is meaningful need of systemic changes in processes relating to the preparation of textbooks. It is unfortunate that states of India and its organs have not only ignored the vital importance of textbooks for cognitive development of students, but have undermined the local cultural spaces (as texts in textbooks) which attract students and parents to understand own self through textbooks also. As students, author(s) should evaluate what has been written by them? If content of textbook is attractive and character of pedagogy is critical, then to an extent the huge number of drop outs and out of school children may be reduced. Textbooks, thus, can be used as those tools by which social exclusion of children of various social categories experiencing marginalization can be minimized. It has already been mentioned somewhere in this discourse that 'child' and socio-cultural frame of 'childhood' (similarly adolescence and adolescent) have not found central place or front stage in textbooks. Thus, without transforming the whole world of textbooks, transformation of school education system is not possible. Textbooks have failed to achieve the basic philosophical purpose of education, which according to Muchkund Dubey is to 'enhance the capacity of the children to comprehend, contest and transform'. The absence of such books for the students at school levels makes a large part of younger generation apathetic and indifferent. Such students do not take human sufferings seriously. As a result, the academic establishments associated with higher education (in which students after school education take admissions) have failed to raise the voice in support of socially excluded categories, developing and underdeveloped nations and ethnic conflicts. All academic establishments – the schools, the colleges, the universities and centres of professional education – have yet to accept the logic that each child/student is a 'socio-cultural document'. Such outcome or appearances undermine the significance of social movements. The caste-centric systems in India and challenges to democratization – secularization processes at global levels do not invite any dominant pattern of resistance. These dimensions make 'sociology of textbooks' an important branch to observe 'culture-society-development interface' in context of younger generation in general and school-goers in particular. These textbooks can be used as tools to analyse the attitudes and perceptions of the students. Since these textbooks do not provide systematic articulation of complex and dynamic interplay between social lives of (in) the communities and related politico-economic context, children develop no autonomous vision about what is happening in the society. Text becomes so descriptive and fragmented that both the teachers and students are not able to locate 'centre(s) of narrative'. As a result, children are not fascinated toward the 'world of textbooks'. Thus, textbooks are representatives of 'poverty of culture linked diversity' and 'poverty of multiple knowledge', making students unstable, undecided and confused. This outcome creates hindrance in the process of awakening. The private-public partnership encouraged by state and private funding in the field of school education system have challenged or raised questions about affirmative action in the state of India. The parallel books taught in private funded schools generally question the ideas of social justice, affirmative action resulting into the continuance of social exclusion. It reveals the intervening roles of powerful sections of society. Such books introduce and establish the neo-liberal logic to 'meritocracy'. Talent and ability can be acquired through rigorous efforts only and it is the logic by which reservation issue along with the value of social justice is not only questioned but projected as anti-developmental.

The above mentioned elaboration never means that textbooks do not play the role as significant agents of appropriate socialization. Since child cannot select what is right/desirable and wrong/undesirable, the production of textbooks by state should be a cautious exercise so that 'inclusive society' could become a reality. With these frames of reference, the possibilities of sociology of textbooks as a branch within sociology can be explored. Sociology of textbooks, in our opinion, emphasizes on the logic that text constructed in the textbooks must provide valid explanation of human activities and societal affairs. Text, first of all, should be framed with the questions and the suspicions regarding human activities and societal affairs in the beginning and should reach, in the end, to valid explanation so that questions are answered and suspicions are ruled out. This effort of author(s) makes textbooks scientific. Each textbook is prepared with a definite design, i.e., class consciousness so that the same could be communicated to the students. It makes textbooks a part of superstructure (culture). Consumerism, individualism, success, competition, social hierarchies and its logic and necessities of authorities in private and public spheres are communicated to the students through textbooks. It also legitimizes 'education as businesses'. In textbooks, how people have resisted oppressive and exploitative tendencies and people's engagement in work activities so that their life struggles are known, should be included. Such text always faces marginalization when text books are prepared. Activities of several social groups like trade unions, political parties of various ideologies and movements of working class(es) linked with unorganized sectors, struggles of peasantry and women and life patterns of special need social categories, etc., hardly find place in the chapters or the content within chapters of the textbooks. It is a deliberate denial of the roles of common persons/marginalized groups in developmental processes. It simply means that production of textbooks depends upon the type of production relations which society possesses. It is essential to examine how textbooks at school education system do provide space for 'suppressing socio-economic' aspirations of deprived and poor sections of society. Exploitative use of social labour is never discussed systematically in these textbooks generally. Thus, textbooks produce three forms of consciousness:

(i) The general consciousness for primary understanding (expansion of common sense and world of information).
(ii) One-sided consciousness (avoidance of life world of several social categories so that the notions like 'mainstream' could appear along with the roles of 'we' in development and change of society).
(iii) False consciousness (misinformation and error based knowledge based on manufactured facts so that biases and prejudices could find place in primary stages of socialization at school levels). It means culture and knowledge produced by textbooks present the world of divisions on the one hand and 'manufactured' inclusiveness on the other.

Conclusions

The structures of arguments, upon which this narration is constructed, can be used for drawing following conclusions about sociology of textbooks:

1. Sociology of textbooks as an organ of sociology of education (old and new) and branch of sociology can be defined as scientific-critical and ideological analysis of interplay of syllabus/curriculum bound books, social biographies of the author(s), students and the parents (families), communicators of the textbooks (educators/teachers), cultural world of the society and political economy of the state. Thus, sociology of textbooks constitutes the text of 'manifesto of education' and educational development (in relation to continuity and change).
2. Sociology of textbooks as 'manifesto of education/educational development' not only expresses myths and realities about dialectics of communitarian civilizations and systems of rule but also reveals what powerful forces wish to communicate or distribute knowledge and information (selective cultures) to the new generation – the students.
3. The changes in the production process of textbooks are helpful in understanding the dynamism in the class character of society and of state.
4. Textbooks and classroom interaction between teachers and students give rise to non-questionable and imitative mindsets amongst students so that legitimacy to 'status-quoism' could continue.

5. Textbooks in terms of content structure, structure of language, chapter-schemes, framing questions and use of symbols are not child/student friendly. As a result, pedagogy in classroom interplay never stimulates a child to make his/her personality multifaceted. These textbooks are prepared for examination purposes resulting into the presence of various kinds of markets of textbooks. These complex enquiries construct the nature and subject matter of sociology of textbooks.
6. The nature and types of state and society in the era of globalization explore possibilities to examine 'textbooks' with comparative orientation. It also invites the attention of academia whether textbooks at school levels make students conscious about education, health, democratic institutions and roles of state in relation to societal welfare.

References

Dubey, Muchkund (2010). 'Academic Dependency: Some Reflections', in Kathinka Sinha-Kerkhoff and Syed Farid Alatas (eds), *Academic Dependency in the Social Sciences*, New Delhi: Manohar.

Kumar, Krishna (2001). *Prejudice and Pride*. New Delhi: Viking.

Nash, R. (1972). 'History as She is Writ', *New Society*, 3 August.

Olson, David R. and Nancy Torrance (eds) (2001). *The Making of Literate Societies*. Oxford: Blackwell.

5

Trends of Youth Sexuality in Globalizing India

Challenge for Curriculum

Swati Shirwadkar

A decade ago, the doyen sociologist, Yogendra Singh (2000) pointed out that the study of cultural changes has not drawn enough attention of sociologists. Today, the forces of globalization and culture change have attracted attention of scholars and its impact on different walks of life are now so evident that researchers cannot miss the emerging trends in society. Processes of change in culture due to the impact of market economy and telecommunication revolution were noted and discussed earlier when its pulse was beginning to be felt. In that earlier stage itself, implication of global market economy and cultural change for the teaching and research in sociology was underscored by Professor Singh.

For understanding of critical issues reflected in the society, not only research but curriculum construction and pedagogical practices are also significant. However, some trends reflected in the cultural and social change fail to make its presence felt in the traditional structured curriculum. However, today's challenges of globalization demand that we need to study the new changes that are taking place in different aspects of the society, such as emerging trends in sexuality and reproductive health. Moreover, in the changing situation, it is also important that these issues should be a part of discursive learning of students.

The paper first contextualizes the issue of youth sexuality with emerging changes of global market economy as pointed out by Yogendra Singh, with a discussion about some emerging issues related to youth sexuality. Further, this paper presents a short review of some studies on emerging trends of youth sexuality around the time of the publication of the book on culture change in India (ibid.). With this, the relation of significant social factors in the process of globalization and cultural change that perhaps propelled the trends in sexuality issues is brought out. It is suggested that the needs and issues of the present-day youth reflected in society, demand that sociology curriculum needs to be more inclusive of the new trends. The paper concludes with a plea that there is a need of capturing these new changes in the curriculum of sociology for students' discursive learning. It is hoped that this may help in exploring a meaningful balance between research and teaching, as suggested by Yogendra Singh.

A lot of research is going on related to this subject, encouraged by insistence of international organizations and the covenants. However, social science curriculum, particularly sociology, has not been given the required space that it deserves, through its curriculum, to the issues related to reproductive sexual health. Since the construction of both femininity and masculinity being a historical process was done through the patriarchal structures, gender studies have given attention to these issues to some extent. Within mainstream sociology in India, however, it is still perceived as an area left for social work and activists. Considering the present context, particularly of the youth in the turmoil of globalization, there is an urgent need of making our curricula more inclusive of issues that deserve urgent attention.

The Need and the Context

A decade back, the changes due to rapid growth in electronic media, accelerated process of migration and consequential mobility has thrown in new challenges as pointed out earlier by Professor Singh. With globalization and unleashing of the forces of media and easier access to the cyber world, the market and the changing culture together are throwing up various processes. Indeed in present social context issues related to sexuality and reproductive health have become more crucial for the youth. The youth need not be seen as a victim in the turmoil of transition but needs to be taken seriously as to how their potential can be directed. The emancipatory potential of knowledge can be used through curriculum practice by educators. A deeper understanding of the youth problems not only reveals its multi-faceted nature but also brings out the complexities that are enmeshed in the structural aspect and the ongoing forces of change in the society. Against this background it becomes imperative to understand and unravel the issues related to sexuality and reproductive health in general, locating it within the socio-cultural context. The historicity of the construction of sexuality brings out its interconnections with the structural aspects of the society.

The Background

Literature on sexuality shows that sexuality refers to the individual and social meaning of sex, in addition to the biological aspects of sex. It is a result of the interplay of biological, psychological, socio-economic, cultural, ethical and religious/spiritual factors. The meaning and practices that are associated with sexuality differ in various societies, in different classes, according to age and gender (Weeks, 1986; Vance, 1984). Foucault considered power relationships as a central aspect of sexuality, not just as a negative force but as inciting and extorting various effects. He sees sexuality as a product of a system of discourses. He shows that what we think of as 'repression' of sexuality is a mistaken hypothesis and actually sexuality is a core feature of our identities (Foucault,

1977, 1978). Complex social relationships and their meanings, interpretations and reinterpretations contribute to the production of sexuality. It is a product of struggles, contestations, negotiations and human agency (Weeks, 1986). However, the cultural and the structural forces of the society create unequal power relationships between the gender roles. Patriarchal social norms create patterns of subordination and exploitation and now are accentuated by capitalist market forces within the process of globalization. The impact of globalization and subsequent cultural change is now visible in India. However, it is argued that though situation in Indian society is changing, the underlying norms remain same at the core (Abraham, 2002; Thapan, 1997). Prof. Singh has underscored the inner resilience of core cultural values in his work.

Recent Happenings

In most of the developed world, particularly the US, the capitalist global mass media promotes, glorifies and exploits sex, which has a far-reaching impact even in the developing world. Norms related to sexuality differ from culture to culture. In many developed countries sexuality and trends in sexual behaviour are a matter of concern. This concern is due to number of reasons, such as high rate of pregnancy among teenagers (CDC, 2001), a significant number of young women becoming victims of sexual violence (Gelles and Straus, 1988; Hines and Saudino, 2003) and the risk of infections because of sexually transmitted diseases (STDs) like HIV/AIDS. In India, issues related to sexuality are no longer hidden in the dark cupboards, which are not to be opened in public. Regardless of parents' wishes the new generation kids are engulfed into the images beamed by the market-world. The consumerist attitude has given rise to the use of most hi-tech tools without much of conscience governing the use of it. With media making the 'unspeakable' issues widely accessed and discussed, adolescents and youth being bombarded with sleazy ads and images through TV, cyber world, lifestyle magazines and page three materials, younger generation is indeed in a tricky situation. With increasing globalization of the market and communication in Asia and other parts of the world, new possibilities and access to opportunities are opening up for the youth. Added to this, as Macionis points out, the capitalist exploitation of skin has driven up the age of kids, reflected in the clothes lines in shopping malls and branded clothes with skin wars (Macionis, 2007). In this increasing emphasis on body show, India is not lagging far behind. Advancement and 'modernity' (understood by general public as being westernized) has not enabled us with discursive understanding of sexuality. The youth is caught between the value system that is undergoing change and the uncontrolled access to tech-viz gimmicks. Cases of misuse of tech-freedom and exploitation through new technology are recurrently appearing in media (e.g., cases of webcam used against girls, 'sms' scandals and sex rackets from Delhi, J&K to Aurangabad, Pune, and now even in smaller towns are just a few examples).

On one hand there is a challenge of rise in sexual crimes and on the other hand there is also a challenge of making sexuality recognized as rights-based issue, not only related to health but also related to other areas of the society and quality of individual life. The absolute number of illiterates is now going down. With literacy, education, socio-economic mobility of young males and females, there is also an avalanche of global media and market reaching the rural places some way or the other. For some sections of population, though perhaps still in small number, the control of family is loosening for different reasons. Though basic needs are not properly satisfied, the consumer goods are fast catching up even in rural communities. There is a change in their leisure activities and different trends are seen today among the youth. Recent reports and trends in media show that the attitude and behaviour related to sexuality show a significant change in youth sexual behaviour. There are other related problems coming up such as sexual violence and abuse, different forms of crimes against women by (spurned) 'lovers', 'boyfriends' or just stalkers, sex rackets and increasing reports of other pathologies that cannot be neglected. Activists and NGOs are trying to sensitize the people as well as institutional practices by documenting the cases and debates on issues (Sakshi, 2005). The possibility of improved reporting notwithstanding, the pervasiveness of the problem, from educated to less educated, moneyed class to lower class, and from metro to semi-urban areas demand attention for serious study.

Whereas the trends' reports throw up new dimensions in sexual behaviour of young, the debates related to the issue and the work of voluntary organizations show a range of issues untouched so far, which are now being addressed. Movement and activism has brought forward the issues of neglected sexual minorities. A review of the actual trends in youth sexual behaviour, the debates around sexuality and the work of voluntary organizations together underscore the need of a better understanding. It is not enough to just impart the scientific information around the issue (by just including sex education in school curriculum). It is necessary to develop awareness that is gender sensitive and inclusive of rights, for informed choice. In this context, the role of curriculum in higher education becomes crucial.

In most societies the issue of sexuality is studied in different ways. Western social scientists, especially renowned Anthropologists explored sexual behaviour, rituals and practices among tribes. With Kinsey report, there was a revelation regarding different practices that were not accepted earlier by the society. Further, with the medical advancement and several other factors there was a change in sexual behaviour of young. AIDS pandemic, however again started a debate related to openness about sexuality in the western world (Weeks, 1986).

Historically, in India, issues related to sexuality have long been the arenas of scholarly discussion and explorations, though it became a restricted issue in public life, in the later period. Right from the descriptions of women's body forms depicted in Vedic literature to the famous Kamasutra by Vatsayan, or even the Khajuraho and other sculptures in many temples show that expressions of sexuality were treated as natural. One finds this view reflected in western writings (Foucault, 1977; Connell, 1997). The issue was later addressed by several Indian researchers, while linking it to other problems or processes such as fertility decline, fertility rate or ratio, colonialism, or even to Gandhian philosophy (Srivastava, 2004). More recent works analysing the construction of Indian sexuality and its linkages to religion or the apparently hidden and neglected folk literature and practices in everyday life have contributed to the understanding of construction of sexuality and gender (Kakar, 1978; Raheja and Gold, 1996). Scholars have expounded on the issue of sexuality in different ways in past.

Western sexuality is usually understood in India as liberal. However, studies point out to the emphasis on 'machismo' masculinity in western culture. Militarism is exploited in the commercial popular culture by the commodities such as Rambo movies and Masters of Universe toys (Connell, 1997). Connell argues that with industrialization, political revolutions and the growth of bureaucratic state, there was a change towards more rational, calculative masculinity. Connell traces the development of these to today's new hegemonic variety of entrepreneur type masculinity and also brings out the turbulence around it due to the dynamics of marginalized, subordinated masculinities and feminism. Giddens agrees that today masculinity is subjected to pressure. The traditional masculine role no longer exists today, in spite of the attempts to revive it. With greater autonomy and liberation of women, men have lost their safety net. Hence he pleads for democratic relationships devoid of power (Kaspersen, 2000). Though the social situation in the western society may not be comparable, certainly there are signs that show the reflection of analysis offered by Giddens. Research studies in India bring out some interesting trends. Studies have traced the history of ideas about sexuality, present trends and new challenges. While Giddens's argument about vulnerability of male sexuality may be found evident in Indian context, Prof. Singh's caution about new challenges of globalization is also another added dimension. An overview of some research studies bring this up to the forefront.

Sanjay Srivastava refers to the earlier studies that explored the invisible terrain of female sexuality. It is not only the female sexuality that is silenced in India, but also there is an anxiety around male sexuality in terms of anxiety of threat from female sexuality (Srivastava, 2004). The European ethnocentric machismo image was seen as coming under threat from South Asian female sexuality of 'lower' race in British India. These aspects of colonialism are reflected in Sudipto Sen's study of tracking racial ideology reflected in sexuality of the colonial times. The study provides details of effort to be saved from the threat of native female sexuality in the 'Raj', barring the aspect of colonialism and racism. Studies in sexuality have thus brought forward the historical context as well as the socio-cultural mediation of construction of sexuality. Contrary to common belief, homosexuality too has been reflected in earlier studies (Sen, 2004). The onslaught and pandemic of HIV/AIDS have generated new attention not only to the subject but also towards the necessity to address the issue from human rights perspective.

These changes are also linked to addressing the issue on international forum. International conventions paved the way to take cognizance of different aspects of sexual violence and exploitation for developing certain standards (Misra and Chandiramani, 2005). The International Conference on Population and Development (1994) and later the Beijing Conference are said to be the turning point for shifting the emphasis on population control to 'rights for development'. Earlier, from the official viewpoint, sexuality was seen only in the context of reproductive health of the population. After the Beijing Conference, sexuality was seen by subsequent forums with more awareness and there was an attempt to reduce discrimination on the basis of sexual orientation.

Field studies related to sexuality and reproductive health underscore the importance of the new approaches and the international provisions which in turn will have to be taken cognizance of, by the state. The studies come out with some facts showing that the burden of facing problems, exploitation, violence are unequally shared by women, vulnerable people due to several reasons ranging from influence of socio-economic and cultural factors to the lack of legal provisions. Such structural as well as institutional imbalances need to be addressed not only through legal provisions but also through discursive knowledge. When a section of population is adversely impacted due to unequal distribution of resources, structured imbalances and state of apathy, there is a need to create awareness about the issue rather than just the dissemination of information, which is seen as a state responsibility. It is necessary to develop a critique and awareness about the issue at a higher level, considering the future role of the students as educators.

Studies in Sexuality: Mapping of the Issues

A review of the field realities gives us an idea about how the issue of sexuality is related to the deeply entrenched structural problems of the society. It also highlights the importance of sociology curriculum being more inclusive for such serious social issues pertaining to the vulnerable groups. Census reports and other surveys have established the correlation of early age of marriage, fertility rate and larger size of family. Micro studies have also pointed out the relation of socio-cultural factors related to fertility transitions (Rajan, 2005). Research studies also highlight that choice of reproductive health and sexuality, family size, hardly rests with women. Regarding this, the contrast in the development in south compared to north is considered significant. Fertility has shown a decline in the South India, while Kerala and Tamil Nadu are far ahead of other states. The importance of socio-cultural factors should be acknowledged while examining the differences in fertility change in different geographical areas. As far as sex ratio is concerned, sexual discrimination seems to be a complex phenomenon where differences in regional culture related to structural economic changes play a part. The socio-economic and the structural factors play a role in female infanticide in Salem in spite of Tamil Nadu's overall better performance in fertility rate (Vella, 2005). Practices related to sexual behaviour too are related to socio-cultural factors apart from other processes of change. Whereas Tamil Nadu could bring down the percentage of people living with HIV/AIDS, Andhra Pradesh's situation has a cause to worry. Male dominated society, exploitative practices combined with factors such as migration and rural-urban mobility are reported as responsible factors (*The Indian Express*, 21 May 2006). Trends of sexual and reproductive behaviour, in northern part of India also underscore the importance of social factors and processes. Though we have improved on reduction of maternal mortality rates in some areas, still there is an increase in HIV/AIDS affected people.

Recent studies are coming out with systematic empirical work related to reproductive sexual health of people with macro and micro studies. The studies are dealing with the magnitude of the problem, its context, trends and also the efforts of support, healing as well as organizing and struggle to establish the rights. While fertility rate being an indicator of development becomes a component of curriculum studies, issues related to early age of marriage and reproductive health choices or sexual violence within marriage does not get the attention it deserves.

In India, sexual activity is largely seen within the context of marriage. Research shows that the field reality, however, may be different. While pointing out to the under reporting by girls and over reporting by boys about their pre-marital sexual behaviour, Jejeebhoy has highlighted the growing evidence from small studies. Studies have reported risky sexual behaviour among different sections of younger population (Jejeebhoy, 2004; Abraham, 2000; Sodhi and Verma, 2003). While pre-marital sexual activity among males is condoned, women face severe restrictions, violence, stigma, exploitation and lack of informed choice (Abraham, 2004; Bott and Jejeebhoy, 2003; Jejeebhoy, 2000, 2004). Jejeebhoy points out to the NACO data and data from different states reporting casual sexual experience, bringing in the risks and violence in the activity. It is also known that sexual abuse and coercion takes place by perpetrators who are known to the victim.

Studies suggest a lack of information and access to safe services for the adolescent and young (Ganatra, 2000; Jejeebhoy, 2000). Obviously, the burden of stigma and exploitation is adversely borne by females. Though data on adolescent and youth sexuality and behaviour trends are difficult to elicit, some research studies have indicated not only the existence but also the related problems, which need attention. Studies report such activities among both urban educated youth and rural youth. There is a change in attitude towards pre-marital sex and sexual activity (Abraham, 2000; Bang et al., 1989; Jejeebhoy, 2000; Straus et al., 2004). The influence of regulatory institutions such as family, religion or educational institutions is declining for males. Work status and spatial mobility reduces family control of urban boys. There is more curiosity, exploration of sexuality and sexual activity among them and yet they tend to engage in unsafe sexual practices (Abraham, 2000). Poverty, illiteracy and migration worsens the access of protective health information to not only women but also to groups of people who have alternative sexualities. Studies of the different aspects of the work being carried out by NGOs to fight HIV/AIDS related issues bring out the complexities of our socio-cultural situation (Ramasubban and Rishyasringa, 2005). These studies show a linkage of all these issues to the larger socio-economic and political processes in the society in which the context of globalization cannot be forgotten.

Connecting sexuality and reproductive health has gains in form of social justice. However, it is warned that such connection can make other non-sexual identities and non-reproductive practices invisible or marginalized (Miller, 2000). Debates around the sexuality issues are not limited to only hetrosexual relations. Issues that are coming up, address an array of areas such as experiences and struggles of lesbian, gay, bisexual and transsexual people fighting for their rights. This is also connected to other issues such as state repression, articulation of rights and stigma. From this different perspective the institutions such as marriage, family are increasingly becoming a contested site (John, 2005). The need of evolving a public debate and a necessity to understand the issues related to sexuality as a discourse cannot be denied. Here, the role of social sciences curriculum is important for analysing the issue.

A survey of the postgraduate courses of Sociology curriculum of the universities in Maharashtra state up to the year two thousand shows that the subjects such as sexuality and reproductive health or related issues like sexual violence, were not included in the curriculum of any university of the state, in spite of the growing social importance of the issue. The department of Sociology, University of Pune introduced courses on 'Sexuality and Human Rights' and 'Reproductive Health and Development' and 'Interpersonal Violence' only for two consecutive semesters, as an overwhelming student response to a seminar organized on the same. (The courses were later included as regular elective courses for Sociology). At the end of the last semester, the students of these courses attended a workshop organized by experts in science. The students were offered an orientation course that helped prepare them for dissemination of scientific information about health, particularly reproductive health. It was observed that as a result of familiarity with the debates about sexuality and reproductive health, the students were raising critical questions about the way the scientific information was imparted. This led the organizers to improve their own content and definitions. This is just one example of how the introduction of the issues related to sexuality and reproductive health in curriculum of higher level can help in understanding the social construction of sexuality and in developing an ability to bring out change.

New Challenges and Curriculum Change

Indian youth today, to a large extent, is engulfed by different processes. These processes are affecting even the interiors of rural society by some way or the other. Globalization, explosion of information, technology and communication system are making the choices more open for the youth. The belief and value systems are becoming destabilized (Giddens, 1990). Decline in community values and alienation of the individual in the expanding global domain is underscored also by Yogendra Singh. Today's situation shows that spatial mobility of youth and compression of time-space through different means are loosening the control of family, kin networks and other such primary influences. At the same time there is a conflict as well as reassertion of the patriarchal value system. Globalization has brought monitory betterment for some but it has also brought a threat of cultural bankruptcy. Contradictory and multiple belief systems are pushing the ideas about sexuality in a flux. At the same time, increasing autonomy of choice making and formation of new individual identities, as Singh predicts, points to the direction of social change. In such conditions, it becomes imperative to develop the expert system that is emancipatory. It is important to accept the challenge of the situation and make changes towards a curriculum, which is inclusive of new voices that are reflected in the society in different ways. Curriculum can be shaped by understanding the voices that are reflected in the new processes. Thus, this will effectively bring in the change from within. Our curriculum should reflect the present context, social changes and the new issues, which affect a section of population that is an essential part of education. It can be a small step towards a democratic society through building up of the reflexivity of individual.

References

Abraham, L. (2000). *Understanding Youth Sexuality: A Study of College Students in Mumbai*. Mumbai: Tata Institute of Social Sciences.

—— (2002). 'Bhai-Behen, True Love, Time Pass: Friendships and Sexual Partnerships among Youth in an Indian Metropolis', *Culture, Health and Sexuality*, 4 (3): 337–53.

Bang, R.A. et al. (1989). 'High Prevalence of Gynecological Diseases in Rural Indian Women', *Lancet*, January 14, 1 (8629): 85–88.

Bott, S. and S. Jejeebhoy (2003). 'Adolescent Sexual and Reproductive Health in South Asia: An Overview of Findings from the 2000 Mumbai Conference', in S. Bott, S. Jejeebhoy, I. Shah and C. Puri (eds), *Women's Reproductive Health in India*. Geneva: WHO.

Center for Disease Control (CDC) (2001). Fact Sheets. National Center for Health Statistics, US Department of Health and Human Services.

Connell, R.W. (1997). 'The Big Picture: Masculinities in Recent World History', in A.H. Halsey et al. (eds), *Education: Culture, Economy and Society*, Oxford: Oxford University Press, pp. 605–19.

Foucault, M. (1977). *Power/Knowledge: Selected Interviews and Other Writings*. New York: Pantheon.

—— (1978). *The History of Sexuality*, Vol. I, New York: Vintage Books.

Ganatra, B. (2000). 'Abortion Research in India: What We Know, and What We Need to Know', in R. Ramasubban and S. Jejeebhoy (eds), *Women's Reproductive Health in India*. Jaipur: Rawat Publications.

Gelles, R.J. and M.A. Straus (1988). *Intimate Violence*. New York: Simon and Schuster.

Giddens, A. (1990). *The Consequences of Modernity*. Oxford: Polity Press.

—— (1991). *Modernity and Self-Identity*. Cambridge: Polity Press.

Hines, D.A. and K.J. Saudino (2003). 'Gender Differences in Psychological, Physical and Social Aggression among College Students using the Revised Conflict Tactics Scales', *Violence and Victims*, 18 (2): 192–217.

Jejeebhoy, S. (2000). 'Safe Motherhood in India: Priorities of Social Science Research', in R. Ramasubban and S. Jejeebhoy (eds), *Women's Reproductive Health in India*, Jaipur: Rawat Publications.

—— (ed.) (2004). *Looking Back, Looking Forward*. New Delhi: Population Council and Jaipur: Rawat Publications.

John, M. (2005). 'Symposium on Marriage, Family and Community: A Feminist Dialogue', *Economic and Political Weekly*, XL (8): 721.

Kakar, S. 1978. *The Inner World*. Delhi: Oxford University Press.

Kaspersen, L.B. (2000). *Anthony Giddens: An Introduction to a Social Theorist*. Oxford: Blackwell.

Lauman, E. et al. (eds) (1994). *The Social Organization of Sexuality: Sexual Practices in the United States*. Chicago: University of Chicago Press.

Macionis, J. (2007). *Sociology*. New Jersey: Pearson/Prentice-Hall.

Miller, Alice (2000). 'Sexual but Not Reproductive: Exploring the Junctions and Disjunctions of Sexual and Reproductive Rights', *Health and Human Rights*, 4 (2).

Misra, G. and R. Chandiramani (2005). *Sexuality, Gender and Rights*. New Delhi: Sage.

Raheja, G. and A. Gold (1996). *Listen to the Heron's Words: Reimagining Gender and Kinship in North India*. Delhi: Oxford University Press.

Rajan, I.S. (2005). 'Introduction: Emerging Demographic Changes in South India', in C.Z. Guilmoto and S. Irudaya Rajan (eds), *Fertility Transition in South India*, New Delhi: Sage.

Ramasubban, Radhika and B. Rishyasringa (2005). *AIDS and Civil Society*. Jaipur: Rawat Publications.

Sakshi (2005). *Walking Wisdom: A Creative Learning Experience*. The Asia-Pacific Advisory Forum on Judicial Education on Equality Issues.

Singh, Y. (2000). *Culture Change in India: Identity and Globalization*. Jaipur: Rawat Publications.

Sodhi, G. and M. Verma (2003). 'Sexual Coercion among Unmarried Adolescents of an Urban Slum in India', in S. Bott, S. Jejeebhoy, I. Shah and C. Puri (eds), *Towards Adulthood*, Geneva: WHO.

Srivastava, S. (2004). 'Introduction: Semen, History, Desire and Theory', in Srivastava (ed.), *Sexual Sites, Seminal Attitudes*, New Delhi: Sage.

Straus, M. et al. (2004). 'Prevalence of Violence against Dating Partners by Male and Female University Students Worldwide', *Violence against Women*, 10 (7): 790–811.

Sen, Sudipta (2004). 'Colonial Aversions and Domestic Desires: Blood, Race, Sex and the Decline of Intimacy in Early British India', in Sanjay Srivastava (ed.), *Sexual Sites, Seminal Attitudes*, New Delhi: Sage.

Thapan, M. (1997). 'Feminity and its Discontents: Women's Body in Intimate Relationships', in M. Thapan (ed.), *Embodiment: Essays on Gender and Identity*, Delhi: Oxford University Press, pp. 172–93.

The Indian Express (2006). 'The Andhra Syndrome', May 21, p. 13.

Vance, C.S. (ed.) (1984). *Pleasure and Danger: Exploring Female Sexuality*. Boston: Routledge and Kegan Paul.

Vella, S. (2005). 'Low Fertility and Female Discrimination in South India: The Puzzle of Salem District, Tamil Nadu', in C.Z. Guilmoto and S. Irudaya Rajan (eds), *Fertility Transition in South India*, New Delhi: Sage.

Weeks, J. (1986). *Sexuality*. Chichester: Ellis Horwood.

6

Society Caught Between 'Tradition' and 'Modernity'

Is India Ready for Sex Education?

Niharika Tripathi and T.V. Sekher

Sex is a very sensitive subject and discussing sexual matters openly is considered as a taboo in Indian society. Given this context, introducing sex education at school level always attracts objections and apprehensions from many quarters. Family life education or sex education refers to a broad programme designed to impart knowledge regarding practices, values and attitudes affecting family relationships. It aims to develop the qualities and attitudes on which successful family life depends. The real purpose of family life/sex education is the transfiguration of a boy child into manhood and of a girl child into womanhood. The education that provides knowledge on physical, mental, social, moral, behavioural changes and developments during puberty is termed as 'adolescent family life education'. It teaches the adolescents about the role boys and girls play in family and society, and responsibility and attitude towards each other, etc., within our social context. Many psychologists believe that sex education begins at an early age and continues throughout the life of an individual. The purpose of sex education should be to facilitate the best possible integration between the physical, emotional and mental aspects of the personality and also between the individuals and the groups.

Sex education includes the information about conception, contraception and sexually transmitted diseases. It is a continuous process of developing attitudes, values and understanding regarding all situations and relationships in which people play role as male or female (D'Souza, 1979). More than biological facts, sex education should also include social and moral behaviour, proper attitudes and values towards sex, love, family life and interpersonal relations in society. Due to increasing incidences of HIV/AIDS, RTIs/STIs and teenage pregnancies, there is a need to impart sex education among youth. The problem of overpopulation in our country also demands family life education, including family planning as a priority, as many of the young people are about to be married and should be aware of responsibilities they have. The study on child abuse in India, conducted by the Ministry of Women and Child Development, reports that 53 per cent of boys and 47 per cent of girls surveyed faced some form of sexual abuse (Government of India, 2007). Therefore, family life education might help the vulnerable young population to be aware about their sexual rights and empower them to protect themselves from any undesired act of violence, sexual abuse and molestation. The National Population Policy also reiterates the need of educating adolescents about the risks of unprotected sex (Government of India, 2000). Furthermore, the provision of family life education might result into multiple benefits to the adolescent boys and girls. This might include delayed initiation of sex, reduced unplanned pregnancies and too early pregnancies and their associated complications, fewer unwanted children, reduced risks of sexual abuse, greater completion of education and later marriages, reduced recourse to abortion and the consequences of unsafe abortion, slower spread of sexually transmitted diseases including HIV (WHO, 2003).

Objectives of Family Life Education/Sex Education

The main objectives of family life education/sex education are:

- To develop emotionally stable children and adolescents who feel sufficiently secure and adequate to make decisions regarding their conduct without being carried away by their emotions.
- To provide sound knowledge not only of the physical aspects of sex behaviour but also of its psychological and sociological aspects, so that sexual experience will be viewed as a part of the total personality of the individual.
- To develop attitudes and standards of conduct, which will ensure that young people and adults will determine their sexual and other behaviour by considering its long range effects on their own personal development, the good of other individuals, and welfare of society as a whole (D'Souza, 1979).

The rapidly changing western society has for a long time recognized the importance of sex education. In 1984, it was found that around 50 per cent of Canadian schools introduced family life education programme (Nolte, 1984). The scenario in India is somewhat different, as sex education is considered as a 'taboo' by many. Children as well as parents feel hesitant and embarrassed while discussing on such issues. Curiosity to know about sex is inseparable and inevitable thirst of humans. Its necessity has been realized and imparted throughout the history of human societies within its variant cultural settings, though with restrictions. But, in the modern society, under the strong influence of mass media, the taboo regarding sex has lost its meaning. Adolescents and youth are getting affected mainly because of various misconceptions on sex. The first organization in India to sponsor sex education was All India Moral and Social Hygiene Association, founded by Keshab Chander Sen, who led the movement for improving the status of women (Forbes, 1963). The

Family Planning Association of India (FPAI) pioneered the population education in 1960s and moved on to 'family life and sex education' thereafter, keeping the need of such education.

Controversy in 2007 over Introducing Sex Education in Schools

In 2007, the scheme promoted by the National AIDS Control Organization (NACO) and the Ministry of Human Resource Development (HRD) that adolescence education should be introduced in the school curriculum led to a major controversy in India. The opponents of sex education argued for a ban of sex education in schools on the ground that it corrupts the youth and offends 'Indian values'. They felt that it may lead to promiscuity, experimentation and irresponsible sexual behaviour. On the one hand, we have a thriving economy and modernization while, on the other, an uneasy debate on sex education. The critics of sex education feel that sex education may be necessary in western countries, but not in India, which has already a 'rich' culture. It will have adverse effects on young minds. On the contrary, the proponents say that conservative ideas have little place in a modernizing country like India where attitudes towards sex are changing rapidly. The states of Gujarat, Madhya Pradesh, Maharashtra, Karnataka, Kerala, Rajasthan, Chhattisgarh and Goa declared that the course content as suggested by HRD Ministry was unacceptable and banned the programme (Motihar, 2007).

Even, while the politicians and religious leaders have opposed the introduction of sex education in schools, studies show that Indian adolescents, youth, even married men and women, do not have enough information about sex, thereby increasing the possibility of marital rape and other forms of sexual violence. TARSHI (Talking about Reproductive and Sexual Health Issues), a non-governmental organization, running a helpline on sexual information, received over 59,000 calls from men seeking information on sexual anatomy and physiology. An analysis of this data showed that 70 per cent of the callers were Hindi-speaking and below 30 years of age, while 33 per cent were in the age group of 15 to 24 which indicates that young people do have the need, but no source to receive appropriate and correct information in a positive manner. The introduction on sex education in schools is opposed on the ground that it being anti-ethical to Indian culture, whereas, the World Health Organization (WHO) reports conversely show that promotion of sex education resulted in delayed age of entering into sexual relationship, reduced number of partners, increase use of safer sex and contraception, and other positive behaviour (Chauhan, 2007). A survey of 35 sex education projects conducted by WHO showed that sex education in schools did not encourage young people to have sex at earlier age; rather it delays the start of sexual activity and encourages young people to have safer sex (Dhiman, 2007).

India has become the second largest hub of HIV/AIDS pandemic in the world. The proponents of sex education stressed the need for providing knowledge about HIV/AIDS, teenage pregnancies and information about sexual health. Both the critiques and supporters of sex education shared same ideology of 'sexual restraint' (Anandhi, 2007). In a survey of college students conducted by the All India Educational and Vocational Guidance Association, it was reported that 54 per cent of males and 42 per cent of females did not have adequate knowledge regarding matters of sex (D'Souza, 1979). Another study (Jejeebhoy, 1998) found that about 30 per cent of males and upto 10 per cent of females are sexually active during adolescence before marriage, though social attitudes clearly favour cultural norms of premarital chastity.

We need to accept the fact that we are living in a complicated world leading complicated lives. Preventing access to pornographic movies or erratic television shows is not practical, but adding a single chapter to the school curriculum is simple and practical (Yashwantha, 2007). Mass media being highly influential has been part of both solution and of the problem in the area of sex and youth. It has been part of the solution because it has helped to bring sexual topics into discussion. Radio and television have been medium in opening doors to the discussions of some topics which were previously considered as taboo. A survey conducted in Mumbai found that among 695 college students, 88 per cent of the boys and 58 per cent of the girls had received no sex education from their parents and the source of information were books, magazines, and youth counsellors (D'Souza, 1979). Internet is the greatest culprit which makes pornography easily accessible in recent times. Research studies have shown that vast majority of parents do not accept the responsibility for providing sex education to their sons or daughters (Devi et al., 1988). Another study states that 68 per cent of the parents believe that they should be the primary sex educators of their children followed by schools (Alexander, 1984). The stigma attached to any discussion on sex in India is due to the fact that people tend to view sex education in a narrow sense, that is, the mere explanation of anatomical and biological differences. Ideally home is the best place for sex education and the attitudes of parents are of vital importance. It is also found that when a child feels the subject as forbidden he/she feels more curious to know about it which can lead to misleading information, if parents feel shameful and embarrassed in talking about sex with their children (D'Souza, 1979).

Review of Literature

A study conducted by Bhasin and Aggarwal (1999) reveals that majority of school teachers were in favour of imparting sex education to school children. Fourteen years of age was considered to be the most appropriate for imparting sex education by 28.6 per cent of school teachers. School teachers and doctors were considered to be the most appropriate persons for providing sex education. A study conducted in Surat city to assess the impact of sex education on the students depicted that doctors were the first choice to impart sex education followed by school teachers; the preferred mean age to start sex education was 15–16 years (Thakor and Kumar, 2000). A study was conducted in seven private co-educational schools in Cochin to understand adolescent attitudes towards sex and sexuality. The study showed a lacuna of knowledge among adolescents on sex and sexuality. More than half of adolescents received information on sex and sexuality from peers. Majority of adolescents were aware about AIDS but adequate knowledge about its spread and prevention was lacking (Unni, 2010).

Majority of mothers believed that discouraging premarital intercourse should be the most important objective of sex education, and those who felt that their own sex education was inadequate were in support of sex education for their children. Children who had sex education were less likely to engage in premarital intercourse than those who did not have (Marsman and Harold, 1986). Another study found that only 68 per cent of parents were the primary source in providing sex education to their children (Alexander, 1984). A study by Forbes (1963) concluded that the understanding of family life varies greatly by the type of residence. Parents should provide sex education to their children in a free and informal atmosphere so that children may get rid of the idea that sex is dirty and be aware of their responsibilities as well as prepare themselves for marriage (Israel, 1967).

A survey conducted in Hyderabad and Secunderabad cities (Moses and Praveena, 1983) found that the major sources of sex information for adolescents were books and films, followed by friends and parents. The study strongly indicates the need for introduction of sex education in the formal curriculum. An important observation emerging from this study is that in spite of exposure towards sex education, many adolescents did not have the correct knowledge regarding reproduction. This shows that sex education in the format being imparted in certain institutions does not have the desired impact on adolescents. Family life education for boys and girls at the adolescent stage should be constructive enough so as to contribute to healthier emotional growth and it must prepare them to enter into a responsible and healthier adulthood (Rao, 1988). Another study carried out in Andhra Pradesh (Devi et al., 1988) concluded that adolescent boys and girls need sound and correct knowledge about sex. The knowledge of boys regarding sex is more than that of girls. It may be so because boys try to satisfy their curiosity more readily than girls. Lack of proper sex education can result in emotional and social disturbances. It was also found that educated parents help their children to clarify their doubts and anxieties about sex in a more realistic way. The findings of National Family Health Survey (IIPS and Macro International, 2007) show that majority of men and women in India favour family life education. More than two-thirds of adults approve of teaching school children about physical changes in their bodies that come with puberty, although there is somewhat less approval of children learning about puberty in the opposite sex.

Need for the Study

Sex education has been one of the most controversial issues in Indian society. Though few micro-level studies have been conducted to examine the knowledge, attitude and perceptions of adolescents towards family life education, yet there exists huge gap in appropriate understanding regarding various issues of family life education and its effective implementation. Few schools and colleges are taking initiative in imparting sex education. Since there are many supporters and opponents in introducing sex education in Indian schools, it is most important to understand the perception and attitudes of youth on this controversial subject. This study is an attempt in that direction using two nationally representative surveys for the first time to analyse the perceptions and experiences of family life education among young women in India. These large-scale surveys conducted across India provide a unique opportunity to gauge the attitudes of younger generation. This may also help the government in formulating appropriate strategies. In this study, the terms sex education, family life education and adolescent life education were interchangeably used.

Objectives of the Study

The present study broadly attempts to gauge the views, perceptions and aspiration of adolescents and youth regarding the issues of family life education. The specific objectives are as follows:

- To study the perception regarding family life education among adolescents and youth, particularly women.
- To examine the awareness and experiences of youth who received family life education.

Data Sources and Methodology

The data for the present analysis come from two major surveys of India. The District Level Household and Facility Survey-3 (DLHS-3) conducted by the International Institute for Population Sciences (IIPS) in 2007–08 is the largest ever demographic and health survey carried out in India with a sample size of over six lakh households covering 601 districts of the country. The perception and knowledge about family life education, family planning, RTI/STI, HIV/AIDS and reproductive health issues were collected from unmarried women of 15–24 years. A total of 1,66,260 unmarried women were interviewed in DLHS-3 using a structured interview schedule (IIPS, 2010).

In this paper, an attempt has been made to analyse the attitudes and experiences regarding family life education among young unmarried women. The final analytical sample is comprised of 1,60,550 unmarried women (15 to 24 years) after excluding the missing cases (5,710) for various socio-economic and demographic characteristics from the analysis. Literature in demography and sociology suggests that the attitudes and behaviour of respondents are usually influenced by individual socio-economic, cultural and demographic characteristics. The pertinent socio-economic and demographic characteristics considered in this study include age groups (15–19 and 20–24), type of locality (rural and urban), religion (Hindu, Muslim, Christian and others), caste (SC, ST, OBC and others), education (non-literate, less than 5 years of schooling, 5–9 years and 10 years or above), economic status of the households as presented by wealth index (poor to rich) and employment status (employed and unemployed). Awareness about contraceptives has been computed based on modern methods (sterilization, pills, condom, IUD, etc.) and traditional methods (rhythm, withdrawal, abstinence, etc.).

The second survey is the 'Youth in India: Situation and Needs' conducted in 2006–07 in six states (IIPS and Population Council, 2010). The main objective of this survey is to gather evidence on key transitions experienced by youth as well as their awareness, attitudes and life choices. The study was conducted in Andhra Pradesh, Bihar, Jharkhand, Maharashtra, Rajasthan and

Tamil Nadu. In all, 50,848 married and unmarried young women and men were successfully interviewed from 174,037 sample households.

Findings

According to the Youth Study in India (2006–07), 83.7 per cent of young men and 81 per cent of young women aged 15–24 years felt the need to impart family life education. There is rural-urban differential in reporting of the need for family life/sex education. Majority of respondents received family life education from schools/colleges. The survey found that 24 per cent of the women had premarital sex for the first time before age 15. Those who received the family life education consisted of only 23 per cent unmarried women and 17 per cent unmarried men (Table 1).

Table 1

Perceptions Regarding Family Life Education among Unmarried Men and Women in India

Topics/Issues	*Unmarried Women*	*Unmarried Men*
Perceived family life/sex education to be important	81.0	83.7
Perceived the best person to provide family life/sex education		
Parent	30.4	5.7
Teacher	34.9	47.7
Family life/sex education	23.0	17.4
Source through which received family life/sex education		
School/College	91.8	81.6

Source: IIPS and Population Council, 2010.

Table 2 presents the composite picture concerning the perceived importance of family life education and proportion of unmarried women who in fact received family life education in India. Results suggest that, on an average, nearly four-fifth of unmarried women, 15–24 years of age perceived the family life education to be important, whereas, only half of them actually received family life education in their lifetime. However, there were substantial differentials in the perceived importance of family life education and receipt of family life education by selected socio-economic and demographic characteristics. For instance, the proportion of unmarried women of 15–24 years, who viewed family life education to be important, were relatively older (20–24 years of age), urban folks, highly educated (more than 10 years of schooling), engaged in non-manual jobs, and belonged to the wealthiest section of society. We found quite similar socio-economic and demographic pattern among unmarried women who actually received family life education in India.

Importantly, the DLHS-3 asked women about their opinion regarding at what age and at what level in school does the family life education should be introduced? Table 3 reveals that majority of women approve that family life education should be provided in the age group 15–17 years (38%) and in the 8th to 10th standards (55%). Nearly 40 per cent of women who had schooling

Table 2

Awareness and Perception regarding Family Life/Sex Education among Unmarried Women (percentages)

Background characteristics	*Perceived family life education is important*	*Received family life education*
Age Group		
15–19	78.7	45.9
20–24	86.8	55.7
Residence		
Rural	77.4	43.4
Urban	85.1	54.8
Education of Women		
Non-literate	50.8	16.2
Less than 5 years	57.9	18.7
5–9 years	77.6	40.2
10 years or above	92.0	65.5
Employment Status		
Not working	81.4	49.5
Agriculture	70.9	34.0
Manual	74.1	36.8
Non-manual	87.6	59.0
Religion		
Hindu	81.2	48.5
Muslim	78.6	43.3
Christian	81.2	57.4
Others	82.7	51.7
Caste/Tribe		
Scheduled Caste	79.3	44.9
Scheduled Tribe	73.9	44.8
Other Backward Classes	79.7	46.7
Others	86.9	54.6
Wealth Index		
Lowest	61.2	25.1
Second	70.2	32.8
Middle	75.9	40.6
Fourth	82.6	50.2
Highest	90.1	61.9
India	80.9	48.5

Source: DLHS-3 (IIPS, 2010).

for more than 10 years and belonged to the wealthiest households were of the opinion that family life education should be provided in standard 10 and above respectively. However, around 37 per cent unmarried women among Christians responded that the sex education should be provided between 12–14 years of age.

Table 3

*Introducing Family Life/Sex Education: Opinion of Unmarried Women**

Background characteristics	*At what age*				*From which standard*		
	Below 12	*12–14*	*15–17*	*18 or above*	*Below 8*	*8–10*	*Above 10*
Age Group							
15–19	7.4	33.7	37.7	16.1	22.9	55.0	13.8
20–24	7.3	31.7	36.3	21.7	22.0	54.7	17.8
Residence							
Rural	7.8	33.1	36.1	17.2	24.7	52.9	12.9
Urban	7.0	33.3	38.7	18.2	20.4	57.2	17.2
Education of Women							
Non-literate	7.5	28.0	31.3	12.6	21.6	21.5	16.0
Less than 5 years	8.0	30.7	32.1	13.9	31.6	24.6	18.0
5–9 years	8.5	33.8	35.5	17.0	28.7	35.4	28.0
10 years or above	6.5	33.4	39.7	19.0	17.5	34.2	45.9
Employment Status							
Not Working	7.8	35.5	39.2	17.6	24.9	59.5	15.6
Agriculture	8.4	33.7	39.2	18.8	27.4	59.1	13.6
Manual	8.0	31.2	38.4	22.4	26.5	58.4	15.1
Non-manual	7.7	34.7	36.5	21.1	25.9	55.4	18.8
Religion							
Hindu	6.7	32.9	38.2	18.2	19.8	57.2	16.2
Muslim	8.8	32.8	35.3	17.0	23.1	51.5	13.6
Christian	12.8	36.9	31.2	14.5	44.6	39.9	8.3
Others	6.0	32.8	40.2	17.7	25.8	56.1	12.8
Caste/Tribe							
Scheduled Caste	6.6	31.8	38.2	18.7	21.1	55.7	15.1
Scheduled Tribe	10.5	35.6	32.4	14.8	37.0	44.1	8.5
Other Backward Classes	6.7	32.0	38.2	18.4	19.4	55.8	16.8
Others	7.0	33.2	37.3	17.7	20.1	58.6	16.0
Wealth Index							
Lowest	8.0	32.1	32.8	15.1	28.4	43.8	7.9
Second	7.5	33.0	34.9	15.5	26.5	49.2	9.7
Middle	8.0	32.2	36.2	17.5	25.5	51.5	12.9
Fourth	8.0	32.8	37.3	18.3	23.4	55.0	15.1
Highest	6.7	34.0	39.2	18.3	19.1	59.4	18.2
India	7.4	33.2	37.3	17.7	22.7	54.9	15.0

*Among women who perceived family life education to be important.

Source: DLHS-3 (IIPS, 2010).

Table 4 presents the information regarding major sources of family life education among unmarried women of 15–24 years in India who perceived family life education to be important. Majority of the respondents felt that the main

Table 4

Sources of Family Life/Sex Education among Unmarried Women who Perceived Family Life/Sex Education important

Background characteristics	*Parents*	*Brother/ sister/ sister-in-law*	*Husband /partner*	*Friends/ peer*	*Health care provider/ sex education expert*	*Youth club/ mandal/ NGO worker*	*Teacher/ school/ college*	*Others*
Age Group								
15–19	81.1	50.0	3.6	29.1	8.5	2.9	54.0	3.1
20–24	81.7	49.7	4.7	4.7	12.1	4.8	57.6	2.5
Residence								
Rural	79.9	50.9	4.2	28.0	8.9	3.2	50.9	2.9
Urban	82.8	48.9	3.7	31.2	10.3	3.8	59.6	3.1
Education of Women								
Non-literate	79.1	54.3	3.4	25.0	2.2	1.7	11.7	4.4
Less than 5 years	80.5	52.3	3.0	25.0	3.7	1.4	22.3	3.4
5–9 years	81.7	50.6	3.6	27.6	6.8	2.6	48.9	3.2
10 years or above	81.2	48.8	4.3	31.7	12.8	4.5	66.4	2.6
Employment Status								
Not Working	81.7	50.3	4.2	28.6	9.7	3.5	56.7	2.68
Agriculture	79.7	54.1	3.7	27.8	7.7	3.0	43.2	3.49
Manual	81.6	51.6	3.1	30.3	7.0	2.8	41.2	3.96
Non-manual	82.2	48.2	4.2	32.4	14.0	4.9	59.8	2.98
Religion								
Hindu	80.6	51.4	4.2	31.2	10.0	3.4	56.7	3.2
Muslim	81.1	51.7	3.2	27.0	5.8	2.3	47.5	3.5
Christian	86.3	30.5	3.3	18.6	13.9	7.0	48.5	1.2
Others	82.9	51.6	4.2	30.0	9.2	3.7	62.1	1.6
Caste/Tribe								
Scheduled Caste	80.0	51.5	3.8	30.2	8.1	2.8	53.5	3.3
Scheduled Tribe	84.2	41.3	4.4	23.8	11.4	5.4	48.3	1.7
Other Backward Classes	79.9	50.2	3.5	30.7	8.9	2.9	55.7	3.5
Others	82.2	53.3	4.3	30.5	10.0	3.6	59.1	2.8
Wealth Index								
Lowest	79.1	51.7	4.0	27.5	5.7	2.2	32.9	2.8
Second	78.7	50.3	3.7	27.9	7.3	2.3	41.2	3.3
Middle	79.5	48.8	3.8	28.4	8.2	2.9	50.2	3.4
Fourth	81.1	50.1	4.0	28.8	9.6	3.5	55.2	3.1
Highest	83.1	49.9	4.0	31.1	11.2	4.2	63.9	2.6
India	81.3	49.9	3.9	29.5	9.6	3.5	55.1	3.0

Note: Among women who perceived family life education to be important.

Source: DLHS-3 (IIPS, 2010).

source for providing sex education should be parents (81%), followed by teacher/school/college (55%), brother/sister/sister-in-law (50%), and friends/peers (30%) respectively. On the other hand, health care provider/sex education experts (10%), husband/partner (4%), youth club/NGO worker (3%) respectively perceivably constituted as other important sources of information on family life education among unmarried women in India.

Figure 1 indicates that among unmarried women who received family life education, an overwhelming majority received either from school or college. The other sources are NGO programmes, youth clubs, government programmes, etc. Furthermore, Figure 2 depicts the experiences of young women who underwent family life education. Majority are of the opinion that family life education answered/clarified many of their questions and the teacher/trainee explained it in a way that can be understood. Forty-two per cent of women aged 15–19 years reported that they felt embarrassed while attending family life education.

Figure 1

Source of Family Life Education Received

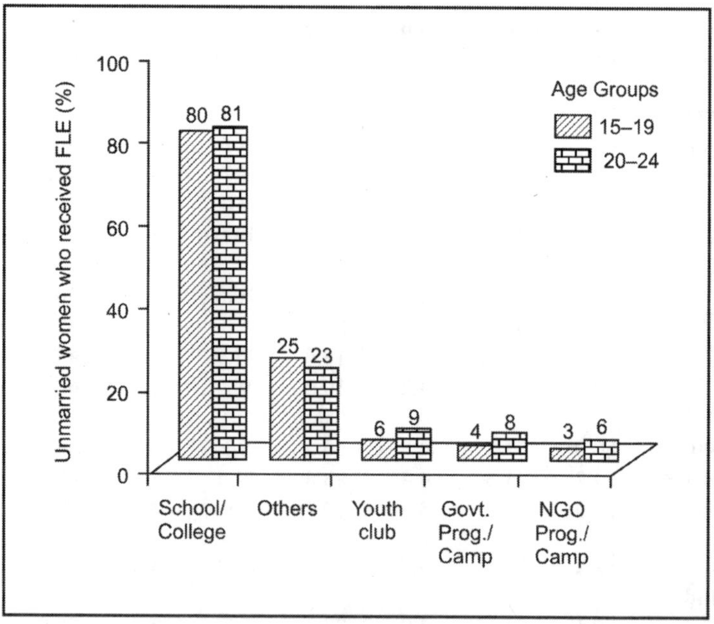

The data on knowledge and awareness on reproductive health issues among unmarried women in age group 15–24 years in the DLHS-3 also indicate substantial differentials in reproductive health issues among women who received family life education and those who did not receive the same according to their selected socio-economic and demographic characteristics. On an average, the women who received family life education had much better awareness on various reproductive health issues like awareness about RTI/STI, possibility of finding out the sex of a baby before birth, and knowledge about reducing HIV, compared to women who did not receive any family life

Figure 2

Experiences of Family Life Education

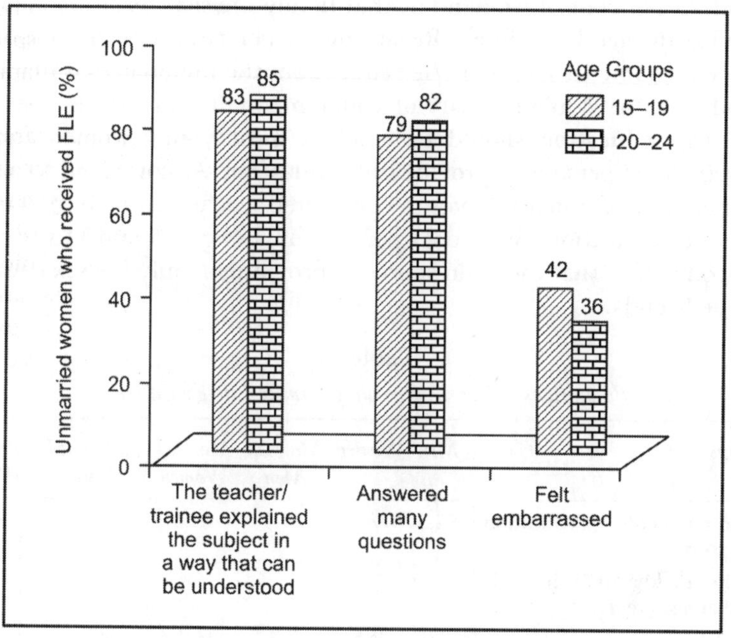

education. Urban women belonging to the households of highest wealth category and those having education of ten years and more have more awareness than their rural counterparts. With the increasing age, education and wealth index, the awareness regarding contraception among women also increases. The awareness level is much higher among those women who have undergone some family life education.

In general, women who received the family life education were relatively more aware about methods of contraception as compared to their counterparts. For instance, among women who received family life education, nearly 98 per cent and 27 per cent women were aware about any modern and traditional method of contraception, respectively. On the other hand, this figure reduces to 89 per cent and 12 per cent respectively among women who did not pursue family life education. Interestingly, with the increasing age, years of schooling and wealth status, the awareness regarding contraception among women also increases. Majority of young men and women who received family life education have better awareness regarding contraceptives, comprehensive knowledge of HIV/AIDS and were aware of reproductive health issues as compared to youth who did not receive such education.

Table 5 illustrates the young people's perceptions on family life/sex education, according to youth study. Around 83 per cent of young men and 78 per cent of young women felt that it is important to impart family life/sex education to youth. A slightly large proportion of unmarried youth (84% of men and 81% of women) as compared to married youth (79% of men and 75% of women) perceived family life/sex education to be important. Majority of young men and women approve that family life/sex education should be provided to adolescents in the age group 15–17 years. Thirty-five per cent of men and 25 per cent of women felt that family life/sex education should be provided at the age 18 or above. Regarding the perception of youth about the best person to impart family life/sex education, the preferences differ among men and women. While majority of young men felt that the best person to provide this education should be teacher, most young women felt that parents are ideal persons to provide such education. As compared to married youth, majority of unmarried youth considered teacher as the best person to provide such education. Around 21 per cent of young men and 11 per cent of young women felt that the main source of providing family life/sex education should be friends.

Table 5

Perceptions of Youths regarding Family Life Education

Perceptions	*Men*	*Women*	*Married Men*	*Married Women*	*Unmarried Men*	*Unmarried Women*
Perceived family life/sex education to be important	82.5	78.1	79.5	75.5	83.7	81.0
Family life/sex education should be provided at age (years)						
Below 12	2.8	2.6	3.3	3.2	2.7	2.1
12–14	12.1	23.6	10.7	22.6	12.6	24.7
15–17	47.5	42.6	41.7	41.5	48.7	43.7
18 or above	35.4	25.5	41.4	25.6	34.3	25.2
The best person to provide family life/sex education is						
Parent	5.9	33.8	7.4	36.7	5.7	30.4
Sibling/sister-in-law	0.4	5.6	0.4	6.5	0.4	4.8
Spouse/partner	0.2	2.4	0.3	4.2	0.2	0.3
Teacher	44.8	27.3	36.7	20.2	47.7	34.9
Friend	21.2	11.4	23.7	11.6	20.2	11.3
Healthcare provider/expert	23.2	14.5	27.1	14.7	21.9	14.2
Youth club/NGO worker	0.9	0.4	0.9	0.3	1.0	0.4

Source: IIPS and Population Council, 2010.

Table 6 indicates that nearly 15 per cent of young men and 14 per cent of young women received family life/sex education (IIPS and Population Council, 2010). Majority received family life education through schools/colleges. Among those who received formal family life/sex education, majority felt that it answered many of their queries and the teacher/trainee explained the subject well. Twenty-one per cent of men and 37 per cent of women also reported that they felt embarrassed while attending classes for family life/sex education. This, in a way, it suggests that we need to modify the curriculum and the method of teaching.

Table 6

Experiences of Youth Who Received Family Life Education

Experiences	*Men*	*Women*	*Married Men*	*Married Women*	*Unmarried Men*	*Unmarried Women*
Source of family life/sex education received						
School/College	80.0	87.9	64.5	77.1	81.6	91.8
Government programme/camp	16.3	11.8	26.2	21.2	15.3	8.3
NGO programme/camp	6.4	5.1	13.6	8.9	6.1	3.7
Opinion about family life/sex education received						
It answered many queries	87.4	90.0	89.7	91.7	87.1	89.3
Teacher/trainer explained well	89.8	91.2	84.8	91.0	89.6	91.3
Respondent felt embarrassed	21.3	36.6	19.3	36.7	21.1	36.6

Source: IIPS and Population Council, 2010.

Discussion and Conclusion

The present paper makes an attempt by using nationally representative sample surveys for the first time to unravel the divergent views, perceptions and aspirations of adolescents and youth regarding the issues of family life education, its perceived importance, and the potential effects of family life education on array of reproductive health issues. By virtue of using unique datasets, this study seeks to address the contemporary boisterous debate on introducing family life education in school curriculum in Indian context.

Young people (aged 10–24 years) constitute about 315 million and represented about 31 per cent of India's population. They not only represent India's future in the socio-economic and political realms, but also largely determine India's achievement of population stabilization and our ability to harness the demographic dividend. In the course of transition to adulthood, young people face significant risks related to sexual and reproductive health and lack adequate knowledge to make informed sexual and reproductive choices. Adolescent life education programme has been started in order to ensure the rights of the large section of population, adolescents/youth, and to develop them as healthy and responsible members of the family and society. Adolescents in all societies learn their responsibilities towards their family by observing and following the behaviour of others. Due to rapid social change occurring all over the world, the young generation is presently facing an enormous challenge in coping with the erosion of traditional family, social life, and values. Under this environment, the family life education can help the adolescents in their transition from childhood to adulthood.

One of the most significant findings of the study indicates that majority of unmarried women (15–24 years) perceived family life education to be important. This highlights that Indian adolescents realize the range of potential health risks and challenges lurking before them and demands the appropriate knowledge, skills and training to lead a responsible and healthy lifestyle. However, the study points out that only half of the unmarried women actually received any form of family life education. This critical mismatch between the potential demand for family life education and apparent lack of facility might lead to a brigade of untrained, ill-equipped and unmanageable group of risky young population who might indulge into array of unhealthy lifestyle practices. Another finding that needs special attention relates to the appropriate age and standard at which this education should be initiated. Our findings based on the opinions of unmarried women between 15–24 years suggest that this education should be started at the age of 15 to 17 years and during 8th to 10th standard in schools. This is a significant finding and helpful from policy perspective to implement the family life education in Indian schools.

One of the crucial findings that deem attention relates to the major sources of this education. The study indicates that majority of unmarried women, who perceived this education to be important, reported parents to be the harbinger, followed by teacher/school/college, brother/sister/sister-in-law and friends/peer respectively. Therefore, it becomes apparent that family life education need not be only part of formal school curriculum; it should also be equally augmented in the first place by parents at home to remove all the misconceptions, inhibitions and doubts of adolescents on various issues of family/sex life. The study also indicates that relatives and friends/peers could also be important avenues that need to be appropriately tapped to help the adolescents learn about the basic issues/rules of family/sex life skills safely and comfortably either at home, school or neighbourhood.

Addressing the debate on the implementation of family life education in school curriculum in India, several scholars, administrators and politicians have mooted the adverse impact of introducing the education and how it is going to denigrate the rich Indian cultural values and ethos. However, our findings effectively nullify all these apprehensions and convincingly illustrate that, among unmarried women who received this education, the awareness about various reproductive health issues and knowledge of contraceptive methods was far better and comprehensive compared to their counterparts who had no such knowledge. This further goes on to show that provision of family life education will benefit not only the adolescents, but many more generations to come by avoiding the menace of RTI/STI, unwanted pregnancies and HIV/AIDS, etc.

The present study further provides evidence to support the argument that even in this era of globalization and modernization, there still persists steep socio-economic divide in the knowledge, attitudes and perception of individuals in Indian society. The same holds true with regard to benefits of family life education. Whether it relates to the perceived importance of family life education, or its actual acceptance among unmarried women in India, we found substantial differentials across socio-economic groups. This indicates that even after more than six decades of planned development efforts in India, large proportion of population living in rural areas, illiterate, marginalized social groups, continue to lag behind when it comes to the adoption of modern attitudes and innovative behaviour. Hence, it is crucial for policy makers and programme managers to remain mindful of these socio-economic hierarchies in Indian society, while implementing any model of family life education.

Finally, we summarize the key issues that emerge from this study. There is no unanimity in India regarding the introduction of family life education in schools. There exists a wide gap between the proportion of women who perceive it important and those who actually received any sex education. It was also true that women who received family life education had better knowledge and awareness on reproductive health issues than others. The study strongly argues the need to formulate a proper policy regarding family life education so as to address the problems faced by the youth. The present study also found that the level of awareness and knowledge regarding family life education is more among the educated, better off sections and those living in urban areas. The growing population and increasing incidences of HIV/AIDS is a great challenge. Youth also get wrong information/messages from media and other sources. In order to prepare the youth to face these challenges, introducing sex education is an important step. The nation-wide surveys clearly illustrate that an overwhelming majority of young women and men are in favour of family life education. The government should initiate a national debate to reach a consensus on this issue among various sections of the society. Imparting sex education in an appropriate manner at school level should be a national priority. We need to realize the fact that family life education makes an important contribution towards strengthening families to fulfil their significant role as the basic unit of society. What is emerging from the analysis presented in this paper is the existing confusion of a society caught in a dilemma of 'tradition' on one hand and 'modernity' on the other.

References

Alexander, S.J. (1984). 'Improving Sex Education Programs for Young Adolescents: Parents' View', *Family Relations*, 33: 251–57.

Anandhi, S. (2007). 'Sex Education Conundrum', *Economic and Political Weekly*, 42(33): 3367–69.

Bhasin, S.K. and O.P. Aggarwal (1999). 'Perceptions of Teachers Regarding Sex Education in National Capital Territory of Delhi', *Indian J Pediatrics*, 66: 527–31.

Chauhan, C. (2007). 'Keep Off Sex Education, Teachers Told', *Hindustan Times*, 17 July, http://www.hindustantimes.com/News-Feed/india/Keep-off-sex-education-teachers-told/Article1–237205.aspx (accessed on 8 June 2010).

D'Souza, A.A. (1979). *Sex Education and Personality Development*. New Delhi: Usha Publications.

Devi, G., N.V. Reddy and M. Laxmanna (1988). 'Knowledge of Sex Education among Adolescents', *Journal of Family Welfare*, 35(2): 55–60.

Dhiman, A. (2007). *Sex Education in India*. Book Summary, www.shvoong.com (accessed on 24 April 2010).

Forbes, G.S. (1963). 'Some Observations on Family Life Education in India', *Marriage and Family Living*, 25(4): 466–68.

Government of India (2000). *National Population Policy 2000.* New Delhi: Ministry of Health and Family Welfare.

Government of India (2007). *Study on Child Abuse: India 2007*. New Delhi: Ministry of Women and Child Development.

International Institute for Population Sciences (IIPS) (2010). *District Level Household and Facility Survey (DLHS-3), 2007–08: India*. Mumbai: IIPS.

International Institute for Population Sciences (IIPS) and Macro International (2007). *National Family Health Survey* (NFHS-3), *2005–06: India*. Mumbai: IIPS.

International Institute for Population Sciences (IIPS) and Population Council (2010). *Youth in India: Situation and Needs 2006–07*. Mumbai: IIPS.

Israel, S. (1967). 'The Purpose, Scope and Method of Sex Education', *Journal of Family Welfare*, 13(4): 6–11.

Jeeson, C.U. (2010). 'Adolescent Attitudes and Relevance to Family Life Education Programs', *Indian Pediatrics*, 47: 176–79.

Jejeebhoy, S.J. (1998). 'Adolescent Sexual and Reproductive Behavior: A Review of the Evidence from India', *Social Science and Medicine*, 46(10): 1275–90.

Marsman, J.C. and E.S. Harold (1986). 'Attitude towards Sex Education and Values in Sex Education', *Family Relations*, 35: 357–61.

Moses, S. and C. Praveena (1983). 'Sex Education: Its Need and Attitude of Adolescents', *Journal of Family Welfare*, 30(2): 34–39.

Motihar, R. (2007). *Between Tradition and Modernity: Controversy in India about the Sex Education Programme in State Run Schools*, http://www.kit.nl/net/KIT-Publicaties-output/ShowFile2.aspx?e=1421 (accessed on 2 June 2010).

Nolte, J. (1984). 'Sex Education in Canadian Classrooms', *Tellus*, 5(3): 13–16.

Rao, M.P. (1988). 'Adolescence: A Perspective and a Need for Family Life Education', *Journal of Family Welfare*, 35(2): 42–47.

Thakor, H.G. and P. Kumar (2000). 'Impact Assessment of School-based Sex Education Program amongst Adolescents', *Indian J Pediatrics*, 67: 551–58.

Unni, J.C. (2010). 'Adolescent Attitudes and Relevance to Family Life Education Programs', *Indian Pediatrics*, 47: 176–79.

World Health Organization (WHO) (2003). 'Family Life, Reproductive Health and Population Education: Key Elements of a Health Promoting School', *Information Series on School Health, Document 8*, Geneva, Switzerland, http://www.who. int/school-youth-health (accessed on 13 May 2011).

Yashwantha, C.P. (2007). 'Need to Move with the Times', *The Hindu*, 13 May, http://www.hindu.com/op/2007/05/13/stories/200705/303521400.htm (accessed on 11 June 2010).

7

Globalization and Civil-Military Relations

A Culture of Peace Process in Kashmir (Case Study of a School Near LOC)

Leena Parmar

The conventional notion of security, in safeguarding territorial integrity from external aggression for the honourable existence of any nation-state, has been and remains state-centric with military as its major instrument. However, there are equally, if not more vital, concerns and facets of security that are often ignored in the specialized security discourse of military strategists, where the concerned area is ravaged by militancy, hatred and innocent killings. Military security through modern arms and ammunitions generally neglects the social structures, people's movements and non-state actors, thus making the entire process elitist, parochial and often insensitive.

This current research on the civil-military relations aims to bring peace to the people of the Kashmir valley.

In any discussion on national security, it would be useful to keep in mind the physical parameters of our concerns. Here, in this context, it would be worthwhile to recount a few facts which though, otherwise, well known, are not adequately kept in view. India, being the seventh largest country in the world, has an area of about 3.3 million sq kms, with land boundaries of 15,200 kms, over 600 island territories, a coastline of 7,517 kms and an Exclusive Economic Zone (EEZ) of 2.5 million sq kms. India has land frontiers with six countries and maritime borders with five countries. Its island territories in the east, 1,300 kms away from the mainland, are far closer to the countries of Association for South East Asian Nations (ASEAN) members. Except Haryana and Madhya Pradesh, all other states and some of the union territories have one or more land or maritime borders which require to be safeguarded. Our borders with Pakistan and China are militarized and those with Pakistan generate a variety of threats to our country. While speaking about India's security concerns, it is also necessary to remember that India represents an immense cultural and geographical diversity and socio-religious traditions, which date back to 5,000 years of recorded history. Every major religion in the world is practised in India. Its Muslim population, being the second largest in the world, is significantly larger than that of Pakistan. The roots of India's secular and pluralistic traditions are embedded deep in our ancient history (Bohra, 2004).

Military professionalism is an influential but controversial concept in the study of civil-military relations. The Indian military has been unique among the armies in the developing world in several ways since the historical background and political context are different in each country. Yet, the framework enables us to study some of the trends of institutional development in Indian military organization. Moreover, no country is immune from the transnational influences that shape civil-military relations. Since the relationship between the military and society in each social system also reflects national and cultural considerations, the need of the hour is to understand developmental trends over time through empirical research findings.

India is the world's largest and most populous developing country with a democratic system. Surrounded by military-dominated and non-democratic states, it represents one of the most interesting cases of firm, stable and authoritative civilian control of the military. It is remarkable that the appalling problems of low economic development, sharp differences in income, mass poverty, overpopulation, illiteracy, ethnic antagonism, absence of linguistic unity, cultural fragmentation, social diversities, and a complex class system do not seem to hinder civilian control of the Indian military. The two neighbours of India – Pakistan and Bangladesh – closely matched to it in a number of ways yet display divergent patterns of civil-military relations (Cohen, 1976: 43–64).

Methodology

Students of civil-military relations, particularly those in the developing countries, admit that they have to work on meagre data. One of the reasons could be the relative newness of this area of study. The study of civil-military relations, in the narrow sense, confined mainly to military coups and interventions, attained importance only after the Second World War (see Perlmutter, 1970; Zimmermann, 1979; Bienen, 1981; Janowitz, 1981 and Martin, 1984).

Broad reviews of the social science literature on civil-military relations suggest that scholarly work in this field has essentially been of two types. First, there are theoretical studies in the form of comprehensive theories and hypotheses and, second, there are empirical studies. The main weakness of the theoretical writings is that they either concentrate on the characteristics of civilian politics and their influence on military intervention while generally ignoring the organizational and professional qualities of the military itself, or give emphasis to the latter to the exclusion or inadequate treatment of the social and political environment (Luckham, 1971: 8–9). The empirically-oriented statistical studies have been criticized for not paying sufficient attention to the quality of data and to the theoretical basis for imputing causality and interpreting the results (Janowitz, 1964: 11).

Assessing the theoretical and empirical validity of Lasswell's influential but utopian construct of possible or probable developments, one finds it refuted, at first glance at least, by the course of events. The Garrison-soldier model has been followed by the liberal and civilian oriented professional soldier model advanced by Samuel P. Huntington. Huntington attempted to explain the nature of the modern military profession in terms of its loyalty to its master – the civilian dominated democratic state. The major contribution of Huntington's general theory of civil-military relations lies in his argument that the rise of military professionalism is inversely related to military intervention. The modern professional sense of mission, military-mindedness and corporate autonomy incline the military against political intervention.

However, Huntington's controversial argument that professionalism inclines the military towards a low political posture has been challenged by several scholars. Nonetheless, Huntington's *The Soldier and the State* is one of the earliest sophisticated attempts to set up a general theoretical framework of civil-military relations. Civil-military relations can best be understood as a process in which there is a great deal of fluidity and informality. The relationship cannot be completely captured by using interest group models alone or by setting large institutional networks contending or co-operating with each other (Kulrija, 1991).

Civil-military relations can range across a broad spectrum and precisely where they fall on that spectrum at any given point of time depends on a multiplicity of variables. Focusing only on a few of them can produce a seriously distorted picture. Moreover, the dynamics of a country's civil-military relations over time can be highly complex, for many factors can spark changes in these relations.

The changing nature of civil-military relations in Asia has been a focus for any serious scholar of peace and security. In recent years, 75 per cent of all terrorism-related casualities in the world occurred in Asia. South Asia and contiguous regions have been the major target areas of terrorism, insurgencies and separatist movements in comparison with other parts of Asia. In South Asia, the number of fatal casualties in terrorist attacks is the highest in the world; internecine ethnic, communal and separatist conflicts pose a serious threat to stability and inter-state relations in this region. Afghanistan, Pakistan, Central Asia, Xinjiang, India, Sri Lanka and Nepal are facing serious problems with terrorist threats. India, Pakistan, Sri Lanka and Nepal are witnessing multiple conflicts in which ideological, ethnic, communal and political issues are intertwined. There are many reasons for these countries to be vulnerable to various forms of violence. But, the main reason is the failure of political management to meet the aspirations of the people that has given rise to dissatisfaction, terrorism and insurgencies, in most countries of the region.

Most terrorist groups, operating in South Asia, are based in Pakistan, Afghanistan and Sri Lanka. The Liberation Tigers of Tamil Elam (LTTE), for example, has generally confined its activities to Sri Lanka but terrorist groups in Pakistan and Afghanistan operate across international borders as a part of the global 'jihad' movement. The Sri Lankan conflict remains as a no-war no-peace situation; Bangladesh is witnessing a collapse of governance and this has given a fillip to Islamic fundamentalism (Karim, 2004).

India–Pakistan Relationship

Terrorist organizations located in Afghanistan–Pakistan belt are supported by Pakistan's Inter-Services Intelligence (ISI) and religious parties. While this situation has remained unchanged for the last few decades, ongoing conflicts between India and Pakistan and cross-border tensions between the two countries largely contribute to the insecurity in the region.

At a time when relations between India and Pakistan are upbeat as never before, it may appear inappropriate to recall the past which has been a long history of enmity between the two countries. But, knowledge of the past helps in understanding the present.

The birth of India and Pakistan as independent nations in 1947 was accompanied by a holocaust, the like of which had never occurred in human history. Millions got killed and uprooted in an orgy of unprecedented communal violence. The partition of India was a pyretic victory of communalism over secularism. Muhammed Ali Jinnah's vision of a nation-state on the basis of religion was achieved in the form of Pakistan. Despite the setback to secularism in 1947, India stuck to its secular ideals, in keeping with its tradition of thousands of years (Sinha, 2005: 183).

There are two constraints at the heart of the Indo-Pakistan conflict. The first constraint is the political utility of the war-like tensions between the two countries, and the second is the mutually sustaining mindsets, which recognize war as the only real solution. Both India and Pakistan are constantly vulnerable to the urge to fight. Millions of people in both countries are beset by the drudgery of peace. Military preparedness and the news of impending war have the unfortunate capacity to give both the young nation-states an instant sense of purpose. One cannot help recalling a time in the 1970s when India derived a similar sense of purpose by acting as a force for world peace. But it began to lose that sense of identity, even as the failure of the economic development projects of the 1960s became all too apparent. A new national identity began to take shape alongside Cold War models. Hunger, poverty and illiteracy gradually ceased to inspire the state planning apparatus. The self-image of military power began to serve a cohesive political role (Stobdan, 1996).

Both India and Pakistan have used education and the media to reinforce hostile attitudes. In Pakistan, school textbooks openly teach prejudice towards Hinduism and equate India with Hindus, forgetting India's struggle for secularism. Elite public schools have a better record, but their products either migrate or learn to live on the margins of a fluid, routinely manipulated public space. That journey to the margin of a rapidly shrinking political space is just beginning for the Indian elite whose children have been raised on the staple scientific diet in a corrupt and chaotic political milieu (Kumar, 2002: 190).

Since 1947, India and Pakistan have fought four wars over Kashmir (1965, 1971, 1999) and Bangladesh (1971). Pakistan openly abets cross-border terrorism and mutual suspicion rules bilateral relations. The rest of the world considers the region a potential nuclear flash-point.

Figure 1

Jammu & Kashmir: Proportional Division of Area

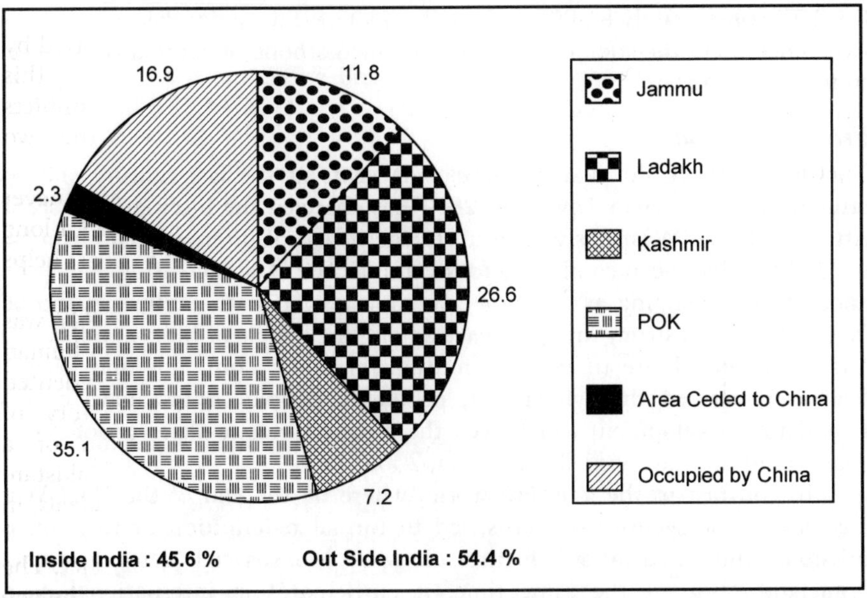

The above diagram shows the actual area of Jammu and Kashmir (J&K). Pakistan-occupied Kashmir (POK) occupies 35 per cent of the area; 26 per cent is Ladakh; 16 per cent area is occupied by China; 11 per cent area is Jammu; 7 per cent is Kashmir valley; 2 per cent area is ceded to China. So, total area within India is 46 per cent and outside India is 54 per cent.

The Historical Perspective

J&K was one of the 565 princely states of India on which the British paramountcy lapsed at the stroke of midnight on 15 August 1947. The rulers of these princely states were given the option to join either of the dominions – India or Pakistan. The ruler of J&K, Maharaja Hari Singh, however, did not exercise the option to join either of the two dominions, and instead, wanted a Standstill Agreement pending final decision on his state's accession. With Muslims comprising a majority of the population in Kashmir Valley, one could easily have expected communal politics to develop but the people of this valley, through centuries of their history had developed tolerance and peaceful co-existence, irrespective of different religious beliefs. The National Conference led by Sheikh Abdullah, a popular Kashmiri leader, believed in nationalism based on community interests and not on religion. Jinnah tried but failed to win the sympathies of the Muslims of Kashmir for his two-nation theory. Perhaps a plebiscite, soon after the partition of India and Pakistan, would have been overwhelmingly favourable to India.

Frustrated by this and with the aim of intimidating the population, Pakistan tribesmen entered Kashmir on 22 October 1947, and indulged in large-scale bloodshed. On 26 October 1947, however, Maharaja Hari Singh signed the Instrument of Accession in favour of India. This instrument was accepted by the Governor General of India, Lord Mountbatten, thereby making J&K a legal and constitutional part of the Union of India.

India took up the issue of Pakistan aggression in J&K with the United Nations, but it was only in 1949 that a ceasefire actually came into operation, leaving approximately 84,000 sq kms (54.4%) of J&K under Pakistan control. Ever since then, the state of J&K has remained a bone of contention between India and Pakistan.

Present Scenario

The end of the Cold War in the closing years of the last century and the crumbling of the Twin Towers in 2001 has changed the international scene. After 2001, the West has woken up to the threat of international terrorism, which India had been combating for over a decade. The increasing perception about India emerging as a major economic power of the future is another factor. There is a strong urge for peace among the people of India and Pakistan and a growing desire to improve mutual relations. Bonhomie and friendly feelings generated through cricket, people to people contact have been a remarkable development which even the most optimistic observers of yester-years could not have visualized (Sinha, 2005: 183).

In contrast to the Western world, where by the end of the Cold War, changes in the security concerns, led to formal redefinition of their major missions, Indian Army still focuses on what Moskos call 'defense of their homeland'. But, at the same time, it participates in international peace keeping operations, and other humanitarian operations. A look into the military functions today, definitely show some minor shift from primarily war fighting or war deterrence to military deployments for peace and humanitarian purposes. This may be due to the change in the threat perception from Pakistan and China.

The shift is towards peace missions, humanitarian activities of the armed forces. This has also led to some changes in public attitude and opinion. Thus, this paper focuses on the school at the India–Pakistan border, as a comparative case study method, choosing the richness of detail provided by the framework of Charles Moscos (2000: 27), to understand military as a developmental construct. Out of the two major projects 'Operation Sadbhavana' and 'Operation Ujala', which are being taken up by the army in Kashmir, this school comes under 'Operation Ujala'.

'Operation Ujala': The Peace Process

'Operation Ujala' is a modest, but extremely purposeful effort to contribute to bringing about normalcy in the Kashmir valley. The central objective of 'Operation Ujala' is also to change the existing largely neutral and sometime hostile perception of a large section of the population by making a meaningful contribution by addressing some of their concerns.

Army has started in a very productive way the process of development in J&K which covers Education, Information Technology, Women Empowerment, Medicare and Community Development. Indian Army is providing basic gender needs to the women to improve their status within the family and community. 'Operation Ujala' has brought self-awareness among the women through social awareness and literacy campaign. 'Operation Ujala' with its philosophy of human development, has done and is doing a great service for the people of Kashmir.

The aim is to act as a catalyst and a facilitator, and provide the initial impetus to the endeavours of the population, in selected ventures. Four areas have been chosen for attention – Education, Self-help, Cooperative ventures, and Healthcare. In each of these areas, selected ventures have been started. For example, in educational projects, schools and hostels for children of victims of terrorism have been given the highest priorities.

All ventures are meant to be collaborative and participative, entirely a partnership between the corporate houses, the people managing the venture and, for the purpose of ensuring smooth functioning and continuity, the Army unit in location. The major portion of the funding is expected from philanthropic corporate houses inclined to be participants in this truly nationalist cause. The basic idea is to create a corpus and provide initial start-up outlay, so that the projects become self-sustaining gradually. In some cases, the start-up capital comes from the Army funds. The funds collected are generally handled entirely by the locals nominated by the corporate houses (the Army provides assistance in identification of trustworthy and efficient persons) to manage the venture. The Army neither receives nor handles any kind of funds directly, however, assists in monitoring their proper utilization. The Army facilitates by providing safety and security of personnel associated with the supervision of the projects to ensure optimum utilization of funds. Army also provides initial accommodation and facilities to the personnel engaged in these ventures in border areas where such infrastructure may not be readily available. Army also provides sanitation and healthcare needs. The Army obtains regular feedback on the progress of the ventures and acts as a monitoring mechanism on behalf of the business house. The Army provides resources for reshaping the curricula of madrassas, sponsors the visits of cultural troupes that can perform both in urban and rural areas. It also provides expertise to cooperatives and self-help ventures, assists in securing a market for these goods to be sold in the open market. Army also plays an important role in sending talented children to exclusive institutes such as National School of Drama and National Institute of Design. It also looks after the provision of sponsorship for artificial limbs project, medical treatment in border areas and up-gradation of existing medical clinics. As part of this noble project, school children from the valley are given the chance to visit other parts of the country and children from other parts of the country visit the valley.

Help from Confederation of Indian Industry (CII) and Their Contribution

In the last few years, CII's thrust in J&K has been on the social sector. The philosophy has been, and is, that there has to be concerned attempts to strengthen the delicate social fabric that exists in J&K today. With this objective, CII has undertaken a number of initiatives. CII's involvement has been through a multidimensional approach. The first of these focuses on the orphans affected by the militancy and violence. These children are between 7 to 15 years of age. It was felt that education was the best way to restore normalcy in their young, bruised, frightened lives.

The second focus group has been women and young girls affected by the violence. CII felt the necessity of working with them to help them regain their sense of dignity and self-esteem, and instilling in them the confidence to be part of a progressive society. Since January 2003, CII, along with 'Sadbhavana Trust', has been mobilizing women into self-help groups with the objective of harnessing a united, powerful force, with more bargaining power, and capability to be effective agents of social change. Introduction of micro-finance help women in starting micro-enterprises, thus ensuring livelihood, self-reliance, and most importantly, a belief in themselves.

The third focus group has been the youth of the state. Playing a pivotal role, the Indian Army mobilized the resources and manpower at its command not only to motivate large numbers of young people to attend the workshop but also worked hard with the youth to transport them from their homes to the training centres for the above purpose.

Goodwill School, Boniyar

In this paper, the Army-Corporate world initiative has been highlighted through the example of Goodwill School, which is situated at the India–Pakistan border near Line of Control (LOC) in Uri Sector (J&K). This school, opened about a couple of years ago, is transforming the people of that area. This effort is meant to be collaborative and interactive, entirely a partnership between the corporate houses and the common people, who lived for years with fear and terrorism. The role of the Indian Army is that of a facilitator.

No sociological study has been done till now taking into consideration the people's perception, aspiration and expectation. The interviewer visited the area in June 2003, 2004 and 2005 respectively and interacted with cross section of the society. The methodology of this paper is case study along with unstructured interview. Extensive interviews have been conducted on 100 students and about 100 parents whose children are studying in the school, and also the community at large. For interviews, men, women and children of different religions along with group meetings at several places gave the interviewer the opportunity to meet maximum number of people within limited time. They were eager to speak very spontaneous and one could see and feel the enthusiasm of those who had remained under pitiable and neglected conditions for years together.

What is so unique about this school? Education plays an important role in shaping the future of any nation. It is pertinent and imperative that people residing in remote areas of Kashmir have access to quality education. To achieve this objective the Pir Panjal Brigade of the Dagger Division has opened Goodwill School at Boniyar in Uri to provide quality education to the children of local villages that have remained impoverished due to lack of communication and proximity to the LOC at the India–Pakistan border. The school was inaugurated on 22 July 2002 by the Army on defense land with a total of 209 children from nursery to 1st class with an expansion plan of increasing one higher class in each academic session. It is an English medium school, which provides ample opportunities to the children for overall development of their personality.

Due to continuous efforts to bring in socio-political and economic equality and also to provide quality education, the school has been declared as a model school in a short span of one year in this region. The salient features of the school are:

- Education for all-round development of their personality
- Co-education(245 students from 28 villages)
- Optimal student-teacher ratio
- Teaching-Learning by Play Way Method
- Teaching based on Three-Language Formula (English, Hindi and Urdu)
- Computer training
- Library and TV facility
- Indoor and outdoor sports facility
- Free education to the needy children –16 scholarships
- Free school bus services to pick and drop the children to school from villages.
- Free boys hostel for poor children of remote villages on LOC (Battalions of 161 brigades sponsor the boys which include tuition fees, stationery and uniform)
- Free medical facility
- Minimal fee structure
- Expansion plan

Table 1

Highlight of the School

Transport from Village to the School
Learning English as Compulsory Subject
Painting and Handicraft
Computer Training to All the Students
Dramatics and Other School Activities
Compulsory Games
Strict Discipline
School Uniform for All
Ethos of Secularism
Gender Sensitivity
Teacher–Student Relationship with the Bondage of Trust, Friendship and Space for Discussing Conflict Situation

The biggest facility which is being provided to the students is the free transport. Table 2 shows that children from far away villages come to the school. The school bus even goes up to 34 kms to fetch some students from the hilly area. This has boosted the image of the army in a very big way.

Table 2

Village-wise Distance from Goodwill School, Boniyar

Village	*Distance by Bus (kms)*	*Village*	*Distance by Bus (kms)*
Rampur	34	Dawaran	03
Thathamulla	15	Gingal	02
Nowshera	20	Trikanjan	28
Pringal	03	Salasan	08
Limber	04	Neelam	08
Ghantamulla	03	Maidanan	08
Mohura	14	Prankutra	01
Chandanwari	03	Hillar Priniya	04
Uranboha	27	Bela	01
Noorkha	13	Lari	01

Children are learning English as a compulsory subject, which is very significant to note as in that area no other language is known/used except perhaps the local dialect. This facility of learning language along with computers has given a lot of confidence to the children as well as the parents. They now think beyond their village and gradually understand that the world is larger than their villages. The army discipline along with smart uniforms is transforming the small children into responsible citizens of the country. Children learn games, dramatics, music, painting, and handicrafts, which is making them self-confident. These children can be compared to the children of any of the best schools of Mumbai or New Delhi.

The ethos of secularism and gender sensitivity of the school help the child move towards the aim of education. This also helps the children in socializing into a democratic set-up through appropriate school co-curricular activities and judicious choice of topics/subjects.

Teacher and Student Relationship

The teachers are well qualified and much more devoted than the teachers of any other public/private schools where the parents help the children with homework. Most of the students are first generation learners and as most of the parents are illiterate, the obligation and work of the teacher increases to make the weaker children come at par with the brighter ones. They are completely dependent on the school and its culture for initiating reading and writing skills. Many children are also vulnerable because of the conditions prevailing at home.

The research shows that these children and teachers share and reflect on their individual and collective experiences without fear of judgement. This enables them to understand and relate to differences instead of fearing them. Conflict and tension are a part of the children's lives. They constantly encounter situations which call for moral assessment and action, whether in relation to subjective experiences of conflict involving the self, family and society or in dealing with exposure to violent conflict in the area where they live. The teachers help these children to deal with conflict and facilitate awareness of its nature and role in their lives. Teachers are not only teaching but are also creating an atmosphere of trust, friendship and a safe space where children can share experiences and discuss which prepares them for taking decisions in the future.

Views of the Parents

Some of the views of the parents whose children are in the school are given below:

- Our children are in the best hands of the Indian Armed forces.
- I (woman) lost my husband in cross-border terrorism; I thought I had lost everything in life. But, Indian Army has picked up my three children for education.
- We can see the change in our children. They are getting wiser, bolder and are learning many good things in the school.
- I never saw a computer in my life. My son says that he is learning computer in the school. He says, 'it is helpful for him for his future'.
- We have full faith in the school teachers. They take extra pains to teach the weaker children.
- We wonder that our little girl is teaching us about cleanliness and sanitation.
- We need not worry about our children's future. Our children would be future officers of the Armed Forces.
- The facility of the bus to pick and drop the children from home to school has assured us that Indian Army is really interested in our progress and development.
- We want more such schools to be opened near the India–Pakistan border so that every child can get the opportunity to go to the best schools.
- The biggest contribution of the school is the dream of our children of becoming something in life.
- The greatest agony is that we cannot help the children in their homework, as we are illiterate.

Views of the Children

- My sister and I did not come out of our small hut for days after militants killed my parents. We were hungry and scared (aged 7 and 8). At that time, the Army personnel came and rescued us, brought us along with them to the hostel.
- I want to join the Indian Armed Forces as an officer. I remember how militants in front of me killed my father. When I grow up, I will make sure that there are no militants in this area.
- The school has separate toilets for boys and girls; this facility is not available in our own houses.
- My parents died in an accident when I was a year old. I used to live with my elder brother. Militants killed him too. I was left with no one. Now, I stay in the school hostel.

- My idol is Colonel (Principal of the school). I want to become like him when I grow up.
- I have learnt to clean up/wash up my hands before eating any food, which I did not know earlier.
- It feels so good to wear the school uniform; my mother says that I look very handsome in it.
- I want to be a school teacher when I grow up (girl student).
- Why some people are killing others? I want to kill those who are killing others.
- My parents are shocked to know that I now dream of becoming an engineer or doctor.
- When I grow up, I would like to work for this village so that all the future children can join this school.

Conclusion

A country can be powerful only when it has educated its citizens. Goodwill school is a small effort in this direction. These small children have grown up amidst war and violence so far and this school is an example of the effort of the army and the corporate world initiative for peace in the valley, to convey the message of love, non-violence and peace.

If analysed honestly, the high budget, high expectations of peace efforts by the politicians have not been successful on the ground level. Instead, the continuing and increasing arms race by both the countries has put more fuel into the fire. And, the built up of distinctive nuclear arsenals by both the countries now threatens the very survival of the planet.

The security environment could be improved only when the state-centric security perspective is abandoned in favour of the society-centric one. And, genuine efforts should be made to ensure democratic and responsive governance, plurality of socio-cultural life of people and autonomy of decision, which is free from external interference and rests on national needs and aspirations. Thus, it is the non-military aspects of national security that need strengthening, not the conventional military aspects of security.

The common man/woman in the area is interested in two times meal, poverty alleviation programmes, and electrification in their homes and road, transport system, and health clinics. Above all, they want a secure future for their children and this school is a ray of hope for them. They want to live in a peaceful atmosphere, as they are tired of cross-border terrorism, militancy and uncertainty. The present structure of violence and aggression needs to be reconsidered from the vantage point of the people at the periphery.

More and more people from all over the world are realizing that the answer to present problem of violence is to be found in a morality which replaces greed with contentment, hate with tolerance, and killing with reverence for life. At the common man's level also, awareness of these dangers of violence is growing. Many protest groups are contributing all their strength in arousing the human conscience further. Principles of Ahimsa, Satya, Aparigraha, Anekantwad, etc., assume great relevance in this context.

There is a feeling that the deep valleys are overflowing with the words of Khawaja Habib, which rendered into English are as follows:

Whosoever realizes his own true Self
Uncovers the vessels of wine,
Overflows with joy, is intoxicated
And forgets his lower self;
He will not know a Hindu
From a 'Musalman' (Muslim)
Thus, the symphony of the traditions and cultures still echoes with its varied melodies (Wakhlu, 1998: 17).

The ongoing operations in Afghanistan and Iraq indicate that technology by itself cannot guarantee victory. National and regional pride can motivate a group to wage guerrilla warfare. The weak, so to speak, can resort to asymmetric warfare. Asymmetric means of waging war are not new. The history of development of defense versus attack, counter technology versus technology, and conventional versus non-conventional shows how numerically inferior or simple technologies have upset the high technology. Decoys, viruses, deception and guerrilla warfare are asymmetric manifestations. Peace loving people can become the most ferocious fighters if motivated with a cause or ideology. Bengali insurgents of the 'Mukti Bahini' or a Tamil fighter of the LTTE have demonstrated this transformation to Pakistan and Sri Lankan militaries respectively. But, at that point of time, very few could have imagined the growth of the suicide bombers and fidayeen squads. This is an important convergence of the motivation and will of humans to fight till the last. This convergence indicates that fighting spirit can be aroused and sustained by any race or tribe if there is sufficient motivation.

The people of Jammu and Kashmir, torn and tortured by tyranny of the militants at the close of the 20th century cast wistful eyes upon their past fulfillments, upon the golden age of Sultan Zain-ul-Abidin of Kashmir and the golden age of Raja Ranjit Dev of Jammu and these splash them with wonder and lead them to hope that the good days of peace and prosperity may return soon on the swift wings of time! All around they see devastation and desolation but no hand of the tyrant could destroy the characteristic spirit of the people or their heritage of spiritual messages of their saints and sages.

Peace operations have become the most important tool for international crisis management. The importance of the project 'Operation Ujala' will continue for a long time, with occasional ups and downs. Given the fact that such missions/operations are likely to be gaining more importance in future, it will be important to ensure that the lessons learnt in such operations are shared as widely as possible.

References

Bienen, Henry (1981). 'Civil-Military Relations in the Third World', *International Political Science Review*, February, II (3): 363–65.

Bohra, N.N. (2004). 'Internal Security Management: Some Concerns', *Security and Society*, Winter, 1 (1).

Cohen, Stephen P. (1976). 'Civilian Control of the Military in India', in E. Claude Welch (ed.), *Civilian Control of the Military: Theory and Cases from Developing Countries*, Albany: State University of New York Press, pp. 43–64.

Janowitz, Morris (1964). *The Military in the Political Development of New Nations: An Essay in Comparative Analysis*. Chicago: The University of Chicago Press, p. 11.

—— (ed.) (1981). *Civil-Military Relations: Regional Perspectives*. Beverly Hills, California: Sage, pp. 10–13.

Karim, Afsir (2004). 'Challenges of International Terrorism', *Security and Society*, Winter, 1 (1).

Kulrija, Veena (1991). *Civil Military Relations in South Asia, Pakistan, Bangladesh, and India*. New Delhi: Sage and London: New Bushy Park.

Kumar, Krishna (2002). 'Alternatives to National Suicide: Peace as Daily War', *The Times of India*, 13 June, p. 190.

Luckham, A.R. (1971). 'A Comparative Typology of Civil-Military Relations', *Government and Opposition*, Winter, VI (1): 8–9.

Martin, Michel L. (1984). 'Introduction', in Michel Louis Martin and Ellen Stern McCrate (eds), *The Military, Militarism, and the Policy*. New York: The Free Press, pp. 1–30.

Moscos, Charles C. (2000). 'Toward a Postmodern Military: The United States as a Paradigm', in Charles C. Moscos, John Allen Williams and David R. Segal (eds), *The Postmodern Military: Armed Forces after the Cold War*. Oxford: Oxford University Press, pp. 14–31.

Perlmutter, Amos (1970). 'The Arab Military Elite', *World Politics*, January, XXII (2): 269.

Sinha, S.K. (2005). 'Jammu & Kashmir: Past, Present and Future', *USI Journal*, April–June, p. 183.

Stobdan, P. (1996). 'Kashmir: The Key Issues', *Strategic Analysis*, IDSA, April, XIX (1).

Wakhlu, Somnath (1998). *The Rich Heritage of Jammu and Kashmir: Studies in Art, Architecture, History and Culture of the Region*. New Delhi: Gyan Publishing House, p. 17.

Zimmermann, Ekkart (1979). 'Towards a Causal Model of Military Coup d'etat', *Armed Forces and Society*, Spring, V (3): 392.

Part II

RELIGION

8

Mobilizing Religion for Dignity and Development

Revisiting the Mahar Buddhists of Maharashtra

Surinder S. Jodhka

> Religion can help to keep everything in its place. But it can also turn the world upside down.
>
> — Christian Smith (1996)

In the mainstream discourse on development and modernization produced during 1950s and 1960s religion was generally conceptualized in negative terms, often viewed as hindering efforts for progress and development of 'pre-modern' societies of the Third World. Such notions of development worked with the popularly held assumptions of the 'modernization theory', which had propagated that the religious worldviews and the framework of values and beliefs it provided could only help the pre-modern communities reproduce their 'traditional' ways of life, invariably characterized by hierarchy and patriarchal authority. Decline of religion, or its 'privatization', followed by institutionalization of a 'rational' value system, and secularization of the public life were thus imperatives for a society to become developed and modern.[1]

It was not only the mainstream functionalist theories of modernization and social change that viewed religion in negative terms, the radical and left-wing thinkers too suspected the role of religious sentiment in human endeavour for progress. Karl Marx, for example, had famously described religion as 'opium of the masses', something that kept those on the margins of social and economic power contained and uncritical of exploitative structures of authority and economic production.

Over the last three decades or so such theories of social change have been extensively criticized and have, more or less, been abandoned. It is now widely recognized that religion is not merely a source of conservation and stability, it can also be a force of disruption and change. Students of social movements have repeatedly pointed to the fact that religion has always been an important source of inspiration for people to mobilize, sometimes to resist change, and at some other times, to demand social change and reform. The symbolic resources of religion are available not only to those in power, but also to the weak, who sometimes deploy them in their struggles for a secure and dignified life, which in turn could subvert the traditional or establish structures of authority.

This change in attitude of the social sciences towards religion could also be seen in shifting trends in empirical research on the subject. Over the last two or three decades we have seen a steady shift towards treating religion as a 'normal' sociological fact, without any teleological presupposition about its pasts or futures (Smith, 1996; Beckford, 1990; Haynes, 1995; Casanova, 2001). It is with this sociologically pragmatic perspective that we wish to study the religious social movements of some of the marginalized sections of Indian society and their role in bringing about social change for a better life.

Much of the available scholarly literature on religion, as also the popular discourses, tend to look at the so-called 'grand religious traditions' like Christianity, Islam or Hinduism. The contemporary revival of religion in the post-9/11 global politics also refers to these grand, civilizational religious systems (for example, Samuel Huntington's thesis on *Clash of Civilizations*). The internal dynamics of religious traditions and movements for change within such traditions, particularly of those located at the margins of these communities, have been relatively less discussed or researched. The historical experience shows that the socially excluded and marginalized struggle not only for equity and entitlements but also for cultural and symbolic resources, of which religion is an important part.

In a country like India, where caste and religion have been the primary sources of identification and social/cultural organization, engagement with religion becomes even more critical for the socially marginalized. Apart from its symbolic value as a source of dignified social identities, religion, at times, also becomes critical for distribution of material resources and state patronage. For example, during the colonial period, movement for social and economic rights invariably raised issues about religious reforms. Several Dalit groups and other marginalized castes also mobilized themselves on religious lines during the later phase of colonial rule. The existing literature convincingly shows that these movements produced profound social, political and economic changes in the traditional social order and, in some cases, significantly raising the social and economic status of the erstwhile marginalized groups (see Juergensmeyer, 1979; Dube, 1993; Hardgrave, 1969).

This study[2] focuses on the neo-Buddhist Mahars of Maharashtra with a focus on their quest for dignified social existence and struggle for material development and empowerment through religious mobilizations.

Religion and Social Movements for Change

As mentioned above, following the post-Second World War writings on development in the Western social science, the mainstream development discourse in India also saw religion in negative terms, a part and parcel of the traditional value system, which needed to be changed if rapid economic growth and social transformation had to happen. However, beyond the 'modernization' and development studies literature, perspectives on religion were quite different.

There are at least three different sets of writings in the social movement literature where religion figures quite prominently.

First, the writings of reform movements during the colonial period directly deal with religion. In fact, most of these movements, even when they mobilized for reforms within their community, used religious idioms for mobilizations (Dua, 1970; Oddie, 1975; Drene, 1991; Jones, 1979; Oberoi, 1994; Chauhan and Barua, 1974). These movements had two dimensions. First, they were identity movements with clear focus on mobilization of a community or a section of community for recognition in the emerging political formations under the colonial rule where representations were increasingly being given on the grounds of demographics of communities (Grewal, 1989). The second dimension of these movements was reformist. Along with mobilizations for identity, the leadership of these movements also pressed for internal reforms in the cultural and religious practices of their communities. They generally campaigned for reforms in traditional practices relating to women and children. Some of these movements also set up schools and faith-based organizations to work for the poor and the marginalized.

The second set of social movement writings where religion appears prominently, were the 'religious revivalist' and identity movements of the 1980s and after. The most important movement in this category is the Khalistan movement among the Sikhs of Punjab. Khalistan movement has also been a well-studied social movement (Gupta, 1982; Singh, 2000; Juergensmeyer, 1988). Equally well-studied movement has been the politico-religious mobilizations of the right-wing Hindutva groups (Zavos, 2000; Katju, 2003; Baber, 2000; Jaffrelot, 1996; Hansen, 1999; Ludden, 1996; Sarkar, 1999; Kanungo, 2002). The relatively less studied in this category has been the separatist movement among the Muslims of Kashmir (Bose, 2003).

The third set of social movement studies where religion figures prominently is in the writings on Dalit movements, which invariably became movements against Hinduism and for autonomous religious identities, or conversion to other faith traditions. Even when they appeared as religious movements, they were also movements for social change and development, with uplift of the historically excluded and marginalized at the core of their concerns. The more well known in this category of social movements were the anti-Brahmin movements in the south of India (Pandian, 1996), the neo-Buddhist/Dalit movement in Maharashtra (Wilkinson and Thomas, 1972; Zelliot, 1977; Omvedt, 1976, 2004; Joshi, 1986; Guru and Chakravarty, 2005; Beltz, 2005), the Buddhist movements among the Tamils (Aloysius, 1998), the Buddhist movements of Western Uttar Pradesh (Joshi, 1977), the Satnami movement in Chhattisgarh (Dube, 1993; Babb, 1972) and Ad Dharma movement in Punjab (Juergensmeyer, 1979, 1988) and elsewhere in India.

It is the work on this third set of movements that the present study intends to take forward. The study attempts to explore the 'development effects' of the a religious movement and the nature of social changes it has been able to produce in the life of the marginalized — an aspect that has not been studied much by students of Dalit religious movements in India.

The Neo-Buddhist Mahars of Maharashtra

Socially and culturally also Maharashtra could be described as one of the mainstream states of India. Its religious demography looks more like the national demography. Maharashtra has an overwhelming Hindu majority (80.2%) with Muslims (10.6%) and Buddhists (6%) its prominent minority populations. Christians too have their presence in the state, being around 1 per cent of the total population. Though small in proportional terms, Maharashtra is also home to the largest number of Jains, Zoroastrians and Jews of India.

Along with Bengal, Maharashtra emerged as an important centre of western education and social reforms during the 19th century. Names of early reformers like G.K. Gokhale, M.G. Ranade and Jyotiba Phule are quite well known to the students of Indian history. It was here that the question of caste inequality was forcefully raised by people like Phule and B.R. Ambedkar. This criticism of caste culminated in an important movement for religious conversion among the Mahars, an ex-untouchable community, under the leadership of Ambedkar.

It was in 1956 that Ambedkar led the conversion of almost the entire community of Mahars of Maharashtra to Buddhism. The census of 1951 had counted only 2,487 persons of Buddhist religion in the state of Maharashtra. This population swelled to 2,789,501 in the next census carried out in 1961. The number of Buddhists has continued to grow in the state. Of the total Buddhist population of around 8 million, counted for the entire country in the census of 2001, as many 73.39 per cent lived in Maharashtra, and with the exception of a small minority they were all neo-converts, also known as the neo-Buddhists (see Table 1). Though some Dalits have converted to Buddhism in other parts of India as well, the neo-Buddhist movement has remained popular mostly with the Mahars of Maharashtra.

Table 1

Rate of Growth of Buddhists in Maharashtra

Year	*Population of Maharashtra (total)*	*Buddhist population of Maharashtra*	*Percentage of total population in Maharashtra*	*All India Buddhist percentage of population in India*
1951	32,002,564	2,487	.01	0.05
1961	39,533,781	2,789,501	7.05	0.74
1971	50,412,235	3,264,233	6.47	0.7
1981	62,783,000	3,946,149	6.39	0.7
1991	78,937,000	5,040,785	6.28	0.77
2001	96,878,627	5,838,710	6.1	0.8

Sources: Patwardhan, 1973; Mahana, 1985 and Economic Survey of Maharashtra, 2005–06.

What prompted such a movement among the Mahars of Maharashtra? Who provided the leadership? What have been the development effects of the movement for the marginalized and poor among the ex-untouchable community of Mahars? What kinds of structures have evolved over the years that facilitate development and socio-economic consolidation of the new community? These are some of the questions that we try to explore in this chapter.

The Mahars of Maharashtra

Broadly speaking, we could identify four different caste clusters in Maharashtra. The so-called upper castes (Brahmins, Banias and Kayasthas, etc.) constitute around 3 to 4 per cent of the total population of Maharashtra. The middle level land owning rural/dominant caste groups, the Maratha-Kunbis, comprise nearly 31 per cent of the total population. The third caste cluster of the Other Backward Classes (OBCs) also has a substantial presence with around 27 per cent of the total state population. The fourth caste cluster is of the marginalized communities – the Scheduled Castes (SCs) and the Scheduled Tribes (STs). Though as many as 59 groups have been classified as SCs in Maharashtra, a large majority of them come from four groups, viz., Mahars, Mangs, Matangs and Charamkars.

According to the colonial census of 1931 Mahars were the most numerous among the 'untouchable' population and they alone accounted for around 11 per cent of the total population of the colonial Maharashtra state (total population of all the 'untouchable' communities put together was 16.47%), higher than any other caste group except for the Marathas (who were 20.2%). The so-called upper castes together constituted only 6.59 per cent of the total population. The predominance of Mahars in the total population of SCs in the state continues even today. As per the 2001 Census, of the 59 castes listed in the schedule, Mahar, Mang, Bhambi and Bhangi together constituted 92 per cent with Mahars alone making for 57.5 per cent (5,678,912 persons) of the SC population of Maharashtra.

Unlike some other 'untouchable' groups, Mahars of Maharashtra were not always identified with a single occupation. They were the 'village servants' but some of them were also engaged with other tasks. They were ranked among the most important *balutedars* (a service caste) and unlike most other *balutedars,* they were entitled for *vatan* (rights over free/common land).

Balutedari, a variant of the *jajmani* system, was a system where various artisan castes (*balutedars*) performed their traditional tasks in the name of serving the village. While in the *jajmani* system, popular in north India, the services were technically for the individual *jajmans,* who in most cases was the landowner from a dominant caste and the service provider (*kamin*) and received payment from his master. The concept of *jajman* was not known in Maharashtra. As *balutedars*, or servants of the village, Mahars were gate-keepers, watchmen, auxiliaries to the police in event of theft in the village, travellers' porters, guides for the people to the next village and boundary referees. They were also in charge of levying taxes and summoning landholders to pay taxes, escorting to the government treasury, sweeping roads, carrying death notices and messages to other villages, bringing fuels to the burning ground and removing cattle carcasses. Though in theory the services of *balutedars* were for the village as a whole, they were often secured by individuals from the dominant caste groups — Patils and Kulkarnis.

As pointed out by Jaffrelot (2004: 20), in terms of the local status hierarchy, Mahars were the first among the last. During the payment in lieu of their service to the village, the Mahars were allowed to take their share from the first row. But, apart from their share in the harvest, they were also granted the right to a *vatan* (an area of land free of tax) in return. This piece of land was often of good quality and therefore they had the privilege to cultivate and do their own farming, unlike *balutedars* from other Dalit castes.

However, despite these privileges Mahars continued to be treated as untouchables. They lived outside the village, in the *maharwada*. The process of their mobility begins only when they move out of the village, into secular occupations. One of the most important occupations that Mahars took to was military service, initially in the army of the local rulers, the Peshwas, and later in the British Army.

According to Stephen Cohen (1990), in the pre-Mutiny years, Mahars constituted a fifth to a quarter of the entire Bombay Army and they fought in several battles for the colonial masters. However, after the Mutiny of 1857 Mahars were de-listed from recruitment when the Peel Commission in its report on army reorganization did not recognize them as a 'martial race', a status bestowed mostly on the locally dominant/upper caste communities. By 1893, the recruitment of Mahars and other untouchable castes was completely stopped. 'We cannot practically ignore it (the caste system), so long as the natives socially maintain it,'[3] was the argument advanced by the Commission. Together with a number of other classes Mahars were no longer be recruited to the army. They could only get enlisted as bandsmen or clerks. The regiment was to be revived again in the year 1945.

Notwithstanding these ups and downs, the experience of recruitment in colonial army played a very critical and positive role in the Mahar social mobility. Mahars benefited from their participation in the British Army in a number of ways. It took them out of village, gave them a sense of autonomy and confidence and opened up avenues of secular education for them, which in turn also opened up employment opportunities for them in other areas of urban economy. They began to abandon their traditional caste-related occupations. As Zelliot observed:

> During the 19th and 20th centuries, a substantial number of Mahars removed themselves from their traditional village service role. The establishment of British rule in Bombay Presidency provided Mahars with the opportunity for the service in the army, employment in cotton mills, ammunition factories, railroads, dockyards, construction work, and as servants in British homes. (1972: 75)

Zelliot also refers to the 1921 Census which recorded only 13.5 per cent of Mahars being employed in their traditional occupations. In contrast, as many as 55 per cent of Chambhars and 33.2 per cent of Mangs, the two other major Dalit castes of Maharashtra, were reportedly employed in their traditional caste occupations (ibid.: 75). This point has also been underlined by Christophe Jaffrelot (2004) in his work on the subject. He refers to an ethnographic study conducted by M.G. Bhagat who reported that in early 1930s only 6.5 per cent of Mahars pursued their traditional role, as against 54 per cent of Chambhars, 62 per cent of Dhors, 79 per cent of Mangs and 100 per cent of Bhangis. Of the 17 untouchable civil servants mentioned by Bhagat, 15 were Mahars and only two Chambhars. In terms of education too, Mahars made up for 67 per cent of the total untouchables who had some knowledge of the English language as against only 16 per cent of Chambhars. This social and economic mobility among the Mahars had an interesting impact on the educational status of the total Dalit population of the region. The highest rate of literacy among untouchables recorded during the 1921 Census was in the Bombay Presidency (4.1%), much higher than Punjab (1.1%) and even Madras Presidency (3.5%).

This understandably had an impact on their personal selves. Those who joined the army experienced much lesser caste prejudice. As Basham observes:

> ... within the closed circle of the regiment, caste prejudice was, if not actually absent, at least officially discouraged. According to army regulations no distinction was made between soldiers on the basis of their caste or community ... Mahar officers were able to command men of the other castes apparently without difficulty. (1986: 167)

Notwithstanding this experience of a small minority of Mahars, their social status in the local society did not experience any major improvement. Economic mobility in a caste society does not translate directly into higher social status. It may be useful to quote Zelliot (1972) once more:

> It was their entry into the British army which proved significant for the subsequent history of the Mahar movement. It is important to gauge this significance. It consists not in any automatic elevation in the social hierarchy through military service, which indeed is ruled out in a hierarchical system governed by considerations of ascriptive status and ritual purity. It rather consists in the fact that military service at such an early date exposed them to British institutions much before the dissemination of the western culture took place on a large scale.

It was this exposure to the western institutions and secular employment that gave a new sense of confidence to a section of the Mahars and created conditions for the subsequent social movements among them, which eventually resulted in movement for religious conversion and search for a new identity in Buddhism. Though it was a newly emergent educated social class within the Mahar community that provided social context for this movement, the role of an individual leader – B.R. Ambedkar – was also extremely critical.

Ambedkar and the Mahar Movement

Ambedkar was born in a military cantonment (Mhow) in the Indore district of the present-day Madhya Pradesh. His father, Ramji Sakpal, rose to become a Subedar Major, the highest rank that an Indian could hold in the British Army at that time. Ambedkar's mother too came from a family of soldiers. Her father and her six uncles had all been in the British Army at the same rank as her husband was. Having grown-up in a cantonment area, Ambedkar escaped much of the prejudice and violence of caste system that his fellow Mahars experienced in a typical rural setting of Maharashtra. However, he could not escape this reality for very long. Ambedkar's biographer, Dhananjay Keer, gives a vivid account of Ambedkar's first experience of the dark reality of caste and the shock it gave him. It happened while he was travelling outside the military environment, and had gone to meet his father in a distant village. Keer writes:

> At the railway station, they hired a bullock cart to take them to the village, but hardly had the cart gone a few yards when the God-fearing touchable Hindu cart-man, to his wrath, came to know that the well-dressed boys were the accursed Untouchables! In a fit of rage he threw them out on the road as one overturns the dust bins; for he felt they had polluted his wooden cart and destroyed the purity of his domestic animals! (1964: 12)

During this trip Ambedkar was also once 'beaten black and blue' when some member of the touchable castes found him drinking water from a 'public water course' (ibid.: 13).

Fighting caste-based prejudice and discrimination was to eventually become a major preoccupation with Ambedkar, a life-long mission. It was in order to fulfil this mission that he turned to religion. His relationship with religion was rather peculiar. He critiqued religion – Hinduism – for sustaining caste divisions and hierarchy in society. He embraced religion – Buddhism – to escape untouchability and humiliation thrust upon people of his community by Hinduism. However, in order to do it effectively, he had to work tirelessly all through his life. Not only did he work as an intellectual and critique of Hinduism but also as a leader and missionary to mobilize his people for dignified existence.

Ambedkar had a long and interesting career as a student. He concluded his primary education at the cantonment school and his high school at Satara town in Maharashtra. Later, when his father moved with the army to Bombay, he got enrolled at the Elphinstone College there from where he obtained his BA degree in English language. In 1913 he joined the army of the princely state of Baroda as a lieutenant. However, his interest was to pursue further studies. Having secured financial aid from the Maharaja of Baroda[4] he went to Columbia University, New York for a Master's degree. From there he moved to London School of Economics (LSE) to study law.

However, before he could complete his studies at LSE, he returned to India in 1917 on the request of Maharaja of Baroda and rejoined the Baroda administration as a Military Secretary to the Maharaja. Once again he was haunted by his caste background and could not find a decent house to live in the city of Baroda. His education abroad and a well-paid job with the Maharaja could not erase his identity of being an untouchable. He eventually resigned from the job in Baroda and returned to England to complete his studies. This time he was supported by another Maharaja – the Maharaja of Kolhapur.

Ambedkar presented his thesis on *The Problem of Rupee* at the LSE in 1922 and was awarded the degree a year later. He was also awarded Ph.D. by Columbia University for his thesis on *The Evolution of Provincial Finance in British India* in 1927. With two degrees from two of the best centres of higher education of the world, Ambedkar was not only the first from an untouchable community to reach that level, he was also among the few Indians at that time to have achieved such a distinction.

Ambedkar returned to India in 1923, registered at the Bombay Bar and started legal practice in the Bombay High Court the following year. However, his caste identity continued to be a factor in the legal profession. Many potential clients would not approach him simply because he was from an untouchable community. To supplement his income, he, therefore, was forced to also teach on the part-time basis.

Like many other Indians of the time who had returned from abroad after completing education, Ambedkar too was attracted to ongoing social reforms and political movements. However, unlike most others who were involved with religious reform and movement for freedom from the British rule, Ambedkar had a single-point programme – to fight against caste system and untouchability, to uplift his people and give them a life of dignity.

Christophe Jaffrelot (2009; also see Jaffrelot, 2004) has identified four different strategies that Ambedkar deployed in his struggle against caste inequalities and untouchability over the three decades of his active political career. First of all he worked for building of a respectable identity for them, to produce an alternative history of them, a history that gives them a sense of dignity and explains their subordination without justifying it. His second strategy was the engagements with 'electoral politics'. He actively campaigned with the colonial rulers in making them recognize the special case of the untouchable population and how they could be represented in the democratic institutions that the colonial rulers were trying to put in place. This also brought him in direct contact with the 'mainstream' nationalist political leaders, who were invariably upper-caste Hindus, such as Mahatma Gandhi and Jawaharlal Nehru. Though his relations with leaders like Gandhi were not cordial, Ambedkar's aggressive emphasis on caste made them recognize the significance of dealing with questions of caste and untouchability in independent India. It was out of these engagements that the present-day system of quotas (reservations) for the SCs and STs in legislative bodies is in place.

The third important strategy that Ambedkar employed to uplift his people was to 'work with rulers – from British Raj to the Congress Raj'. Unlike the nationalist leaders, Ambedkar did not take an oppositional stance vis-à-vis the British. As Jaffrelot writes, he 'tried hard to influence the governments in his personal capacity, whether they were of the British or Congress, for better serving the cause of the untouchables'. He had no hesitation in rejecting the movement for independence, which he saw as being dominated by the upper-castes Hindus. He worked with British in various committees with the hope of getting a better deal for his people. However, when he was offered a ministerial berth by Jawaharlal Nehru, India's first prime minister, he accepted it. He was also the chairman of India's Constituent Assembly and had played an active role in framing the Constitution of independent India.

Finally, and most importantly for us, was his decision to embrace along with his people Buddhism. Though it was in 1956, only a few months before his death that he converted to Buddhism, he had never been comfortable or happy with being a Hindu. It was in 1927, at a public meeting in the town of Mahad in the Konkar region of Maharashtra that he had first declared:

> We want equal rights in society. We will achieve them as far as possible while remaining within the Hindu fold or, if necessary by kicking away this worthless Hindu identity. And if it becomes necessary to give up Hinduism it would no longer be necessary for us to bother about temples. (cited in Gore, 1993: 91)

It was also the year he began his political career and started mobilizing Dalits of Maharashtra against the practice of untouchability. In his first appearance as a political activist at a conference of 'the depressed classes' on 20 March 1927 in Mahad, he demanded the abolition of untouchability and the caste system. He was also supported in his efforts by some caste Hindus. It was during this series of protests that along with his supporters, he decided to go and drink water from a public water source in the town where those belonging to Dalit communities were not allowed. Ambedkar's choice of the public water source was deeply symbolic. It was to show to the world the extent of discrimination faced by the people of his community. The caste Hindus did not treat the untouchables even at par with the animals. Water, after all, was freely accessible to animals and birds.

However, this act of Ambedkar resulted in a near rioting situation in the town. The caste Hindus performed rituals to purify the tank for it having been visited by untouchables. This made Ambedkar even more angry and critical of Hinduism. A few months later, on 26 December 1927, he planned another demonstration in the town and along with a large number of Dalits he burned the *Manusmriti* (the Hindu law book presumably written by Manu). To spread his message to the larger public Ambedkar also started publishing a weekly *Bahiskrit Bharat* (Depressed India) where apart form articulating his position on the caste question, untouchability and Hinduism he also wrote critically about the failure of the British government in its duty towards the untouchables.[5]

As it appears, Ambedkar's opposition to Hinduism and his desire to convert out of it was primarily driven by instrumental reasons. Given that the Hindus practised caste system and treated certain communities as untouchables and that this practice was sanctioned by the sacred texts of Hindu religion, there could not be any place for him and the people of his community within Hinduism where they could feel dignified members of the faith.

Though Hindu reformers of the times criticized the practice of untouchability Ambedkar had little faith in their ability and even suspected their intentions. His frequent disagreements with Gandhi on this are quite well known to the students of Indian history. For Gandhi and other Hindu reformers, it was important to keep untouchables within the Hindu fold for the larger politics of numbers. It was precisely for this reason that Gandhi did not want the untouchables to have separate electorates and went on fast unto death in Pune in 1932. After the famous Poona Pact between Gandhi and Ambedkar, it was agreed that there would be no separate electorates for the untouchables, as had been allocated to the Muslims and some other religious minorities, but they would have seats reserved for them where electorate would be mixed.

As rightly pointed out by Jaffrelot, for Gandhi, Poona Pact was not an agreement about giving due representation to the untouchable communities in the electoral process but about making them ready that they are a part of Hinduism. This is clearly evident from his comment to Ambedkar in 1933:

> In accepting the Poona Pact you accept the position that you are Hindus. (cited in Jaffrelot, 2004: 67)

Notwithstanding his differences with Gandhi and other Hindu reformers, Ambedkar continued his 'movement for acceptance by the caste Hindus' for several years. He supported the movements for temple entry being organized by his fellow untouchables. He himself organized a large procession to enter the Kala Ram Temple in Nasik in 1930. Though he was largely unsuccessful, he continued this movement for nearly five years and was able to mobilize thousands of untouchables. Even when he was fighting for civil rights for the untouchables, he did not loose sight of the religious dimension of their subordination. He often attributed untouchability to Hindu religion and its ideology. Radical reforms in Hinduism that would accommodate and include the untouchables were simply not possible. He articulated it quite clearly and loudly in his speech delivered at a conference of the representatives of depressed classes held on 13 October 1935 in a small town of Yeola:

> Religion is for man and not man for religion. If you want to organize yourself, change your religion. If you want to gain self-respect, change your religion. If you want to create a society that ensures cooperation, and brotherhood, change your religion. If you want to achieve power, change your religion. If you want equality, change your religion. If you want independence, change your religion. If you want to make the world in which you live happy, change your religion.
>
> Why do you want to remain bound to a religion, which does not treat you as a human being? Why do you want to remain in a religion which prohibits you from entering its temples? Why do want to remain under the religion which prohibits you from drawing water from public wells? Why do you remain in that religion which bars you from decent occupation and jobs? Why do you remain in that religion which insults you at every step?
>
> The religion that teaches man to behave with man in an inhuman manner is not religion but infamy. The religion which does not recognize a human being as a human being is a curse. The religion in which the touch of animals is permitted but the touch of a human being pollutes, is not a religion but the mockery of religion. The religion that precludes some classes from education, forbids them to accumulate wealth and to bear arms, is not a religion but tyranny. The religion which compels the ignorant to remain ignorant and the poor to remain poor does not deserve to be called as a religion. (cited in Das, 1963: 61)

For himself, Ambedkar made a declaration in this meeting that though he was born a Hindu, he would surely not die a Hindu. He declared:

> ... Unfortunately for me I was born a Hindu Untouchable. It was beyond my power to prevent that, but, I declare that it is within my power to refuse to live under ignoble and humiliating conditions. I solemnly assure you that I will not die a Hindu. (ibid.: 108)

Notwithstanding his anger and despair, Ambedkar did not want his exit from Hinduism, or conversion to anther religion to be an individual affair. He wanted it to be a social movement. He was aware of the fact that while he was ready to leave Hinduism, the large masses of his community also needed to be prepared for it. It was perhaps for this reason that he continued to support the campaigns for entry into Hindu temples. It was only after the failure and disillusionment of these campaigns that he proposed conversion out of Hinduism to the leaders of the 'depressed classes'.

From Untouchables to Buddhists

Even after the declaration of his intent Ambedkar took more than 20 years to convert to Buddhism. However, what changed after this declaration was that he stopped participating in efforts directed at reforming Hinduism. While it was easy to reject Hinduism, finding an alternative was not. Further, though Ambedkar had been criticizing Hinduism, he did not criticize religion *per se* and did not see alternative in a 'secular community'. Though he was aware of Marxist writings, the idea of communism did not appeal him much. The alternative to Hinduism had to be another religion, which could give them a new religious identity.

Though Islam and Christianity had attracted sections of the untouchable communities in the subcontinent, but he was not very keen on choosing them. Apart from the continued experience of discrimination by Dalits in these religions, Ambedkar was also sensitive to the Indian nationalist sentiments. The Indian nationalists, even some of those within the Congress, saw Islam and Christianity as foreign religions and given the weak economic position of Dalits in different parts of the country, Ambedkar did not want any kind of schism to develop between the dominant groups and the Dalits (Keer, 1994; Jaffrelot, 2004). He seriously considered the possibility of converting to Sikhism and spent a good deal of time to assess the advantages and disadvantages of converting to it. He finally gave up on Sikhism also. Despite its theological opposition to the Brahminical caste system, its practice had not gone away from Sikhism and it was also confined to only a small region of the subcontinent.

Buddhism appeared to be the most viable alternative. Apart from it being a part of the Indian native tradition, as a religious system, Buddhism was also less dogmatic and philosophically quite open. Given that there was hardly a strong Buddhism community anywhere in India at that time he thought the neo-converts would be able to make claims over it much more than any other religious tradition. As Gail Omvedt (2004) points out, Ambedkar's interpretation of Buddhism was not only a challenge to Brahminical Hinduism but also to the existing interpretations of Buddhism. In fact, Ambedkar called it 'Navayana Buddhism', to mark its distinction from the three accepted 'ways' of Buddhism: the Theravada (or Hinayana), the Mahayana and the Vajrayana. Navayana Buddhism was to eventually emerge as a powerful expression of Buddhism in India.

It was in the year 1950 that Ambedkar for the first time asked his followers to celebrate Buddha Jayanti and the same year contributed an article in the *Mahabodhi* journal of Calcutta under the title 'Buddha and the Future of His Religion' where he argued that he liked Buddhism because he found the religion of the Buddha being rational, scientific, and epitome of liberty, equality and fraternity (cited in Ahir, 1998: 112). The same year Ambedkar participated in the First Conference of the World Fellowship of Buddhists held at Kandy in Sri Lanka. In the year 1954, he again visited Burma to participate in the Third World Fellowship of Buddhists held at Rangoon. It was after his return from Burma that he started concentrating all his attention on the plans of his conversion to Buddhism. On 4 May 1955, he founded the *Bhartiya Bauddha Mahasabha* (The Buddhist Society of India) to undertake preaching and propagation of Buddhism. Then, he very thoughtfully selected the day of his conversion on October 14 as it was the auspicious day of 'Dhamma Vijaya', the day on which Asoka the Great had embraced Buddhism in 262 BC, and requested the most venerable U. Chandramani Maha Thera of Kushinagar to lead to the religion of Buddha. Even the place, Nagpur was selected because he considered it as the land of Nagas, the earlier Buddhists.[6] About four lakh people gathered for the ceremony. After the *deeksha* rites were performed, he took twenty-two vows. Important to note is that the first eight vows were dedicated to the renunciation of Hinduism and all the Hindu Gods. Addressing the vast gathering, Ambedkar, after the conversion, said,

> I started the movement of renouncing the Hindu religion in 1935 and since then I have been continuing the struggle. This conversion has given me enormous satisfaction and pleasure unimaginable. I feel as if I have been liberated from hell. (ibid.: 114)

For those who attended the ceremony and converted to Buddhism along with him also it was a moment of liberation. We were able to speak a woman who was part of the historic Nagpur conversion ceremony in Solapur during the fieldwork and described her experience to us in following words:

> I went to Nagpur to attend the conversion ceremony when I was in the sixth month of my pregnancy. Along with me were many other women from Solapur. I remember the names of Sona Bai, Tai Bai, Shivsharan, Guna Bai, Khar Bhandare. Most of them are not there any longer. We all felt very proud and were singing the song, 'Neela Zhanda Oonch Dhara, Dalitanchi Gatna Gadha, Junmaroodicha Deun Dhola, Jai Bhim Bola'. (Speak loud the name of Babasaheb; keep the blue flag straight; start a movement of Dalits; come out of the old dogmatic traditions and say 'Victory to Bheem')

Another participant provided us with a more detailed description of the ceremony:

> ... even the poorest, came clad in the spotless white shirts and saris that had been prescribed for the occasion by their beloved leader. Some families had had to sell trinkets in order to buy their new clothes and meet the expenses of the journey, but they had made the sacrifice gladly and set out for Nagpur with songs on their lips and the hope of a new life in their heart ... . By the end of the week 4,000,000 men, women and children had poured into Nagpur, with the result that the population had nearly doubled and the white-clad Untouchables had virtually taken over the city. (Sangharakshita, 1986: 129–30)

For lay members of the community it has become a sacred day. Many of them proudly claimed this to be the 'only event in world history till date where so many people converted to a different religion in one go'. The place where conversion took place is named as *'Deeksha Bhoomi'* and has become the most sacred place of pilgrimage for the neo-Buddhists of Maharashtra. They have erected a grand memorial *'stupa'* at the venue. Every year the neo-Buddhists from Maharashtra and other states of India visit the place to celebrate day, *Dhammachakrapravartan Divas*.

A few months later, on 6 December 1956, Ambedkar died at his residence in Delhi at the age of 65. Ten days after his death, another mass conversion was organized by his comrades in Bombay. By the time the census enumerators began to collect population data for the 1961 Census, 80 per cent of the Mahars of Bombay reported new religious identity as Buddhists (Zelliot, 1994: 73). Though they had not yet been able to organize themselves properly as a community, they felt sufficiently inspired and confident to distance themselves from Hinduism. It was only later that the community of neo-Buddhists began to consolidate itself.

Building the Community for Dignity and Development

As we have argued above, Ambedkar's attitude towards religion was instrumental. He criticized Hinduism because its ideology and practices were discriminatory and denied a dignified membership to the caste communities that were treated untouchable. However, notwithstanding his quest for a 'rational' alternative, he consciously distanced himself from Marxist politics of class, which could have been an obvious choice for him. He understood the specifics of Indian society well. Caste could not be reduced to class and class unity was virtually impossible in society divided on caste lines. While economic deprivation was a fact of life for a large majority of Dalits, caste prejudice worked independently of the poverty of his people. He had learnt it through his own experience of being discriminated against in urban professional life despite being well-educated and well-employed.

It was in this background that one should understand his efforts of taking his people along and working towards building a community of believers and united around a symbolic identity. When he converted to Buddhism along with hundreds of thousands of Dalits, he also made them swear by certain principles that distance them from Hinduism, and make them a community of believers around certain universal values. These principles were:

1. I shall not recognize Brahma, Vishnu and Mahesh as Gods, nor shall I worship them.
2. I shall not recognize Ram and Krishna as Gods, nor shall I worship them.
3. I shall not recognize Gauri and Ganapati as Gods nor shall I worship them.
4. I do not believe in the theory of incarnation of God.
5. I do not consider Buddha as the incarnation of Vishnu.
6. I shall not perform *Shraddha* (a Hindu rite that one carries out for the safety of the deceased) nor shall I give offerings to God.
7. I shall not do anything which is detrimental to Buddhism.
8. I shall not perform any religious rites through the agency of a Brahmin.
9. I believe that all human beings are equal.

10. I shall endeavour to establish equality.
11. I shall follow the eight-fold path of the Buddha.
12. I observe the ten 'Paramitas' (observances) of the Buddha (the virtues in which a follower of the Buddha has to restrain himself/herself).
13. I shall be compassionate to all living beings and I shall nurture them with care.
14. I shall not steal.
15. I shall not lie.
16. I shall not commit adultery.
17. I shall not drink liquor.
18. I shall lead my life striving to cultivate a harmonious blend of the three basic principles of Buddhism (enlightenment, precept and compassion).
19. I thereby reject my old religion, Hinduism, which is detrimental to the prosperity of human kind and which discriminates between man and man and which treats me as inferior.
20. I fully believe that Buddhism is Saddhamma.
21. By my embracing Buddhism I am being reborn.
22. I hereby pledge to conduct myself hereafter in accordance with the teachings of the Buddha.

Before Ambedkar died he worked on providing his fellow Buddhists with a text on Buddhism with which they could relate. During the last days of life he worked hard and completed the writing of a book, *Buddha and His Dhamma* (Buddha and His Teachings), where he presented Buddhism as a religious philosophy for social action and social change. Buddhism, according to Ambedkar, was a social and political emancipator. However, the book could be published only after he died but has become a sacred text for the neo-Buddhists. It has become virtually mandatory for every neo-Buddhist to keep the book before them along with the images/statues of Buddha and Ambedkar.[7]

This community of neo-Buddhists has continued to grow ever since. Though most of those who converted to Buddhism in Maharashtra have come from a single caste of ex-untouchables, the Mahars, to which Ambedkar himself belonged, have over the years become sources of inspiration for Dalit movements all over the country. Apart from Maharashtra, we can find a large number of Buddhist Dalits in states like Uttar Pradesh, Andhra Pradesh and even Punjab. As shown in Table 1, the total number of Buddhists has grown by many folds.

Conversion to Buddhism, however, was not a one-time affair for the neo-Buddhists. They have over the years worked hard to consolidate their community. They have evolved their own cultural and symbolic resources and institutions for economic, social and political development of the community.

One of the first things to emerge as a source of symbolic identity among the neo-Buddhists was a literary movement, an independent and autonomous groups of Dalit writers, which has shaped a new intellectual tradition in the region. This movement was started by a group of around 35 to 40 leading Dalit writers, poets, journalists, college teachers, lawyers and others who came from relatively prosperous sections of the community. They put together a platform for articulating the interests of the Dalit masses and their own ideas about the progress and development of their community. They started holding annual conferences under the banner of *Bouddha Sahitya Sammelan* (Buddhist Literary Conference). This was an attempt to evolve a parallel body which could challenge the *Marathi Sahitya Sammelan* (Marathi Literary Conference) dominated by upper castes. Dalit writers portrayed in their writings the glorious historical past of the ex-untouchables, especially Mahars, and also eulogized their past cultural achievements. Some of them have emerged as iconic figures and their writings have been translated into Hindi, English and many other foreign languages (Bhoite and Bhoite, 1977: 60–75).

While the Dalit writers provided an intellectual leadership to the new community and attempted to write an alternative history of the ex-untouchables, several other initiatives helped the community consolidate itself socially and culturally. The new community evolved several structures and organizations with the intention of initiating the process of institutionalization of the neo-Buddhist movement as a separate religious community with its own rituals, institutions and identity. The foremost of these was the Buddhist Society of India (BSI).

Buddhist Society of India (BSI)

As mentioned above, the Buddhist Society of India (*Bhartiya Bauddha Mahasabha*) was set up by B.R. Ambedkar in May 1955, nearly a year before the conversion. After his death the leadership of the BSI was taken over by his son Yashwant Rao Ambedkar (popularly known as *Bhaiyasaheb*). The headquarters of BSI is in Mumbai and its stated mission is to convert entire India into a Buddhist society, a *Prabuddha Bharat* (Buddhist India). It thus promotes Buddhism and has been trying to re-invent Buddhist rituals in its own way. In the year 1968, the BSI organized a *Dhammadaan*, a long procession from the birthplace of Ambedkar with the purpose of spreading the message of Buddhism and building a funerary monument at the *Chaitya Bhoomi.* In the same year, he also organized a national conference on Buddhism in Mumbai and released a book *Bauddha Jeevan Samskar Paath* (Life and Path/Teachings of a Buddhist) where the supreme leader of the faith, Dalai Lama, was also invited. The book gives a detailed set of directives to the Buddhists on how to organize their everyday life and rituals to be followed on various occasions, from life to death. They also bring out an annual calendar of important days for various rituals and festivals. The main focus of the BSI during this period was to develop a code of conduct for the neo-Buddhists for which they started organizing classes and study circles on Dhamma – the Buddhist philosophy and its interpretations by Ambedkar. After the death of Yashwant Rao Ambedkar in 1977, his wife Miratai Ambedkar took over leadership of the organization.

Over the 50 years or so BSI has organized six national conferences on Buddhism. It has also translated the *Bauddha Jeevan Samskar Paath* in Hindi and made it available to the larger population of India. Today, there are many other organizations which promote Buddhist *samskar* (culture), but it is the BSI, which has the largest following and institutional set-up in Maharashtra and outside the state.[8]

Bauddha Jan Panchayat Samiti (BJPS) is another important institution created by the community that has been actively involved with the spread of Buddhist religion in Maharashtra during the post-Ambedkar period. Though it could be seen as an offshoot of the *Mahar Jati Sewa Sangh* (a caste association of the Mahars), set up in 1938 by the Mahar military pensioners, Ambedkar had transformed it in 1941 into an institution for social change for development of the Buddhists. Since then, it became BJPS and has taken the task of spreading Buddhism and Buddhist practices. The BJPS today has almost 750 branches in Mumbai and its surrounding areas. Each branch works as a community organization with a membership ranging between 100 and 500. Its active link with the Buddhist community has made it a potent force working for change in the social consciousness of the Mahar Buddhists. According to Srikant Talwadkar, the General Secretary of the organization,[9] the prime purpose of the organization was to create awareness about education among students and parents; provide financial support and other assistance for the poor students; settle family disputes; eradicate blind faith and superstitions; and raise consciousness among community members (awakening of the society).

The BJPS is particularly active in urban areas. It is one of the most important Buddhist organizations that has helped people accept the new Buddhist traditions, from offering prayers to marriage to any other thing. However, in terms of impact, its domain has largely been in cities like Bombay, Nagpur, Aurangabad, Pune and some areas of the Konkan region of Maharashtra.[10]

Another institution established in this category was Bhikkhu Sangha's United Buddhists Mission, which also acts as the regional centre for World Fellowship of Buddhists. This was established by Bhadant Rahula Bodhi, who works and lives in Mumbai. As he told us:

> Bhiku Sangh is an organization that creates Bauddha Bhikshus (Buddhist priests), who explain the principles of Buddhism to lay people; make them understand the five precepts, ten virtues and teach them how to celebrate Buddhist festivals.
>
> Every Buddhist locality should have a Buddha Vihar and every Buddha Vihar must have a Bauddha Bhikhu. In Mumbai there are more than seven hundred Buddha Vihars. There is a small Buddha Vihara in every locality. There are Budha Vihar in other parts of Maharashtra also but not everywhere ...

Though they claimed to be working for producing Buddhist priests, they seem to be doing much more. As she elaborated on their activities:

> First we started going to different slums and started collecting children to teach them about how to live their life as Buddhists. Every Sunday our vehicle used to go to these places and bring children here at the Sarvodaya Vihar.
>
> Though we follow the syllabus, our main focus is to infuse a sense of confidence among them. We tell them that even by living in a slum or a village, you could become a doctor or a lawyer. This has had a good impact. Today even the children of poor can read and write. Anybody who is ready to struggle can become a big name. Our main purpose is to encourage them to study hard, to change their attitude towards education. We tell them stories, how Babasaheb and others have struggled hard to reach to the top.

They also educated them on the need to be philanthropic. It was important to donate for the society, even if one is poor. '... even one rupee, one fistful of rice, one bread was enough'.

Trailokya Bauddha Mahasangh Sahayak Gan (TBMSG) (Association of the Friends of the Buddhist Order of the Three Worlds) is another important organization that has played an important role in promoting neo-Buddhist movement in Maharashtra. Sanghrakshita, an English Buddhist monk and an admirer of Ambedkar, established it in 1979. Initially active in the Nagpur district alone, its work has spread to the entire state under the name of Trailokya Bauddha Mahasangha (TBM) with its head office in Pune. Like other Buddhist organizations, TBM is also involved with cultivating a distinct cultural and spiritual life among the neo-Buddhists of Maharashtra. They underline the need to understand Buddhism as about building a good and just society. As one of their activists said:

> Buddha was actually a human being like us, and when he practiced his philosophy he just developed himself as the biggest example of today's world as to how one can grow in today's world. All the Buddhist practices emphasize on the value of how we treat another human being. That made me to understand that nobody can be a born Buddhist, it has to be learnt and practiced.[11]

TBM is not only a religious body, it also has a number of social programmes. They established the Bahujan Hitay Trust (majority welfare trust) in the year 1986. It runs hostels for students, crèches, kindergartens, clinics and community libraries; and also organizes lectures, health camps, adult education programmes and cultural programmes. It also has programmes for self-employment and runs thrift societies *(bachat garh)* for women. Most of their social programmes are funded by London-based Karuna Trust. Its work is carried out through community centres of the neo-Buddhists, most (72) of which are located in Maharashtra and another eight in Goa, Uttar Pradesh and Gujarat.

Apart from these relatively big organizations, there are also local level groups that promote Buddhist philosophy and rituals and have been working for building a neo-Buddhist community.

Education and Development

One of the most important slogans given by Ambedkar to India's 'untouchables' was 'to educate, organize and agitate'. Of the three, education came first. Ambedkar's personal mobility to a large extent was made possible by the fact that he was able to study well. As a role model, even today, he inspires his followers for his ability to get top degrees from some of the best educational institutions in the world. The Peoples Education Society (PES) established by Ambedkar in Bombay in 1945 has been working as the champion for this cause and has produced several Buddhist elites by establishing a chain of educational institutions in the state. Before he died in 1956 PES had already set up seven such institutes. PES has continued to be actively pursuing the agenda of building educational infrastructure and has established another 28 institutions during the post-1956 period.

Apart from enabling Dalit students to go for quality higher education, the PES also provides free hostels, scholarships, books and other facilities to the deserving students from the SC background. We visited two of the colleges being run by PES, one each in Mumbai and Pune. In Pune, we visited the Dr Ambedkar College of Arts and Commerce and in Mumbai we went to

Siddhartha College of Arts, Science and Commerce, the oldest college established by the PES.

Besides the general teaching, the college also organized special lectures on Buddhism, celebrated Buddhist festivals and made students participate in Buddha prayer in the morning. Though the college had students from all castes and communities, we were told they have never had any case of caste antagonism of conflict inside the campus.[12]

Siddhartha College of Arts, Science and Commerce was established in Mumbai in 1946 by Ambedkar himself. However, it could get affiliation from the Mumbai University only in 1960. The total number of teaching staff in the college is 85 and the number of students is 3,700. The principal of the college, a non-Buddhist, told us about the contribution that the college has made to educate the poor and marginals:

> We have a majority of students from SC (primarily Buddhist) communities. We do not deny admissions to students from other communities. However, the number of non-SC students seeking admission to this college has always remained very low. The college has several schemes of scholarship for the SC students and it always makes additional effort to uplift these students educationally.

One could also observe the 'education movement' among the neo-Buddhists in smaller towns. In fact, opening and running school has also emerged as an entrepreneurial activity among the educated neo-Buddhists of Maharashtra. For example, for Rajabhau Sarvode, an MLA of the RPI (Athavale) group, running schools has become a lucrative business and he runs several schools in Solapur. This was accepted by Sarvode himself, who said that 'although I prefer Buddhist and SC students, it is also my source of income'. However, for most private schools being run by the neo-Buddhists, funds were a serious problem but they did not wish to give up for political reasons. Most of them are into education with a spirit of dedication. Following Ambedkar, they see 'education' as important source of liberation for the ex-untouchable communities.

This emphasis on education among the neo-Buddhists has made a difference. As is evident from the official data of the 2001 Census, educational status of the neo-Buddhists was significant when compared with the Mangs, a Hindu SC (see Table 2).

Table 2

Educational Levels Attained by Major SCs of Maharashtra (2001)

Name of SC	*Middle School*	*School Graduates (up to class X or XII)*	*College and University Graduates*
All SCs	16.6	20.5	4.8
Neo-Buddhist/Mahars	17.2	22.1	5.3
Bhangis	18.8	13.5	1.6
Mang	14.1	14.2	2.4

Source: http://censusindia.gov.in/Tables_Published/SCST/dh_sc_maha.pdf (27 July 2009).

Mahars also had larger proportion of children in the age group of 5–14 years attending schools (81.5% against 79.3% for all the SC population of the state of Maharashtra).

Religious Mobilizations and Economic Development

While education has been rightly identified as an important area of intervention for infusing confidence and skills for better social, cultural and economic life, the neo-Buddhists have also been investing in alternative ways of economic development and undertaking initiatives to enable individual members of their community to move forward. One of these was to set up a co-operative bank in Pune, the Siddhartha Sahkari Bank Ltd. Vilas Vagh, Chairman explicated the thinking behind setting up the bank:

> ... In the post-liberalized era, reservations or quotas in government jobs is not going to be of much use for the Scheduled Castes. Though education in India is expanding, employment opportunities, particularly in the government sectors, were actually on decline with growing privatization and liberalization. So we, the Buddhist people, dalit people, the Schedule Caste people, thought that we should find our own resources and create jobs by our efforts. We cannot improve our social condition unless we can improve our economic conditions. We have been poor for long but we would not like our next generation to remain so. It was with this in mind that we started our bank. With bank we can provide financial support to the educated and talented young members of our community to start their own businesses, small businesses like purchasing a vehicle for transport business, opening a small shop, etc.[13]

It was in the year 1997 that some fifteen members of the community met in the city of Pune[14] and decided to start a co-operative bank. The bank had completed 12 years when we were doing our fieldwork and appeared to be working smoothly. Being a bank of the 'backward classes', it had been allowed a 50 per cent concession on reserve deposit capital with the condition that it would maintain 50 per cent or above membership from the SCs.

The bank currently has five branches in the Pune city. Except for the Sadashiv Peth branch all other branches are located in areas where the Buddhists/SCs/have large population. Declaring its motto in bold letters as 'a new economic direction for the development of the society', annual report of the bank for the year 2008 proudly claims:

> ... the bank is running with a deposit capital of Rupees four hundred billion and a total reserve capital of Rupees twenty billion. There are six thousand four hundred and twenty two share holders and it has disbursed loans of Rupees two hundred and twenty-eight billions. The running capital of the bank is in 10.41 billion.[15]

Bahujan Hitay Sangh[16] (Association for the Welfare of Majority) is another organization that is working for development of the community through religious mobilizations. It was started in the year 2007 by the senior government officers from the community.[17] All the members on its governing body are Buddhist converts.

> This organization has a *panchsutri karyakram* (five-dimensional programme). First, to propagate Dhamma; second, to education accessible; third,

strengthening economic profile of the Buddhist community; fourth, empowering women; and fifth, building a co-operative movement.

Concluding Remarks

Caste has for long been viewed as an important aspect of India's social order. Notwithstanding significant variations across regions, the institution of caste has shaped structures of opportunity and access across the subcontinent. It has been an important aspect of the Indian culture and religious life, particularly for majority population of the Hindus. The ritual and religious life of a common Hindu has been governed by the logic of caste differences and division. As has been pointed out by students of caste system, the core feature of the system has been the centrality of the ideas of 'pure' and 'impure', their dialectical unity that structured the Hindu mind and produced a hierarchy of social groups marked by a rigid form of social inequality.

Given that the caste hierarchy was legitimized and reproduced within the religious framework of classical Hinduism, those who propagated egalitarian values had to invariably confront the dominant Hindu religious establishment. Though caste system is often presented as an unchanging ancient reality, which began to undergo changes only during the colonial period, a closer look at the pre-colonial history of the subcontinent would present us with several instances of social and religious movements against caste.

Some of the so-called Bhakti poets and saints not only questioned the legitimacy and relevance of Brahminical ritualism but also offered alternative religious value system and modes of social organization (Patwardhan, 1973; Omvedt, 2008). More important, they were not mere cases of individual 'revolts'. Some of them even attracted large masses of people and became popular social movements for change.

It was indeed during the colonial and post-colonial period that the caste system began to be attacked politically and more systematically. Interestingly, even during this period anti-caste movements invariably took and continue to take religious form. However, even as religious movements, they are movements for social change and development, with uplift of the historically excluded and marginalized as their core concern.

B.R. Ambedkar, who has hardly ever professed religion in his public life, chose a religious identity as a route of emancipation for his people. Interestingly, Ambedkar had extensively read and engaged with the writings of Karl Marx. However, for him, alternative to Hinduism and caste could not be communism. It had to be in another religion, which could replace Hinduism and could give an alternative identity and dignity to his people.

Ambedkar spent last months of his life in writing a book on his notion of Buddhism – *Buddha and His Damma*. His followers have been working hard to develop their own rituals and codes of a Buddhist way of life. A lot of work is being done by the local Buddhist organizations towards developing new elite in the community that could articulate an alternative way of life, a religious ideology, and become role model for other members of the community. Apart from running their own schools and other skill imparting educational centres, these organizations also arranged regular sessions to socialize adult members of the community into the Buddhist religion and culture. They recognize the crucial role that education plays in modern times in enabling the younger members of the community to explore new possibilities of living a life of dignity. However, along with building these secular resources, they are also investing in cultural consolidation. They have invested their material resources in constructing new Buddhist *stupas* and places of pilgrimage in different parts of Maharashtra.

Acknowledgements

The research for this paper was undertaken as part of the Religions and Development Research Programme based at the International Development Department, University of Birmingham. The programme was funded by UK Aid from the UK Department for International Development (DFID) for the benefit of developing countries. The views expressed are not necessarily those of DFID.

Notes

1. A good example of this kind of position could be seen in Inkels and Smith (1974) and Hoselitz (1960).
2. The study is based on qualitative data, collected mostly through primary interviews conducted with relevant informants and through 'non-participant' observations. The study focused specifically on the development-related institutions set up by the community of 'followers' and activists. Fieldwork for the paper was spread over a period of around eight months, beginning from September 2008 to April 2009, primarily in three urban centres, viz., Solapur, Pune and Mumbai and some neighbouring centres of neo-Buddhist activism in Maharashtra.
3. See Cohen (1990: 36). It was not appointed to examine the role of caste, but it soon understood that the caste structure of the Indian society would be a central problem.
4. The ruling dynasty of Baroda (the Gayekwars) was itself of a low caste – Marathas, and had already established schools for untouchables and supported the studies of the promising young low caste men (see Jaffrelot, 2004: 27).
5. See Damle (2003). Ambedkar had already started a weekly, *Mooknayak* (Dumb Leader) in the early 1920s. In the later phase he also started *Prabuddha Bharat* and *Janta* (The People).
6. As argued in Ambedkar's book *The Untouchables: Who They Were and Why They Became Untouchables*, first published in 1948.
7. In our field trip to Solapur, we had the opportunity to attend a retirement 'felicitation' ceremony of a Buddhist Branch Manager of Dena Bank. The function started with garlanding the statues of Buddha and Ambedkar and offering flowers on the book *Buddha and His Dhamma*. The functions though were not performed by a *bhikkhu*, a trustworthy man, who owed respect from all, recited all the Buddha prayers and everybody present at the gathering followed him. It was then followed by giving bouquets to the host, and a vegetarian dinner, without alcohol.
8. As told to us by Mr Jagdeesh Gawai, the National Secretary of BSI, Mumbai.
9. Whom we met as the librarian of the Siddhartha College in Mumbai. This is our second meeting with him. We had met him once at the BJP's office during our study of the 'Religion, Politics and Governance' component.
10. All information provided by Mr Talwadkar during the interview.

11. In an interview with Maitrainath in Pune.
12. While celebrating festivals on two occasions, when the turn to say 'Victory to Ambedkar' came, some of the students shouted, 'Victory to Shivaji Maharaj'. Shivaji Maharaj owes respect among the Marathas.
13. In an interview with Vilas Vag, the Chairman of the Siddharth Sahkari Bank, Pune. He is also one of the 15 founder members.
14. The names are: N.K. Jagtap, P.B. Pole, S.T. Gayekwad, Vilas Vagh, A.K. Bhalerao, A.N. Gayekwadm, S.N. Kamble, B. Sarode, S. Kavade, M.S. More, M.B. Vaghmare, U.H. Selar, Nirmala Vanshiv, S.S. Nagnoor and M. Kamble.
15. The annual report of the bank as provided at the head office of the Siddhartha Sahkari Bank.
16. All the information on this organization is based on our discussion with Dr Krishna Handore, Mr V.D. Gaikwad, Mr B.S. Tanhalikar, Dr M.D. Shinde, Dr Sahji Gayekwad and Prof D.S. Kamble. However, most of the information regarding this was shared by Mr Shinde, who himself was an office bearer in the organization. Some of the information was also given by Mr Vilas Vagh, who was appointed as the Chief Editor of the newspaper *Bahujan Maharashtra*, started by the Bahujan Hitay Sangh.
17. Sushant Kamble, Deputy Collector, Solapur was the Chairman of Solapur Branch; Deepak Wagade (Revenue Officer) and Suryakant Tarkade (another officer in some office) were members of its governing body.

References

Ahir, D.C. (1998). *India: 50 Years of Independence: 1947–97; Status, Growth & Development; (6) Buddhism,* Delhi: B.R. Publishing Corporation.

Aloysius, G. (1998). *Religion as Emancipatory Identity: A Buddhist Movement among the Tamils under Colonialism*. New Delhi: New Age International Publishers.

Babb, L.A. (1972). 'The Political Involvement of a Religious Movement: The Satnamis', in J.M. Mahar (ed.), *The Untouchables in Contemporary India*, Arizona: University of Arizona Press.

Baber, Z. (2000). 'Religious Nationalism, Violence and the Hindutva Movement in India', *Dialectical Anthropology*, Volume 25, Number 1, March, pp. 61–76.

Basham, Ardythe (1986). 'Army Service and Social Mobility: The Mahars of the Bombay Presidency in Comparisons with the Bene Israel and Black Americans', Ph.D. Thesis, University of Columbia as quoted in Richard B. White, 'The Mahar Movement's Military Component', *South Asia Graduate Research Journal*, Spring, 1 (1), accessed at http://asnic.utexas.edu/asnic/sagar/spring.1994/ 1/1/TEST_fn.html

Beckford, James (1990). 'The Sociology of Religion and Social Problems', *Sociological Analysis*, 51: 1–14.

Beltz, Johannes (2005). *Mahar, Buddhist and Dalit*. New Delhi: Manohar.

Bhoite, Uttam and Anuradha Bhoite (1977). 'The Dalit Sahitya Movement in Maharashtra: A Sociological Analysis', *Sociological Bulletin*, March, 26 (1).

Bose, Sumantra (2003). *Kashmir: Roots of Conflict, Paths to Peace*. Cambridge, MA: Harvard University Press.

Casanova,José (2001). 'Civil Society and Religion: Retrospective Reflections on Catholicism and Prospective Reflections on Islam', *Social Research*, Winter, 68 (4): 1041–80.

Chauhan, S.K. and S.L. Barua (1974). 'Religion and Social Change: Neo-Vaisnavite Movement in Assam, *Social Action*, January–March, 24 (1).

Cohen, Stephen P. (1990). *The Indian Army: Contribution to the Development of a Nation*. Delhi: Oxford University Press.

Damle, Y.B. (2003). 'Dr B.R. Ambedkar: Critique and Reconstruction', Speaking at the Ambedkar Memorial Lecture at Pune University. Collected during the fieldwork in Pune, also available at (cssh.unipune.ernet.inHistorySociology.... A%206%20Primary%20sources....B.Damle....A%206%20C%202%2003.pdf)

Das, B. (ed.) (1963). *Thus Spoke Ambedkar*. Vol. 4, Bangalore: Ambedkar Sahitya Prakashan.

Drene, Steve (1991). 'Purifying Movements and Syncretic Religious Movements: Religious Changes and the 19th Century Munda and Santhal Peasant Revolts', *Man in India*, 71 (1), special issue.

Dua, Vina (1970). 'Social Organization of the Arya Samaj: A Study of Two Local Arya Centres in Jullundur', *Sociological Bulletin*, 19 (1).

Dube, Saurabh (1993). 'Caste and Sect in Village Life: Satnamis of Chhattisgarh', Occasional Paper 5, Shimla: Indian Institute of Advanced Study.

Gore, M.S. (1993). *The Social Context of an Ideology: Ambedkar's Political and Social Thought*. New Delhi: Sage Publications

Grewal, J.S. (1989). 'Changing Sikh Self-image before Independence', in P.C. Chatterjee (ed.), *Self-images, Identity and Nationalism*, Shimla: Indian Institute of Advanced Study, pp. 187–200.

Gupta, Dipankar (1982). *Nativism in a Metropolis-Shiv Sena Movement in Bombay*. Delhi: Manohar.

Guru, Gopal and Anuradha Chakravarty (2005). 'Who are the Country's Poor? Social Movement Politics and Dalit Poverty', in Raka Ray and Mary F. Katzenstein (eds), *Social Movements in India: Poverty, Power and Politics*, New Delhi: Oxford University Press.

Hansen, T.B. (1999). 'The Vernacularisation of Hindutva: The BJP and Shiv Sena in Rural Maharashtra', *Contributions to Indian Sociology*, 30 (2).

Hardgrave, Robert (1969). *The Nadars of Tamilnad*. Berkley: University of California Press.

Hoselitz, Bert F. (1960). *Sociological Aspects of Economic Growth*. Chicago: The Free Press.

Haynes, Jeff (1995). 'Religion, Fundamentalism and Ethnicity: A Global Perspective', United Nations Research Institute for Social Development Discussion Paper 65, May 2.

Inkles, A. and D.H. Smith (1974). *Becoming Modern*. Cambridge, MA: Harvard University Press.

Jaffrelot, Christophe (2004). *Dr Ambedkar and Untouchability: Analysing and Fighting Caste*. New Delhi: Orient Longman.

—— (2009). 'Dr Ambedkar's Strategies against Untouchability and the Caste System', Working Paper, New Delhi: Indian Institute of Dalit Studies.

—— (1996). *The Hin du Nationalist Movement in India*. New Delhi: Oxford University Press.

Jones, Kenneth W. (1979). 'Social Change and Religious Movements in Nineteenth Century Punjab', in M.S.A. Rao (ed.), *Social Movements in India*, Vol. II, New Delhi: Manohar.

Joshi, Barbara R. (1977). 'The Buddhist Movement of Western Uttar Pradesh', Mimeographed Paper, March 27.

—— (ed.) (1986). *Untouchable! Voices of the Dalit Liberation Movement*. London: Zed Books.

Juergensmeyer, M. (1979). *Religion as Social Vision: The Movement against Untouchability in 20th Century Punjab*. Berkeley: University of California Press.

—— (1988). *Religious Rebels in the Punjab: The Social Vision of Untouchables*. Delhi: Ajanta Publications.

Kanungo, Pralay (2002). *RSS's Tryst with Politics: From Hedgewar to Sudarshan*. Delhi: Manohar.

Katju, Manjari (2003). *Vishva Hindu Parishad and Indian Politics*. New Delhi: Orient Longman.

Keer, D. (1964). *Dr Ambedkar: Life and Mission*. Bombay: Popular Prakashan.

Ludden, David (ed.) (1996). *Making India Hindu: Religion, Community and the Politics of Democracy in India*. New Delhi: Oxford University Press.

Mahana, P.P. (ed.) (1985). *Census of India 1981 Series 12,* Maharashtra; *Household Population by Religion of Head of Household*, Bombay, Government Central Press as quoted in Jaffrelot (2005).

Oberoi, H. (1994). *The Construction of Religious Boundaries: Culture, Identity and Diversity in the Sikh Tradition.* Delhi: Oxford University Press.

Oddie, G.A. (ed.) (1975). *Religion in South Asia: Religious Conversion and Revival Movements in South Asia in Medieval and Modern Times*. New Delhi: Manohar.

Omvedt, Gail (1976). *Cultural Revolt in a Colonial Society: The Non-Brahmin Movement in Western India – 1873 to 1930*. Bombay: Scientific Socialist Education Trust.

—— (2004). *Buddhism in India: Challenging Brahmanism and Caste*. New Delhi: Sage.

—— (2008). *Seeking Begumpura: The Social Vision of Anticaste Intellectuals*. New Delhi: Navayana.

Pandian, M.S.S. (1996). 'Towards National-Popular: Notes on Self-Respecters Tamil', *Economic and Political Weekly*, 31 (50).

Patwardhan, Sunanda (1973). *Change among India's Harijans*. Delhi: Orient Longman.

Sangharakshata (1986), *Ambedkar and Buddhism,* Glasgow: Windhorse Publications.

Sarkar, Tanika (1999). 'Pragmatics of the Hindu Right: Politics of Women's Organizations', *Economic and Political Weekly*, 31 July.

Singh, Gurharpal (2000). *Ethnic Conflict in India: A Case Study of Punjab.* Basingstoke: Macmillan Press.

Smith, Christian (1996). 'Correcting a Curious Neglect, or Bringing Religion Back In', in Smith (ed.), *Disruptive Religion: The Force of Faith in Social-Movement Activism*, London: Routledge Paperback.

Wilkinson, T.S. and M.M. Thomas (eds) (1972). *Ambedkar and the Neo-Buddhist Movement*. Madras: Christian Literary Society.

Zavos, John (2000). *The Emergence of Hindu Nationalism*. New Delhi: Oxford University Press.

Zelliot, Eleanor (1972). 'Gandhi and Ambedkar', in J.M. Mahar (ed.), *The Untouchable in Contemporary India*, Tuscon: The University of Arizona Press.

—— (1977). 'The Psychological Dimension of the Buddhist Movement in India', in G.A. Oddie (ed.), *Religion in South Asia: Religious Conversion and Revival Movements in South Asia in Medieval and Modern Times*, London: Curzon Press.

—— (1994). *From Untouchable to Dalit: Essays on the Ambedkar Movement*. New Delhi: Manohar Publications.

9

Kalpathy Heritage Village

Sacred and Modern

Susan Visvanathan

Palghat or Pallakad, as the Malayalis call it, is a town which is associated with activities like music, dance, drama and ayurveda. It is across the blue line of hills that separates it from Coimbatore. And, the village of Kalpathy is associated with heaven itself. The popular saying goes, 'Bathe in its river, and you will go to heaven.' The temples of Kalpathy are famous for its *rath* (car or chariot) festivals. The guide books describe it as a melting point for all the people of Kerala during the period of the 'Rath Uttsavam' or temple car festival. Kalpathy is a Brahmin enclave. The Brahmins are Tamil Brahmins. They are said to have arrived 600 years ago. To avert a famine and illness which was raging among his people, the Pallakad Rajav (king) asked his astrologers what he should do. They told him to build a temple. But then, the Rajav could not work with his Namboodri priests, so he invited the Tamil Brahmins, who came from Mayavaram near Tanjavore. Eighteen villages were set up in Pallakad, and the temples were identical with those of Tamil Nadu, except that the *gopuram* of the Tamil temples is missing. In these temples the Devan is important, while in Kerala it is the Devi who is usually emphasized.

A woman from Kalpathy, called Lakshmi Ammal, went to Varanasi (Benaras) on pilgrimage and brought a stone, the original stone, dedicated here in the Kalpathy Viswanatha Swamy Temple. The Kalpathy village is now a heritage site. For residents like Lakshmi Narayan, Kalpathy is their home, associated with the temples and the tradition of music. 'Veda and music are like railway tracks,' he says, running parallel to each other. He mentions Challakudi Narayan, Mridunga Subbier and Pallakad Mani Iyer. I have already visited the residence of the kinsman of Pallakad Mani Iyer. That gentleman has a large portrait in his house of the famous *mridangam* player, and when I ask him the history of the community, he tells me that he has a website! All the details on the website provide the description of Kalpathy, its history and its environs, including the five temples, for every ward has its own temple, and also the river which forms the boundary of the village. So very early, I have found my local historian.

Kalpathy temples are a tourist destination, for their beauty as well as their cultural vitality. In November, the inner lanes of Kalpathy become packed with residents, visitors and tourists, all of whom are excited by the rituals and the market that springs up for the *rath* festivals. The huge *raths* lie in the street otherwise, testimony to the grandness of ritual. Kalpathy consists of a community of Brahmins who are now Malayalis by virtue of their residence, but their original Tamil Brahmin identity is well asserted. They were once agriculturists, but the enclave is now associated with *pathshalla* or teaching work, specially of accountancy, Vedas, literature, music and science. Families have been associated with clerical work as much as with more powerful roles in administration. Residents believe in caste, for that is their heritage and capital, but they do not believe in communalism. Caste, they say, is the classification of actions and duties. They are impoverished by modernism, and yet the poor Brahmin is the icon of hard work and integrity. How do they cope? One of the residents, Ram Narain tells me, 'In Kali Yuga, one must be silent and observe.' He also tells that Hinduism is about meditation, trance, vision, knowledge and the inner voice. May be this is why music is such a strong part of the vocabulary of the young and the old in Kalpathy. In the evening, one can hear singing coming from almost every street, and many young children can be seen carrying violins. For Ram Narain's son, there are four Gods who must be worshipped: they are the parents, the village deity, the family deity and the *ishta devta* (the God of one's choice).

This gentle world was recently disrupted by the offer of 'heritage site' by the state government, but the residents say that it was not an offer, it was imposed on them without warning. Lakshmi Narayan says it is the 'culture of the people' which is the heritage, and any insensitive display of political power, which does not take community representatives into consultation, will always create problems for residents. As this is a highly literate and informed community, many of whom are bureaucrats, clerks and administrative heads, Eldersveld, Jagannadham and Barnabas write in their pioneering classic, *The Citizen and the Administrator in a Developing Democracy*: 'The greatest pockets of actual, potential, discontent or alienation seem to be in certain social categories of the urban populace and among residents in the large villages which are undergoing a modernization process. This is in keeping with an index they have developed which is the relation between high confidence of the community and low support to policies which are against their interest' (Eldersveld et al., 1968: 52).

Roads in Kalpathy were dug up, the open sewage system which was previously the community responsibility, was cemented up, so that the blockages and general inconvenience are now frequent, and cannot be cleared. The government had offered the families three lakhs of rupees as renovation money, but then said they would have to move out, to accommodate tourists. 'Who would agree to that?' Before the heritage papers could be cleared in official quarters, people started selling their houses to builders. So, Kalpathy will lose its quaintness, and accommodate outsiders in a volume that the water and sewage capacities cannot handle. So much of urban planning is done without consulting the residents, who are completely ignored as if they have no will or intelligence, that it leaves the sociologist quite baffled. A heritage site should be protected and conserved, not redone in an untidy slipshod manner with crumbling cement over original granite. There was no interaction between the tourist department and the electricity department, and between the tourist department and the water department. For the inhabitants of Kalpathy, tourism and modernism have meant the suggestion by the state government that their houses be mortgaged for 'improvement' when they love their traditional homes, and then given over to the state for use as tourist homes in four or five years! This is so absurd a suggestion that people are left aghast at the idea of a heritage site.

A.R. Venkatachalapathy quotes from a fragment from Sangam Literature, Purananuru 243:

> 'To think of the past
> gives much grief.'

He writes that reminiscences of those days are usually about how Brahmins spent their time listening to Ramayanan, Maharbharatham, Bhagavatham and the Puranams, 'when women's education was uncommon, when villagers were resourceful stout hearted and well built,' when women were controlled by their in-laws, when Tamil numerals were in use, when transport was not freely available, when snacks such as bread or biscuits were not available (Venkatachalapathy, 2009: 40, 41). The significance of 'engal oor', he says, cannot be minimized. 'Those days' and 'these days' are often contrasted, and these terms, *antha kalam* and *intha kalam* are on the lips of the diaspora Tamils. The concepts of home, native place, village, town, city, people of the town, region, hometown all interchange according to the context. The idea of *engal oor* according to him is of a place which is spatially and geographically present, but actually only in memory, for everything has in reality changed. People left their *oor* in search of work, and then settled down in other towns and cities to earn. What remained was like a sediment, but according to literary writers who documented this, such as Kalki, it was more like a passion, not merely nostalgia (ibid.: 42, 43).

'Visits to the *oor* were often limited to making annual trips for temple festivals, to meet ageing parents, sending wives for childbirth or packing off bored children during annual school vacation. The more they were caught in the vortex of urban living, the more accentuated was the feeling of losing their oor and its sense of belonging. In a way it was a double loss, not only was the oor lost because of migration, but also the oor in itself was lost due to social transformation which tended to stare at them starkly during their increasingly infrequent visits' (ibid.: 43).

In Ram Narain's youth, spatial maps were a symbol of the close interaction between neighbours for there was a continuity between the houses. On festival days, the plantain leaves for community feasting would be spread in a single line, and every one would eat together.

The car festival is a replica of rituals performed in the original hamlet in Tanjavore. All the Gods are celebrated in Kalpathy. There are no boundaries between castes in the Rath Uttsavam. Muslims and Christians have been traditionally present as shopkeepers. The music festival is a national festival which brings thousands into Kalpathy. It is known as Kalpathy Sangeetha Uttsavam.

I was in Kalpathy on 14 April 2007. It was Tamil New Year. In Kalpathy, the sense of jubilation was evident in the evening. Because of the temples in every street, and the row of shops near the Siva-Parvati temple, there was a sense of bustling joy. The houses are arranged in this 'grammam' or village in a concentration, a nucleated village, as in Mylapore, or in any traditional Tamil town with a temple. Each room leads to another, and in the evenings, the occupants sit on the ledge, or even on the road.

The afternoons are very hot. This year the temperature is unusual, but it also rained quite miraculously. Kalpathy river rushes along at the edge of the *agraharam*, as the settlement of Brahmins is called. From 4 a.m. onwards, bathers arrive, wash their clothes on the steps, have their baths, and then with towels tied on their head, the women make an obeisance at the Bhagyawathi temple. There are two temples side by side on the edge of the river, one to Bhagyavathi, the patron Goddess of Kerala, and the other to that constant visitor who never discriminates, Krishna.

I ask Lakshmi Narayan, and his wife, who is the elected councillor for Kalpathy, whether there is a Pallakad Rajav anymore; they reply that 'Vamsham ondu, Rajav Illa!' (There is a lineage, but no king).

15th April is Vishu, the Malayalam New Year, and the culmination of the a harvest. There is an honouring of fruits and leaves and flowers. The Malayalis have been bursting crackers continuously since early morning. They bathe at the crack of dawn, and go to the temple wearing new clothes, flowers in their hair and are generally jubilant and adorned.

K.N. Lakshmi Narayan, the local historian, believes that the downfall of the Vijaya Nagar empire was accompanied by North Indian invasion, a Muslim invasion which caused the Tanjore Brahmins to migrate. 'The Pallakad Rajav was pleased to see them for this reason, since he (according to the stories), a royal family member, had a liaison with a tribal woman, therefore, the Namboodiris refused to serve in the temple. The migrants from Mayavaram served in their place.' Since they were well versed in the Vedic tradition, including mathematics and the scriptural arts, they were welcomed.

Krishnan, an eminent lawyer, living in Ooty (whose son practises in the Supreme Court visits the Kalpathy Viswam Temple for thanksgiving when a son is born), says that the Tamil Brahmins who came from Mayavaram were 'hydraulic victims'. The drought had made them leave their natal territories, and being informed in the Vedas, they were welcomed by the king. 'Legend has it that when crossing Tamil Country they were given Kanji (Gruel), the border now known as Kanjikode. This suggests they were penniless refugees ... Can these agraharams be settlement of refugees who were unsettled in their native land or was it a planned migration ... How did they bring masons and carpenters to duplicate their villages when only means of transport must have been bullock cart?' (Krishnan, 2010: 58, 59). The Pallakad Brahmins became well known for the Tamil they evolved with a mixture of Malyalam words, for their cuisine, and for their contribution to society in every sphere, particularly in government, literature and music. 'Though they showed their remarkable brilliance in many fields, it was carnatic music in which they excelled. Chambai Vaidhiyananthа Bhagawathat, Kalpathy Ramanathan, Pallakkad Mani Iyer, Mridhingam Raghu, K.V. Narayana Swami to mention a few. Kalpathy has its own Thiagaraja Sabha and it is for over a hundred years conducting Music Festival ... It was said even if you throw an 'Ammi' in Kalpathy River (grinding stone) it will float, if you kick a boy, he will sing. This gives an idea of their love for swimming and music' (ibid.: 60). They were literateurs, and more than sufficient readers. 'Tamil magazines Kalki and Ananda Viketan sold more copies in Palakkad than in Coimbatore. Strangely, only women took to reading Kalki and Ananda Viketan. There was not even an agent for Malayala Manorama, which has a Pallakkad edition now. Hardly any one knew to write Tamil, but almost all knew to read. They wrote Tamil letters in Malayalam script. Kalpathy has its own Book Publisher R.S. Vathiyar and Sons who are also book distributors' (ibid.).

Since this is a heritage village there are tourist potentialities that include ritual, music, astrology, ayurveda, etc.

The music festival in Kalpathy was started in 1986. Gigi Thompson was the Collector, and he helped in setting it up. Both Narayan and Thompson collected money. Gigi Thompson was the chairman of the first committee and T.V.S. Sundaram was the co-ordinator. Later, the government, then the Tourism Promotion Board, got involved.

21 May 2008

Before one's eyes the landscape changes. Everywhere modernization brings its own story. It effaces the past without a murmur, or so it seems, the old changes, and gives way to the new. The new is sometimes very brash. In New Kalpathy, the old houses in the hamlet are being demolished and new cement and florid paint comes in its stead. The street changes its face from month to month. Some people say, explaining the rapid transformation, 'Only Old Kalpathy is a heritage sight.' Old shops are replaced by new ones. The old people in the agraharam, sit outside their porches, looking like the ancient scribes, recording the past in memory. The ancient snake circle near the river has gone. Ancient stones under the peepal tree, representing Shiva, Shakti, faceless Gods and Goddesses as well, snakes and flat stones, are now replaced with a brand new Ganesha. Only three stones remain of the many in the circle, Shiva, Shakti and one cobra.

The street is quiet during the day. No one comes out. The agraharam is silent, like a ghost town. In the evening, visitors to the temples begin filling the streets, standing at the rims of the temples, worshipping the Gods. The shopkeepers are well-stocked traditional grocers. They now keep eggs along with bakery bread. In Kalpathy, traditionally, no one could keep non-vegetarian foods. The bakery sells excellent fresh bread. The most popular place for food is the small shop in the middle of the agraharam, *Easwarya,* where breakfast and 'tiffin' which means savouries at tea time, are served.

An old woman sitting in the enclosed verandah of her house smiles toothlessly at me. I stop to talk to her. She reminds me now of Michael Ignatieff's reminiscence of King Lear:

'How dost, my boy? Art cold?
I am cold myself
Where is this straw, my fellow?
The art of our necessities is strange,
That can make vile things precious.' (Shakespeare cited in Ignatieff, 1994: 41)

'Has your fever gone?', the old lady asks me.

I smile, and say, 'Yes,' knowing she has mistaken me for someone else.

'And are you well? (Sukam anno?)', I ask her.

'What well being can I have at this age?' she says, 'I just exist. Whatever comfort I have (sukam) is in my mind. What about you?' she says to me.

'Shantam Aa.' (I am in peace.)

'So how many days?'

'Just today and tomorrow.'

We part, with me saying, 'I'm happy to have met you.' Diaspora communities recognize the stranger not as alien but as someone familiar, someone passing by someone who is recognized as different. This difference is celebrated rather than derided. Ghettoization does not necessarily in these circumstances create the stranger as someone to be wary of, or someone to keep at a distance. Rather, the person is integrated in by virtue of his or her difference. He or she however has the status of a passer-by. In Britain, the foreigner is often brought into society by virtue of his/her ability to contribute to such a society. In such cases new emigrants are inducted into time share arrangements, where the care of old people is made a voluntary engagement in return for benefits such as spending time with an older inhabitant and interacting with them for purposes of being part of a community. Posting a letter may receive the gift of repartee and joking, a meal, a language skill interaction, etc. Taking a house guest might mean an enhancement of these in various ways, of which currency exchange is only one aspect.

Globalization has led to new facets of land and capital transactions. The sale of land while regulated has yet resulted in advertising for upmarket flatted housing, since Pallakad during the first decade of the 21st century has experienced a promise of boom economy with the possible coming of a railways coach factory. Zygmunt Bauman writes:

> Where family and communal businesses were once able and willing to absorb, employ and support all newly born humans, and at most times secure their survival, the surrender to global pressures and the laying of their own territory open to the unfettered circulation of capital and commodities made them unviable. Only now do the newcomers to the company of moderns experience that separation of business from household which the pioneers of modernity went through hundreds of years ago, with all its attendant social upheavals and human misery but also with the luxury of global solutions to locally produced problems – an abundance of 'empty' and 'no man's lands' that could easily be used to deposit the surplus population no longer absorbed by the economy emancipated from familial and no communal constraints: a luxury not available to the latecomers. (2004: 72)

There is great poverty in some of these traditional houses. Many are derelict and many are being rebuilt in modern fashion, with cement and kaleidoscopic paint. Love for tradition and love for the past are not abstractions in the face of rapid change of the face of the street in New Kalpathy. Ground coffee, a valued commodity, in this neighbourhood, for instance, is sold by Coffee Day – a modern enterprise.

I spoke to the grand old man Dikshitar. He is the best known and most respected of the Vidvans or scholars of Kalpathy. He has milky blue eyes, a top knot and diamonds in his ears. He must be 80 and more.

'I wish to write a book on Kalpathy.'

He points to the ledge, adjacent to him, beckoning me to sit.

'What about?'

'It's history. Can I speak with you?'

'You need to talk to old people who know. It's an old history that goes back and back.' He makes whorls with his hands, indicating spirals.

'I'm a sociologist – we record, we inscribe. Everything is changing very fast, so we must describe it. Whatever you tell me, wish to tell me I will write it down.'

'I have no time,' Dikshitar say.

I take his leave and go away. He is a very great scholar, and when we see each other everyday, we wave to one another.

I ask the priest who has come to circumambulate the peepal tree near the Kalpathy river where the snake circle was, and he says, 'All gone, only three left.' The guard at River View apartments, where I stay, tells me that an insane man came and broke the ringed lamp as well as the stones. He crushed the stones with a heavy stone. He damaged the ancient stones at the Shiva temple as well.

The treasurer of the block of flats adjoining the river Kalpathy says that Indra Nooyi, Pepsi Cola chief is a Kalpathi girl and has donated to the making of a *gyanamandiram* or meditation chamber. Nooyi's grandfather, Justice Narayanan was from Kalpathy, so her mother gave three lakhs and a plaque which is inscribed in his name.

K.N. Lakshmi Narayan runs a kiosk for telephones, and a courier service, and is the local historian, with a website, kalpathyviswam. com. He is on the managing committee of the music festival in Kalpathy, which is an annual feature, taking place during the *ter* or car festival in November, when the village becomes the centre of attraction for pilgrims and tourists. Lakshmi Narayan:

> For the last two years, we have had only Carnatic Music, no dance performances, though in the early years, we did have dance as well. As you know, dance and music are temple arts. The Car Festival is not yet a National Festival. Puri, Jagannath Temple has achieved national festival status, so has Trichur Guruvayoor. They are conducted on a larger scale. Here it is smaller, but I would say, three lakhs visit in ten days. The decorated cars of our temples come together. The decoration is done with paper pulp, The main car is pushed by an elephant. The people put all their strength, but the elephant is necessary for the car is too big.

The festival is associated with commercial activity, and this meets the needs of the villages. For four or five centuries, Tamil Nadu merchants have been coming with cloth, vessels, pulses and return with spices. Now, the marketing system has changed, everything is available everywhere. So, the festival provides a market which provides glittering things, which the villagers look forward to: ribbons, vessels, women's items like bangles and such. The Ter festival (rath or car) takes place on the last ten days of the Tamil month of Epishi. The rituals echo the ones which were typical of Mayavaram, the original place from which the Kalpathy residents come from. Some people continue to visit, for every house has a kuladevam, and since rituals to the kuladevam continue, they do return to villages in Tamil Nadu. Some have property there, some have marriage relations. But this is an individual relationship with Tanjore, one cannot generalize.

Regarding the music festival, Lakshmi Narayan says that committees are formed in June and July. Shamianas are constructed in Chatapura. Auditorium named after Pallakad Mani Iyer is a little away from the village. The music festival is a costly business, musicians are invited, but the cost is heavy, and the committee pays Rs 8–10 lakhs for the purpose of the ten-day festival.

Lakshmi Narayan escorts me to the Viswanatha Temple. I have never been inside before. He takes me around, where tourists and non-Hindus may go. 'You have to enter a valley.' We go down a flight of steps. Everything is in a process of dismantling and construction. The Kumbha Abhishekam has just been completed. The thatched shamiana (pandal or tent) has been dismantled, so have the makeshift altars built for the purpose. Huge stainless steel pillars have come up, light pink tiles roof the building, ornate woodwork with the images of Gods and devotees are to be seen. 'A lot of work remains to be done', Lakshmi Narayan tells me. 'We have spent one crore rupees. I'm not a modernist, so I feel a sense of loss that old carvings have been substituted by new ones.' Irschick (1994) has an interesting discussion on temple renovation, and the inability of Brahmins to engage in farming, while hiring others to work on their lands.

The inhabitants of Kalpathy believe in change and transformation, Lakshmi Narayan is happy and proud of the new temple, and his website (kalviviswam. org/kalpathy) says that a temple according to the Shastras must be renovated every twelve years. It is more than twenty-five years since it was improved upon. There are some old carvings, the wood piled in the corner, there are ancient stone carvings of snakes and Gods under a stone pillar. They may be reintegrated later. The carpenters are at work. The temple priests are inside tending to devotees.

Interestingly, in Kalpathy, the residents knock down their houses, and watch neighbours doing the same. One man sitting outside his house fanning himself in the hot still evening, the sky still fiercely blue and cloudless, laughed when I said to him, 'I heard this settlement is 700 years old.'

'Is that what they told you?'

Then very reasonably, he said, 'May be there were people who lived here seven hundred years ago. These houses are nor more than 150 years old, in fact probably renovated much later, and very frequently. Old houses were made of mud, the living conditions were very bad, there was no air or light, they were like guhas or caves.' He likes the new houses, say they are convenient, and have light and air.

A. Satish, in his article on the website newindpress.com (4 April 2008), writes of *Heritage Village Turning Nightmare for Residents:* 'The restriction imposed on the repairs and alterations of the houses in Kalpathy agraharam as part of it being declared a heritage site was turning out to be a bane for the residents.' No one in the heritage village can construct or modify without a go ahead from the municipality in consultation with the Art and Heritage Commission in Thiruvanathapuram. However, the subsidy of 25 per cent offered by the tourism department will be made available only to those who 'are providing homestays'.

Clearly, the report says, the inhabitants of Kalpathy who find maintenance of their traditional homes expensive are disturbed by their applications for renovation lying for long periods in municipality offices.

Kerala now depends on tourism as a non-polluting industry. Much of the beauty of the natural landscape has depended on craft, agriculture, fishing, and now information technology, functioning from laboratories. Heritage sites need protection, but so do inhabitants. My own data, as well as Satish's show that the large amounts of money which have been spent on Kalpathy are not seen as helping the villagers. It is time that inhabitants are taken on as representatives of government committees and have a say collectively about what their future is.

27 June 2009

The local historian Lakshmi Narayan has promised to take me inside the Kalpathy Viswanath Swamy Temple, since as a Syrian Christian I cannot access its interiors without permission. He says that I can circle the interior of the temple, like tourists do, but not present myself before the sanctum, since that is not permitted. While we are waiting for him to get ready, we go inside the temple precincts which has a shopping area. This, as we have been told, is open to anyone. Inside, there are some residences on either side of the temple ('squatters!' according to the trustee, since that is where the Tamil and Malyali divide becomes most obvious), a tailor's shop and another which sells holy pictures, oil and beads.

Rajan Narayanan, a priest doing rituals for the dead, says that Lakshmi Ammal, a widow had returned from Benares, given coins to the temple and left the stone there. The stone is a lingam, it is about six feet tall. It had inscriptions but now these are gone. ('We have photographs of the inscriptions', a temple spokesman says comfortingly. Since Kerala has a wood tradition, it is possible that the medieval script was not seen as significant by the asari who polished the stone. On the other hand, it could be that the inscription on the stone and the oral history clash. This would be for epigraphists to find out.) Kalpathy websites discuss the legends pertaining to the origins of the temple and its historical dating. Itty Komban Achen, the Pallakad king, was trustee to the widow Lakshmi Ammal's wishes that a temple should be built as a memorial of her visit to Benaras.

Kalpathy is the place where Lakshmi Ammal established the lingam brought from Benaras, and so it is called the Benaras of the South, for those who cannot take ashes to Benaras, may visit Kalpathy Viswanath Swamy Temple for the mortuary ceremonies of their kinfolk. The connection with Benaras continues, and Lakshmi Narayan tells us that in Viswanath Swamy Temple in Benaras, every evening rituals and songs support the Tamil pilgrims under the umbrella of the Shankaracharya of Kanchi.

We walk around the renovated Kalpathy temple. Lakshmi Narayan is very proud of the changes, and old ladies coming for evening worship, congratulate him on the continuous work of modernization. Every twelve years it is renovated (or should be), according to him. Only one rafter of the old temple has been incorporated into the new structure. The rest have been built back into the wooden portals of a building, like a shed, with an aluminium roof, at the rear courtyard. They are pretty wood carvings with simple motifs of flowers. Surrounding this, facing the river, is a small sacred garden which is kept scrupulously clean by the old attendant. The snake stones are venerated here.

Lakshmi Narayan tells me that Kalpathy is a convenient ritual site for many families in Kerala, to carry out their *agamams* or funerary rituals. The priests are called Shivacharyas and are trained in the *agamams*. Originally, they were from Mayavaram, but now some come from Coimbatore. They must be trained in the scriptures, and also recognized or accepted by the serving priests. The Smartha Iyers, who live in Kalpathy, are not equipped to deal with mortuary rituals being householders. However, they are very learned in scriptures, and there are some very well-known Dikshitar families.

Nicholas B. Dirks (2008: 293) writes, ‘Although there is a general consensus that caste is a retrograde force, there is also widespread acceptance of the social fact that caste is the natural focus of political mobilization and economic redistribution, as well as the somewhat illicit marker of cultural identity and traditional pleasure. Indeed, caste identification is a form of pleasure that negotiates the contradictory faultlines between embarrassment in the face of colonial criticism and nostalgia over the comforts of home’.

We walk towards the river. It is terribly stagnant, in spite of the myth surrounding it, that to bathe in Kalpathy is to know heaven. The river is blocked, silted up, crammed with weeds and sludge and water hyacinths. Who will clean the river? Sand mining is creating a block. Further up, there are three small dams which further obstruct the river’s flow. About the sand miners, Lakshmi Narayan only says, ‘One cannot say anything! That is how they make a living.’ I read later in the newspapers that there have been death threats to those who obstruct the miners. Akber Ayub in his web column has written an interesting account, ‘Swansong of the Nila’ which refers to Kalpathy village with regard to the problem of a dying river. The Hindu webpage, under the title ‘Alternatives to Riversand’ describes the escalating costs of construction and the dying of the Bharatapuzha of which Nila is one tributary (21 April 2007). Further up, garbage blows into the river. After the election, no one has come forward to help with river maintenance. This is unlike Rajasthan, where water debates are always foregrounded.

29 June 2009

I have been buying needles, shampoo and other things from one of those ubiquitous stores in Kerala which are called fancy stores. They have everything from soap and washing powder to artificial jewellery, buttons and baubles and toys. The owner is a man called Sethu Madhavan who worked in Pallakad station for decades. It is a success story that Kerala knows so well, for he came to Pallakad for work, bought a house and settled down. His son-in-law, Achutanandan Prasad, is an accountant with an eye for antiques. The house is beautifully embellished with old things, each lovingly carved from wood, bought from demolished Kalpathy houses, from shops and stores in New Bazaar. Prasad used to come to bathe in Kalpathy river when he was a boy, and studied in the local school. Each of the objects he has bought costs a great deal. Sethu Madhavan is extremely proud of his new house, constructed with tiled roofs, marble floor and his son-in-law's good taste in antiques. They have been written about in a well-known Malayalam magazine.

Prasad, the antique collector, says that the Brahmins are going through a decline which happens to many communities during historical periods. The subject of the 'poor Brahmin' is of great interest to the community. They have lost traditional occupations and skills, and have become auto-drivers, shopkeepers and labourers.

Lakshmi Narayan tells me that his father was a Sanskrit scholar who had the ability to cross over and weave and plait scriptural texts. 'Jedda' they used to call him. Opposite his house, where now the owner has built a pretty cottage with a charming garden, which has a coniferous tree, there was once a printing press which published Sanskrit works. He says, 'Some people in the gramam may still have copies. In the 1920s, it shut down for lack of buyers and a new press opened. They print texts, but not necessarily Sanskrit. When people say 'Heritage Village' today it is limited to taking some foreigners for a walk around Kalpathy. Preservation of culture is not limited to buildings, it is not only about buildings it is about Vedic culture, about music, mathematics and scriptural knowledge, that is, Sanskrit.'

The Tamil Brahmins in Kalpathy remain migrants in Kerala, though they have been here for centuries. Mayavaram, or Mayiladathura remain extolled, though not many people may visit the ancestral *oor*, which is a well-known site for cultural and ritual activities existing in Tamil Nadu since the Chola period. The temple is 650 years old, and by the records in the memory of residents, it is the woman Ammal (or Lakshmi Ammal) who established the stone, by decree of the king, so that Kalpathy and the river became embodiments of Shiva-Shakti of Benaras Viswanath Swami and the Ganges respectively. Achutanandan Prasad says a dip in Kalpathy is worth half of a dip in Benaras. No one is ready however to take any action over the increasingly polluted Kalpathy river. Prasad says, 'It cannot be done by a single individual.' The Kalpathy river is dependent on the Mallampuzha dam for its rapid flow. During the summer months, water is diverted from the dam to the town for drinking purposes, so the farmers and the pilgrims have to manage with the minimal flow, silted trees growing in the middle on garbage islands, and stagnation. In a later part of this paper, I will discuss the significance of the Mallampuzha dam for Pallakad and its inhabitants.

People still come from far to bathe in the Kalpathy river, and women can be seen carrying their buckets of washing in the early morning, and jumping into the river with their children and women friends, long hair washed in the river. Cows are washed in the afternoon. The men come after a day's work, as do boys in the evening.

The transformation of a Brahmin *agraharam* into a modern house is very visible in the recent past. Mala, a trained homeopath, who has been living in the same house for 26 years, says that they have not renovated their home, because one has to go to Thiruvanthapuram to get the papers to do this. She looks around, where by the day, houses are being demolished and rebuilt. Most of new Kalpathy has become vividly commercial, there is a herbal beauty shop, an ayurveda clinic, two telephone and internet shops, a private milk depot, a food shop (canteen and caterers), an old age home and office. It then merges with the temple complex, and the shopping arena which has a series of grocers' shops very well stocked with provisions, a tailors shop, a fancy store for women and children, a kitchen wares store, a cycle repairs shop, and a Milma or government milk depot, a bakery and three eateries for tourists and pilgrims. There are two pickle stores, one of them is run by two ladies who are local residents, and sell fried savouries in packets along with pickles and *appalams* or *pappads*. There are also coir and broom dealers, a carpenter's shop, a publishing house and a clothes store, and of course well-stocked medical stores. Fruit and flower merchants have push carts stationed in front of the temple. There are also two shops selling betel leaf, fruit, lemon drinks and eggs. The last is a representation of changing times, since eggs and non-vegetarian food were traditionally not to be found in Kalpathy. However, the former residents are selling their homes to others, and new mosaics of residence and food customs are now to be found. Ezhavas and Nairs, traditionally meat eating, are now found serving the Brahmins in their homes, and one of them laughed and said, 'In the flats if the tenant wants to eat and cook meat, the Board cannot say anything.' However, while diaspora Tamils may indeed eat eggs, there is a circular taken out, if meat or fish are cooked, saying that this is strictly forbidden. Those who eat meat say that the rule is for Kalpathy, not for Vaidyanathpuram which is outside Kalpathy. At the entrance of the heritage village, near the mainroad is an eatery which serves the truck drivers and manual labourers and also sells curried fish on banana leaves to the Malayalis.

The flats are taking over the heritage village rapidly, and the sky line is beginning to change, as people return to Kalpathy because it is a sacred site, but still remember neighbourhoods in Delhi or in Bombay with affection. I have had interesting conversations with diaspora Tamil women (always perfectly dressed in fine silks or expensive handloom cottons in the calm of their homes) who accompanied their bureaucrat husbands to various parts of India, and who speak Hindi with felicity, while being nostalgic about the shops in Sector 1 of R.K. Puram, which I too know well. Many of them still have children in big cities in India, or more likely in America or Singapore, the citadels of the IT professionals.

It is not necessary to cook meals at home in the *agraharam* of the Brahmins of Kalpathy since there are excellent caterers who bring food right on the doorstep on request. Even the cakes sold at the bakery were 'ghee cakes.' Outside the local eateries which are crammed with clientele, mainly the working class and the middle class pilgrims from outside the village, the Brahmin men and women congregate outside the 'Mess' where caterers sell *appam, dosas, vadas*, coffee and all sorts of sweets and delicacies known to them such as *shoondal, sewai* and *parram vada*. As if this were not enough, there are *pakoda* sellers doing brisk business too. On my first visit to Kalpathy, I made an awful hybrid type language mistake. While my daughters asked for dosas, I said very grandly, 'Ennika Thali Vennam!' I imagined that a plate with steaming curries and rice would appear. It was 5 p.m. The owner of the café looked totally aghast, and then perplexed. 'Tali Vennam?' I had asked for a plate of food using a Hindi word, but he converted it into a word that Brahmins and Nairs must have had in common for many centuries, i.e., a marriage locket. My secular Syrian Christian identity was immediately undercut. A kind woman eating with her husband said 'Shaddam Vennam' which means rice. Malayalis would have used the word 'Chor', since that is what they use in everyday language for rice. Being Malayali, in erstwhile Madras Presidency I am often confounded since my earlier work was in Travancore. The questions of language, politics and identity are too large to present here, but would include the questions of the historical location of Pallakad both in medievalism and after the merger, when it came to Kerala: agriculture and caste and language are the key motifs of that ensemble. Dikshitar, the most eminent of the men in the *agraharam*, asked his relative who I was, and the man answered 'Angadikar' which could mean a resident, but was traditionally used for Syrian Christians, who lived in settlements known as *Angadi*, as opposed to *Agraharam*. The Syrian Christians as pepper merchants were traditionally allowed into the *agraharam*. It may be noticed that caste as exclusionary is the subject of fiction writers attention, and in modernism the problem reappears in new ways which are yet to be analysed. Niels Brimnes (1999: 9) speaks of the significance of the relationship between colonialists and the upper castes, 'In general, it seems most fruitful to look at the relations between colonial power and indigenous inhabitants as the result of a dialogue in which both sides participated. They did not, of course, participate from the same motives, and rarely did they participate on equal terms. The specific relations of strength between the colonial power and various indigenous groups determined the extent to which each part could assert themselves, and it seems reasonable to assume that the Indian voices in the colonial dialogue weakened as colonialism consolidated'. Satish Saberwal makes much the same point in 1972, and so does Christopher Bayly. What is important for us to remember is that Kalpathy provided much of the clerical staple of the work force in the colonial government. Brimnes further writes, 'A prime example of the Indian component in the discourse is the role of the Brahmins assistant to the great gatherers of knowledge ... It seems that the codification of Indian society was thanks to the continuous possibility of participation from privileged groups of Indians – at the same time a process of Brahminization took place. In this process a particular indigenous interpretation of the nature of Indian society – or one of the Indian voices in the colonial dialogue – began to dominate over other interpretations' (ibid.: 75).

Similarly, for the Dalits, Gundimeda Sambaiah (2009: 108) writes, 'For the present purpose, it is sufficient to note here that the SC category is part of the colonial project of reconstructing Indian society in the lines of the Brahminical world view, with the help of both British and Indian officials alike in the service of the colonial state, especially in the context of law and order, education and political representation'. Class and caste become read in Kerala through the motifs of dispossession of land and property, for the *agraharam* Brahmins after 1956. Today, the *agraharam* resembles an emptied out landscape as the old and infirm remain stationed in picture book houses, for relatives who have made new lives elsewhere. Tradition is crystallized in motifs of archival significance: texts, architecture medicine and music being some of them.

The street in New Kalpathy remains completely empty in the afternoon because of the heat, the bright white light, and an unblemished azure sky. During the early morning it is busy with school children waiting for the bus, with parents, old people reading the newspapers, women drawing the ornamental and sacred *kollam*. Evenings are markedly different, everyone comes out to chat and talk. Families sit at their verandahs, the women wear jasmines in their hair, the children play and sing and chatter. The men are often comfortable in their white *sarongs*, bare chested with only the sacred thread as upper vestment. The street is a public thoroughfare with fruit vendors and vegetable sellers, jasmine merchants carrying their fragrant ware on bicycles or on their heads in baskets. Kalpathy is rapidly becoming a flatted area. The residents in the flats, which are now elbowed in with the *agraharam* homes, are professionals who have retired from Bombay, Calcutta, Delhi or Chennai. Elderly couples with children abroad, or in the metropolis (Bangalore is a hub for professionals' children, many of whom are in the Sciences, Industry or in Electronics), spend their day as other retired professionals in India do cooking, cleaning, reading newspapers and watching television, chatting to one another, over balcony walls or in the corridors. They often visit their children in cities and towns in India and abroad. They hurry back because they are wealthy enough to be able to afford to live in Kalpathy, or culturally inhabit one of the most valued places on the tourist map of Kerala. Valentine Daniel (2010) has an interesting concept called the 'territo-rial-limit-indicator'. This helps us to understand how a map of memories is organized around space. It is similar to Evans-Pritchard's concept of structural time, and space-event maps, where lineage and territory combine to coincide in concentric circles of expansion (ibid.: 318, 319). Daniel uses this with regard to the diaspora world of Tamils, but it can be used significantly to understand occupational migrants as much as refugees of war. He quotes Adi Ophir, 'Whenever the disappeared is not replaceable, and as long as it has no replacement, it is a loss. Loss is a singular type of disappearance, of some irreplaceable thing.'

October 2009

Kalpathy has the sense of a picture postcard. The colours are always placid and bright. The breeze blows cool, as if there was a beach close by. The houses are set in such a way that the horizon extends and is fullfilled by the temples. (As an ethnographer, it seems coincidental to me that I studied Puthenangadi, a Christian hamlet with five churches, in 1980 and here in Kalpathy are five temples in sequence with its local legends!).

Suddenly, the empty road ends and there is the warmth of people and activities and lights, colour, sound, fragrances. The solitude of the street and the appearance of the crowds comes as a surprise. Somewhere the mosaic of people, men and women, of different castes and communities appears, as a map of Kerala as it is changing with urbanization. The calm and peacefulness is marked by the appearance of the cows as they desultorily walk down the lanes, rummaging in the occasional garbage consisting of plantain leaves outside the cafetarias – for the rest, the streets are extremely clean, the *frangipani* and the *parjyathi* lies noticeably on the streets, uncrushed by the occasional passerby.

In the evening, the families sit outside sharing gossip – front to front – as the houses are adjoining, the entire street now begins to resemble an open courtyard. Fried *vadas* and *bhajjis* or *pakodas* are most frequently bought, neighbours participating in the commerce of the everyday, buying what is popularly called 'tiffin' together. Perhaps because they love to eat fried foods, a great deal of this is easily available. *Dosas, vadas, bondas* (these are seasoned potatos, dipped in a pulse batter and fried) and a delicious sweet called *adai*, which is rice flattened on a banana leaf, on which is placed cooked jack fruit with jaggery and coconut, then folded and steamed in banana leaves. A carnival sense fills the market place every evening. The temples at the end of every street are brightly lit, people thronging them, and the children playing. As a lot of Kalpathy since British times has had people visiting from Bombay, Calcutta, Delhi or Chennai, so 'gole guppa' and 'bhel puri' typically northern delicacies or urban foods can be bought at the street corner. The bakery has soft springy white bread, warm and delicious, tray loads of fresh bread and buns, appearing at noon, rapidly sold at 4 p.m. along with fruit cakes, treacly and sweet icing pastries in vibrant pinks and chocolates, and the traditional sponge cakes, for which Malayali bakeries are famous. The local eateris also provide rice and *sambhar* and vegetables on banana leaves. The Milma supplies excellent hot *idlis* and *vadais* to the auto-drivers and pilgrims who haunt the shop for good coffee and butter milk. As they say about Paris, there is never a bad meal in Kalpathy. Eswarya Mess is the most popular of these eateries. Crowds gather in the early morning and late afternoon, happy to get large quantities of coconut chutney with their *vadas* and *bondas*. The family living adjacent to the Easwarya Mess has put up a trestle table. Easwarya continues to get its loyal Brahmin clientele, but the vendors next door seem to get enough customers. Especially during the *ter* or the annual temple chariot festival, profits are substantial never mind the size or custom of the eateries, mobile (as on push carts or pedaled on bicycles)or stable as in cafes.

13–18 November 2010

Kalpathy is ready for the annual *ter* or *rath* (chariot) festival. The *agraharam* prepares slowly day by day. Bamboos line the street. On these advertisements come up, banners fluttering in the wind. The houses receive the ramshackle additions with aplomb. Everything looks makeshift. Diwali is over, the *ter* festival is what Kalpathy looks forward to with excitement. I visit the ayurved doctor who practices in new Kalpathy, and has a factory in Ambikapuram, and a hospital too. He has been practising since 1934, in Kalpathy. His father established a practice, now he, his son and daughter circulate between three clinics in Pallakad.

The Arogyadayam Ayurveda Hospital is a modern double storey house with two patients, and a clientele of outpatients. The older Dr K.K. Kumaran Vaidyan, studied with his father Vaidyan K.R. Krishnan Ezuthachatan who was born in Kuthanoor village of Pallakad in 1903. In 1934, Krishnan Ezuthuchathan set up a clinic in Kalpathy. He also started the production process of the medicines used by the present doctors. Earlier, they got the herbs from gatherers and foragers, who were 'local people' who went in for any kind of work: gardening, cleaning of courtyards, paddy agriculture, cement labourers. Now, the government protects the right of the tribals, so the Arogdayam pharmacy buys from shops in Pallakad, and there is a main outlet in Trichur, to whom they place orders either by post or on phone. I visit his factory. It is adjacent to his house. His wife Seethalakshmi comes out to greet me. His manager Shakkit takes me upstairs where there is a laboratory which checks each bottle for its purity content, and its alcohol base content. Downstairs are the vats for boiling, and for storing distilling and for bottling.

The bottles are collected by two or three agents from New Bazaar, and then washed with soap and water, and dried in the sun. It is a small unit, occupying the floor space of one house of medium proportion (2000 square feet). Production varies by the day. The output is dependent on all the factors being in place. The laboratory check for each batch is to provide for the standardization certificate required from the government.

Seethalakshmi amma, who is the Vaid's wife, is rolling the small balls that go into the making the cough medicine. The manager tells me that he cannot explain the application and use of the medicine since these are very complex and take years to learn. The medicines come from the town, from individual shops, and are stored in big plastic buckets. Each herb is classified by its Sanskrit name, Malayalam name and Latin name. Some herbs look very similar, so they have to be identified by the specialist.

The Vaid tells me on a subsequent visit (on 17 April 2011) that he has nine brothers, all of whom are or were practitioners of ayurveda. Seven brothers practise in Chennai, and he with another one inherited the Kalpathy practice. The two brothers were very compatible, but the sibling died very recently. All the nine brothers meet often, discuss cases and these were very useful for them as individual practitioners.

The temples are getting ready for the event, lots of lights, people, shops, in spite of the drizzle. The sky is very dark blue. The river is flowing fast and sure. It is very different from the summer, when the river was a mere polluted trickle, and sand miners abounded.

In every house, guests have arrived, the accumulated slippers, outside of every house with its fragrant interiors, show how many are gathered. The children cycle in the rain, the girls wearing beautiful long silk skirts. Their mothers are dressed in flamboyant silks too, with diamonds glittering in their ears. The men are no less demonstrative and also wearing new clothes.

These rituals serve to integrate the five wards of the village. Tomorrow at 12 midnight, there will be a meeting of *raths* in the street. Some say tomorrow, 12th November, others say 13th November.

12 November 2010

The women at the river wash clothes late in the morning after the domestic chores are over. The talk is about ration shops, electricity bills, one woman has forgotten to bring her husband's clothes for wash. The children have lost handkerchiefs, the mothers are laughing and complaining. One mother says that her son uses his handkerchief to clean the seats of the bus, another says her daughter always gives away everything she owns – handkerchiefs, bangles, even rubbers and pencils, or the expense of it all! The men chat desultorily at the back, robing and disrobing with ease. The bathing space is not divided, water weeds grow to divide the river, and while the women are to be found near the steps, the men venture deeper into the water. The women are detached, and do not look at the men who are oiling themselves, they slip into their petticoats and stand in the water continuing their baths and clothes rinsing, and scrubbing the younger children who have accompanied them. The young girl, who is already dressed in bright blue silk, after her bath, is waiting for her mother to finish and complaining that the ants are following her.

The shopkeepers in the street are beginning to stock the ribbons, buttons, clips, bells, bangles and toys. One of them is called Saladri. Portly, dark, handsome, he has spent twenty years in the Gulf, in Saudi Arabia, as a courier agent, but the work was very hard. So he shifted back to Wadakencheri and is an itinerant seller of toys at fairs. He says he was 12 years in Bombay as well. Since he suffered from back ache from carrying loads for the courier agency he worked for, he is now happy to earn a little everyday, stay with his family, and now keeps in good health.

The day is very hot. Bright white hot. The only person venturing out in the verandah is the Dikshitar, the wisest and most learned man in the village. He has grown older year by year. His sole diamond in one ear gleaming harshly against his ancient creased wise face. He is the most knowledegeable of the Sanskrit scholars. Other than him, the other person who is outside in the afternoon heat is a woman, making a pattern on the ground. She stops to gaze at the *kollam* she has made, and wonders if she had made it perfectly. A man feeds a cow and chases the bull calf away. The street is completely silent. At the chemists, the shop girls are excited. It is the fifth day of the *ter* festival. All the Gods will gather at midnight at Kalpathy Viswanath Temple.

13 November 2010

Pushpa who cleans my flat, gave a graphic account of the *rath* festival. 'There will be crowds. Pushing and pulling. Gold-chain snatchers and alcoholics will move about freely. For the *prasadam* people come from miles around. The shops will be busy. Everything that you want!' However later she brings me a huge and delicious *laddu*, along with pomegranate kernels, which are a novelty for her. She too has stood with the devout, and is happy that it is festival time.

People gathered yesterday, the 5th day of the *ter* at D.K. Pattamal Street, known commonly as Chattanapuram.

The music festival at Chattanapuram is supported by Kerala Tourism. The singers were well known and exceptionally talented. Each day is dedicated to the memory of a traditional musician. The simplicity and joy of the musicians is matched by the devotion of the listeners, mainly residents, the women dazzling in their diamonds and silks, the men urbane and detached. They sit on plastic chairs under shamiana roofing. Local TV unblinkingly records every moment for the captive audiences at home, mainly old people and housewives.

Each pandal is embossed and decorated with the name of a patron. Allukas, the Syrian Christian gold merchant who has vulgarized Kerala's urban landscape with his shops, has emblazoned the Kalpathy Viswanath Temple. The industrialist Bajaj has his name up on Lakshminarayan Temple in old Kalpathy. The music pandal is sponsored by Mathrubhumi, and the state government to promote tourism in Kerala.

The sellers of toys, ceramics, cold drinks, picnic foods like pop corn have started to line the road. Each day brings new vendors, some from as far away as Kodaikanal and Ooty.

At 12 p.m., the mini *raths* with the Gods arrive. Two from the streets adjoining Shiva-Shakti Temple, known as Viswanathaswamy, and the other from the New Kalpathy Ganesha Temple. The Shiva-Shakti *rath* is drawn by white cows with perfect horns. All the white cows look mythic, perfect and identical. They are used to the crowds, though there is some essential pulling and straining. The people have been waiting for hours, sitting on ledges outside the houses or on any odd crook of wall. There is a sense of excitement, the boys race past on cycles or in gangs, the girls are dazzling in their synthetic clothes with spangles and sequins. A new dress culture has evolved among the children: keds, t-shirts with logos and shorts for the boys, ubiquitous choodidar-kameez for the girls. Young women wear silk saris with jasmines in their hair accompanied by siblings, parents, in-laws and husband. Families move together in large groups, many have come from other places.

14 November 2010

Yesterday, the 'chiefs' appeared on the dias – minister for tourism, MLAs, cultural secretary, police officers. The minister for tourism has sanctioned three lakhs rupees for the festival. Propogation of cultural values, the importance of heritage, the celebration of religion, difference and diversity, the adaptation of traditional culture to internet and other technologies and the significance of inter-religious, and inter-community dialogue, were the main themes of the talks. After the speeches, Sharrat, a famous film musician, who has supported classical music in films, introduced a young musician, who sang to a very musically enlightened audience, for three hours. He passed the test, and people went home satisfied at 10 p.m. The *ter* is out again, travelling slowly from Ganesh Temple to Swaminathan Temple. People continue to flow into the streets, like a steady river of human beings, and excited by the presence of the gods. The normally quiet street is packed with visitors. Rajshri, who is an associate professor at Anna University, Coimbatore, tells me that during *ter* people continuously visit them, all their relatives and friends assemble together. They all eat together, everywhere else, people return home for Diwali and Christmas, but here they assemble together for *ter*. Her parents have gone to d the visiting priests and teachers and gurus, vadayar at the temple.

Rajshri takes me to her house, and introduced me to her cousins and aunts. Everyone has collected here – cousins, aunts, in-laws. The house is large, with glass fitted into the tiles. So, a lovely dim light comes in. It is a hushed tinted light, keeping the house incredibly cool. There are no partitions, no separations, no alcoves or hidden spaces. In a joint household, everything is shared. Collective or joint living means that every room is accessible to every one else. At the back there is a large garden. It extends with adjoining gardens, to a boundary wall. Each house stands in close proximity to the neighbours, in such a way that the wall of each house shares bricks with the next. The government does not allow renovation of the front part of the house any longer, however inside and beyond can be renovated. Rajshri explains the route of the *ter*:

Shiv and Shakti have two *ters*, Ganapathy has one.

They meet in the same street in New Kalpathy with Ganapathy setting out to meet his parents.

Ambikapuram has its own *ter*, related to Guruvayur.

Old Kalpathy has Lakshmi Narayan.

Chattapuram has Krishna.

Each *ter* with its God or Gods will meet the people.

The main function of the *ter* is to have the gods meet the people. There are people who cannot come to the temple, so once a year, the gods come to visit the people to see them in their homes. Rajshri says that when the Pallakad king invited them to live in the 18 villages, the migrant Brahmins had only one condition: that the *ter* festivals which they celebrated in their village in Mayavaram, should be celebrated in the Pallakad villages in every detail. Rajshri sends me an e-mail outlining the said events. It consists of seven pages, and has a long list of recipients all having a personal interest in the Kalpathy *rath* festival, and mentioning the cultural music festival events by date and event.

The festival is described as starting with Dwajarohanam (flag hoisting) and ends with Rathasangamom according to the publicity circular sent by e-mail to several residents and diaspora Tamilians. To quote,

> This year, the Kalpathy car festival is scheduled to be held from 8–16 November 2010. The Dwajarohanam (flag hoisting) will be held on November 8th. The Ratha Sangamom will be held before the Viswanatha Swamy temple on the evening of November 16th. The main attraction of the car festival is on the last three days, i.e., from 14–16 November 2010. On these three days the chariots are ceremoniously drawn through the streets.
>
> On the first day (14th November) the three chariots carrying the deities of Sree Viswanatha Swamy temple is taken out in procession. The first chariot is of Lord Shiva and Parvathi. The second chariot is of Lord Vigneswara and the third is of Lord Subramanya. The chariots set out on Grama Pradikshanam, which is the village tour, around 10 in the morning for a small distance and

continues its journey to all the four nearby *agraharams* and returns to its base on the 3rd day evening, where the Ratha Sangamom takes place.

On the second day (15th November) Lord Maha Ganapathy, which is the presiding deity of New Kalpathy temple, is taken out on procession.

On the final day (16th November) Lord Maha Ganapathy, which is the presiding deity of New Kalpathy temple, is taken out on procession.

On the final day (16th November) the deities of Lakshmi Narayan Perumal of Old Kalpathy and Mahaganapthy of Chatapuram villages are taken around the villages on their chariots.

In the evening on the final day (26th November) Deva Ratha Sangamom – the congregation of all the chariots – will take place in front of the Sree Viswanatha Swamy Temple.

The *raths* are covered with flowers and fruits, which are well known to South Indians, such as jasmines, *kannakambaram* (a small delicate orange hued flower with trumpet formed flowers) and of course the maroon banana flowers. Fruits and vegetables adorning the *rath* are of many varieties of bananas and gourds, and the sense is certainly of rich and bountiful harvest. They are heavy and need hundreds of people to pull them around, sometimes an elephant appears for ceremonial purposes to the delight of the crowd. The people are delighted by the beauty of the *rath*, small boys sitting on the top, delighted to be in a place of power, with their families waving out to them. A small girl who climbs up will hasten down because of the heat and the danger of the rocking *rath*, which teeters sometimes in the narrow lane. When it rains, the work does not stop, but the men and women continue the hard task of steering the *rath* with heavy ropes, with the understanding that what they do is for the Gods. The usually silent streets are thronging with people and the sellers of food and trinkets. The noise level is very high, as those who enter the *agraharam* are revellers, who increase the decibel of noise with their slogans, both Saivite, extolling the holy family of Siva, Parvati and Ganesha as well as in favour of Lord Ayyapa, the bachelor God, who shuns women, and rules Sabarimala. Is there an opposition between the familial traditions of the Tamil Brahmin *agraharam* dwellers, and the large numbers of Malayali youth who enter the streets on festival days, yelling and dancing with great enthusiasm for Ayyapa Sharanam! Not necessarily. Michel Maffesoli writes, 'Cultures exhaust themselves, civilizations die; everything becomes inscribed in the mechanization of saturation ably described by Sorokin' (Maffesoli, 1996: 114). But, if equilibrium is lost, then destruction only leads to construction. 'Returning to a balance I have already evoked earlier, we can say that the unity of bourgeois society is succeeded by the unicity of the masses – the masses not as an historical subject, as in the case of the bourgeoisie or the proletariat, but rather as a contradictory entity; or as a daily practice in which evil, the strange, the "other", are not exorcised but integrated, according to varied measures and norms, be they homeopathic even.' He demands that we acknowledge a natural plurality, a plurality of natures. 'This is what I mean by conflictual harmony, since an equilibrium is more difficult to attain when passion triumphs over reason; this is a phenomenon quite easy to observe in both everyday and civic life' (ibid.: 115). The *vahanam* rituals are perhaps the most interesting in appearance because they integrate totemically the animal world and that of the Gods and humans.

Websites on Kalpathy are interesting to the extent that they communicate the significance of the rituals, and the importance of tradition. In *Rethinking Maps*, Martin Dodge, Rob Kitchin and Chris Perkins write about community map formations, where the idea that tourism and ceremonies, political, secular or ritualistic, can inform those who are interested about events. 'From tourist and leisure spaces, public space, to cyberspace and the domestic arena, play allows capitalist accumulation to progress. And further, everyday culture matters, style matters and language become the field of play' (Perkins in Dodge, Kitchin and Perkins, 2009). Combining the notion of work and play (*'their work, the development of sustainable mapping'* by Dominica Williamson and Emmet Connolly in the same book), the authors usher in an analysis of why local knowledge and direct experience give us new democratic and local mapping practices, which are narratives towards sharing and emancipation of communities. Pierre Bourdieu in *The Logic of Practice* has an interesting discussion on how traditions in the habitus motivate people to action, where the grammar of the future is already in place.

'The homogeneity of habitus that is observed within the limits of a class of conditions of existence and social conditionings is what causes practices and works to be immediately intelligible and foreseeable, and hence taken for granted' (Bourdieu, 1990: 58). When the Brahmins had their lands taken from them in the 1950s, since they were not the cultivators, they became impoverished. The cultivating castes, including farmers with small holdings and agricultural labourers, are dependent on the nearby Mallampuzha dam, which is 8 km from Kalpathy.

Appukutty Masha, a retired school teacher, whom I interviewed in 2006, near Kannadi village, explains the process of what cultivation means to him. Love for agriculture is his legacy. The Mallapuram dam, which came in 1956, made the farmers independent to some extent, from the rain. But, the dam lacks water because the monsoon was not sufficient, so the water is sent every 15 days, with regular breaks in between. For three days at a time, the canals have been dry and everything, consequently, shrivels up. Masha loves farming, and since he has a pension, he can manage even in the years when there is loss from drought or unseasonal rain. But, what about the others? He says that by putting the fertilizers himself, without hiring farm labourers, he had saved five hundred rupees a day. He is 65, but he said he really enjoyed paddy cultivation.

In 2006, the farmers in Kannadi village had told me that water for the fields comes from Mallampuzha dam, and that in the summer, the water is not released so that paddy cultivation suffers. Bettina Weiz has given a detailed analysed of how dams for local farmers become located in a complex frame of social relations around the aspect of land, the sluice and the hierarchies of ownership of tools, motor and land and the biographical notations of actors in the context of redistribution of water (in Mines and Yazgi, 2010: 130). Similarly, Jyothi Krishnan gives us an elaborate and detailed description of wells, ponds, tanks and fields in Pallakad, showing the importance of fields, location and type of harvesting.

Padmaja Sasi Kumar, who works in the panchayat of Kannadi says that Virripu (kharif) from June to September and Mandakkam (rabi) from November to December are the two main cropping seasons. Poonja is from February to May, and this is when the farmers are advised to go for short crop duration, 90 days, 130 days, or for mixed cropping seasons. Farmers are given a schedule of the water release plan from Mallampuzha dam authorities. Because of fragmentation of land, unlike the Tamil Nadu farmer, who works with hundreds of acres, the Kerala farmer works with 5–10 cents, sometimes 25 cents. Labour charge is too high, so farming is actually dependent on other activity such as school teaching, employment in private firms or government service. It is supported not only by mixed cropping (coconuts, arecanuts, yams, banana) but also keeping of cattle and fish in ponds or in rice fields. Earlier, Bharatapuzha had water, now rivers are drying up because of plants and trees which are not cleared, sand mining which aggravates the condition, paddy lands converted into real estate, so no water drains into the soil but is cemented up. December 15th onwards water is released from the dam.

Mallampuzha dam is also a recreational site where families gather for picnics. The dam supplies Pallakad town with drinking water, so in the summer months, there is no diversion to agriculture, but only piped water to the town. The water is locked in, it is a peaceful lake, fenced off from tourists. Against the backdrop of the sky and the Nilgiris, the water is a beautiful expanse of clear blue. There is an electric wire trolley car which gives an aerial view of the dam, a snake museum and an aquarium, and a garden which is closed for renovation. There is most significantly a temple of Hidimba, the rakshasa wife of Bhima.

Colonel Venu, who accompanies me to the dam the first time, believes that the poor Brahmin has no opportunity to believe in secularism. He says, 'Though there is no evidence of the Tamil Brahmins' criminality, he has been excluded from all things economic or beneficial, particularly in Tamil Nadu.' His father was an entomologist in the state of the king. Once he asked his father for one anna to buy a pencil of German make, because the poor boys in the class got free books and new pens, but since he was a scientist's son, he was excluded. He longed for a pen, his father agreed to give him the money to buy one. When he went to school, his friends said, 'Let's buy peanuts instead.' Before he knew what was happening, he was persuaded. A large quantity of peanuts was bought and distributed among the boys. Trailing home he went to his father's laboratory and asked his father's assistant to loan him a pencil. When his father came home, he asked to see the new pencil, so Venu showed him the pencil. His father said, 'This is a glass marking pencil!' (interview 18 April 2011). On the subject of Brahma's lie, it would be useful to look at *The Children of Nature* (Visvanathan, 2010).

Sanjay Subramanium, David Shulman and Narayana Rao, while discussing the emergence of folktales in Tamil Nadu, write in their book, *Symbols of Substance* that the poor Brahmin pits his wit, lies and survives. The folktale is a parody of, not a foil to high caste, Sanskritic modes. Parody pivots on a hinge that swings in two directions, both towards and away from the subject. Satire works in a linear fashion. Parody mingles domains and superimposes or interweaves contrasting visions, including competing notions of the real. There is real kingship and there is illusory kingship. Both wield power. What are the contexts in which we can see parallel structures at work? (Rao et al., 2004: 21).

While the legendary Pallakad raja and the Tamil Brahmin are the possible two subjects of analyses, yet on the other hand, we cannot understand agriculture without the serf, who wins in the end, as land redistribution, party politics and the displacement of Coco Cola have shown in Pallakad district.

23 May 2011

The Mallampuzha dam was established in 1956 as part of India's development project. It provides drinking water to Pallakad town, and water to the farmers, from November to March. From April onwards, the dam water is released on specific days.

There was a conference going on the day that I visited (19 April 2011) So, while I was not permitted to attend the meeting (in fact so confidential that the engineers were locked in) the discussion was around the question of increased surveillance, CCTV cameras, etc. There has been no trouble, the dam site is peaceful. It is a 'large dam' for Kerala, but in comparison to others in India, a small dam. People are in a state of agitation because the garden is closed for renovation. There are many people from Tamil Nadu who come to the dam after visiting Kanayakumari and Guruvayur and other temple sites. Busloads of gaily dressed peasants, including honeymooners, arrive and visit the pleasure booths (rides, food, lucky dip and toy stalls.) There is a fish aquarium and a snake zoo. Since it is ticketed, some of the poorer citizens sit despondently but even so, the dam conveys a sense of a leisure zone.

On the way back I caught a bus to Kalpathy. The old woman sitting next to me was in traditional Syrian Christian dress: white *mundu* or *sarong*, and white shirt or jacket, and a cotton drape over it, also white. I asked her, 'Are you alone?' She pointed to a boy at the back. He was about 14 years old.

'Isn't it too hot to come to a tourist site?' I asked in a conversational tone. She looked blankly at me.

'I live here,' She said.

'Where?' I was totally puzzled.

'Behind the dam. In a village called Annakallu (Elephant Stone). Elephants still come down the hill. We have to fence it. The agriculture is good. We grow everything that we did in Naadu (that is Kerala before 1956). Its not hot here, the cool breezes come down the hill. The rain falls, and we have planted many trees. We came from Moovatapuzha and bought the land cheaply 35 years ago from farmers who feared the dam. I am going for an eye check up. My son will meet me in Pallakad. The boy accompanying me is his son, my grandson, training to be a Kappiar (a deacon). We belong to the Patriarch of Antioch's party. No, he cannot visit us, since there is a war. (She is referring here to the Iraq war.) He will be killed if he comes by sea. (There could be a cultural signifier here since a Jacobite bishop was killed at sea in 1664). He could come through the forest. People of all religions, Hindu Muslims and Christians live peacefully in Annakalu.'

I had to leap off the bus, since, the *agraharam* where I stay, had come. Kurt Iveson writes that, 'For Simmel, then, the stranger is the product of an arrival which has both spatial and temporal dimensions. The stranger has moved from one place to another, at some moment passing across the boundaries of a pre-existing group with the hope of staying. This arrival brings strangers into contact with other individuals to whom they are not connected through ties of kinship, locality and occupation' (Simmel, 1950: 404 cited in Binnie et al., 2006: 72). The diaspora Brahmins have made their homes in every corner of the world, and today, they have had to open their doors to tourists, pilgrims, anthropologists and anyone who can afford to buy a flat or home in Kalpathy. This is not a matter of 'cultural pessimism' but the Brahmins' innate ability to integrate into the new vocabularies of postmodernism without losing their sense of self-validation regardless of personal circumstances.

Acknowledgements

To Prof. Yogendra Singh who once told me that 'Othello's occular proof' (the matter of the handkerchief) does not work for Sociology, Prof. T.K Oommen for his early and valued work on land relations in Kerala, Prof. Modi for inviting me to write in this collection, to UGC and JNU for supporting the costs of research, and to friends, family, students and teachers for their patience and kindness in all things related to my work, to Smt Rajshri, to Shri K.N. Lakshmi Narayan, Colonel Venugopal and many resident Pallakadians for their constant and assured presence in allowing me permission to share ideas and work with them and to Shri K.V Krishnan for making his essay on Pallakad available to me very early on. I am extremely grateful to the agricultural officers in Pallakad town and the government employees at the Mallapuram dam site for their kindness, since the debate is significantly around reservoirs versus large dams, and the success of the small dams is significant to the water debates.

References

Aloysius, G. (2005). *Interpreting Kerala's Social Development*. Delhi: Critical Quest.

Bauman, Zygmunt (2004). *Wasted Lives: Modernity and its Outcasts*. Cambridge: Polity Press.

Bennet, Oliver (2001). *Cultural Pessimism: Narratives of Decline in the Postmodern World*. Edinburgh: Edinburgh University Press.

Bhatt, G.S. (2010). *Cult, Religion and Society*. Jaipur: Rawat Publications.

Binnie, Jon et al. (2006). *Cosmopolitan Urbanism*. Abingdon: Routledge.

Bourdieu, Pierre (1990). *The Logic of Practice*. Stanford, CA: Stanford University Press.

Brimnes, Niels (1999). *Constructing the Colonial Encounter: Right and Left Hand Castes in Early Colonial South India*. London: Curzon Press.

Brodbeck, Simon Pearse (2009). *Gender, Culture and the Royal Hereditary*. Farnham: Ashgate.

Chekki, Dan A. (1997). *Religion and Social System of the Virasaiva Community*. Connecticut: Greenwood Press.

Daniel, Valentine E. (2010). 'The Lost Ur', in Diane P. Mines and Nicolas Yazgi (eds), *Village Matters*, New Delhi: Oxford University Press.

Dirks, Nicholas B. (2008). *Castes of Mind: Colonialism and the Making of Modern India*. Ranikhet: Permanent Black.

Dodge, Martin, Rob Kitchin and Chris Perkins (2009). *Rethinking Maps: New Frontiers in Cartographic Theory*. Abingdon: Routledge.

Eldersveld, Samuel J., V. Jagannadham and A.P. Barnabas (1968). *The Citizen and the Administrator in a Developing Democracy*. Dallas: Scott Foresman and Company.

Firth, Raymond (1963). *We, the Tikopia*. Boston: Beacon Press.

Ignatieff, Michael (1994). *The Needs of Strangers*. London: Vintage.

Irschick, Eugene F. (1994). *Dialogue and History: Constructing South India, 1795–1895*. Delhi: Oxford University Press.

Iveson, Kurt (2006). 'Strangers in the Cosmopolis', in Jon Binnie et al. (eds), *Cosmopolitan Urbanism*, Abingdon: Routledge.

Krishnan, K.V. (2010). *KVK's Take: Honesty is still the Best Policy*. New Delhi: Dayan Krishnan.

MacIver, Robert and Charles Page (1937). *Society: A Textbook of Sociology*. New York: Farrar and Rinehart.

Maffesoli, Michel (1996). *The Time of the Tribes: The Decline of Individualism in Mass Society*. London: Sage.

Mines, Diane P. and Nicolas Yazgi (2010). *Village Matters: Relocating Villages in the Contemporary Anthropology of India*. Delhi: Oxford University Press.

Morris, Lydia (ed.) (2006). *Sociological Perspectives*. Abingdon: Routledge.

Muthaiah, S. (2009). 'Its Time to Put Down Memories', in Vijaya Ramawamy and Yogesh Sharma (eds), *Biography as History*. Delhi: Orient BlackSwan.

Oommen, T.K. (1972). 'On the Distinction between Micro and Macro Studies', in Satish Saberwal (ed.), *Beyond the Village*. Shimla: IIAS.

Perkins, Chris (2009). 'Playing with Maps', in Martin Dodge et al. (eds), *Rethinking Maps*. London: Routledge.

Prasad, Leela (2007). *Ethics in Everyday Hindu Life: Narration and Tradition in a South Indian Town*. Ranikhet: Permanent Black.

Ramaswamy, Vijaya and Yogesh Sharma (2009). *Biography as History: Indian Perspectives*. Delhi: Orient BlackSwan.

Rao, Narayana, Sanjay Subramanium and David Shulman (2004). *Symbols of Substance*. Delhi: Oxford University Press.

Rao, Yagati Chinna (2009). *Dividing Dalits: Writing on Sub-categorization of Scheduled Castes*. Jaipur: Rawat Publications.

Rude, George (1974). *Paris and London in the 18th Century: Studies of Popular Protest*. London: Fontana.

Saberwal, Satish (ed.) (1972). *Beyond the Village: Sociological Explorations*. Shimla: Indian Institute of Advanced Study.

Sambaiah, Gundimeda (2009). 'Madiga Dandora: A Social Movement for Rationalisation of Dalit Reservations', in Yagati Chinna Rao (ed.), *Dividing Dalits*. Jaipur: Rawat Publications.

Venkatachalapathy, A.R. (2009). 'Making a Modern Self in Colonial Tamil Nadu', in Vijaya Ramaswamy and Yogesh Sharma (eds), *Biography as History*. Delhi: Orient BlackSwan.

Visvanathan, Susan (2010). *The Children of Nature: The Life and Legacy of Ramana Maharshi*. Delhi: Roli.

Visvanathan, Susan (1993). *The Christians of Kerala: History, Belief and Ritual among the Yakoba*. Chennai: Oxford University Press.

Weiz, Bettina (2010). 'The Man Makes the Village Makes the Mad: The Story of Varandan, the Common Irrigator of a Village in Northern Tamil Nadu', in Diane Mines and Nicolas Yazgi (eds), *Village Matters*. Delhi: Oxford University Press.

Williamson, Dominica and Emmet Connolly (2009). 'Their Work: The Development of Sustainable Mapping', in Martin Dodge et al. (eds), *Rethinking Maps*. London: Routledge.

Youngsters' Association, Newkalpathy, Palakkad. www.kalpathyfestival.blogspot.com

Zimmerman, Francis (2009). 'A Hindu to His Body: The Reinscription of Traditional Representations', in Axel Michaels and Christoph Wulf (eds), *The Body in India: Ritual, Transgression, Performativity*. Berlin: Paragrana, Internationale Seitschrift fur Historische Anthropologie, Akademie Verlag, Freie University.

10

Jagannath Temple Organization

Symbiosis of Hindu Religiosity, Inter-Sect Understanding and Social Values

Ramanuj Ganguly

We start with the premise by looking into an observation made by Yogendra Singh[1] on the issue of impact of globalization on the cultural and social identity of people, in context of Indian society, where he explains that 'India has been exposed to cultural contacts with other civilizations since millennia. It has been continually making adaptive changes in the cultural styles, traits and forms as it encountered other cultures. It has a history of accommodating identities. The cultural impact of globalization on the identities of local cultures, therefore, is bound to be mediated by this resilience. There are several reasons for this observation. In the first instance, the historical conditions of the Indian social structure have been unique. It is characterized by immense plurality of communities, languages, cultural diacritical symbols and ethnic styles. A variety of cultural traits and cultural styles have over centuries given identity to communities but not in total isolation. Cultural interaction among regions and communities has persisted in a mode of co-sharing and mutual accommodation. This commonality has existed beyond the religious and ethnic divides despite the plurality of identities or, in other words, a macro-linkage of cultural bonds has existed in India throughout the history. It continues to subsist even today, and constitutes the cultural unity of India despite plurality of local identities. The cultural impact of globalization gets enmeshed within this process of internal dynamics and resilience of the local cultures. The perception that globalization threatens local culture is being increasingly invalidated. It is observed that in the process of globalization local cultures are reinforced, and also globalized. It is in this context, this paper undertakes to examine the Jagannath Temple Organization of Puri, Orissa.

The principles of any religious tradition perhaps do not grow on their own; rather, they evolve over a period of time, depending on the efforts of the (reflective members of the) society that provides patronage to the religion concerned. Such efforts are, for sure, collectively interactive; the process of this evolution is, therefore, built upon a myriad of factors established and examined by many hours of deliberations, observations, opinions, events and consequences, and finally, political and social conditions. In search of more appropriate ideas, changes were continually made, and further demands were forwarded to effect more changes. Sometimes these efforts were even deliberate and calculative (as in cases of all other religions) to make the tradition more compatible with the pan-Indian Hindu philosophy. The obvious consequence of such a process has thus led to an incorporation and amalgamation of various components and parameters from diverse sources.

Thus, here, we would like to understand the dynamic process of emergence and evolution of culture of the Jagannath Temple, under the influence of various external and internal forces of change related to society, religion, philosophy, trade, politics and governance. On the other hand, the purpose, therefore, is not to venture into spheres of Religion, Theology, Scriptures, Archaeology or Indology, although secondary reference may be made to outline the present extent of knowledge.

Multiculturalism and plurality have always been a hallmark of Indian society that has been highlighted by social scientists of every hue and colour. An attempt is being made here to understand the symbiotic nature of Hindu religiosity that tolerates both unity and difference, the basis of inter-sect understanding, and the embedded social values that guide a person to move with their everyday life.

Though temples and sacred places have worked as unifying forces for all Indian traditions, but the methodological insulation amongst the sociologists, Indologists, historians and social anthropologists has led to a situation where in dichotomically isolated concepts have been juxtaposed to show the cultural developments of India. This has been pointed out by A. Eschmann and others, when they state, 'Both disciplines (Indology and Social Anthropology) thus have mainly concentrated their research on the 'outer portions' of the continual spectrum of India's tradition, that is, its local and all Indian aspects ... both disciplines have tended to avoid the various regional traditions of the South Asian sub-continent, although they form not only literary the 'central position' of India's tradition, but also the true melting-pot of the local and all-Indian tradition.'[2]

The perspective that this paper adopts, using the words of Malory Nye[3], is that '... those who study religion and culture do not become bogged down in finding a definition, but instead work on the assumption that in many cultural contexts there is a field of cultural activity that is labeled as "religion". If we accept this as something that is given, then the purpose of our study is to see how the activities that go by this loose term are practised *as part of*, not separate from, the rest of cultural life ... terms "religion" and "religious" is based, therefore, on their common usage as a way of describing certain aspects of human activity ... In this way, the study of religion and culture helps us to make sense of the contemporary world. Not only does it tell us about the diversity of these discourses on religion (how and why people talk of what they do as religion), but also how such religion works as part of the lives and cultures of people in so many different contexts. In short, religion is not something mystical and detached from the human sphere – it is what people do, and how they talk about what they do.' This approach allows us to stay clear from finding the 'ultimate truths or answers' of divine principles, that otherwise would have put this work on a "God centred" theological plane. The present paper takes the venerated temple of Jagannath at Puri as part of the socio-cultural milieu of Indian society, and is, therefore, not judgemental about its quality or importance. This paper accepts, taking the long history of the temple into account, that people of India have chosen Jagannath Temple at Puri as their own selected cultural product, thus investing it with meaning and significance.[4] In this way the paper intends to address the issue as to how the temple of Jagannath at Puri, as an expression of Indian culture, has been functioning, and how it has been adjusting at different levels to the changing socio-cultural aspects of Indian society, though not breaking away from the particular tradition where it is located. Further, this study instead of restricting itself only in exploring the egalitarian practices of the temple goes on to explain how this egalitarian philosophy is 'belied by the real relationships of inequality between groups'.[5] The approach of the current study is not to highlight a particular aspect of religion in India, nor does it stress to identify an 'influential cultural product'.

The Field: The Jagannath Temple at Puri

Puri, a quaint township on the east coast of India, has been renowned for being the seat of Lord Jagannath – one of the incarnations of Lord Vishnu, the *preserver* God of the Holy Trinity. For ages, the temple has attracted devotees and pilgrims, from all over India in great numbers, to seek and acquire merit, purity and expiation.

The present temple complex of Lord Jagannath at Puri was constructed after 1135 AD by the Ganga king, Anantavarman Chodagangadeva (1078–1147) on the ruins of an earlier temple built by the Kesari king, Yayati Kesari.[6] The temple has survived the ravages of time and the onslaught of different adversities, primarily because of the serious religious esteem with which it has been regarded for over nine centuries. The temple, having always occupied a significant position in the religious life of the Hindus over a considerable period of time, has therefore also played an eminent role in influencing contemporary religion, moral philosophies, economic and social environment – interpretations, opinions and practices, not only in the region in vicinity but across the world.

Why Study a Temple Tradition? Theoretical Frame of Reference

Classical thought in sociology and social anthropology has uniformly tried to explain religious phenomenon in human society, pointing out its importance over the ages. Explanations of evolutionary scholars like Taylor, Frazer, Morgan, etc., in understanding religion, seem not so relevant in today's context because of their definition in evolutionary terms, which does not explain why religious organizations and rituals still remain a major component of all organized religions, even today. Functionalists like Durkheim, Malinowski, Radcliff-Brown, Evans-Pritchard and others studied religious organizations and rituals in terms of their functions and roles within the society. Religion as a concept was explained as an embodiment of the social order from which humans derive 'we-feeling', and working within this solidarity honours and sustains all of them. Talcott Parsons characterized these by their essentially transcendental nature that exists outside the means-end relationship. Cultural anthropologists like Edmund Leach not only see what the religious organizations and rituals do but also try to understand them as symbolic statements of social and cultural dimensions. Max Weber, on the other hand, tried to understand what meaning the followers of different religious traditions ascribed to their activities, and how the greater society interpreted these activities. Gerald James Larson briefly describes various traditions of theorizing religion and supplementing them with his own perspective of religionization as follows:

> Although the importance of religion is recognized by all of the types of theorizing ... no one of the approaches adequately deals with the high salience of the religious question. Modernization-secularization theorizing focuses on the disappearance of traditional religious perspectives but has little to say about how religious perspectives come into play beyond rather thin theories of functionalism (or structural-functionalism, largely following Durkheim) or an unapologetic historicist positivism (so-called substantive accounts like that of *Peter Berger*). Orientalist theorizing tells us a great deal about the great premodern 'world religions', especially as these classical 'essence' are described in the belief systems of the great textual traditions, but such theorizing seldom takes us beyond essentialist formulations, as Roland Inden has cogently shown us in his *Imaging India*. World-system theorizing clearly recognizes the importance of religious perspective as a crucial component in many 'anti-systemic movements' but then treats the perspective in a reductive fashion, as something other than what it appears to be. Finally, subaltern theorizing realizes that the 'religious consciousness' is a 'vital subject of study' but frankly admits that it has not made a great deal of progress in treating it ... What is missing in all of these traditions of theorizing, however, is what I would call a religious studies perspective. By a religious studies perspective, I mean a perspective that focuses on the high salience of religious experience, not simply in terms of its manifestation in historical, social, economic and political contexts, but also in terms of its substantive content, that is, its basic intellectual and spiritual claims. This is not to blame or censure any of the other traditions of theorizing, since, after all, they do not intend nor, for that matter, should they intend to do a religious studies analysis.[7]

The problem what Larson explains above is that of oversimplification and partial stereotyping, regarding religion in India, in terms of Western world view/experience.

Therefore, it is our position that in any study before going into an exploration on Indian society, its religious life and institutions, it will be important to remember certain cautions. To grasp the Indian way of life, the scholars of Western countries, with a few exceptions, and following them, the Indian scholars have drawn simplistic generalizations. In his extensive critique of past scholarship in India, Ronald Inden[8] claims that it has produced distorted images, because of both the epistemological assumptions of Western scholarship and the political biases inherent in the 'imperial formations' of which this scholarship was a part. At the core of Inden's analysis is an attack on the notion of essences: attempts to reduce the complexities of human life to a few factors that serve as the key to understanding a social reality. His main objective to the search for such essences is that they eliminate human agency. History becomes the playing-out of various kinds of supposedly ageless forces – whether it is caste society, the Hindu mind, the Asiatic Mode of Production, Oriental Despotism or whatever – rather than the outcome of historical actions of complex human agents.[9] In a similar vein, much earlier, A.K. Coomaraswamy[10] countered the overemphasis on 'spirituality' and 'otherworldliness' that was labelled on Indian society.

Drawing attention towards another aspect of scholarship on Indian society, Indradeva and Shrirama say that, '... most serious difficulty seems to be that it leads to a comparison of entities which do not belong to the same order ... the construction of a continuum with two polar types ..., implies an unwitting faith in unilinear evolution – a doctrine hardly acceptable to contemporary social science.'[11]

Religion remains vital to the Indian way of life was also highlighted by G.S. Ghurye when he states that 'the Indic Civilization and its affiliated Hindu Civilization, as correctly stated by Toynbee, display a "manifest tendency towards a habitus which is predominantly religious", and the history of the development of this complex must form a major constituent of these Civilizations ... almost the whole of the complex of Hinduism, its shrines, its iconic deities, its particular mode of worship, was fixed by about the beginning of the Christian Era ... Emotional devotion to a personal deity has been conclusively proved to have been a glorious evolutionary achievement whose steady and progressive march spreads over the long span of time that lies between Svetasvatara Upanishad, one of the ten older ones of that class of literature, through the Bhagavadgita to the works of Ramanuja, Jnanesvar, Ramanand, Chaitanya and others and may be said not to have yet halted'.[12] Thus, it is true that the various aspects of Hinduism are not the entire of the same provenance, equally enduring and equally old, but what is remarkable is its tolerance for diversity, and a source and guarantor of identity.

Interaction and accommodation among various diverse groups, though not smooth and complete, gave rise to the beliefs and practices of Hinduism – a way of life that had a federal character, allowing the local, regional and heterodox cultural traditions to thrive within its fold. Therefore, in contemporary Indian society, we witness the existence of reality on diverse plains. In the words of Gerald James Larson, there is '... on one level (hidden or latent), one of the world's oldest collections of cultures with its *kavya* (formal poetry), *vyakarana* (science of grammar), *purana* (old tales), *itihasa* (tradition), *darsana* (philosophical reflection), its Yogins and *sadhu*-s (holy men) and pilgrims, and its plurality of tongues, old and new, still "abiding"... on another level (apparent or manifest), that same culture celebrating its identity by cloaking itself with the symbols of imperial power, pageantry and ritual reenactment borrowed from the "eventide" of Western civilization's expansion ... there are two levels of truth in contemporary India, one level representing the changing, empirical dimensions of everyday life (*samvrti-satya*), another level representing what truly is, or what truly is the case – namely, the level of absolute truth (*paramartha-satya*) ... whether one argues that the "flux-level" of India as a modern secular nation-state is ultimately illusory or is, rather, a provisional, empirical formulation that has a certain plausibility within an appropriate context, all would surely agree that it is crucial to take full account of the "permanence-level" of Indic civilization within which the "flux-level" operates and to attempt to understand the manner in which the permanence-level and flux-level interact historically, ontologically and epistemologically'.[13]

Religious organizations and rituals constitute the major component of any organized religion. These function with the specific intention of spiritual fulfilment of human members of the society. Day-to-day behaviour pattern, and the present social structure and ideology of Indians, are still supported by ideals of '*dharma*' and '*moksha*'. Personal worship, worship in temple, guidance of spiritual authorities and pilgrimage still hold the imagination of the Hindus. Studies on temples in India, therefore, can go to a large extent in explaining the reality, and answer queries regarding apparently incongruent forces within the society.

Srinivas, in his essay on a South Indian deity Ayyappa,[14] advises that an open mind and statement of facts by the researcher, notwithstanding what has been stated before, is the best hope for knowing the reality as well as for future theory building. He says, '... the student of Indian social institutions has to take great care to see that he treats the field situation or "the ethnographic reality", as a novel one, and not as something which either reflects or ought to reflect what is in the books, sacred or otherwise. There is an implicit assumption, all the more dangerous because it is implicit, that practices ought to correspond with what is in the books, and this has a dangerous effect on observation as well as on theory.' His conclusion in the essay on the South Indian deity Ayyappa is relevant and applicable to the Jagannath Temple tradition of Puri as well, when he states that, 'The story of Ayyappa illustrates clearly how local cults all over India are woven into Sanskritic Hinduism. Such a process produces numerous inconsistencies and oddities which irritate people with tidy minds, but what is important for the sociologist is the fact that due to this process a local group becomes part of an all-India community and at the same time retains its individuality.'

Srinivas feels that religion in India does not need to be seen as an antithesis to the changing environment of post-colonial India because like in the past, religion remains a dynamic phenomenon that will adapt itself according to the requirement, as evident in the emergence of 'cult of new Godmen', etc. He concludes that,

> ... Hinduism, with caste and the worship of many gods and goddesses, and its pristine syncretistic bent, is a live-and-let-live religion, and this may be still seen in some local festivals and pilgrimages. Also, at the local level, particularly in rural areas, people not only belonging to different castes and other ethnic groups but to different religions, are economically and socially interdependent. In such interdependence lies the best hope of coexistence.[15]

Cultural Dynamics of the Jagannath Temple

There has been a tendency to fix the nature of Indian identity in particularistic terms, which exhibit less delicate sensibilities on the part of the researchers towards the distinctive pattern of 'continuous accretion' that have taken place in the growth of Indian civilization. We can now turn to see how this pattern of 'continuous accretion' takes place by looking into the cultural dynamics of Jagannath Temple at Puri, Orissa.

The antiquity of Puri as a sacred place of pilgrimage was established even before the present shrine of Lord Jagannath was constructed in the 12th century. This is evident from the following:

- Satyendra Patnaik found, '... in the Bhaumakara period (for two centuries from 736 AD) we come across the names of Purusottama and Balabhadra for the first time in the records. The discovery of a stone slab depicting the Car Festival further strengthens this contention'.[16]
- 'The Sarasvati-Temple Inscription of Maihar' of erstwhile Madhya Pradesh clearly presents, according to D.C Sarkar and V.S. Subramanyam, that 'the god (Purusottama) was enjoying the same celebrity as in early as the middle of the 10th century and probably even some time earlier'.[17]
- From distant places like Madhya Pradesh and Gaya, pilgrims visited the place.[18]
- The 'Vedi' on which the Pandavas prayed on to acquire divine prowess, mentioned in the tirth-yatra section of 'Vana Parva' the Mahabharata, is supposed to have been a place of worship in Puri as clarified by K.C. Mishra. He also pointed further to three dilapidated temples on the Mahendra hill, which according to local tradition, were constructed by the Pandavas.[19]
- According to one of the debatable theories proposed by many researchers, the Chinese traveller Hiuen Tsang referred to Puri when he talks of 'Uchang–na'. His visits to India were during 630–44 AD when Harshavardhana (606–47 AD) was the king of Kanauj.[20]
- Historically, it is held to be true that Shankaracharya (788–820 AD) had come to Puri and played a vital role in consolidating Hindu faith and reinvigorating the influence of Brahmins in this area.[21]

However, it must be mentioned that researchers have agonized to establish the essential and authentic historicity of the tradition. But, the present researcher feels that it is not right to equate tradition with antiquity as because a tradition is not necessarily less compelling if its origin does not go back to the distant past. The following description may establish the basis of this feeling.

Hindu sacred centres, by tradition, have classical shape, like Varanasi, in the shape of a 'half moon', Viraja Kshetra (Jajpur, Orrisa), in the shape of a 'bada', etc. Similarly, Puri is considered as Shankha (conch) Kshetra, drawing parallel to the holy conch of Lord Vishnu.[22]

'What is most characteristic of such cities, according to Wheatley,[23] is the "cosmo-magical" thought and symbolism they represent. Such symbolism presupposes a strong parallelism between heaven and earth. Duplicating the divine order, the city draws forth the power of that order into the cities and the kingdoms of the earth.'[24]

According to O.M. Starza,[25] in the Puranas, 'Puri was imagined to be a massive conch full of sand, from the sea. Diameter of its largest symbolic circle was ten miles long and the Shankha Kshetra was four miles wide, extending right up to the seabed. It commenced from the Mango Forest at the top of the conch on the western extremity of the town to the Nilkantha shrine on the front tip in the southeast. The tirth is traditionally divided into three geographical sections consisting of the head of the Shankha, the middle which is known as antarvedi and the tip, which stretches beyond the silted-up estuary to the Balagandi. The circumference of the inner symbolic circle around the Rohini well and the banyan tree on the Blue Mountain covers a distance of two miles and stretches from the sanctuary of Kapalamocana on the west to that of the Goddess Ardhasani in the middle of the Shankha Kshetra, the Rohini Kunda on the Blue Mountain and that of Manika near the Kapalamocana shrine. The antarvedi is as holy as the heart of Vishnu itself and is said to give mukti to all mortals. It is guarded by eight Saktis and Sivas who stay in the eight directions of the city. Mangla lives under the Vatamula tree, while Vimala resides in the western part of the inner enclosure of the Jagannath Temple. Behind the conch-shell dwells Sarva Mangla, while towards the north stay both Arddhasini and Lamba. Kalaratri Legend relates that when Rudra saw the eight manifestations of the Devi he prayed for similar divisions of his own being. Hence, Visnu himself remaining at the centre, set up the eight sambhus: Kapalamocana, Ksetrapala, Jameswara, Markandeya, Isana, Vilvesa, Nilkantha and Vatesa.'

'According to Tantric philosophy, the Sankha Kshetra is made up of seven concentric folds. The inner most or first fold, as the navel of the Kshetra is the seat of the divine platform on which Lord Jagannath with his elder brother Lord Balabhadra and their sister Goddess Shubhadra are installed. The second fold ... is hexagonal in shape and provides the seats for four goddesses of power (Bimala, Kamala, Sarbamangala, and Uttarai), two tirthas (Rohini kunda and Pranito daka kunda), two sacred trees (Kalpapadapaaud and Salmalitaru), Garuda (the vehicle of Lord Vishnu) and the top of the Nilgiri Hill which is convex like the back of a tortoise. The third fold ... is the central part of the lotus-like structure having eight petals, each inlaid with a Shiva and a goddess ... these deities are responsible for watching and guarding the first fold having the Supreme Lord of the Sacred Complex. The fourth fold ... forms the convex surface of the temple precinct (Mahakurma) and the inner compound wall. The fifth fold ... is the seat of eight Sivas and eight goddesses ... in charge of watch and ward functions of the sacred complex. The sixth fold ... includes the noted five tirthas and the four original monastic seats of Ashram. The five tirthas are: Manikarnika (a Shiva temple), Swetaganga (a tank), Indradyumna (the tank and the temple of Indradyumna), Markanda, Mahodadhi (the sea). The four ashrams are: Angira in the east, Pandu in the west, Markandeya in the north, and Brigu in the south. The seventh fold, which is the outermost zone, consists of the sentries (Nilkantheswara, Narasingh, Ardhasosani, Bileswar, Lokeswar, Kapileswar) of the Sankha Kshetra and two pilgrim centres (Chakratirtha, Sargadwara)... Of all the sacred centres located in different parts of the country Puri is considered to be the most holy and therefore regarded as heaven on earth. It is the abode of the Supreme Spirit (Narayan), which is installed in the great temple of Jagannath in the form of the wooden idol and by having his darshan a person, becomes free or is released from the bondage and the effects of Action (Karma). Therefore, Puri is outside the jurisdiction of Yamraja and Yameswar ... For these reasons Puri is looked upon as the supreme pilgrim centre (Tirthraj) among all pilgrim centres in India ... if a person dies in Puri he is released for good from the cycle of births and gets himself merged in the body of the Almighty.'[26]

Nothing specific has been found from archeological and epigraphical sources about the Jagannath Temple tradition at Puri before 10th century AD. 'The entire early period of 600 years from the 4th century to the beginning of the 10th century AD ... has as yet not yielded inscriptional references in any part of Orissa or Kalinga that could provide the slightest clue to the existence of a Purusottama kshetra in Orissa or of a Purusottama temple on sea shore.'[27]

The stone inscriptions of Kalindindi grant of the eastern Chalukya king Rajaraja I (of mid-11th century), Nagpur stone inscriptions (of 1104 AD), Pujaripali inscription (end of 11th century approximately) and Maihar stone inscription (unknown), according to von Stietencron,[28] corroborate the tradition that the Purusottama temple, constructed by Yayati I, existed since the middle of 11th century K.C. Mishra[29] is of course of the view that Yayati II was the founder of Purusottama temple at Puri. According to Starza,[30] unlike Bhubaneswara, during Somavamsi reign, Puri was not a centre of artistic creativity though culture flourished there too. Somavamsis were absolute in their silence, in their 160–year rule, about anything on this subject. Yet, it is a fact that a widely known Purusottama temple existed in Puri, within their kingdom. The case may be that the conquering Somavamsi king Yayati, in order to legitimize his rule in this region, and to connect ritually to his homeland, constructed the Purusottama temple in Puri, although they continued to worship Lord Shiva primarily as their original 'kula'. This explains the neglect and the ruin of the temple.

Following the same principle, Anantavaram Codagangadeva (1077–1147) took up the construction of the present shrine of Jagannath at Puri after 1135 AD on the ruins of the earlier temple. Though Shaiva in personal faith, Codaganga exhibited foresight and religious inclusiveness. More with an eye for socio-political acceptance and consideration, he harnessed co-existential tendencies, and started his reign basing on rising Vishnuism that was making inroads in the region from south and west. 'The conviction that Codagangadeva completed the temple is based on the evidence of two inscriptional passages. One of them occurs for the first time in the Dasgoba copperplate grant of Rajaraja III ... issued in 1198 AD ... The second inscriptional passage contained in the same record, refers to the coronation of Jatesvara Kamarnava VII (1147–1156)... This argument however, which has been repeated over and over again, is based on a wrong translation of the text ... This verse does not contain any hint of the completion of Codaganga's Purusottama temple, nor does it say that Kamarnava was crowned at Puri ... Gangesvara certainly started building the great temple, but he probably did not live to see its completion. The Utkalakhanda of Skanda Purana mentions the "garba pratistha" of the temple ... The Utkalakhanda tell us that this was not yet completed when the king ... died. Since the text also seems to indicate that the progress on the temple construction was slow after Codaganga's death, it seems likely that the temple was indeed completed towards the end of the reign of Anangabhima II. The mukhasala must have been added still later, possibly by Rajaraja or Anangabhima III. The Natamandapa was added after 13th century and Bhogamandapa was an addition of the 15th century .... It has to be noted that the great temple is mentioned for the first time in the Dasagoba copper plate grant of Rajaraja III, son of Anangabhima II. This also strengthens our view that Anangabhima II probably completed and consecrated the main temple tower ...'[31]

K.N. Mahapatra[32] has pointed out traces of Buddhist element in the worship of Jagannath. Various factors have been highlighted to establish this position:

- First, in the work 'Jananasiddhi' by Indrabhuti, the king of Uddiyana of 8th century AD, who was the founder of the Vajrayana system of Buddhism, Jagannath of Puri supposedly can be identified to Jagannath, a manifestation of Buddha.
- The car festival of Lord Jagannath has been identified with the tooth festival of the Buddhists.
- Third, the disregard of *jati*, *dharma* and commensality barriers in case of 'mahaprasad' of Lord Jagannath also has been credited to the Buddhist practices and ethos.
- Subhadra has been identified with Sangha, and Balaram with Dharma, in order to maintain consonance with the concept of identifying Lord Jagannath with Buddha.
- Kailash Chandra Singha[33] has argued that the fact that the eastern gate (the Lions Gate) is the main entrance to the temple, proves the Buddhist origin further. It is relevant that in Hindu temples, the main doors are usually located in the south or the west while the main doors to Buddhist *stupas* are always in the east.
- The 'ratnabedi' where the three idols stand is considered a *stupa*.
- Finally, the existence of a temple without openings within the Jagannath Temple precinct and the Bauddha Bijaya painting in the Lakshmi Temple are also presumed to accentuate the Buddhist connection to this cultural tradition.

It is assumed that by 7th to 8th centuries AD, Buddhism got overrun by Vaishnavism; the domination was perpetuated and Buddhism got assimilated more and more into Brahminism under the influence of Shankaracharya by 9th century AD. Rajendralal Mitra, in this regard, states, 'Looking moreover to the history of Buddhism in other parts of India and the way in which the Buddhist doctrine of the identity of the human soul with the divinity was appropriated by some of the Vedantists, the Buddhist belief of the sanctity of the *bo* tree made a part of the Hindu religion; the Buddhist repugnance to animal sacrifices taken up by the Vaishnavas; and the Buddhist practices appropriated for Hindu usage; it is impossible to resist the conclusion that Puri was like Gaya, a place of Buddhist sanctity and gradually converted to Hinduism.'[34] In this regard, Starza[35] reviews the opinions of various people, like A. Cunningham, A. Coomarswamy, J. Stevenson, H.K. Mahatab and J.W. Laidley, who were convinced of the admixture of Buddhism and Brahminism in the Jagannath tradition, and concludes that, '... there is no evidences to support the belief that the great temple of Puri occupies a former Buddhist site. Nor do any of the manifestations of the cult of Jagannath, such as the great car festival, the icon with the supposed relic of Krsna, the absence of caste rules in the temple, or the identification of the God with the Buddha Avatara of Vishnu, suffice to establish a Buddhist origin of the worship of Jagannath.'

Nilakantha Das[36] advocates, contrary to above, a supposedly Jaina origin of Jagannath. He connected the Nilamadhava legend to what he called Kalinga Jina that can be 'explained as Nila (black, nothingness) Ma (Mother, creative energy) and Dhava (white, i.e., the phenomenal universe). Some other reasons forwarded are summarized below:

- The 'natha' affix of Jagannath is also common to the names of many Jaina Tirthankaras.
- The famous 22 steps of the temple are said to symbolically represent the 22 Jaina Tirthankaras.
- The Jaina Kaibalya is supposed to be the pseudonym for mahaprasada.'[37]

However, reverting to Starza,[38] '... the general paucity of evidence makes it difficult or even impossible to assess the degree to which Jainism influenced the cult of Jagannath at Puri. Conceivably it did so during several different periods through contacts between Jainas and the worshippers of Jagannath. However, in any case it is clear that the Jagannath cult was not Jaina in origin.'

D.C. Sircar[39] is of the view that Lord Jagannath, like many other deities of India (Venkateswara Balaji of Tirupati, Minakshi at Madurai, Kamakhya in Assam, to name a few), has an aboriginal origin. The tribal origin of the Jagannath tradition is pretty emphatic and clear. The Hinduized uniconical symbols of aboriginals has shaped the present iconography that cannot be linked to a particular Hindu deity is further strengthened by Indradyumna legend. 'The idea of Jagannath seems to have come from "Jaganaelo", the tribal prototype of Jagannath, amongst the Sabaras, living in the forest tracts of Ganjam, Koraput and Dhenkanal districts. They still believe that of all the ten kitungas (Gods), "Jaganaelo" is the greatest and He is therefore, called the Lord of Lords and the Lord of the universe. His wooden image is found coloured with different colours like red, white and yellow, and he is affectionately also known as "Madala", meaning a wooden log without any limbs except the face. It is not unlikely that Jagannath was originally worshipped in the form of tree by the Austrics or the Proto-Austroloids and later in the form of "Daru", and still later on in the form of "Madala" which was converted to an unknown image.'[40] The presence of Daita and Patimahapatra priests of Jagannath, who claim tribal descent, till the present day, also point towards the tribal origin of the tradition. Nevertheless, this connection cannot be so simplistically explained. Hinduization took place by identifying the tribal deity with Narasimha, adding a head with arms. This occurrence is nothing unusual as, since Gupta period, Purusottama, being a title of Vishnu, can be invoked through Narasimha who also is an 'avatar' of Vishnu. Even to this day, Narasimha plays a vital role during 'anabasara' and 'navakalevara' rituals connected with the shaping of the images. Stietencron[41] feels that '... there was a period of at least 80 years during which the cult subsisted (till the end of

12th century) – if at all – on a reduced scale. By the end of this period a revival of Purusottama cult could well have been accompanied by a combination of the cult of the wooden God with that of the Hindu Purusottama. Such an amalgamation of the two cults, out of which one was living and popular, and the other almost extinct but replete with the memory of an ancient glory required royal authority and certainly involved the legitimatory aspects ... The scenery for such a process of transformation required:

1. a pre-existing Brahmanic Purusottama cult in neglected state;
2. a pre-existing semi tribal cult of a wooden God Bhairava/Narasimha; and
3. a conqueror that is powerful monarch and requires legitimization by joining two cults ...

The intention to join them should be attributed to Ananatavarman Codagangadeva. It was put into practice only in later generation.'

The layout of the sacred inhabitation of Puri conspicuously shows the *'shaiva'* and *'shakta'* connection to the temple of Jagannath that lies on a high land, encompassing which are the Shiva temples. This unusual constellation of Vishnu and Shiva temples can be understood only in terms of the Shakti connection. The temple of Vimala within the precincts of the Jagannath Temple, offering of 'prasada' of Jagannath first to Goddess Vimala, central position of Subhadra in the sanctum, and the 'tantric' tradition of Vimala being shakti of Puri and Jagannath the corresponding Bhairava, are the pointers indicative of Vimala being the presiding deity of the place, metamorphosed with the changing times and conditions.[42]

In this connection, it is interesting to note the striking similarity between the iconography of Ekapada Bhairava and Jagannath. Stietencron[43] and Starza[44] opine that the transformation occurred under Shaiva auspices, which is even conceded in Purusottama Mahatmya of Skanda Purana, recorded around 1300 AD. Stietencron further explains that, 'when at a later stage the Vaishnavas accepted the Wooden God; they emphasized only the Narasimha elements while the Bhairava elements were largely excluded from theology and ritual. This may partly explain why only the iconography of Jagannath has retained traces of Bhairava ... It is likely that two gods of same shape were simply juxtaposed ... In later Pancaratra interpretation ... they became the brothers Balabhadra and Jagannath ... The third image of Puri triad, the image of Subhadra ... may have been related to Bhairava at an early stage. Being his *Shakti* she stands at his left side. She retained this position, which is that of the wife of Siva (who changed to Balabhadra) till today. And till today she is considered as Durga Bhubaneswari with whose mantra she is worshipped ... In the course of the Pancarata re-interpretation she was renamed as Subhadra and officially considered as the sister of Balabhadra and Jagannath.'[45] K.C. Mishra[46] points out in reference to the stone inscription of Gopinathpur of the time of King Kapilendradeva, '... that even in the 15th century AD, the goddess Subhadra was treated as Bhagavati Durga.'

After Anantavarman Codagangadeva, the Vaishnava influence was more systematically used on the triad of Puri mainly under the influence of Ramanuja, and was consolidated by the Pancarata system of interpretation connecting Purusottama with Krishna, Subhadra with Ekanamsha Durga, and

Balabhadra with Samkarsana. Sudarsana weapon of Vishnu, present with the triad, may have been originally the 'chalanti-pratima' of the early Jagannath-Narshima icon, is interpreted as the 'kriya-shakti' of Vishnu.

In words of G.C. Nayak[47] we can say that the significance of shrine of Jagannath 'lies in the fact that it is a successful attempt in the form of an image to express the reality of the Upanishads which is both nirguna and saguna and in whom the salvation of mankind rests ... Jagannath is a unique expression of the ultimate reality of the Upanishads, which having a form is at the same time formless ... (it) has the capacity to express the formless in a way which is unique in the history of mankind.' Mystical analysis of Jagannath also explain the trio as Purusha, Prakriti and Kala; as Sat, Chit and Ananda; and Prema, Gyana and Shakti.'[48] 'It is no wonder that Jagannath being the expression of such reality has proved himself to be capable of fulfilling the aspirations of varieties of races and cults through out the ages. And only in this background one can understand how diverse, antagonistic, and mutually contradictory theories are built and flourish side by side in connection with one and same reality, i.e., Jagannath.'[49]

The identification of Lord Jagannath at Puri with Lord Krishna, though all along prevalent, was popularized by Caitanya only after 1512 AD when he visited Puri. Imprint of Caitanya's philosophy can still be seen in the temple. The marginalized and the outcaste among Hindus were accepted by Caitanya, providing them a relatively secured place in the social order. Caitanya propounded Vaishnavism attached no importance whatsoever to the socio-economic background of the people in their spiritual tryst. Preaching universal fraternity, Caitanya emphasized faith on and love for Krishna (Hari), therefore, in reality denounced caste-based orthodoxy. 'The possibility is strong, then, in preaching Vaishnavism to the masses at the time when Brahminical Hinduism was under pressure, the Gaudiya Vaishnavas were in fact seeking to promulgate Brahminical rules of social ethics through a medium with which people of all classes and social levels could identify.'[50] Caitanya as the 'bhakta' (devotee) of Lord Jagannath, in reality, had a lasting enough impact on the Jagannath tradition at Puri, still evident in the practices – within 'anandabazar' (where the sacred offerings to the Lords are available for the pilgrims), the undefilable 'mahaprasad' (sacred offerings to the Lords), the daily 'kirtan' (sacred songs) where any one can join, etc. – has liberated the temple tradition further, adapting its expansion to the changing demographic, political, economic and cultural features of the society. In fact, Caitanya made the Jagannath Temple more amenable to the aspiration of the masses by popularizing the identification of Lord Jagannath with Shri Krishna, thereby utilizing the reach of the latter as a vehicle for propagating their liberal views, ultimately strengthening the place of the Jagannath Temple at Puri within the cultural tradition of India.

The tradition of Jagannath Temple at Puri imbibes religiosity, but is tolerant enough to be sobered with the ideas of different faiths, cultures, religions and allied influences. The consequence that this tradition imparts is one of confederation of faiths, united despite diversity, and presenting a tangible beacon of co-existence and peace.

The sanctum sanctorum in all Hindu temple architecture is commonly known as the sacred *garbha griha*, where the presiding deity is enthroned on a raised platform, facing the east side inside the tower, clearly identifiable from outside; the platform is surrounded by a narrow passage for the observance of the ritual of circumambulation, and is faced by an antechamber and a hall with roof and pillars. As Hindu temples are endowed with social responsibility, they tend to expand in form and content as new necessities crop up. Therefore, Hindu temples usually function also as forums of performing arts and sites of congregation; besides, they house many secondary and subsidiary temples, permitting concurrent practice of diverse faiths and sects.

In the period from the 7th to 13th century, India witnessed the erection and construction of most large and renowned temples. The practice has continued till date (the 'rich' replacing the 'monarchs') although it suffered a steady decline after political power shifted to rulers of the Muslim faith, in the wake of the invasions from the northwest of the subcontinent.

It is relevant to note here that the temples in India usually housed a central deity. The enshrined images were considered to be the embodiment of either one of the incarnate forms of the Mother Goddess, or those of the two of the trinity – Lord Shiva and of Lord Vishnu. A successful pilgrimage to these sacred sites was recognized both by society and the leaders of the religious faith as a commendable achievement in the process of spiritual salvation; that the pilgrimages also did not subject the common devotees to the much harsher conditions of restraint and discipline of asceticism, made them only more expedient. Quite naturally, therefore, such pilgrimages attained the status of a primary benchmark in the overall socio-religious life of the general population.

The architectural design of these Hindu temples did adhere to some preordained conventions, but gradually they also came to learn, adapt and assimilate newer and different methods, materials, effects and influences, corresponding to creative versatility and availability of resources. It would not be unreasonable to assume that architectural ideas and principles from other distant countries also percolated in from the experiences and writings of travellers and ambassadors. The resultant architecture applied to these temples have given rise to two distinct forms, one in northern India and the other in southern India, with specifically discrete forms of the temple structure above the sanctum sanctorum.

At this point, it becomes a necessity to clarify briefly the major aspects and inclusive philosophical interpretations of the architecture and constructions at the Jagannath Temple:

- The temple – the abode of Lord Jagannath, viewed as the ruler of the universe – is conceptualized as a fort. It has been provided with four gates, namely the Lions Gate (Simha Dvara), Horse Gate (Ghotak Dvara), Tiger Gate (Byaghra Dvara) and the Elephant Gate (Hasti Dvara). The main entrance – Lion Gate – is on the east of the temple, symbolizing strength. On the southern gate, horses are placed on either side, symbolically exhibiting military prowess. The Tiger Gate on the west showcases energy. Finally, the Elephant Gate on the north, indicating prosperity. In consonance to the traditional Indian practice of circumambulation (*pradaksin*) by the pilgrims where the sacred object should remain all the time on the right side of the circumambulator, we therefore see the process of going round the temple from east to south, to west, and then to north. The local tradition also says that the four gates of the temple signify *dharma* (east/lion), *kama* (south/horse), *moksa* (west/tiger) and *artha* (north/elephant). Lord Jagannath, the Supreme Master of the universe, is also assumed to accord to his devotees the 'Chaturvarga' (dharma, artha, kama and moksa) through these four gates of the temple. According to another school of thought, these gates in different directions of the temple represent *dharma* (east/lion), *jnana* (south/horse), *vairagya* (west/tiger) and *aisvarya* (north/elephant). This view claims to find its resonance in the ritual prayer of the *Sevayats*, who while worshipping the gates as part of their daily ritual services, offer Pushpanjali to the four gates by saying Dharmaya Svaha, Jnanaya Svaha, Vairagya Svaha and Aisvarya Svaha.

- The second significant aspect relates to the planning of the layout of the temple on the lines of a fort; one example is the lofty strong walls; wells dug up in the four corners of the complex, provided a perennial source of water at the times of siege, ensuring the survival of the blockaded civilians seeking refuge in the temple from Mohammedan invaders.
- Standing near the Garuda pillar devotees pray to Lord Jagannath and other deities. The Garuda pillar believed to house the famous Samantakamani with miraculous curative power. Pilgrims for this reason are known to embrace the pillar leading to body contact, and also bathe in the water used for washing the pillar. On the walls of the Bhogamandapa, laterally behind the Garuda pillar, ten incarnations of Vishnu are sculpted, peculiarity of which is that in one incarnation Jagannath and Buddha stand juxtaposed. In all probability, such identification was under the influence of the continuous assimilatory attempts of Hinduism. It is interesting to know that the local Pancaskhas still claim that Lord Jagannath at Nilachala, in the Kaliyuga, would take birth as the Buddha.
- The sanctum sanctorum or 'Manikotha' where the presiding deities are placed on a raised platform (known as the 'Ratnavedi', 16 ft long, 13 ft wide and 4 ft high) which according to tradition supposedly contains one lakh 'salagramashilas'. According to a tradition, the temple has been conceived as a 'yogic purusa'. As a yogi has to pass through the eight-fold of yoga or stages of life, similarly, the temple has eight organs (astanga) such as (from below to the top) *pabhaga, bandhana, jhangha, gandi, garbha, beki, khapuri* and *kalasa*.
- The images worshipped inside the vimana are of two kinds, namely, *arca* images and *tattva* images. In the temple three kinds of images are found, i.e., *dhyana* images following the sastras (Narayana, Ananta, Purusottama, Vimala, Laksmi, Bhuvanesvari), *avarana tattva* images following the silpa sastras (Ksetrpala, Tapasvimahavira, Vaikunthesvara, Patalesvara, etc.), and decorative images (Gopesvara, Ganga-Yamuna, Jaya-Vijaya Ramabhiseka, Yoganarayana). The images of presiding deities (of Jagannath, Balabhadra and Subhadra) do not conform to the dhyanas as

well as to the traditional iconographic texts in an attempt to symbolically present the Infinite.

- The Jagannath Temple, like many other Hindu temples, is located in higher altitudes on top of hills or raised natural platforms/hillocks as a site of greater spiritual excellence and appreciation symbolizing the importance of spirituality over worldly life.
- The various segments of the temple of Jagannath, as seen above, according to a tradition, represent different organs of the human body (e.g., *garbha graha* or sanctum sanctorum symbolizes womb and sometimes the human heart). In this way, the temple epitomizes God in his supernatural as well as natural. It, therefore, symbolically links the mortal humans to the immortal God, draws the connection between the material plane and the spiritual plane, and tries to show the obvious and the ideal side by side.
- There are relatively few erotic scenes depicted inconspicuously on the outer wall of the Jagannath Temple. They can be interpreted as the expressions of general exuberance, a form of thanksgiving to the Gods who created us all. However, it can also be seen to reflect the concern that one must set aside the worldly temptations upon the threshold of the temple. In fact, such carvings simultaneously express a celebration of *samsara* (worldly) and a movement towards *moksha* (otherworldly).
- The outward appearance of the Jagannath Temple raises the expectation of meeting with God. However, the temple was not designed necessarily with an eye towards maintaining a harmony with its surroundings; the construction rather seems to be a break in the continuity, for starkly manifesting the sacred exception. Jagannath Temple, which is thought to be an opening towards heavenly direction ensuring communication with the Gods, is the manifest representation of a cosmic pillar and its site is said to be a navel of the world.

Lastly, we now turn to the *Sevayats* (temple ritual servitors) and their organization within the temple that also exhibits principles that are not seen elsewhere in India. Since the inception of this tradition, it may be noted that in the face of social, economic and political ups and downs, the *Sevayats* have survived and emerged as the strongest upholders of this enigmatic religious tradition based on inclusive principles, designed as a symbol of universal goodwill and synthesis of diverse religious trends, besides acting as a message of peace. Anangabhimdeva (1211 AD) foresaw the need for disciplined administration of the temple and introduced the system of '*Chattisa Niyoga*' (thirty-six types of *Sevayats*) in place of original nine types of *Sevayats*. *Niyoga* is an association of each category of *Sevayats* with distinct duties, organized for effective execution of daily rites and rituals within the temple. Proportionate to their ritual functions *Sevayats* enjoyed part of the '*Amrit Mahoni*' (rent-free land) and '*Khei*' (*Kotho Bhog* offering). In the course of time, increasing endowments made to the temple necessitated greater elaboration of ritual services and worship. This led to a sub-division and bifurcation of the various *niyogas* to independent *niyogas*. In the Record of Rights (L. Panda, 1955), 119 categories of *Sevayats* are indicated but the census of the *Sevayats* conducted by Sri Jagannath Temple

Administrative Committee in 1988 showed 63 types. The *Sevayats* of different castes, regardless of their contemporaneous social rank, were accorded equal status and importance considering their association and engagement in the temple. Though this did not affect their ethos, the unique method of organization among the *Sevayats* in the Jagannath Temple reflected a virtual liberalism and imparted a democratic character to the entire organization.

The *Sevayats* of the Jagannath Temple have never allowed the tradition to retreat itself in the private sphere, or get segregated or marginalized. In fact, here we see that there is a continuous effort to de-privatize it, thus providing an alternative to the masses to fulfil their religious obligations. In contemporary India, to overcome the mutual incomprehension of multicultural Indians, the *Sevayats* ensure that the temple remains mainstream fold by fashioning a new form of hybridism that will integrate people in the midst of diversity. Going beyond the doctrines and dogmas, the *Sevayats* are trying to place the Jagannath Temple tradition in such a manner that a communitarian ethic is evolved to counter individualism. Therefore, the outward permanence of the organization is permeated by the vitality and dynamics in the assimilative matrix of the tradition.

The *Sevayat* organization within the temple provides us the following insights:

1. The organizational practices of the Jagannath Temple at Puri disproves the fact that *jati*-based divisions hindered pluralistic interface. The *Sevayat* organization in the temple exhibits the dynamic process of 'sanskritization' where people from multiple *jatis* and tribes claim equal status though their functions in the temple are *jati*-ordained. Further, they work together maintaining a complex work roaster and work shift, thus, they have an obligation to cooperate and share with each other. Such practices over the ages have safeguarded Indian society from external threats as well as internal corrosion and ossification.
2. Despite the fact that the Jagannath Temple at Puri represents a pan-Indian Hindu religious organization but the process of acculturation and integration seen within the organization has been mostly at work at the regional level. On the one hand, we see each group or community with a distinctive identity and ethos but on the other they do not exist in a social vacuum and, therefore, is part of an extended and dynamic network. Often, interaction, exchange and integration characterize this. The Jagannath Temple at Puri often bridges the gaps in inter-community relations allowing them to share space, and uphold regional culture and ethos binding people of the region despite their religious and sectarian differences.
3. Better transport and communication now allow disparate groups and communities to influence and exchange with one another, thus increasing the opportunity for better understanding. Ritual functionaries of the Jagannath Temple today are much more open in their interaction with outsiders despite their ortho-praxy.
4. Pluralistic interface in India has gone beyond the restrictive religious substance, has become less value-loaded in its form, allowing people to

interact and influence each other without hurting their closely held sensibilities.

5. Rigidity and closed practices are a passé today as people are going to make choice, compare and judge in relative terms. Therefore, institutionally and individually religious beliefs and practices have to take into consideration the privatized religious necessity of its clientele.
6. Volition and identity are two important factors that have gained importance at present than in past.

Conclusion

The tradition of Shri Jagannath Temple at Puri, as discussed above, shows its capacity to absorb and respond to the expectations of the society. This may be the reason that we can speculate about the cause of the continued reach and popularity of this tradition. In this context, it seems pertinent to look at what Nye observes: '... religious organisations and religious cultures are as subject to change and influence as any other human activity ... When anthropologists and other cultural analysts describe such processes of hybridity they are not implying that the mixing is a problem, rather they are trying to describe a reality that they perceive. That is, cultures and religions are rarely as "pure" and unmixed as their members would like to think they are.'[51] This is what Rosalind Shaw and Charles Stewart (1994) describe in context of religion, as the antithesis between "syncretism" and "anti-syncretism". Thus, they argue that 'all religions have composite origins and are continually reconstructed through ongoing processes of synthesis and erasure'.[52] This happens all the time, and any religion ... is particular and unique: made up of specific historical and cultural processes that make up of specific historical and cultural processes that make it distinct from other religious cultures, even of the same religion ... so in this sense, all religious cultures are syncretic, and there is no such thing as a non-syncretic religion. Even so, this does not mean that a particular religious tradition cannot also be authentic, since for Shaw and Stewart: 'authenticity' or 'originality' do not necessarily depend on purity ... is a separate issue, a discursive matter involving power, rhetoric and persuasion. Thus, both putatively pure and putatively syncretic traditions can be 'authentic' if people claim that these traditions are unique.

The regional tradition of Shri Jagannath Temple at Puri mirrors the Indian spiritual vision of 'Sanatana Dharam' and 'Sarva Dharma Samanwaya Dharma'. It has absorbed and assimilated all those various tenets that divide the Indians at mundane level, thus envisioning us with the same Indian spirit that brings *samanwaya* amongst aboriginal tribalism to Vedic Hinduism, to Buddhism, to Jainism, to Shakta, Shaiva and Vaishnava mode of worship, to *'advaitavad'* of Shankara to *'dvaitavad'* of Ramanuja to the *'bhakti'* of Caitanya. Religion being part of our culture, we can expect that strengthening of pluralistic tendencies would allow us to celebrate the commonality of major differences. Pluralism of India variety with eclectic social ingredients both at macro and at micro levels holds out hope for better fulfilment of individual aspirations by enlisting their initiative and participation.

Notes

1. Yogendra Singh (2004). *Ideology and Theory in Indian Sociology*. Jaipur: Rawat Publications, p. 11.
2. A. Eschmann, H. Kulke and G.C. Tripathi (eds) (1978). *The Cult of Jagannath and the Regional Tradition of Orissa*. New Delhi: Manohar, p. xiii.
3. Malory Nye (2003). *Religion: The Basics*. London: Routledge, pp. 17–18.
4. Ibid., p. 31.
5. Ibid., p. 34.
6. Dr Satyanarayan Rajguru (1992). *Inscriptions of the Temples of Puri and Origin of Shri Purushotama Jagannath*, Vol. I. Puri: Sri Jagannath Sanskrit Visvavidyalaya, pp. 95–156.
7. Gerald James Larson (1997). *India's Agony over Religion*. Delhi: Oxford University Press, pp. 42–43.
8. Ronald Inden (1990). *Imagining India*. Oxford: Blackwell.
9. As quoted in Jr. M. Milner (1994). *Status and Sacredness*. Delhi: Oxford University Press, pp. 12–13.
10. A.K. Coomaraswamy (1948). *The Dances of Siva*. Bombay: APH Publishing and H. Zimmer (1952). *Myths and Symbols in Indian Civilization*. London: Routledge & Kegan Paul.
11. Indradeva and Shrirama (1999). *Society and Culture in India*. Jaipur: Rawat Publications, pp. 21–22.
12. G.S. Ghurye (1962). *Cities and Civilization*. Bombay: Popular Prakashan, p. 170 and 177.
13. Gerald James Larson (1997). op. cit., pp. 2–7.
14. M.N. Srinivas (1954/2002). 'A Brief Note on Ayyappa, the South Indian Deity', in K.M. Kapadia (ed.), *A Collection of Essays*, New Delhi: OUP, pp. 349–54.
15. Ibid., p. 370.
16. Satyendra Patnaik (1987). *Brahmanical Religion in Ancient Orissa*. New Delhi: Ashish Publishing House, p. 102.
17. Dr Satyanarayan Rajguru (1992). op. cit., p. 96.
18. See O.M. Starza (1997). *The Jagannath Temple at Puri: Its Architecture, Art and Cult*. Leiden: E.J. Brill.
19. See K.C. Mishra (1971). *The Cult of Jagannath*. Calcutta: Firma KLM, pp. 6–7.
20. Romila Thapar (1966). *A History of India*, Vol. 1. New Delhi: Penguin Books, pp. 143–46.
21. See K.C. Mishra (1971). op. cit., pp. 151–52.
22. See S. Pani (ed.) (1984). *Jagannath Consciousness*. Cuttack: n.p., p. 126.
23. Paul Wheatley (1971). *The Pivots of Four Quarters: A Preliminary Inquiry into the Origins and Character of the Ancient Chinese City*. Chicago, IL: Aldine.
24. See Diana L. Eck (1987). 'The City as a Sacred Centre', in B. Smith and H.B. Reynolds (eds), *The City as a Sacred Centre: Essays on Six Asian Contexts*, Leiden: E.J. Brill, p. 3.
25. O.M. Starza (1993). op. cit., pp. 8–9.

26. Nityananda Patnaik (1977). *Cultural Tradition in Puri*. Shimla: IIAS, pp. 26–30.
27. Eschmann, Kulke and Tripathy (eds) (1978). op. cit., p. 15 (*Note: Henceforth will be mentioned as CJRTO*).
28. See H.V. Stietencron, CJRTO (1978). pp. 17–20.
29. See K.C. Mishra (1971). op. cit., pp. 31–32.
30. O.M. Starza (1993). op. cit., p. 4.
31. H.V. Stietencron, CJRTO (1978), pp. 75–77.
32. K.N. Mahapatra (1954). 'Antíquiry of Jagannatha-Puri as a Place of Pilgrimage', *Orissa Historical Research Journal*, Vol. III, p. 7.
33. Kailash Chandra Singha (1923). *Sri Darubrahma*. Calcutta: n.p., p. 55, as quoted in Ishita Banerjee-Dube (2001). *Divine Affairs*. Shimla: Indian Institute of Advanced Study, p. 33.
34. Rajendralal Mitra (1880). *Antiquities of Orissa*, Vol. II. Calcutta: Wyman, p. 107. As quoted in Jagannath Padhi (2000). *Sri Jagannath at Puri*. Puri: SGN Publications, p. 44.
35. O.M. Starza (1993). op. cit., pp. 53–61.
36. See Nilakantha Das (1958). 'Hints on the Significance of Jagannath', *Orissa Historical Research Journal*, Vol. VII, Part I, pp. 1–36; and Ishita Banerjee-Dube (2001). op. cit., p. 35.
37. Himanshu S. Patnaik (1994). *Lord Jagannath: His Temple, Cult and Festivals*. New Delhi: Aryan, p. 86.
38. O.M. Starza (1993). op. cit., p. 63.
39. D.C. Sircar (1971). *Studies in the Religious Life of Ancient and Medieval India*. Delhi: Motilal Banarsidass, pp. 69–70.
40. Satyendra Patnaik (1987). op. cit., p. 100.
41. H.V. Stietencron, CJRTO (1978), p. 73.
42. Ibid., pp. 25–27.
43. Ibid., pp. 120–23.
44. O.M. Starza (1993). op. cit., p. 6.
45. H.V. Stietencron, CJRTO (1978), pp. 120–23.
46. K.C. Mishra (1971). op. cit., p. 50.
47. G.C. Nayak (1999). 'The Unique Vedantic Synthesis in Jagannath as Lokayata Bramha and Vaishnavism: A Philosophical Approach', *The Quarterly Journal of the Mythic Society*, Bangalore, July–September, p. 82.
48. See Gopabandhu Mohapatra (1981). *God in Three Images at Puri*. Dharma Puri: Jyoti Pitha, pp. 27–31.
49. G.C. Nayak (1999). op. cit., p. 83.
50. M.H. Klaiman (1983). 'Religious Tradition and Religious Revolution: The Case of Vaishnavism in Bengal', *South Asia: Journal of South Asian Studies*, June, Vol. VI, Part 1, p. 38.
51. Malory Nye (2003). op. cit., pp. 44–46.
52. Rosalind Shaw and Charles Stewart (1994). 'Introduction: Problematizing Syncretism', in Shaw and Stewart (eds), *Syncretism/Anti-Syncretism: The Politics of Religious Synthesis*, London: Routledge, as quoted by Malory Nye (2003). op. cit., p. 46.

11

Hinduism

Exclusivist or Inclusivist?

Hetukar Jha

J.H. Hutton, in the 1930s, observed that in Tamil Nadu Dalit women were not allowed to wear gold and silver ornaments, use sandal paste and flowers; similarly, Dalit men were prohibited from wearing clothes below the knee and above the waist, etc.[1] Many such examples of the field views of discrimination against Dalits and the practice of untouchability one may find among Hindus particularly during the colonial period. Ambedkar, however, considered untouchability as a 'permanent hereditary stain' of Hinduism, 'which nothing can cleanse.'[2] Hinduism, he asserted, has no concern with moral basis, liberty and equality.[3] Perhaps, the extreme level of dishonour to which the Scheduled Castes (SCs) were being subjected in the name of religion, prompted Ambedkar, Gaekwad of Badodra, Anant Krishna Aiyar and others to hold such a view against Hinduism.[4] Hindu social order of *jati/varna* system that held SCs as untouchable was proclaimed by Max Weber as a product of Brahminical theodicy.[5] Later, Louis Dumont reinforced Weber's view and held Brahminism encompassing all other economic and political domains of society in India.[6]

The understanding of Hinduism based simply on *Dharmashastras*, that is, according to D.D. Kosambi, 'tunnel vision'[7], led the British authorities and indologists to hold Brahminism as the essence of Hinduism as a whole. However, to consider this notion of Hinduism of one particular period (the colonial era) as valid for all ages of Indian history seems to be, according to Bourdieu, 'substantialist' or 'naively realist', which 'is inclined to treat the activities and preferences to certain ... groups in a society at a *certain moment as if they were substantialist properties, inscribed once and for all in a sort of biological or cultural essence leads to ... error*[8] (emphasis added). For a realistic understanding of Hinduism in the context of the tradition of exclusion (of SCs in particular), it, therefore, seems necessary to search for variations in the notion of Hinduism in different periods of history.

The word 'Hindu' or 'Hindutva' has not been mentioned in any ancient Indian literature such as the *Vedas*, *Upanishads*, *Sutras*, *Smritis*, etc. In none of the *Puranas*, it has been referred to. Only Arabs used this word for the inhabitants of India since late ancient and early medieval era. There is no evidence to indicate that people of India also adopted this identity as soon as Arabs began to call them 'Hindu'. The idea of Hinduism can be supposed to be valid only after it became based on social reality, that is, when people (Hindus) began to identify themselves as Hindu and practise certain ways of life in the name of Hindu *dharma*. In this context, it may be pointed out that there are only two books, not written before the 14th century AD, one *Keertilata* by Vidyapati and the other, *Prithviraj Raso*, in which the word 'Hindu' was first used by Hindus for Hindus.[9] It seems, thus, that this identity had been widely adopted by the people of India by the 13th century. David Lorenzen contends in this context that following the advent of Islamic politico-religious forces, in the 13th century, 'the Hindus developed a consciousness of a shared religious identity based on the family resemblance among the variegated beliefs and practices cutting across the boundaries of sect, caste, chosen deity or theological creed'.[10] Pt. Hajari Prasad Dwivedi also holds a similar view in this regard and asserts that the social base of Hinduism that emerged at that time became much broader than that of anyone of its constituent religious or sectarian traditions, sects/cults, which had originated and developed in India, such as Sanatani tradition, Vaishnava, Shaiva, Shakti and Tantric cults of Lokayata tradition, etc., since all of them (except Buddhism and Jainism) came to constitute a common fold of Hinduism by the 13–14th century.[11] Besides, Vidyapati, a great poet and statesman of Mithila (north-eastern part of Bihar) at that time, also gave a dictum regarding the notion of the emergent (Hindu) dharma in terms of private and public contexts. According to it, one should follow the tradition of his/her own family/lineage. In public sphere, one should follow *sadharan dharma*, that is, not to commit violence against any living being, not to think of others' property and women.[12] He did not include any *jati/varna* consideration in this context. Hinduism, thus, began as a very liberal *dharma* to allow its followers (of different sects and cults) to live together peacefully and coexist with the followers of other religions in harmonious atmosphere. It may be pointed out here that until the end of the 18th century after Vidyapati, Nanak, Kabir, Chaitanya and others, preached their doctrines of love for all against *jati/varna* consideration.[13] Under the circumstances, the Sanatani tradition cannot be supposed to have enjoyed supremacy among Hindus since Bhakti cult, Shakti cult, Shaiva cult, etc., according to Hajari Prasad Dwivedi, flourished quite visibly opposing Vedic or Brahminical influence.[14] Lokayata tradition has been continuing since ancient days which included different Tantric cults (in which the question of untouchability did not ever arise) and maintained anti-Vedic or anti-caste/varna philosophy quite rigorously.[15] Further, so far as Dumont's contention that Brahminism encompassed all other domains of society (mentioned before) is concerned, it may be pointed out that the age-long association (following Sanatani *shastras*) of *jati*/varna with kingship was virtually eroded in early 14th century, according to K.P. Jayaswal, a famous indologist of the last century.[16] Now, anyone (of any caste) who could look after *praja* (people) was qualified to become a king. In fact, according to R.S. Sharma, a number of non-Kshatriyas such as Vardhans, Kharwars, Palas, etc., came to occupy ruling positions in north India.[17] Dirks writes on the basis of his study of a south Indian kingdom, Pudu Kotai, since the end of the 17th century, that '... kings (of Kallar caste) were not inferior to Brahminas; the political domain was not encompassed by religious domain. State forums ... were powerful components in Indian civilization'.[18]

Hinduism remained a common religious identity of the followers of the traditions of different sects and cults of both orthodox and liberal nature. In north India, one finds Hinduism as quite liberal before the colonial rule. For example, in the crowded streets of the market place in the city of Jaunpur (in Uttar Pradesh), Vidyapati observed in early 15th century the sacred threads of Brahmins hanging on the bodies of (untouchables) Chandals.[19] Untouchability, it seems, used to be practically ignored in urban areas. In the 17th century, Banarasi Das, a Jain merchant, wrote in his autobiography, *Ardha Kathanaka*, that once, on way to Patna from Agra, he had to stay for a night in a village that was known as a village of thieves (belonging to SCs). He had been advised before to wear a sacred thread and introduce himself as a Brahmin while entering such a village. He accordingly prepared himself and, then, approached the villagers who gave him shelter and behaved quite respectfully.[20] The account of Banarasi Das suggests that Brahmins were respected by lower castes and they (Brahmins) also had no hesitation in accepting food from them or in living with them. Besides, the sects and cults professing against *jati/varna* order were also very popular. Buchanan, who conducted his famous survey of Patna-Gaya, Bhagalpur, Purnia and Shahabad districts of Bihar during the first two decades of the 19th century, found quite large number of non-upper caste groups following Vaishnavism, Kabir Panth, Aghor Panth, Sheonarayani, Dariya Panth, etc.[21] G.W. Briggs noted that people of Chamar caste in Uttar Pradesh had increasingly become the followers of Kabir Panth, Nanakshahi, Rai Das and Sheonarayani sects.[22] Ramakant Chakrabarty compiled a list of 56 sects which arose in the 17th and 18th centuries in Bengal, of which the Baul, the Jaganmohini, the Kartabhaj, etc., became well known, whose 'following was predominantly ... among the lower castes'.[23] The rise in the number of SCs following such Hindu sects as those (mentioned above) opposed to or independent of Sanatani order indicates the extent to which the SCs groups asserted their existence. This, at least indirectly, implies the feeble grip of Sanatanis over socio-cultural life in the society. This is also supported by the fact that a number of SCs families occupied ruling positions in different regions. For example, Pasis are said to have had their kingdoms at different places at Uttar Pradesh around 14th century.[24] Dusadhs were rulers of large areas in Bihar in the medieval period the ruins of whose forts were visible until the second half of the 19th century.[25] They also held important positions in Shahabad (in Bihar). In the zamindari of Jagadishpur, which was the largest zamindari in the district, Buchanan observed that 'The agents (officers) he (Shahebzada Singh – the *raja*, father of Kunwar Singh, who took lead in 1857 war against British power) employs ... Dusadhs and other low caste people ... everything is at the disposal of a Dusadh'.[26] Dusadhs also had almost monopoly of priesthood of the sacred order of village Gods.[27] Buchanan observed in this context that 'the Brahmins will not acknowledge the authority of these deities, but send offerings…'[28]. It may, further, be pointed out that in the village schools of Bengal and Bihar, which had been existing since long and were estimated to be about one lakh in number in the 1830s situated in the villages, the students of all caste groups (including SCs) sat together and received instruction together from *gurujis* (teachers) belonging to even SCs.[29]

One may, thus, infer from the account given before that the practice of Hinduism was not dominated by Sanatani orthodoxy until about the middle of the 19th century. Later, Sanatani orthodoxy was promoted by the colonial authorities. Caste identity was catapulted to become most important of all other identities. Caste consciousness was institutionalized by the end of the 19th century. One U.N. Mukherjee wrote a book, *A Dying Race* in 1909 regarding the position of lower castes. O'Malley wrote in the Census Report of 1911 that 'the present popularity of the term "untouchable" appears to be largely due to this writer's … monograph'.[30] The growing caste consciousness implied increasing consciousness regarding untouchability. Hinduism, thus, came to be circumscribed and defined as mere Brahminism.[31]

However, it may be mentioned that efforts were also made in the colonial period by such eminent persons as Swami Dayananda, Swami Vivekananda, Max Muller and others for highlighting the liberal and spiritual elements drawn from Upanishads and Vedanta as the true foundation of Hinduism. Probably due to this the campaign for eradicating untouchability and uplifting the conditions of SCs was started in the first quarter of the last century, which continued to gain ground in the following decades.

In the context of eradication of untouchability, however, an important event occurred in Bihar (now Jharkhand) in 1934. The *Dharmashastra* was used for the first time, perhaps, to challenge and invalidate the legitimacy of orthodox approach (proclaimed so far to have been based on the precepts of the same *Dharmashastra*) regarding untouchability. The disputation held in this context in 1934 is of historical importance. A detailed account of it was prepared and published by Nathmal Sinhaniyan, one of its organizers, in 1961, in the shape of a small book *Gandhiji ki Deoghar Yatra* (in Hindi).[32] This is the only source of information regarding the said disputation and it also contains a long description of Gandhiji's visit to Deoghar to lead SCs to the Shiva temple. It is a small book of only 88 pages, in the beginning of which a few words regarding the authenticity of its contents and their value written by B.N. Jha, Chief Minister of Bihar in 1961, are given. A summarized account of all that is described in this book is given here.

Arya Samaj and All India Hindu Mahasabha activists launched a sort of movement against the practice of untouchability in Bihar in 1923. In the beginning of the 1930s, SCs men were led to enter some temples to worship deities in Gaya and Shahabad. The movement spread to almost all districts of Bihar by 1932. In November 1932, *Asprishyata Virodhi League* was formed and in the following December it was named Harijan Sevak Sangh, the leading members of which were drawn mostly from upper caste groups. Their activities were, however, opposed at different places by those subscribing to orthodox view (*kattarpanthis*).[33] By 1934, Mahatama Gandhi himself began to lead the campaign against untouchability. It was in the course of this venture that he was requested to visit Deoghar (in the district of Santhal Parganas, Jharkhand). Nathmal Sinhaniyan, a very devoted worker of Congress at that time, was the *pradhan mantri* of the district Harijan Sevak Sangh of Santhal Parganas. Deoghar temple is one of the most sacred centres of Hinduism in the country. Thousands of pilgrims visit it from different corners of India. Sinhaniyan and others of Harijan Sevak Sangh felt that the question of Harijans' entry into the sacred places of Hindus would not be raised on religious ground if they could be led to worship the *Jyotirlinga* at Deoghar. So, they decided to invite Gandhiji to lead the Harijans to the said temple. Gandhiji arrived at Deoghar on 25 April 1934. But soon after his arrival, there was violent reaction of Sanatanis (organized by *pandas* of the temple). The security arrangement of the Harijan Sevak Sangh was always prompt and protected Gandhiji. He, however, remained quiet and composed and made it clear in his public speech (delivered on the following day) that he would not go to the temple unless Sanatanis would change their mind in favour of their Harijan brethren. After that, public meetings were organized in different places to condemn the attack on Mahatma by *kattarpanthis*. The latter, particularly *pandas*, then, began to invite pandits to deliver lectures in the premises of the temple in favour of untouchability. Harijan Sevak Sangh men also began speaking against Sanatani version. This continued for some time and, then, it was decided by both the parties to resolve this issue by holding *shastrartha* (disputation).

So, Harijan Sevak Sangh leaders wrote to Dr Bhagvan Das, a great indologist at that time, requesting him to come to Deoghar and hold disputation on their behalf. He, however, suggested the name of Pt. Lakshman Shastri Joshi for this and requested him personally to go to Deoghar. Harijan Sevak Sangh leaders also approached Joshiji who accepted the proposal. Pt. Joshi was a great scholar of Sanskrit learning and had conducted the marriage ceremony of Gandhiji's son (Vaisya) and Rajaji's daughter (Brahmin) earlier following Vedic way of marriage. One Pt. Akhilananda represented the Sanatani group. The disputation was held at Rajendra Bose Library at Deoghar and attended by hundreds of people.

First, Pt. Joshi said that according to *Shastras* the castes said to be untouchables can enter the temple and worship the deity. He quoted Vedic *mantra*, and, then referred to *Vishweshwara Sanhita*, *Vaidyanath Mahatmya* and *Shiva Purana* in support of his argument.[34] Akhilananda considered Vedic evidence irrelevant in this case and tried to impress the audience by his own interpretations. Joshi contradicted his views on the basis of *Nirukta* and 'Kedar Khanda' of *Skanda Purana*. Akhilananda continued to argue on the basis of interpretations generally popular among the orthodox Sanatanis. The disputation continued for a few hours. Sinhaniyan does not say how it came to an end. However, one thing became clear that in the *Shastras*, there is no unanimity of views regarding untouchability. So, if one cites one text in its favour, another text is there to oppose it. One important consequence of this disputation was that the entry of SCs in the temple of Vaidyanath Dham, and, perhaps, also in other temples (in Bihar) was not opposed in the following decades by the *pandas* in the name of *Shastras*. Thus, Hinduism has many shades, which together constitute what Amartya Sen, a great intellectual of the present era, calls 'Hindu spectrum'[35] including various cults/sects/traditions. However, one of them may appear to have hegemony over others in a particular period due to some specific socio-economic and political conditions. For example, one may consider the rise of Brahminism after the 1850s. But, this should not be considered to be the essence of Hinduism in the light of the history of its existence among the people of India since its emergence in the medieval era that signifies it as being more inclusivist than exclusivist.

Notes

1. J.H. Hutton (1977). *Caste in India: Its Nature, Function and Origin*. Bombay: Oxford University Press, pp. 205–6.
2. Quoted in Padma Velaskar (2000). 'The Politics of Untouchability and Social Change: A Study of the Scheduled Castes of Maharashtra', *Journal of Indian School of Political Economy*, XII (3 and 4), July–December, p. 483.
3. Valerian Rodrigues (1996). 'Making a Transition Critical: Ambedkar's Readings of Buddhism', in Peter Robb (ed.), *Dalit Movements and the Meanings of Labour in India*, SOAS Studies on South Asia, Delhi: Oxford University Press, p. 307.
4. Prasanna Kumar Chaudhary and Srikant (2005). *Bihar Mein Dalit Andolan* (in Hindi). New Delhi: Vani Prakashan, pp. 84–93.
5. Ramkrishna Mukherjee (2002). "Caste in Itself', 'Caste and Class' or 'Caste in Class", in Hetukar Jha (ed.), *Perspectives on Indian Society and History: A Critique*, New Delhi: Manohar, p. 16.
6. Nicholas B. Dirks (1996). *The Hollow Crown*. Ann Arbor: The University of Michigan Press, p. 4.
7. D.D. Kosambi (2002). 'Combined Methods in Indology', in Brajdulal Chattopadhyaya (ed.), *Combined Methods in Indology and Other Writings*, New Delhi: Oxford University Press, p. 4; first published in *Indo-Iranian Journal*, 6, 1963: 177–202.
8. Pierre Bourdieu (1998). *Practical Reason*. California: Stanford University Press, pp. 3–4.
9. For details in this context see Hetukar Jha (2006). 'Who Created Casteism and Communalism? Hinduism under Raj', in Surendra Gopal (ed.), *Colonial India: A Centenary Tribute to Prof. K.K. Datta*, Arrah (Bihar): V.K. University, p. 272, pp. 38–39 and 265–77; Besides, according to Rajat Kant Ray, 'It is not until 1352 that we find a Hindu ... referring to himself as Hindu in an inscription'. See Rajat Kant Ray (2003). *The Felt Community*. New Delhi: Oxford University Press, p. 85.
10. David Lorenzen (1999). 'Who Invented Hinduism?', *Comparative Studies in Society and History*, 41(4): 655.
11. Namvar Singh (1989). 'Bharatiya Sahitya ki Pranadhara aur Lokadharma (in Hindi)', in *Doosri Parampara Ki Khoj* (in Hindi), New Delhi: Rajkamal Prakashan, p. 6.

12. Hetukar Jha (2002). *Man in Indian Tradition: Vidyapati's Discourse on Purush*. New Delhi: Aryan Books International, pp. 75–77.
13. Hetukar Jha (2006). op. cit., p. 272.
14. Hajari Prasad Dwivedi (1950). *Nath Sampradaya* (in Hindi). Allahabad: Hindustani Academy, pp. 145–46.
15. Debi Prasad Chattopadhyaya (1959). *Lokayata: A Study of Ancient Indian Materialism*. New Delhi: People's Publishing House, p. 80, 269 and pp. 322–24.
16. K.P. Jayaswal (1936). 'Introduction', (in English) in Jayaswal (ed.), *Rajaniti Ratnakara by Chandeshvara* (in Sanskrit), Patna: Bihar and Orissa Research Society, p. 25.
17. R.S. Sharma (1974). 'Social and Economic Conditions (AD 550–1200)', in B.P. Sinha (ed.), *Comprehensive History of Bihar*, Vol. 1, Part II, Patna: K.P. Jayaswal Research Institute, p. 362.
18. Nicholas B. Dirks (1996). op. cit., pp. 4–5.
19. Vasudeo Sharan Agrawal (ed.) (1962). *Kavi Vidyapati Krit Keertilata* (in Avahatta). Jhansi: Sahitya Sadan, p. 76.
20. Nathu Ram Premi (1970). 'Bhumika', in Premi (ed.), *Kavivara Banarasi Das Virachit Ardha Kathanaka* (in Hindi), Bombay: Hindi Grantha Ratnakara Pvt. Ltd., p. 29.
21. For details in this context, see Hetukar Jha (2000). 'Promises and Lapses: Understanding the Experience of Scheduled Castes in Bihar in Historical Perspective', *Journal of Indian School of Political Economy*, XII (3 and 4), July–December, p. 427.
22. G.W. Briggs (2004/1920). *The Chamars*. Delhi: Low Price Publications, pp. 206–12.
23. Partha Chatterjee (1993). *The Nation and Its Fragments*. NJ: Princeton University Press, pp. 181–82.
24. Prasanna Kumar Chaudhary and Srikant (2005). op. cit., p. 50.
25. Hetukar Jha (ed.) (2001). *Mithila in the Nineteenth Century: Aina-i-Tirhut of Bihari Lal 'Fitrat'*. Darbhanga (Bihar): MKSK Foundation, pp. 135–38.
26. Francis Buchanan (1934). *An Account of the District of Shahbad in 1812–13*. Patna: Bihar and Orissa Research Society, p. 368.
27. Ibid., p. 216.
28. Ibid., p. 77.
29. A.N. Basu (ed.) (1941). *Reports on the State Education in Bengal (1835 and 1838)*, by William Adam. Calcutta: University of Calcutta, p. XI, 251.
30. L.S.S. O'Malley (1913). *Census of India 1911*. Report, Vol. V, Part I, Calcutta: Bengal Secretariat Book Depot, p. 230.
31. Hetukar Jha (2006). op. cit., p. 230.
32. Nathmal Sinhaniyan (1961). *Bapuji ki Deoghar Yatra* (in Hindi). Patna: Bihar Harijan Sevak Sangh.
33. See Prasanna Kumar Chaudhary and Srikant (2005). op. cit., pp. 110–21.
34. Nathmal Sinhaniyan (1961). op. cit., pp. 63–66.
35. Amartya Sen (2005). *The Argumentative Indian*. London: Penguin Books, p. 46.

Part III

CREATIVITY

12

Literature, Society and the Calling of Creative Public Spheres

Towards a New Art of Cross-Fertilization

Ananta Kumar Giri

We seek certainly for that sort of expression which is self-expression. When an individual feels himself hedged in he recognizes the necessity of getting a situation in which there shall be an opportunity for him to make his addition to the understanding, and not simply to the conventionalized 'me.'

—G.H. Mead (1934), *Mind, Self and Society*, p. 212

He who takes his stand in relation shares in a reality, that is, in a being that neither merely belongs to him nor merely lies outside him. All reality is an activity in which I share without being able to appropriate for myself. Where there is no sharing there is no reality. Where there is self-appropriation there is no reality.

—Martin Buber (1958), *I and Thou*, p. 63

Who is my audience? It took me a long time to understand that the 'public' I am waiting for is the same that I am living for: humanity at large.

—Raimon Panikkar (1995), *A Dwelling Place for Wisdom*, p. 85

What would the world be if there were no needle and thread? Naturally, no stitched garments!

—Kapila Vatsayan (2010), *Sui Dargha: Crossing Boundaries*, p. ix

Literature and Society

Exploring and realizing creative relationship between literature and society is an adventure in co-realizations and transformations going beyond the logic of the fields of both literature and society. It also calls for understanding their manifold conceptualizations and realizations. Our conventional understanding of literature is that it is created by men of literature. It is not always realized that literature is part of life and society; when it is done so it is usually conceptualized and represented in a language of mirror and adaptation: literature is either a mirror of society or it adapts to the logic of society. But literature is not only a mirror of society but also a field of creative expressions and confrontations which breaks existing mirrors of society and creates new languages of self and social realizations and new landscapes of imaginations. Both literature and society are not only fields of adaptation but also of transcendence and transformations in which individuals and groups strive to go beyond adaptation and create new conditions of self-, co- and social realizations. These are fields in which there is interrogation and confrontation of the existing logic of literature and society. Literature is thus not only a field of murmuring but of grumbling and a field of contestation and confrontations of the existing grammar of society based upon a higher grumbling of self and awakened social groups and movements.[1]

In exploring relationship between literature and society, the language of interdisciplinary transaction, as it happens in conventional academic corridors, is not enough. We need a new language and practice of transdisciplinary cultivation, beyond adaptation and meditative verbs of transformations. In this striving for a new language and relationship, realizing the distinction between noun and verb is crucial. In our conventional languages, literature, society as well as such important terms of personal, cultural and national identity as person, nation, writer, India, Shakespeare, etc., come to us as nouns which we also uncritically use, adopt and adapt to. These nouns already from the beginning are imprisoned in a logic of possessive pronouns – this is my self, this is our literature – and any foundational critique of such possessive pronouns are met with resistance and sometimes violent annihilation. But literature, society as well as such fundamental fields of life as self are not only nouns but also verbs. They embody verbs of unfoldment, emergence and realizations.[2] But as verbs they are not only activistic (which is the way verbs are constructed and realized in modernity) but also meditative (Giri, 2009). But these meditative verbs of action, expression, communication and co-realizations are manifold-sitting, walking as well as dancing verbs of life. Literature and society are verbs of co-realizations and meditative transformations involving walking, sitting and dancing verbs (Giri, 2011b). Public sphere is an important sphere in which such verbs of co-realizations and transformations are at work.

And in such transformative co-realizations the nature of 'and' plays an important role. If we conceptualize 'and' in a logic of juxtaposition, as it mostly happens in the logic of interdisciplinarity, the terms and fields on both sides of 'and' do not get mutually interpenetrated and transformed. 'And' becomes a helpless presence repeating the logic of 'end' (which simultaneously means end of meaning as well as ultimate end or purpose). But if our conception and realization of 'and' is one of mutual interrogation, transmutation and mothering bridge then our inhabitation, meditation, dance, walk and work in the space of the 'and,' the space of the middle, becomes a work of transformation – transforming a one-sided conceptualization, realization and organization of fields such as literature and society. While our conventional understanding and work in the space of 'and' reproduces a logic of 'end' and 'noun,' in beyond adaptation and meditative, interrogating and mothering verbs, 'and' is a space of transformations. 'And' is a space of quest for infinity from the actors and fields on its two sides rather than a reiteration of the totalizing logic of totality of either of them.[3] 'And' is a mothering ground and bridge of quest for and embodiment of responsibility. In his work, *Sahitya O* (Literature and ...) Chitta Ranjan Das (1923–2011), a creative seeker, writer and experimenter from Odisha, who has written more than two hundred books on different aspects of literature, society, education and social criticism, suggests such a transformative, interrogative and mothering meaning and realization of 'and' (Das, 1989a; see also Giri, 2011b). This also comes out in a joint work of co-creation in which the poetic critic and essayist Chitta Ranjan Das and poet Srinivas Udgata co-create poems and reflections on poetry together in the work *Ebam* which also means 'and' (Das, 2009).[4]

Public sphere helps us in realizing such a meaning of 'and' beyond the adaptive, already determined and ultimate logic of 'end'. Literature helps us to express ourselves to ourselves as well as to the others and the public. Expression in the field of literature is simultaneously self, mutual and public and helps in the creation of public spheres in societies. In the creation of modern public spheres, as Jurgen Habermas (1989) himself tells us, literature has played an important role. He calls it literary public sphere. But it is one thing to talk about literary public sphere as a type of public sphere or even as a segment of public sphere and it is another thing to realize the integral literary dimension of public sphere itself. In later conceptualizations and realizations, literature becomes an integral part of public sphere through work of rhetoric, language, style of argumentation and mutual co-presence in such modes as co-walking and co-labouring.[5] In their vision and practices, writers such as Chitta Ranjan Das, U.R. Ananthamurthy and Mahesweta Devi from India embody this later realization of public sphere. They are tireless participants in public discourses and public spaces through speech, writing and in case of Das through regular columns in newspapers. They not only help us realize the literary dimension of public sphere but also recreate public sphere through creative and critical literary interventions.

Unfortunately, our understanding of public sphere in social sciences does not fully appreciate its literary dimension and constitution. It has a very prosaic and intellectualist rendering of public sphere without realizing public drama and public poetry in it. The other limitation of contemporary social science understanding of public sphere is that it is part of an uncritical telos of modernity; originating in modernity, it can only become part of an 'unfinished agenda of modernity'. Such conceptualizations of public sphere do not help us realize the work of public sphere in pre-modern and non-modern societies (cf. Giri, 2002, 2008; Uberoi, 1996). But literature in all societies has created public spaces and public spheres for mutual communication though depending upon the nature of social arrangement and mode of government, the nature of such social manifestation of creativity has varied. In societies where creators of literature seeking critical public dialogue with their literature of protest and alternative imagination are not tolerated, humiliated and killed, meditative verbs and streams also dry up and die. Such conditions existed in the past in many societies, especially those under authoritarian regimes, and it does continue to exist even in liberal modern democracies.

Literature and Society: Beyond Adaptation and Dynamics of Creative Expressions

In order to understand the relationship between literature and society, we need to understand the transformed understanding of both these fields. Society is a field which helps individuals to come together and express themselves. In sociological theorization of society, there is an acknowledgement of the fact that society is not just a field of *apriori* determination and embeddedness but also a field of self-realization, co-realizations and creative emergence (cf. Sunder Rajan, 1998). G.H. Mead, one of the pioneers of modern sociological thinking and author of *Mind, Self and Society*, helps us realize the limits of the 'social' and urges us to realize that neither 'I' nor 'me' is a reiteration of the existing conventions of society. As Mead (1934: 209) tells us:

> [...] me may be regarded as giving the form of the 'I.' The novelty comes in the action of the 'I,' but the structure, the form of the self is one which is conventional.
>
> *This conventional form may be reduced to a minimum*. In the artist's attitude, where there is artistic creation, the emphasis on the element of novelty is carried to the limit. This demand for the unconventional is especially noticeable in modern art. Here, the artist is supposed to break away from convention; a part of his artistic expression is thought to be in the breakdown of convention.[6]

Among contemporary philosophers and sociologists we also get an intimation of a post-conventional and post-social conceptualization of society. Jurgen Habermas (1990) tells us that morality is not just reproducing the conventional logic of society, rather, it is to learn how to think and act in post-conventional ways taking into consideration the calling of universal and universalizable justice. Alain Touraine (2007) tells us about sociology beyond society which explores the way individuals become subjects. For Touraine, becoming a member of society is integrally linked to the process in which one becomes a subject but to be a subject is to have the ability to say 'no' to the existing logic if this does not allow creative self-realization. But what Touraine and Habermas have not explored sufficiently is how by cultivating the literary field on the part of self and society one can realize the post-conventional dimension of society, have the capacity to say 'no' in the face of an overwhelming compulsion for 'yes,' and go beyond the logic of an *apriori* social. What they have not explored is how practice of creative literature can contribute to co-creating society as a field of creative expression, co-realizations and confrontation. This we find in the works of seekers and experimenters such as Chitta Ranjan Das.

From the field of literature, we also have a connected move to realize society as a field of self-expression and co-realizations. Das, for instance, urges us to realize that society has been built by those who do not confirm. Personality and self for him is not just a logic of adaptation and socialization; it is a field to realize an emergent wholeness building upon one's quest for self-realization, co-realization and world realization (Das, 2010). Touraine's appeal for sociology beyond society finds a creative resonance in Das who urges us to realize how boundaries of sociology are now being transcended in creative experiments and adventures.[7]

The Calling of Creative Public Spheres

We usually look at literary creativity in an individualized way but now we need to link both to fields of creative public spaces and spheres. For our *tapasya* of creativity in literature and society, we need the spheres of the creative self, intimate groups of mutuality as well as public spheres. But, in each of these spheres, we continue the modernist logic of linearity. Despite the language of sphere in public sphere our conceptualization and organization of it is linear. It is hardly a sphere where the spherical nature of our being is at work or finds an expression.[8] In this context, we need to conceptualize and realize public spheres as manifold circles and *chakras*. Public spheres as *chakras* bring interested people together where people through creative sharing and contestation generate mutual energy. Literature can help realize public spheres as *chakras* where individuals and groups can express themselves and through processes of communicative dialogues and contestations can generate mutual energization. These *chakras* can inspire and enable the participants to bring together their vertical dimension such as quest for transcendence and horizontal dimension such as commitment to fellow beings and realizing solidary praxis with others. The concept and organization of public sphere in modernity is also bound to a logic of double contingency and dualism. For example, we look at self, other and society through the logic of what Strydom (2009) calls 'double contingency' of self and the other, this double contingency is also imprisoned within dualism. But now we need to bring the concept of 'triple contingency' to each of these spheres. In triple contingency, along with self and other, there is also a public (ibid.). But this public is not fixed, it is emergent; it is not only observing but also participating. Triple contingency does not lie only outside but also works inside. Triple contingency is also a bearer of transcendence as it transcends the dualistic logic of double contingency of self and the other.

In literature, spiritual traditions and creative imaginations we are familiar with the concept and reality of third eye. This third eye exists not only in Shiva, the meditative *tapaswee* and dancer, but also in all of us. Triple contingency can be linked to the work of third eye. Literature and creative public spheres can help us realize and cultivate not only the triple contingency of life thus going beyond the arrogance and exclusionary assertion of either self or other but also develop and realize our third eye – a challenge missing in contemporary theorization of society and public sphere. Public sphere and creative meditation can help us realize both triple contingency and third eye and then move it further to the fourth, fifth and further dimensions of our contingencies, aspirations and struggles.[9]

Life Worlds and Living Words

But for this we would have to recreate the link between what is called life worlds and system worlds through the categories of lived worlds and living words. Our lived worlds everywhere are multiplex and plural but the language of life worlds and system worlds as it comes in sociology and in the works of critical theorists such as Habermas usually present a one-dimensional logic and rationality such as the primacy of rational in modernity and hierarchy in traditional societies. Life worlds everywhere are also subjected to dominant logic of the system worlds such as market, state, caste and gender. In this context, to cultivate lived worlds with their creativity, courage, transcendence and multidimensionality is a challenge which calls for us to go beyond the existing logic of life worlds and system worlds. The challenge of creativity is simultaneous: simultaneously nurturing lived worlds of vibrancy, energy, soulful togetherness and meditative solitude and living words which move us not to hatred and annihilation but to mutual blossoming and co-realizations. Both lived worlds and living words do *tapasya* for and with beauty, dignity and dialogues in the face of and in the midst of ugliness, indignity and violence.

Living words work as new *mantras* of life, to put in the words of Sri Aurobindo, and embody what Martin Heidegger (1994) calls 'way making movement'. They just do not mirror 'forms of life' but create new ways of life. They just do not reproduce existing language but create new languages of self and social realizations.[10] They just do not reproduce the rationality of either tradition or modernity but possibly embody strivings towards what Latin American thinker Enrique Dussel (2010) calls 'transmodernity'.[11] They are not just part of either the logic of transcendental awe in tradition or 'linguistification of the sacred' in modernity (see Das, 2004).[12] While they seek to make the Divine and Nature part of the communicative field of humans and express it in ways understandable to modern rational mind, it nonetheless does not reduce either of them only to what is comprehensible in the language of modern rationality. It seeks to cultivate the ineffable and ever-present and dynamically moving beyond in both lived worlds and living words while at the same time making them part of our everyday conversations. Both lived worlds and living words become sites of courage, creativity and transcendence working in between and in the margins of fear, drudgery and pull towards an imprisonment in closed walls which is often justified in the name of immanence.

Going beyond the 'linguistification of sacred' (cf. Habermas, 1990) in modernity and the consequent disenchantment and dualism between the religious and secular, both life worlds and living words embody new border crossing between rational and emotional, religion and reason, nature and human, mental and supramental. The life worlds and living words embody such a new border crossing among human, nature and divine in continuously emergent ways.

Towards a New Art of Cross-Fertilization

Literature, society and public spheres are fields of living words and lived worlds.

Living words and lived worlds can make us pregnant, pregnant with a new creativity. While our existing space and time are empty and continuously being emptied out with the logic of the system such as money, market and capital, life worlds and lived worlds help us cultivate pregnant spaces and pregnant times. Both lived worlds and living words work as seeds for a new pregnancy thus helping us realize the concept of immaculate conception in new ways. Our living words can impregnate us as our lived worlds of *tapasya* can make each other fertile which is an embodiment of a new spiritual eroticism.[13] Our compassion and confrontation can make us conceive new ideas and new relationships.

Our fields of literature, society and public sphere have become dry and deserted and we need to make these fertile. But for this available fertilizers from the market and external world are not adequate. We need to make them fertile through self, mutual and cross-fertilization in which our quality of life, relationships and living words play a crucial role.

It is earthworms which make the land fertile but today we need to be earthworms to each other as well as to ourselves. But once the land is fertile we would have to cultivate it as a garden for which we need to be gardeners. But both earthworms and gardeners can remain bound only to the field thus uncritically reproducing the logic of embeddeness which also becomes hostile, opposed and violent not only to forces of emergence from the field itself but also to other fields. In this context, the calling of cross-fertilization and cross-pollination calls us to grow wings and be simultaneously birds and bards, fly and sing together, wonder and wander.[14] Literature, society and creative public spheres can help us simultaneously become earthworms, gardeners and birds.[15] It can also help us become Socratic gadflies, as Socrates, Antigone, Gandhi, Chitta Ranjan and many other seekers and fighters of humanity have embodied, striking the powers which hinders our potential, aspiration and efforts for self-realization, mutual blossoming and world transformations.

Acknowledgements

This paper builds on my presentations at the National Seminar on 'Literature and Society: Interdisciplinary Transactions,' North-Eastern Hill University, Shillong, March 2010 and the workshop on 'Philosophy, Literature and Social Transformations,' Madras Institute of Development Studies, Chennai, February 2011. I am grateful to Dr Sukalpa Bhattacharjee for her kind invitation for the Shillong seminar and to participants in both these occasions for their kind interest and comments.

Notes

1. In our seminar at Shillong in his keynote address, Professor Mrinal Miri said that literature is an act of murmuring. In my presentation I said that literature is also an act of grumbling, especially higher grumbling of self and awakened social groups. In offering this argument I am building upon the work of Chittaranjan Das (2010) who talks about the work of higher grumbling in personality and society based upon the work of Abraham Maslow.
2. We may note here that in different philosophical, cultural and spiritual traditions, body, mind and Being are considered verbs. As Tu Weiming writes about body in Chinese culture and philosophy: 'There's a beautiful term, *ti*, which means the body. But, that word, *ti*, can also be used as a verb. It means just my

body, but also to embody. The embodiment is a process of understanding other human beings experientially as well as intellectually and spiritually' (Weiming, 2000: 50). In his *Art and Experience*, John Dewey also writes about mind: 'Mind is primarily a verb' (quoted in Elbridge, 2000: 244–45). And theologian and philosopher Raimon Panikkar writes about Being: 'Being is a verb, an action, and it has rhythm' (Panikkar, 1995: 26).

3. This resonates with the thoughts of Emmanuel Levinas. Franson Manjali (2001) also explores such pathways in his *Literature and Infinity.*
4. So does poet and novelist Rabi Narayan Dash (2008) in his book of poems, *Ebam Kadha* (and buds).
5. While Habermasian public sphere is mainly one of the spheres of argumentation I make it plural by bringing such activities as love and labour into it (cf. Giri, 2008).
6. As Mead (1934: 221; emphasis added) tells us:

> The value of an ordered society is essential to our existence but there also has to be room for an expression of the individual himself if there has to be a satisfactorily developed society. A means for such an expression must be provided. *Until we have a social structure in which the individual can express himself as the artist and the scientist does, we are thrown back on the sort of the structure found in the mob, in which everybody is free to express against some hated object of the group.*

7. Note what Touraine, a sociologist, and Das, a creative practitioner of literature, write about sociology. For Touraine (2007: 191):

> One of the main themes of sociology is therefore the reversal of the conception and role of institutions. These were defined by their function in the integration of a social system. They defined and imposed respect for the norms and instruments for the defense of individuals which enable them to defend themselves against norms. Our society is less and less a society of the subjected and more and more a society of volunteers.

About sociology Chittaranjan Das (2009: 579–80) shares with us the following:

> The story of all real sociology is one of breaking open the boundaries. The discipline was originally bound strictly to its specific lines and limitations, and it is great that transgressions have been happening all the time. It is becoming more and more clear that society, people, do always matter more than the study of society. The older definitions and contours are fast changing and there are more and more people who are less shy and hence willing to transgress the boundaries. More mature days are in the offing and the recluses till now working in the laboratories are becoming more courageous. Yes, courage, more than anything else, always helps us to ask questions and rewrite our canons of enquiry. Intellectuals are rethinking and as it were from within more ready to revise their roles. Albert Camus has once made a remark that the intellectual's role will be to say that the king is naked when he is and not to go into raptures over his imaginary trappings. And look, all around now there are hegemonies, kings all round who are visibly naked! The intellectual's laboratory has now to come down in proximity to people where they really are, move and have their beings, suffer all the time waiting for an appropriate remedy. The academics could not as a rule do that. Shri Ramakrishna of India had once observed that 'some people climb the seven floors of a building and cannot get down.' But some can, he did hope, really climb and then come down. They are always of greater worth.

8. Philosopher Peter Sloterdijk urges us to realize the distinction between a spherical approach and a linear approach.
9. This calls for cross-cultural dialogue and border-crossing dialogue between critical theory and religious and spiritual ways of thinking. It would be interesting to explore further dialogue between the concept of triple contingency in critical theory and trinity in Christian religious and spiritual tradition. For Panikkar, 'Trinity is not a number but the depth and unfolding of the riches of reality, which is a living relationship' (cited in Pikaza, 2010: 119). 'Panikkar thereby seeks to move beyond a form of dualism, following the best *advaita* experience (of non-dualism), opening a way to dialogue [...]' (ibid.). In the same way we can realize triple contingency not as a number but as the depth and creativity of relationship beyond the dualistic logic of self and other. But triple contingency also urges us to realize that Trinity whether it is in Christian tradition or Hindu tradition is also confronted with the challenges of public – an observant and meditative public.
10. As expressed in the following poem:

    Oh friend
    You said
    We need a new language
    A new *sadhana* of words and *tapasya* of worlds
    This is not a language of victory
    Nor is one of self-advertisement and aggrandizement
    Neither is it a language of doomsday
    This is a language of walking our ways together
    Walking our dreams, *sadhana* and struggle

    II

    In our co-habitations of affection
    Of compassion and confrontation
    Words become *mantras*
    Of a new life, a new responsibility
    Of wiping tears from our eyes and
    Again taking each other into our laps
    Renewing our strength from embrace
    We create new paths by walking
    We create new language
    Our language is the language of walking
    Stars of *mantras* leap from our lap

    (a poem originally written in Odia by the author and then translated)
11. The following quotation from Dussel (2010) helps us to understand transmodernity:

    > Europe began to function as the 'centre' of the world market (and therefore to extend the 'world system' throughout the world) with the advent of the industrial revolution; on the cultural plane, this produced the phenomenon of the Enlightenment, the origins of which, in the long run, we should look for (according to the hypothesis of Morrocan philosopher Al-Yabri, who we will discuss later) in the Averröist philosophy of the caliphate of Córdoba. Europe's

crucial and enlightened hegemony scarcely lasted two centuries (1789–1989). Only two centuries! Too short-term to profoundly transform the 'ethico-mythical nucleus' (to use Ricoeur's expression) of ancient and universal cultures like the Chinese and others of the Far East (like the Japanese, Korean, Vietnamese, etc.), the Hindustanic, the Islamic, the Russian-Byzantine, and even the Bantu or the Latin American (though with a different structural composition). These cultures have been partly *colonized* (included through negation in the totality, as aspect A of Diagram 1), but most of the structure of their values has been excluded – *scorned, negated and ignored* – rather than annihilated. The economic and political system has been dominated in order to exert colonial power and to accumulate massive riches, but those cultures were deemed to be unworthy, insignificant, unimportant, and useless. The tendency to disparage those cultures, however, has allowed them to survive in silence, in the shadows, simultaneously scorned by their own modernized and westernized elites. That negated 'exterior,' that alterity – always extant and latent – indicates the existence of an unsuspected cultural richness, which is slowly revived like the flames of the fire of those fathoms buried under the sea of ashes from hundreds of years of colonialism. That cultural exteriority is not merely a substantive, uncontaminated, and eternal 'identity.' It has been evolving in the face of Modernity itself; what is at stake is 'identity' in the sense of process and growth, but always as an exteriority.

These cultures, asymmetrical in terms of their economic, political, scientific, technological, and military conditions, therefore maintain an alterity with respect to European Modernity, with which they have coexisted and have learned to respond in their own way to its challenges. They are not dead but alive, and presently in the midst of a process of rebirth, searching for new paths for future development (and inevitably at times taking the wrong paths). Since they are not modern, these cultures cannot be 'post'-modern either. They are simultaneously pre-modern (older than modernity), contemporary to Modernity, and soon, to Transmodernity as well. Postmodernism is a final stage in modern European/North American culture, the 'core' of Modernity. Chinese or Vedic cultures could never be European post-modern, but rather are something very different as a result of their distinct roots.

Thus, the strict concept of the '*trans*-modern' attempts to indicate the radical novelty of the irruption – as if from nothing – from the transformative exteriority of that which is always Distinct, those cultures in the process of development which assume the challenges of Modernity, and even European/North American Post-modernity, but which respond *from another place, another location.* They respond from the perspective of their own cultural experiences, which are distinct from those of Europeans/North Americans, and therefore have the capacity to respond with solutions which would be absolutely impossible for an exclusively modern culture. A future *trans*-modern culture – which assumes the positive moments of Modernity (as evaluated through criteria distinct from the perspective of the other ancient cultures) – will have a rich pluriversality and would be the fruit of an authentic intercultural dialogue, that would need to bear clearly in mind existing asymmetries (to be an 'imperial-core' or part of the semi-peripheral 'central chorus' – like Europe today, and even more so since the 2003 Iraq War – is not the same as to be part of the postcolonial and peripheral world). But a post-colonial and peripheral world like that of India, in a position of abysmal asymmetry with respect to the metropolitan core of the colonial era, does not for this reason

> cease to be a creative nucleus of ancient cultural renewal which is decisively distinct from all of the others, with the capacity to propose novel and necessary answers for the anguishing challenges that the Planet throws upon us at the beginning of the twenty-first century.
>
> '*Trans*-modernity' points toward all of those aspects that are situated 'beyond' (and also 'prior to') the structures valorized by modern European/North American culture, and which are present in the great non-European universal cultures and have begun to move toward a pluriversal project.

12. Habermas (1990) talks about 'linguistification of the sacred' where sacred becomes part of ordinary language and conversation. But in this there may be a danger of reduction of sacred to language that Habermas does not explore.
13. Note here what philosopher Luc Irigaray (2002: 115–17) writes:

> Carnal sharing becomes then a spiritual path, a poetic and also a mystical path [...] Love takes place in the opening to self that is the place of welcoming the transcendence of the other. [...] The path of such an accomplishment of the flesh does not correspond to a solipsistic dream [...] nor to a fin-de-siecle utopia, but to a new stage to be realized by humanity. [...] Nature is then no longer subdued but it is adapted, in its rhythms and necessities, to the path of its becoming, of its growth. Caressing loses the sense of capturing, bewitching, appropriating [...] The caress becomes a means of growing together toward a human maturity that is not confused with an intellectual competence, with the possession of property [...] nor with the domination of the world.

For Irigaray, 'sharing breath' is an important aspect of this aspired for spiritual eroticism, giving birth to life and each other and making of a spiritual community. For Irigaray, 'This proto-ethical plane of shared breath is the eternal germ of a spiritual community, i.e., a community of embodied individuals, caring for each other' (quoted in Skof, 2011: 136).

14. A poem written by my friend Francis Regis Bouquiz about 'Le Troubader,' the wandering musicians in medieval France can be of interest. The following line from the poem in French tells us how the troubader visits from place to place:

> Je suis le troubader du chemin qui me mene vers Lui
>
> Et le passager des temps visibles, invisibles [...]

Also this poem 'On Wings' by Rabi Narayan Dash (2007) can help us realize many meanings of growing wings:

> When I emerged
> Broken and aimless
> She came out on to her terrace
> To ask if I had seen a flying cat
> And a little sparrow crying in sorrow
> If I knew leaves are already yellow.
> The world I came of, seeking
> Care, if I am I love with
> Money or work with a
> Passion for becoming
> Somebody and something
> I have already read

'the child is the father to man'
Sharing her words and unending dream
I started to scream:
'God! Return me to her,
To child, the mother!'

About wings, Rumi tells us about its significance in the following ways: 'Something opens our wings, something makes boredom and hurt disappear.'

15. When I present these three modes of being, I always ask what are the words in local mother languages. While presenting it in Hanoi, my Vietenese partiticpants told me thất the word for earthworm is *Konchin*, for gardener is *Kechia* and for bird is *Lantivuan*. During our conversation we created a symphony of *knochin*, *kechia* and *lantivuan*.

Appendix: Crocodile and Sabari *Sukta*: Shankara, Buddha and Ambedkar

Oh Crocodile
Pull my leg
As you had pulled
The tiny legs of Shankara
If you pull my legs
Towards the other shore
Across deep waters
My *Sannyasi* soul
Would surrender
I would be a *Sannyasi*
With the ways, with light
With home and the world
With self and non-self
A new blossoming of relationship
And the world
A new *Sannyasa*
Transformation of Life!

2

New Encounters
With Soul, with the *Chandala*
But the *Chandala*
Does not turn into Shiva
Chandala Becomes Buddha and Ambedkar
A new Constitution in the hands of the Chandala
Meditating he asks:
Oh Shankara
You had said
We are neither body nor intellect
Chidanada Rupa
But where is here
The festival of soul

In the sacrificial pyre
Of Caste systems
So many souls get killed and burnt
Shnakara embraces Chandala
Holding hands together
Buddha, Shankara and Ambedkar
Walk together
A new Sannyasa of begging of life

3

Walking together
They feel hungry
Says Shankara:
I am supposed to have only my own cooked food
But I do not know how to cook
Would you know?
Buddha the Enlightened says no
Says Ambedkar:
I had coordinated the writing of the Constitution
But forgot to learn how to cook
In hungry stomachs
They meet Sabari
But Sabari does not give them fruits
Brings the three Greats to
The kitchen
By the fire
Blowing the rods of Sabari
Shankara, Buddha and Ambedkar
Learn to make rice and *dal*

4

Cooking and eating
Rice and dal
Around the kitchen
A new *Sannyasa*
Singing *Saundraya Lahari* and reading
Tripitaka Sutra and Constitution
We join them in
This path of *tapasya*
We learn the *sadhana* of cooking
We transform the tears of history
A new garden of creativity
Holding the hands of crocodile
And around the kitchen of Sabari
A new *sannyasa* of Life.

(a poem originally written in Odia and translated by the author)

References

Buber, Martin (1958). *I and Thou*. New York: Charles Scribner's Sons.

Das, Chittaranjan (1989a). *Sahitya O …* [Literature and …]. Berhampur: Pustaka Bhandar.

—— (1989b). 'Ethara Udiba Neta', in Chittaranjan Das and Srinivas Udgata, *Ebam*, Cuttack: Books & Books.

—— (2004). *Mahimandalara Gita: Sri Arakhita Das, Eka Adhyana* [The Mahimandala Gita of Sri Arakhita Das: A Study]. Bhubaneswar: Odisha Sahitya Akademi.

—— (2009). 'Afterword', in *The Modern Prince and the Modern Sage: Transforming Power and Freedom*, Delhi: Sage.

—— (2010). *Byakti o Byaktitya* [Person and Personality]. Bhubaneswar: Pathika Prakashani.

Dash, Rabi Narayan (2008). *Ebam Kadha* [And buds]. Balasore, Odisha: Samara Graphics.

—— (2007). *On Wings and Other Poems*. Huddinge, Sweden: Prima Verba & Balasore and India: New Race.

Dussel, Enrique (2010). 'Transmodernity and Interculturality: An Interpretation from the Philosophy of Liberation', paper presented at the International Symposium on 'Learning Across Boundaries', University of Luxembourg, June.

Elbridge, Richard (2000). 'Dewey's Aesthetics', in M. Cochran (ed.), *Cambridge Companion to John Dewey*, Cambridge: Cambridge University Press.

Giri, Ananta Kumar (2002). *Conversations and Transformations: Towards a New Ethics of Self and Society*. Lanham, MD: Lexington Books.

—— (2008). 'Civil Society and the Calling of Self-Development', *Sociological Bulletin*.

—— (2009). 'Beyond Adaptation and Meditative Verbs of Co-Realizations: Toward Creative Nurturance of 'I,' 'Me,' and 'You' and the Transformative Fellowship of Non-Duality', *Journal of Indian Council of Philosophical Research*, XXVI(3): 109–30.

—— (2011a). 'With and Beyond Plurality of Standpoints: Sociology and the *Sadhana* of Multi-Valued Logic and Living', in *Sociology and Beyond: Windows and Horizons*, Jaipur: Rawat Publications.

—— (2011b). 'A New Morning with Chitta Ranjan: Adventures in Co-Realizations and World Transformations', *Social Change*.

Habermas, Jurgen (1989). *The Structural Transformation of the Public Sphere*. Cambridge, MA: The MIT Press.

—— (1990). *Moral Consciousness and Communicative Action*. Cambridge, MA: The MIT Press.

Heidegger, Martin (1994). 'The Way to Language', in Farrell Krell (ed.), *Basic Writings: Revised and Expanded Edition*, London: Routledge, pp. 393–426.

Irigaray, Luc (2002). *Between East and West*. New York: Columbia University Press.

Mead, G.H. (1934). *Mind, Self and Society*. Chicago: University of Chicago Press.

Manjali, Franson (2001). *Literature and Infinity*. Shimla: Indian Institute of Advanced Study.

Panikkar, Raimon (1995). *A Dwelling Place for Wisdom*. Delhi: Motilald Banarasidass.

Pikaza, Xavier (2010). 'Raimon Panikkar (1918–2010)', *Concilium*, (5): 117–20.

Strydom, Piet (2009). *New Horizons of Critical Theory: Collective Learning and Triple Contingency*. Delhi: Shipra.

Sunder Rajan, R. (1998). *Beyond the Crises of European Sciences: New Beginnings*. Shimla: Indian Institute of Advanced Study.

Skof, Lenart (2011). 'Pragmatism and Deepened Democracy: Ambedkar between Dewey and Unger', in Akeel Bilgrami (ed.), *Democratic Culture: Historical and Philosophical Essays*, Delhi: Routledge, pp. 122–42.

Touraine, Alain (2007). 'Sociology after Sociology', *European Journal of Social Theory*, 10: 184–93.

Uberoi, J.P.S. (1996). *Religion, Civil Society and State: A Study of Sikhism*. Delhi: Oxford University Press.

Weiming, Tu (2000). 'The Complex Bridges between China and the West', in Michael Tobias, J. Patrick Fitzerald and David Rothenburg (eds), *A Parliament of Minds: Philosophy for a New Millennium*, Albany: State University of New York Press, pp. 46–59.

Vatsayan, Kapila (2010). *Sui Dargha: Crossing Boundaries through Needle and Thread*. Delhi: India International Center and Wisdom Tree.

13

Time and Creativity

Towards a Sociological Perspective

Indra Deva

From a sociological angle, the categories both of time and creativity are social constructs. Since human experience and action occur in time, every human society tends to develop certain ways of perceiving and organizing time which are consistent with its cultural and structural pattern. Time is perceived through changes that occur in man and nature, and there are various systems of measuring it in terms of human and cosmic cycles. Apart from the varying conception of time as cyclical or linear, the perception of time involves certain concepts of sequence and duration which vary from society to society. Societies have their own systems of scheduling and allocation of time for individuals and groups. Most traditional societies have certain *rites de passage* marking various stages in a man's life from birth to death. The Hindus, for example, have an elaborate system of *samskaras*. These points of time in each individual's life cycle punctuate his/her changing social roles and status. They are accompanied by rituals that underscore and give vitality to his multifarious changing relationships not only with his kinsfolk but also with other functional and cast groups in society. Apart from a large number of *samskaras*, the Hindu scriptures prescribe the division of a person's lifetime into four portions or *ashrams*. Together with such scheduling of time for individuals, the time of the community as a whole is marked by numerous calendaric festivals. These festivals too are accompanied by various rituals and other symbolic and aesthetic expressions like singing, narrating of myths and paintings on walls and floors. Thus, the accounting of time in different societies clearly has social and cultural concomitants.

Besides this, each culture has as a part of its world view, a pattern of attitudes towards past, present and future. It appears to me that the chief difference between traditional and modern societies is that the former have their golden age in the past, while the latter have it in the future. This difference has widespread implications for their attitudes and behaviour. For instance, while there is a tendency in traditional societies to stick to customs, even though they may be unreasonable or oppressive, just because they are old, there is a tendency in modern society to be attracted by fashions, even though they may be ugly or uncomfortable, just because they are new.

However, the basic notions of time and space which are implicit in each culture are seldom made explicit. Apart from the fact that people belonging to a given culture are contained and carried on by its basic beliefs and values as fish by water, so that they can seldom see beyond them, it appears to me that this has to be so because making these explicit would mean exposing them to questioning and scrutiny, which may shake a culture from its very roots. It is not surprising, therefore, that in each culture the validity of its own conception of time is taken for granted and the people in general are unaware even of its specific character. This seems to be true also of the modern Western culture despite all its claims to rationality and the scientific spirit. And, the modern Western notions of time and creativity inevitably colour, and perhaps distort, all sociological discussions of such problems.

The Notion of Creativity: Ethnocentric Overtones

The current notion of creativity seems clearly to be a product of the modern age and it appears to be bound by the culture to which it belongs. The prevailing concept of 'creativity' emerged in the West during the Renaissance and was first given formal expression by the philosophers of Enlightenment.[1] It seems to be imbued with an exaggerated sense of individualism. The following statement in the International Encyclopedia of Social Sciences of the real task of sociology of creativity sums up well the predominant attitude in modern social science: 'it would seem, then, that sociology of creativity (however creativity may be defined) should consist in the study of those social conditions which either favour or impede the appearance of creative individuals.'[2] One important and, to my mind, pernicious aspect of such theorization, whether it be in the field of sociology or economics, is that there is a tendency to regard the generalizations or 'laws' as universal.

However, when we consider the process and conception of creativity in a non-modern non-western culture, the traditional Indian culture for instance, the picture is strikingly different. Traditional Indian culture gives little importance to the individual in the process of creation. This is true not only of the folk tradition but also the highly sophisticated and articulate elite tradition. The supreme examples of human creativity, such as the breathtaking architecture of Hindu temples and the innumerable pieces of exquisites sculpture that form their integral part, the monumental epics and mythological works, numerous meticulously worked out law books, and treatises on various mundane matters, are, for all practical purposes, anonymous. It is usual to attribute them to mythical personages. Even when the authorship or a literary work goes by the name of a particular person, little importance is given to the author as an individual. This is why we seldom find any authentic biographic account of Sanskrit poets and dramatists. Ananda K. Coomaraswamy, the eminent scholar and connoisseur observes: 'the Indian artist, although a person, is not a personality; his personal idiosyncrasy is at the most a part of his equipment, and never the occasion of his art. All of the greatest Indian works are anonymous, and all that we know of the lives of Indian artists in any field could be printed in a tract of a dozen pages'.[3]

Creativity: The Evidence of Folk Literature

As regards the folk stream of culture, the emphasis on individual creativity is conspicuous by its absence. The significance of this cannot be minimized, for the bearers of the folk tradition have constituted the bulk of the total population in countries like India, and indeed of all peasant civilizations, since the dawn of history. To get an insight into the unity and diversity of culture of the common people, it would be worthwhile to consider some aspects of the oral literature of the folk.

Contrary to what the romantic eulogists of folk culture would like us to believe, the folk song does not spring 'directly' from the heart. A similar opinion about the nature of the folk culture, and its constituents like the folk song, is held by detractors of the illiterate folk, though they couch it in a different vocabulary. For them these are crude products of raw impulses. This is not the only instance where the opposite extremes of opinion tend to agree. But such agreement is no proof of the truth of that view.

The fact is that each folk song or any other item of folk culture is a part and product of an established and elaborate tradition. Though it undoubtedly gives expression to the thought and feelings of the singers (otherwise they wouldn't sing it), it nevertheless conforms to the traditional form and style of expression of the *genre* to which it belongs. A living tradition of folk literature comprises numerous varieties of folk songs, folktales, folk epics, proverbs, riddles, mnemonic formulae and so forth. These broad categories consist of many types and sub-types, each of which has specific stylistic characteristics and particular situational linkages. For example, special types of folk songs are connected with various kinds of work (like planting and weeding), seasons, calendaric rituals and festivals, and *rites de passage*. Among the songs connected with *rites de passage* of the marriage songs alone I collected twenty major types from one region of northern India. Each of these types has a particular established form, both in terms of song words and music, and is sung as a part of a specific ceremony of wedding.

In view of such complexity and crystallization of traditional forms in the stream of folk culture, it would be puerile to assume, whether in praise or derision, that the unsophisticated folk give vent to their feelings as they are, without any restraint, through their songs and other modes of expression. The fact on the other hand is that even the ordinary language of the unlettered folk makes greater use of symbolism and imagery for expressing subtle feelings in a precise manner.[4]

Each person in folk society does have a creative role to play, but this he (and, of course, she too) does as an active bearer of the tradition. He works through the tradition, but the bearer of a living folk tradition does not carry it as a congregation of unchanging museum pieces. While a folk song is being sung, a tale is being told, or an epic lay is being rendered, it is continually reworked in the process of performance itself. The creativity of the folk is amply brought out by the manner in which modern events and objects, and even new images like those drawn on the railway train, have found their way in the folk literature of various parts of India.[5] In response to strong and recurring experience caused by the impact of modern forces, even certain new *genres* have come into being. An example of this is the emergence of the folk opera, Bidesia, in the Bhojpuri-speaking area like eastern Uttar Pradesh and western Bihar. This region has experienced for a long time heavy emigration of able-bodied men who go to distant cities in search of employment leaving behind their wives and other members of the family.

Thus, there is enough evidence of creativity in folk literature. But this creativity is related to tradition. It makes use of the material and techniques provided by the tradition. The performance and composition of heroic poetry, in India and elsewhere, clearly illustrate this process. A good singer of a heroic poem or folk epic, like the Alha, does not depend on a memorized text. He composes instantaneously during performance, so that he can take a whole night in describing upon the response of audience and other circumstances. But while he composes, he does not do so just on his own. The traditions have provided him the broad frame of the story, a rich repertoire of stock descriptions, and techniques of composition and presentation. Through a mastery of these, he gets the freedom to create; and the better the mastery, the greater is his creativity.[6]

It is noteworthy that this character of heroic poetry is not peculiar in India. This has been broadly so for the tradition of heroic poetry not only of various peoples of Central Asia like the Kara-kirghiz, the Kalmuk and the Uzbek but also of the Teutonic and Greek heroic poetry. In the technique of composition and rendering, in the spirit of the hero, the cycle of his life, the description of battles and weapons – in all these there is astonishing similarity in the heroic poetry of numerous societies which, in terms of space and time, are very far apart from each other. The heroes of living Indian heroic poetry are in the same way heroic as the Greek hero, and belong to the same family as do the French *chevalier,* the Spanish *caballero,* the Anglo-Saxon *campa,* the Old German *held,* the Norse *jari,* the Russian *bogtyr,* the Serb *yunak,* the Albanian *trim*, and the *Uzbek paylan.*[7]

These enigmatic similarities in heroic poetry and other *genres* of folk literature and folklore bring to the fore the question of the relationship between time and creativity. These products of human creativity are so similar to each other, and yet they seem to belong to such different times. The tradition of heroic poetry is still vigorous in many parts of India and some other countries of the world in the 20th century, and yet it shares in common so many basic features with poetry in cultures which existed several centuries or even several millennia ago. Why is this so? It appears to me that the answer to this lies in the difference between astronomical time and socio-cultural time. Though these societies are widely separated by astronomical time, they seem to belong to similar socio-cultural eras. In the world today, and even in the same country, various segments of people are living in very different socio-cultural times. While in metropolitan cities like New Delhi and Mumbai some sections may belong to the 20th century in terms of socio-cultural time, a good many people in the interior villages are still living in medieval times both in terms of material and non-material culture, and certain groups like those in the Abujh Madh in the Bastar district may even now be in prehistoric times. While considering creativity, socio-cultural time, rather than astronomical time seems to be more relevant.

That creativity is related to socio-cultural time, i.e., variable properties of socio-cultural systems, and is not merely a matter of an individual's intrinsic qualities, is also shown by the fact that a given type of creativity that was common in a country in a particular historical era ceases to be possible in these very lands when those times no more exist. For example, the English ballad is no more being created in England. All the genuine English and Scottish ballads have been finally collected and put in the volumes edited by F.J. Child.[8] The ones that are being composed now are, according to experts, only counterfeits. As the noted scholar of English folk song, Cecil J. Sharp has said: 'The English ballad is moribund; its account is well-nigh closed.'[9] The Society of Antiquaries of Newcastle-upon-Type has reached a similar conclusion in 1855 when they set about the collection of Northum brain ballads and recorded in their first report that they were 'half-a-century too late'. Robert Graves says that in England the ballad proper gradually ceased to be composed after the Tudor times.[10] This does seem to show that creativity is not just a matter of an individual's capabilities, it is also a question of the times – the socio-cultural time.

The typical folk song is seldom an individual's creation. The German scholars, Herder and Grimm brothers put forward the theory of communal authorship of folk songs and ballads. Herder was comparatively cautious but the Grimm brothers in their *Altdeutsche Walder* (1813) were bold in their assertions. It is not creation whether the Grimms ever used the phrase, '*Das Volk di chtet*' (the folk, or people, makes the poetry), commonly ascribed to them, but Jacob Grimm did say that 'every *epos* must complete itself, must make itself, and can be written by no poet'. The Grimms held that 'epic poetry is not produced by particular and recognized poets, but rather springs up and spreads along time among people themselves, in the mouth of the people' and that the folk-poetry was slowly and unconsciously evolved in the same way as language. 'How does a race make its language?' they asked, 'In mass or by deputy?' C.L. Kittredge in his introduction to the selected edition of Child's work published in 1904 supports the communal argument in a modified form. He concedes that the majority of the existing English and Scottish ballads were in the first instance the work of individual authors but holds that these authors 'were not professional poets or minstrels, but members of the folk'. He points out that the process of oral tradition amounts to a second act of composition, which can be called 'collective composition'. Working about the English ballad, Robert Graves observes, 'Ballad proper is best understood not primarily as a narrative poem or a song, but as a song and chorus evolved by the group-mind of the community, a group-mind which is more than the sum of the individual mind that compose it, more than the conviction of the strong or most active clique'.[11]

Even if we do not wholly agree with these statements about the creation of the folk song and the ballad, the fact remains that the actual form in which we find a true folk song, ballad, folktale, folk epic, or proverb, is not the creation entirely of any one individual. During their performance or use by the folk they are freely re-worked. This involves the introduction of new elements as well as the deletion of some old ones that do not appeal to the person or the group concerned. The numerous versions in which all genuine pieces of folk literature are found bear ample testimony to the re-working by the folk, and this re-working surely amounts to communal re-creation. It has rightly been said that folk songs grow like trees. In fact, the genuine pieces of folk literature acquire their smoothness and characteristic shine by being passed on from one generation to another through time. Just as no amount of chiseling and grinding can give the same kind of gleam to a pebble that it acquires from the flow of the waters of a river through time, so also it is impossible for an individual outside the folk stream to compose a folk song at one stroke.

Originality of the Individual and Factors of Socio-cultural Existence

In the early phases of modern era, whenever new victories over the forces of nature, and conquest of far-flung lands in all parts of the globe, had given the elites in the West an unprecedented sense of confidence in themselves and their civilization, it was natural for them to raise slogans like 'Where there is a will, there is way'. The guiding faith was that an individual could achieve whatever he wished irrespective of the circumstances or the social setting. That was the heyday of individualism and rationalism. It was assumed that ideas could be understood solely on the basis of rationality and irrationality, or knowledge and ignorance; and that creativity is a matter of individual acumen and originality. This bias persists even to this day in the institutionalized social science, as is shown by the fact that the bulk of research on creativity is concerned with psychological attributes which are supposed to make individuals creative to a greater or a lesser degree.

However, as cracks began to appear in the capitalist order, questions arose about the autonomy of ideas. Karl Marx was perhaps the first to give forceful and systematic expression to the part played by other existential factors in determining the nature and emergence of ideas. In his famous 'Preface' to the *Critique of Political Economy*, Marx made the assertion: 'It is not the consciousness of men that determines their being, but, on the contrary their social being that determines their consciousness.'[12] Freud too drove a big hole into the impervious faith of the modern Western elites in the rationality of human, and particularly their own, thought and action. But it was perhaps due to the shattering impact of the First World War, and later on of the great depression of the early 1930s, that there was widespread realization that modern Western thinking, behaviour and social arrangements may not be based solely on unassailable principles of rationality.

The disillusionment, besides producing prophets of doom like Spengler and Toynbee, also impelled a realistic search from the social, economic and ideological factors that lie behind human thought and belief; and led to the rise of *Wissenssoziologie* or sociology of knowledge, which seeks to study systematically the relationship between ideas and other existential factors in society and culture. The growth of sociology of knowledge has undoubtedly been helped by the increasing distrust among various groups having different and conflicting interests. Instead of judging merely the truth or falsehood or a statement, it becomes more and more important to assess the reasons behind making it. The obvious obtrusiveness of organized advertisement and propaganda made such questions all the more pertinent. No statement, attitude or belief can be accepted at face value. It has to be explained by or imputed to particular interests and conscious or unconscious motives.

In this climate of thought, it is not surprising that a discipline is growing which seeks not merely to explain the motives behind particular viewpoints, but to study generally and systemically the relations between mental productions and other social and cultural factors. The coming up of this discipline inevitably implies a consensus that thought and creativity are determined or conditioned in some way by socio-cultural structure. This is true whether one takes a position inspired by Marxism or opposed to it. A good example of the latter is provided by Sorokin's extensive and meticulously worked out magnum opus, *Social and Cultural Dynamics.*[13] Sorokin is strongly opposed to relating ideas to the material base or the mode of production, but he nevertheless traces in great detail the common characteristics of various artistic creations of particular historical eras. Though, of course, he attributes them not to the mode of production but to the different phases of socio-cultural dynamics which he designates as ideational, idealistic and sensate. The view that artistic and other types of creativity of one era have certain common and distinguishing characteristics is not confined to Sorokin. It is shared also by other eminent thinkers and scholars like Spengler and Tyonbee, who take positions that are opposed to Marxism and hold cyclical and not a linear view of history. Thus social thought seems to have come round to the recognition of a nexus between time and creativity, irrespective of whether the conception of time is linear or cyclical.

Traditional cultures seem to have given due importance to considerations of time for all forms of human action. In Hindu tradition, the sacred duty (*dharma*) is not the same for everyone at all times – it varies according to difference in space, time and person (*desa, kala, patra*). Traditional cultures do not harbour illusions about the omnipotence of the individual irrespective of time. When times had changed, Arjun, the unequalled archer hero of the great epic, *Mahabharata*, could not protect from a gang of tribals the women whom he was escorting. This incident is referred to in a proverb which is popular over large parts of India:

> It is time that does a thing; what can a man do?
> Time is very powerful.
> The Bhils took away the cowherd women,
> Though it was the same Arjun, and his arrows were the same.

Time and Eternity

The traditional Hindu conception of time, like that of many other traditional cultures, is cyclical. According to Hindu mythology, each world cycle is divided into four *yugas* or ages comparable to the four ages of the Greco-Roman tradition. In both the traditions each succeeding age is lower in moral virtue than the preceding. The Greco-Roman ages were named after the metals, i.e., Gold, Silver, Brass and Iron. Similarly, the Hindu world ages are named after the four throws of Indian dice, i.e., Krta, Treta, Dvapara and Kali. In the first age Krta, conceived to be perfect Dharma which is symbolized as a bull stands on all the four legs. In each succeeding age it stand on three, two and one leg respectively, thus signifying the decline of virtues in each age. The moral and the social degradation of the last and the lowest age, Kali Yuga, is characterized thus in the Visnu Purana, which was composed some one thousand years ago: 'When society reaches a stage, where property confers rank, wealth becomes the only source of virtue, passion the sole bond of union between husband and wife, falsehood the source of success in life, sex the only means of enjoyment, and when outer trappings are confused with inner religion ...'.[14]

Let us remember, however, that the Kali Yuga is the shortest of the four yugas. It is believed to have a duration of 4,32,000 years, and our times have been computed to lie at a point which is a little short of the middle of the Kali age. Each of the preceding yuga has a duration which is the double of the following yuga. Thus, the total duration of the four yugas taken together, which is called a Maha Yuga (the Great Yuga), is 4,320,000 years.

But, a single day of Brahma, known as a 'Kalpa', is made up of one thousand yugas, i.e., 4,320,000,000 years of human reckoning. With each day of Brahma a new creation in terms of the human world *(srsti)* begins, and it is terminated at the end of Brahma's day with a re-absorption (*pralaya*) which is followed by the night of Brahma. This cycle of Brahma's day and night, i.e., creation of the world (*srsti*) and its re-absorption (*pralaya*), goes on. The events recounted in the mythological texts are believed to take place again and again in each Kalpa (Brahma's day or one creation). The lifetime of a Brahma endures for one hundred Brahma years and concludes with a universal dissolution; and then a state of total re-absorption prevails for another Brahma century. After this the entire cycle of 311,000,000,000,000 human years begins again.

Obviously, in such a huge perspective, time merges into eternity; and even Gods, not to speak of human individuals, are reduced to insignificance. There is a magnificent myth in the Brahmavaivarta Purana[15] which tells how Indra – the king of Gods – was made to realize his insignificance when he became too proud of himself after he had slain the dragon and was being acclaimed by the Gods as their saviour. To bring Indra back to senses, Vishnu assumed the form of a Brahamana boy and told him that there had been many Indras before him and there will be many others after him. He was shown a long procession of ants, in a column which was four yards wide, and was told that each one of these ants was once an Indra.

It seems that the conspicuous indifference of Hindu tradition to dates and biographic details stems from this huge perspective of time. It is well known that it is extremely difficult to determine the date of composition of important texts of Hindu tradition. For example, regarding the date of composition of such an important work as the *Arthasastra,*[16] differences among scholars range to as many as five or six centuries. But what do a few centuries matter if the perspective of time is as big as that of the Hindu tradition. It may be mentioned that in this tradition, the perspective of space too is very big. I heard a Nirgun song[17] from an unlettered villager in the interior of the countryside which personified illusion (Maya) as a belle and promised to cover her breast with a blouse which had the sun and the moon as its buttons.

The Nature and Extent of Originality

Though much more exploration is needed for understanding the exact manner in which creativity is related to socio-cultural time, the idea that creativity depends solely on the individual artist's originality is perhaps a part of the aberration in human history which the modern Western civilization seems to represent. Traditional civilizations do not seem to share this view of creativity and originality. Of course, traditional societies do not attach positive value to novelty or newness, and are not likely therefore to subscribe to the current meaning of originality. Traditionalistic scholars like Ananda Coomaraswamy explain originality in an entirely different manner: 'what we mean by "original" is "coming from its source within", like water from a spring. The artist can only express what is in him, what he is. It makes no difference whether or not the same thing has been expressed a thousand times before. There can be no property in ideas. The individual does not make them but finds them; let him only see to it that he really takes possession of them, and his work will be original in the same sense that the recurrent seasons sunrise and sunset are ever new although in name the same.'[18]

Even though we may not accept this view of originality, it appears to me that the amount of newness that an individual can really contribute is extremely small and marginal in relation to the accumulated resources of culture which he has inherited – and, of course, even his own small contribution is made possible because of that heritage. This is perhaps true even of the greatest innovators. While the crest of a wave may look high to us on the surface, its height from the trough is almost negligible in relation to the real depth of the waters of the ocean on which this wave rises in its transient glory. No poet, howsoever original, invents the language in which he writes, and unless he does that, to my mind his originality is seriously limited.

That creativity even in the sphere of physical sciences is related to time, is shown by the numerous instances of the same inventions made independently by different individuals almost at the same time. For example, in 1641, Galileo has described a pendulum clock, and in 1656 Huyghens invented it independently. Regarding the priority in the successful construction of watches with spiral balance spring, there was a fierce controversy between Huyghens and Hooke.[19] Though there are many other examples of simultaneous independent discoveries in various fields, the case of parallel inventions of clocks and watches is specially interesting because it brings out rather clearly, some of the factors which lead to such inventions and discoveries.

One of the obvious reasons of simultaneous discoveries lies in the stage of development of knowledge itself. A given level of knowledge provides similar opportunities for the solution of a problem, and since the available alternatives for solving it are limited, persons independently working at it may arrive at the same solution. This has been realized for a long time. As far back as 1828 Macaulay, while discussing Newton's and Leibniz's invention of calculus, said: 'Mathematical science, indeed, had reached such a point, that if neither of them had existed, the principals must inevitably have occurred to some person within a few years.'[20]

In addition to the imperatives of the intrinsic growth of science, there are the impelling pressures of economic and social requirements. The history of simultaneous inventions concerning clocks and watches illustrates this well. There is a lot of evidence to show that in the 17th century Europe, because of the growing needs of global navigation, scientific research was focused on developing a dependable method of finding the longitude at sea. The inventions relating to the pendulum clock and the watch with a spiral spring were clearly a response to this ardently felt social requirement. But, besides the broad practical needs of the society, the accounts of these inventions also reveal the part plays by direct economic inducement in motivating research in a particular direction.

However, human creativity in the fields of natural science, philosophical theorizing, and fine arts and literature, is not always guided by practical considerations or by conscious realization of broad social needs. Even when the artist, the scientist, or the philosopher is not conscious of the social needs, his work may nevertheless have certain implications for the social system. For instance, it appears to me that the persistent and widespread appeal of the story of Rama is due basically to its glorification of the cardinal virtue of the patriarchal family and society, namely, unflinching and unquestioning obedience to the patriarch. Rama obeyed the command of his father, even though it was unjustified and involved giving up the kingdom and going to the jungle for fourteen years. The story of Rama has been told since ancient times in numerous Sanskrit works, and in innumerable forms in various languages and dialects of all parts of India. Patriarchal family is the pivotal institution of the traditional Indian society, and perhaps of all civilizations based on plough agriculture. Unquestioning obedience of the patriarch is an essential requirement for the stability of this type of family. The story of Rama seems to owe its unparalleled sway to its efficacy in ensuring the internalization of this fundamental value, indispensable for stability of the social system. But, the innumerable composers of epics, dramas and other forms depicting the story of Rama may not have been conscious of its latent function. In fact, if they were to be really conscious of this, much of their inner reverence and inspiring faith would have gone. Not only myths, but even metaphysical theories seem to be related to and functional for, the social system to which they belong.[21]

There are, thus, a number of levels at which creativity and products of creativity are related with the socio-cultural context. In fact creativity finds expression only through outlets provided by society and culture. Potentiality can take shape as creation only when the requisite resources and conditions are available. We often talk about those creative works which have failed to receive the attention that they deserve, but we seldom think of the infinite potentialities which have not been able to find expression. Mirza Ghalib, the great Urdu poet, thought of these unexpressed possibilities. His perceptive couplet can be loosely translated as follows:

> Just a fee, not all, have found expression as flowers,
> Who knows of the forms which have remained submerged in dust?

Even when products of creativity have come into being, their recognition, as such, depends upon complex socio-cultural factors. One well-known example of this is the paintings of Vincent van Gogh which could not find a buyer in his lifetime, but are prized today as great works of art. Obviously, it is not only the intrinsic quality of product but also its acceptance that makes it an object of creativity. However, it would perhaps be incorrect to conceptualize these discrepancies primarily as a conflict between society and individuality. Such discrepancies seem to have their roots in the varying tendencies of differential socio-cultural times. The artist or author may be representing a rising trend which may not have gained wide acceptance by that time. In his early paintings van Gogh courageously depicted the most sinister aspects of the life of 19th century industrial centres. He painted, for instance, minors with stupor or their faces bent over the dinner of potatoes. He used colours that brought out the gloom and poverty that surrounded their lives. It is likely that the elite at that time were so sure of the all-round progress of their civilization that they had no use for such paintings, but as the disillusionment with the 'march of progress' grew, the same works began to become meaningful. Though one may not agree with the inference drawn from this particular example, the general contention that the acceptability of products of creativity changes greatly with the passage of socio-cultural time may still be valid and it is possible that a creative work representing a trend which does not find acceptability during the lifetime of its author may become famous when the time is ripe.

Though creativity is related in many ways with socio-cultural time, it has to be recognized that great creations remain valuable far beyond the age of their creation. This is true of artistic and philosophical works, as well as those on physical and social matters. Though no one today can write just like Kalidas or Shakespeare, we still enjoy their creations in the field of poetry and drama. This may perhaps be due to the fact that like scientific laws artistic creations too have different levels of generalization. The penetration of classics is so deep that they reach levels where the dividing walls of cultures and societies cease to exist, that is, their level of generality (or abstraction) is so high that their images and themes have an appeal that goes far beyond the society and culture where they were born or worked.

However, any artist or writer works with the raw material and tools which his own cultural tradition have provided him. Any artist or writer living in another society or cultural era does not have at his disposal those materials and tools, and cannot therefore make the thing – if he tries to make similar things, these are generally counterfeits. But thinkers, artists or poets working with different material and tools handed to them by their respective cultural traditions, can reach those depths where the comparatively superficial dividing lines of cultural differentiation vanish and the more commonly shared substratum of human thought and feeling begins.

Creativity and Deviance

Creativity, in many fields, that was acclaimed as excellent in later times was in numerous instances considered deviance in its own day. We know many outstanding persons like Socrates and Copernicus who were condemned as deviant in their own time, and were later worshipped as a genius. But we have no means of knowing about many others whose creativity may have been branded as devilish by their own age and buried deep enough to be forgotten for all time to come.

Many studies have shown that those marginal men and groups, who are not fully integrated with the larger community, are more creative and innovative. In modern societies where there is a great emphasis on success, man is induced to achieve it (primarily wealth and power) through innovative means; and in many cases it is difficult to decide whether an innovative business strategy constitutes deviance or not. As Thorstein Veblen has put it, 'It is not easy in any given case – indeed it is at times impossible until the courts have spoken to say whether it is an instance of praiseworthy salesmanship or a penitentiary offense'.

In the newly developing societies persons who are otherwise deviants, that is, who do not conform to their traditional norms, are often the first to adopt new technological practices. An interesting example of this is provided by a beautiful short story by Phanishwar Nath Renu. This story is entitled 'Panchlight' that is 'The Light of Panchayat'. In this story, almost every caste of a village had acquired a pressure gas lamp for its panchayat, so that it was known as 'Panchlight' or the light of panchayat. One lowly caste which did not have it also managed to purchase such a lamp by pooling various resources like the money collected from fines imposed by the panchayat. The money that was left after purchasing it was set aside for expenses on ritual so that its intricate mechanism may work properly. There was great enthusiasm among the people of the caste. When everything was ready, and the men, women and children had congregated at the door of the head of the Caste Panchayat for celebrating, and singing together *kirtan*, in the glow of the 'Panchalight' – gloom descended on the assemblage. Though certain persons belonging to other castes knew how to light a pressure gas lamp, asking them to light it on the inaugural day would put the whole caste to shame, and make its members the object of their ridicule. No one knew what to do. In the hushed silence, a girl whispered that a rather delinquent youngman, Godhan, knew how to light it. Godhan had been punished by the panchayat for making advances towards that girl by singing film songs directed at her. The panchayat had imposed a fine on that youngman and on his refusal to pay it he was expelled from the panchayat. But now everyone thought that since the prestige of the whole caste was under a threat, this boy should be invited and asked to light the new lamp. The boy agreed to come only when the mother of the girl herself went to his hut to persuade him. When the boy finally came and lighted the lamp there was all-round applause for him. The head of the panchayat called him nearby and said: 'You have saved the honour of the caste. You deserve pardon even if you commit seven murders. Sing as many film songs as you like'.

Time Lags and Creativity

In Ogburn's concept of cultural lag, a lag is caused because the material culture changes first and the non-material culture cannot keep pace with it.[22] However, in the Third World countries of today, which are undergoing social change at an unprecedented rate, we find the opposite kinds of lags also – certain parts of non-material culture, such as aspirations and legislations, sometimes march far ahead of the material culture which can sustain them.

But such analyses of lags are concerned primarily with different rates of change within one society. In today's world there is another kind of lag which has significance all of its own – the lags between different societies. Though these societies exist at the same point of astronomical time, in terms of socio-cultural time there are sharp and wide differences among them. Due to the modern means of transport and communication, and perhaps even more basically because of the propensity of the modern industrial society for continued expansion, the societies which are in very different periods of socio-cultural time come in contact with each other in various ways. Thus, many socio-cultural worlds are battering against each other. This is bound to have many implications for creativity, which have not received the attention that they deserve. In certain situations, such lags in socio-cultural time seem to have stifled creativity, while in another they may open up unprecedented possibilities of creating a whole new civilization. We shall briefly discuss an example of the former, and also the latter possibility.

An example of how creativity in one society may be stifled when it is confronted by another which is more advanced, is provided by a conspicuous lack of creativity in the field of social science in countries like India. Looking upon the state of the social sciences in India, one is struck by their protected barrenness. The social sciences have been taught in Indian universities for a fairly long time to an increasingly larger number of students. But fundamental contributions to social science have been rather rare. One may be able to recall a few contributions of a high order but, on the whole, the record remains surprisingly disappointing. This general paucity of fundamental contributions to social science is not to be explained on the basis of any inherently inferior intellect of Indians. Inadequacy of resources and facilities may explain the situation – but only partially; for, many fields and methodological approaches that have been in vogue in the past do not require huge financial support and material equipment.

What then is the reason for this sterility? It seems to be primarily sociological. It has perhaps something to do with the historical context in which modern social sciences were brought to India and the class that pursued them. Modern social sciences did not originate in India. They have their roots in the Western society, and have been shaped in their spirit and content by the ethos and the processes of that society. It should not be surprising if they have, by and large, failed to grow and yield fruit when planted in a radically different social soil and cultural climate. More than the question of any fundamental difference between the cultures of India and the West,[23] it is a problem of the gap between the different socio-cultural times.

When the British introduced English education in India, which included the study of modern social sciences, the country had a social structure which was basically different from the social structure of contemporary England and other advanced countries of the West. The social science that was taught in India had developed in an utterly different context. It is understandable, therefore, that even if the Indian teacher or student was able to understand and remember theories imported from the West, he could seldom contribute to their fundamental growth.

A question that suggests itself at this stage is: why was it then that social sciences continued to be studied in India despite their irrelevance? An adequate answer to this question is provided not much by any detached love of learning, either on the part of Indian students or that of the British rulers, but by the fact that education was assigned a different function, which it continued to perform. This function, as is well known, was the creation of an English-educated middle class through which the British could govern their vast empire. Not that this class always remained content to perform the task of supporting the British empire. On the contrary, it spearheaded the Indian national movement. But when it comes to accomplishments in the field of social sciences, it fails to show a bright record.

The English educated middle class was seriously handicapped by the lag in time. Even when it came to its own and showed signs of being related to the social dynamics of contemporary India, it found itself too backdated to make a significant contribution to the social sciences. It seems that movements comparable to the Renaissance and the Reformation overtook sizeable parts of India only in the latter half of the 19th century. It will be seen that these movements in Europe go as far back as the 15th and 16th centuries.

The transformation of parts of Indian society, from traditional state to comparatively modern one, did imply the emergence of certain movements comparable to the European Renaissance, Reformation and nationalism. But it would be a folly to think that the ideas underlying them were bodily lifted from the West. Influence of the West, primarily British in the context of India, surely acted as a catalyst, but the elements that reacted were mostly indigenous. For example, the reformist Arya Samaj movement played a role similar to Calvinism in promoting puritan and activistic ethics conducive to the growth of capitalism in western and central parts of northern India. It primarily drew upon ancient Indian texts. In fact, it sought support from the most primeval texts – the Vedas – for their attack on medieval values and institutions, though of course the interpretation of these texts was stretched to suit its case. The Arya Samaj did not consider any form of Christianity acceptable.

This movement and many other reform and renaissance movements that sprouted up in the 18th and 19th century India, and played a remarkable part in its transformation towards modernism, nevertheless remained basically Indian. They engendered an attitude of resistance against Western dominance in the field of ideas as well as those of politics and economy. They nourished beliefs about India's 'glorious past' that strengthened nascent nationalism. Such beliefs were often at variance with the history and other humanities and social sciences taught in schools and colleges under official patronage. These movements could therefore be expected to provide the basis for the growth of indigenous schools of social science, but they failed to do this. The reason for this failure lies not only in the absence of official support, but also in the lack of adequate strength and sophistication to compete with the more modern trends in social science that continued to be pursued under the auspices of the British government.

However, even though the Indian renaissance, reform and nationalistic movements failed to throw up any parallel system of social science, they do seem to have prevented a fuller participation by the Indian intelligentsia in the growth of social sciences that were brought to this country as a result of the British rule. Indians belonging to the new middle class who taught and studied these social sciences were mostly in the grip of one or the other of these nascent nationalistic movements, and they did not really believe in much of what they had to teach or study for earning their livelihood. In such circumstances, they could hardly make any creative contribution to its growth. Thus, on the one hand, they were unable to give a disciplinary status and systematic form to their own ideas about society, and on the other they remained incapable of making substantial contribution to current social science. This situation largely continued till the first half of the 20th century.

Possibilities of a New Civilization in Countries that have Lagged Behind

It would be unwarranted to take for granted that the societies which are lagging behind today are bound to remain in the same position for ever. It is often assumed that those societies which have reached a more advanced stage are bound to the next higher stage earlier than those which have lagged behind. On the contrary, I have put forward a hypothesis on the course of social change,[24] according to which not only is this not necessary but the reverse is more likely to be true provided we take a sufficiently large perspective: 'A culture which has attained stability at a high stage feels no need or compulsion to move to the next stage. On the other hand, a culture that has remained a step lower may have greater impetus than the more advanced culture to move to the higher stage. The society which has lagged behind does not usually have favourable conditions for arriving at the stage already reached by the advanced society, but it may have features which make it more suitable for the next higher stage. The transition becomes easier when it has at its disposal the accumulated fund of knowledge and ideas developed by the advanced society. While the vested interests and norms that have taken root in the stable, advanced society resist transition to the next stage, the underdeveloped society can move to it without these hurdles to overcome. Insofar as the assertions made by the rhythmic theories of social evolution are correct, underdeveloped societies may also be favourably placed to reach the next higher stage because their spirit and values correspond to the ones required.[25] Thus, in the course of socio-cultural evolution, it is not that a particular civilization continues to be first in reaching the successive stages of development once it has gone ahead in the race. On the contrary, once it has attained stability at a high stage of socio-cultural development, it is not this civilization but the civilization at a lower stage which has a greater chance of passing to the next higher stage, leaving the former behind'.

This hypothesis indicates a possibility of passing on of the creative initiative from the more advanced civilization to the less advanced ones. However, this passing on of the initiative would usually imply communication between these civilizations, and the utilization of ideas developed in the more advanced civilization by those that are less advanced.

Let us consider, for example, the possibilities of the growth of a new type of civilization in the countries of the contemporary Third World. We find today in these countries a constellation of forces which seems to be altogether new. The highly sophisticated and mellowed down forces of contemporary modernism are interacting with folk traditions which have vigour enough to combine with new elements and bring forth new forms. The forces of modernization, which trampled over the folk traditions in European countries around the 18th century, were very different from the modern forces as we find them today.

In the 18th and 19th centuries, when coal was the only source of power, industries had to be concentrated around coal mines, thus, giving rise to gigantic industrial centres and turning villages into markets for insipid goods of mass production and suppliers of cheap raw material. This is not unavoidable now. Electric power can be taken to villages and small-sized labour-intensive industries can be set up there itself. These industries need not employ outmoded technology. On the contrary, they can make good use of the most modern developments (like those in the field of electronics) which have made possible reduction in the size of machines to an unprecedented degree. In view of the scarcity of capital and abundance of unemployed labour in the developing countries, it will be far more economical to keep the machines labour-intensive.[26]

Thus, it is no more necessary to uproot the people from the countryside on a large scale to make industrialization possible. The settled life of the folk people in which, there is traditionally a balance between agriculture and industry can be given a new orientation for human ends by imaginative use of the most sophisticated technology.

The ideological elements too are not so hostile now to the folk way of life as they were in the early phase of modernism. The limitations of rationalism are widely recognized. Numerous ideological movements emphasize the value of cooperation and security. This is not to say that modern elite are going back to the values of the folk communities. They, however, do not harbour that self-righteous indignation which impelled their predecessors to combat and suppress traditional folk values. Under these changed material and ideological circumstances, it is not impossible that folk forms find certain new avenues of growth. Of course, we cannot expect them to remain just as they have been traditionally. They will have to raise themselves to a new level by interacting with the contemporary modern elements.

If there is any chance of such interaction it is much brighter in the newly developing countries than in the highly developed parts of the world which set out on the path of modernization more than a couple of centuries ago. In the latter the folk way of life seems to have languished beyond the point of revival. In the highly industrialized countries today, even though the dismal aspects of unlimited acquisitiveness, competition and individualism are recognized by some of their more perceptive elites, it is scarcely possible for them to reconstruct the folk mode of life, the destruction of which they may sincerely lament. It seems that in those countries the attraction towards folk forms is likely to remain rather romantic, as in the case of hippies and their communes in the USA; for nascent forces of the 18th and 19th century industrialization and modernism have already destroyed long ago much of their folk patterns.

Only future can tell us whether the folk traditions in the developing countries will really be able to attain a new level by creative harnessing of the technological, economic and ideological resources made available by the closing decades of the 20th century. A number of factors, however, exist which should deter us from rejecting such a possibility out of hand. The peculiar pattern of social change, with a lot of overlapping of different cultural eras, has brought vigorous folk traditions in close proximity to modern forces which have attained a high degree of maturity. These countries may therefore chart out a new course in their march towards modernism.

This is all the more likely because many of the ways taken by the countries which were the first to industrialize and modernize them are no more open to the newly developing countries. It is well known for instance that the industrial revolution in Western Europe was made possible largely with the help of the capital acquired through the exploitation of colonies. To the newly developing countries of today neither colonies nor virgin lands are available. Due to the prevailing ideas regarding welfare of labour it does not seem possible for these countries to accumulate capital on the same scale even by the exploitation of their inland labour as was done in the Western countries during the 18th and 19th centuries. But, the developing countries have an abundance of unemployed labour, though the capital available is very scarce. Thus, these countries are being compelled by circumstances to think in terms of labour-intensive small-scale industries. As we have noted, the new sources of power like electricity and developments in the field of technology make it possible to disperse industries throughout the countryside, thus doing away with the need to disrupt the settled life of folk society.

The idea, often unstated but taken as axiomatic, that the Third Word countries which have just started following the path of development are bound to follow the same course as was taken earlier by the countries of the West, implies an unwarranted belief in unilinear evolution. The long strides of socio-economic changes in the developing countries of today may permit the skipping of some of the earlier steps of large-scale industrialization. These countries face a unique challenge, and it is not impossible that this may evoke a magnificent response and lead to the growth of a new and healthier civilization.

Such a development appears to be desirable also. Large-scale capitalist industrialization based on individualistic acquisitiveness has led to various maladies, such as alienation of work from life, schism between utility and beauty, commercialization of leisure and recreation, sapping of aesthetic sensibility from everyday life, general uprootedness, and creation of human ant-hills in the form of gigantic urban centres swarming with a variety of problems. Folk culture, on the contrary, is marked by a balance between considerations of beauty and utility. For the folk craftsman work is not alienated from life and the object produced by him has both utilitarian and aesthetic aspects. In folk society the artist is not a special kind of man, but every man is a special kind of artist. Almost everyone sings (not merely listens) and artistic expressions like singing are not put on a separate niche – they accompany work and socially significant rituals. Though it would be impossible and also undesirable to try to preserve folk culture just as it has been, it is necessary to work out the possibility of developing those of its aspects which have abiding value for man.

It must however be stated that the above analysis does not regard the current interest of urbanized people in folk culture as the basis of our hope for its growth. In fact, such romantic interest and praise for folk culture often stems from a type of sensibility which is totally foreign to the ways of thinking of the folk. Instead of ensuring the vitality of elements of folk culture, such interest may result in their turning into museum pieces. Romantic glorification and nostalgia are signs of uprootedness. A true member of the folk does not glorify his song – he sings it, often without giving it a name. On the other hand, people, who praise the folk song, are very often those who look at it from a distance. They are outsiders to the tradition. They can be compared to the antiquarian who does not worship the icon but puts it on a pedestal in museum. The rise in number of such admires of folklore and folk culture in a community may not be a sign of the vigour of tradition; on the contrary, it may suggest that the tradition is losing its vitality and its elements are being reduced to the status of antiques.

Notes

1. *International Encyclopedia of Social Sciences*, 1968, Vol. 3, p. 442.
2. Ibid.
3. Ananda K. Coomaraswamy (1969). *Introduction to Indian Art*. Delhi: Munshiram Manoharlal, p. 80.
4. For a more detailed statement of this view, see, Indra Deva (1977). 'Cultural Level of Unlettered Folk', *Diogenes*, 100, Paris: UNESCO, pp. 26–47.
5. For some examples, see, Indra Deva (1956). 'Modern Social Forces in Indian Folk Songs', *Diogenes*, 15, Paris: UNESCO; Deva (1972). 'Folklore Studies: A Trend Report', *A Survey of Research in Sociology and Social Anthropology*, Indian Council of Social Science Research, Bombay: Popular Prakashan; Deva (1974). 'Oral Tradition and the Study of Peasant Society', *Diogenes*, 85, Paris: UNESCO; Deva (1980). 'The Future of Folklore', *Folklore Studies in the Twentieth Century*, UK: Boydelle & Brewer and USA: Howman and Littlefield; Deva (1981). 'Popular and Folk Culture in Contemporary India: An Attempt at Perspective', *International Popular Culture*, II (1), New York: Station Island.
6. The presentation of the *ragas* of classical Indian music involves a similar process. Those who have attained a reasonably high level of mastery in the classical tradition invariably improvise and create new patterns during performance.
7. Cf. C.M. Bowra (1952). *Heroic Poetry*. London: Macmillan & Co.

   The common characteristics on the basis of which C.M. Bowra analysed the heroic poetry of various Asian and European peoples were earlier brought out by the Chadwicks. See H. Munro Chadwick (1912). *The Heroic Age*. Cambridge: Cambridge University Press; and H. Munro Chadwick and N.K. Chadwick (1932). *The Growth of Literature*. Cambridge: Cambridge University Press.

8. F.J. Child (1898). *The English and Scottish Ballads*. Boston: Houghton Mifflin.
9. Cecil J. Sharp (1954). *English Folk Song: Some Conclusions*. London: Methuen & Co., p. 102.
10. Robert Graves (1927). *The English Ballad*. London: Ernest Benn Ltd., p. 22.
11. Ibid., p. 9.
12. Karl Marx and Frederick Engels (1950). *Selected Works*, Vol. I. Moscow: Foreign Languages Publishing House, p. 320.
13. P.A. Sorokin (1937). *Social and Cultural Dynamics*, 4 Vols. New York: American Book Co.
14. This is condensation of the long descriptive passage in Book IV, Chapter 24 of the *Visnu Purana*. See Heinrich Zimmer (1963). *Myths and Symbols in Indian Art and Civilization*, edited by Joseph Campbell. New York: Bollingen Foundation, p. 15 ff.
15. Brahmavaivarta Purana, Krsna-janma Khanda, 47.50–161, summarized in H. Zimmer (1963). op. cit., pp. 3–11.
16. Cf. Indra Deva and Shrirama (1980). *Growth of Legal System in Indian Society*. New Delhi: Allied Publishers, pp. 28–29.
17. Nirguns are songs about the 'Non-qualifiable Absolute'. It is customary to impute the authorship of such songs to the great mystic poet Kabir, who himself was unlettered and a weaver by profession.
18. A.K. Coomaraswamy (1969). op. cit., p. 80.
19. Robert K. Merton (1975). 'Science and Economy of 17th Century England', *Social Theory and Social Structure*, New York: Macmillan, pp. 661–81.
20. R.K. Merton (1957). 'Sociology of Knowledge', *Social Theory and Social Structure*, New York: Free Press, p. 523.
21. For a discussion of how the metaphysical systems of Samkhya and Vedanta imply a view of women that corresponds, and provides legitimacy, to the position given to patriarchal society, see Shrirama Inder Deva (1966). 'Correspondence between Woman and Nature in Indian Thought', *Philosophy East and West*, XVI, Hawaii, pp. 161–68.
22. W.F. Ogburn (1922). *Social Change*, Parts IV and V. New York: The Viking Press.
23. Many sociologists, European, American as well as Indian seem to have made too much of the supposed 'spirituality' and 'otherworldliness' of Indian culture. It is doubtful to what extent the Indian culture is more spiritual than that of other countries including those of Europe in pre-modern times. The work of scholars like A.K. Coomaraswamy and H. Zimmer suggest that the predominant worldview in all traditional civilizations has been similar.
24. Indra Deva (1966). 'The Course of Social Change: A Hypothesis', *Diogenes*, 56, Paris: UNESCO, pp. 74–91.

    The theory of social change presented through this paper has received wide attention from sociologists in all parts of the world. Paul. F. Lazarsfeld (1970) has discussed it as one of the four major contributions to macro-sociology, *Main Trends of Research in Social and Human Sciences*, Vol. I. Paris: UNESCO, p. 87.

25. There are numerous rhythmic theories of social change which can be variously classified according to the different criteria that we choose. Sorokin has also classified them according to the number of their phases: two-phase rhythms, three-phase rhythms, four-phase rhythms, and five-phase rhythms and still more complex rhythms (P.A. Sorokin (1962). *Social and Cultural Dynamics*, Vol. IV. New York: Bedminister Press, pp. 398–421).

    From the viewpoint of our hypothesis, a society which is only one step lower than the most advanced society is in an advantageous position for moving a stage beyond it, showing a two-phase rhythm. This argument can obviously be extended further.

26. For a more detailed discussion, see, Indra Deva (1981). 'Impact of Modern Economic-Technic Forces on Small Industries and Traditional Crafts: The Perspective of Growth in India', *Petite Enterprise at Croissence Industrielle dans de Monde aux XIX et XX Siecles*, Commission Internationale d'Histoire des Mouvements Sociaux et des Structures Sociales, Editions du CNRS, Paris, Tome II, pp. 937–54.

14

The Art of Sharadchandra Chattopadhyay

M.S. Gore

I was asked by the editor of the *New Quest* why I thought of translating a story by Sharadchandra Chattopadhyay when I did not know Bengali – the language in which the author wrote – from its Marathi translation into English. This question is legitimate because if one does not know the language in which the first author wrote his books, one has to depend solely on the authenticity of the first translation – not only in respect of its faithfulness to the text but also in terms of the first translator's ability to convey the nuances of expressions and sentiments of the characters of the story in the second language. Since I do not know Bengali I cannot say to what extent the Marathi translation on which my translation is based meets these criteria.

My only answer to the Editor was that I had liked the translations that I had read and thought that they were worthy of translations in their own right so that they would be available to a wider spectrum of Indian readership – particularly the one which normally thinks and communicates in English.

I did not undertake the translation with any noble intention of doing a service to my readers if there are any. Like any writer I have always a hope that what I write will be read, but I write or translate because I feel impelled to do so and I enjoy doing it. This is particularly true of my translations. My professional writings have generally been done in specific response to a request or for some scholarly goal that I had in mind.

The translations I have done are however largely because of the fact that I have enjoyed the original in the language in which I read it and wanted to render it in English. I have by now translated about half a dozen stories of G.A. Kulkarni and the stories by Kusumagraja edited by Shanta Shelke. But, a larger part of my translations have been secondary translations of the works of Sharadchandra Chattopadhyay as translated by Mama Warerkar in Marathi. I became familiar with Sharadchandra's works when I was in High School and

College. I was fascinated by them, but I can now say that I had not really understood them until after I had retired from active work and began to reread them with a view to translate them. Though Sharadchandra is easy to follow at the story level, there is a much greater depth to his character development and to his social comment that is not easily grasped at an early age – especially by one who is not familiar with the social context of the Bengal society and the period in which Sharadbabu was writing.

It is possible to say that there is a pan-Indian social reality at a certain level and in certain social contexts – particularly in the traditional middle class familial context and in the traditional concept of caste hierarchy. In a very general way, one could say that in a large part of the country the patrilineal and patriarchal three generation joint family pattern prevailed through a good part of the late 19th and early 20th century. Even today the situation is not as changed as one might imagine though the subjective world of a middle class woman has undergone a great deal of change in the middle classes. The joint family was based on the two facts of pre-industrial India with land as the base of the economy and joint family as the social unit among the landowning classes. The men belonged to the family, the women were outsiders and had to be subjugated to conform and adjust to a new family and also to make for a clear pecking order within the house. Familial units never adhere strictly to the model but the model is clearly spelt out. And even then there were systemic and idiosyncratic variations from one area of the country to another and between the mainstream caste society and the tribal societies in different parts of the country.

Sharadchandra was writing primarily about Bengali society in Bengal in the first half of the 20th century – though some of his novels are located in Burma and one in Agra. But, when you take the whole of his work you find that he has written about nearly every stratum of Bengali society though the point of vantage is that of a member of the middle class. I am not suggesting that he has sought to justify or idolize the middle class, but only that he was himself located in the urban middle class. But, he strides across the rural-urban divide, across the rich-poor divide, and across religious-ideological divides. He wrote naturally about the society that he saw and experienced. But, his life experiences must have been so varied and so steeped in genuine humane values that he takes you into nooks and corners of Bengal society – the Bengal in the large metropolis of Kolkata, the Bengal of the zamindari villages, the Bengal of the district towns, the Bengal of the revolutionary movement, the Bengal of the Bhadralok, the Bengal of the village of untouchables and the Bengal of the urban working class and he is able to project with sympathy the varied lifestyles and does so without imposing preconceived notions of morality.

In his novels, two types of issues are raised almost constantly – one relating to the poor and the deprived and the other relating to the status of women within the family and in society. As a novelist, he is not concerned with offering ready solutions to any of these problems but rather with depicting the situations in which his characters are placed, why they behave the way they do and how they cope with the situations in which they find themselves.

In discussing Sharadbabu's work, I have not followed a chronological sequence of the publication of his work. I have considered some of the works of his period of maturity. I begin first with – *Pather Dabi* (1926), *Vipradas* (1935) and *Shesh Prashna* (1931).

In Savyasachi (*Pather Dabi*) – a novel he wrote in the last phase of his career as a writer, he presents the revolutionary's perspective of how social and political change might be brought about, why political change is critically more important than social change and how violence is the most promising way of bringing about political change. Working directly with the poor and the oppressed are considered by Savyasachi as of no significance in terms of bringing about a political change which for the revolutionary is the prime objective. This perspective is counterpoised in the novel by Bharati who is closely associated with Savyasachi but cannot see violence as a way of solving the problems of the world either politically or socially. The novel is located in the pre-Gandhian era of Indian political life but was written at a time when Gandhi was already a potent political force in the country. In a tangential way, Bharati and Apoorva are projected as planning to initiate a movement after their return to India for peoples' awakening through rural social work thus building up a force for change from below. Savyasachi himself is interested only in a worldwide revolutionary change and in bringing down established regimes. He would rather depend more on the privileged middle class to play a critical role in bringing about a political revolution than on the industrial working class and the rural peasantry. Large portions of the novel are dedicated to the discussions between the middle-aged Savyasachi and the young Bharati – whom he treats as his younger sister – on the pattern and modality of the revolutionary movement. In India's own struggle for independence, the middle class played an important role but had it not been for Gandhi's rousing of mass consciousness it is doubtful whether they would have had the leverage to persuade the British to leave.

The theme of love between the very orthodox Brahmin, Apoorva, and the young Christian girl, Bharati, is kept as a secondary strand, though the novel begins with it in the first part. Bharati's love for Apoorva remains inexplicable and almost one sided because Apoorva is constrained by his religious orthodoxy and his love and consideration for his even more orthodox widowed mother. In quite a few of Sharadchandra's novels and stories, the heroines are seen as the more eager and more active initiator's of a love bond. Even otherwise Apoorva is a timid character and fails to measure up when it comes to standing up for his inchoate political leanings and is found totally unfit for being a part of a revolutionary group. Yet, Bharati's love for him remains constant and she shields and tends to him through many difficult situations both in his personal life as well as in his brief but dangerous political involvement with the revolutionary group.

The novel *Shrikant,* which is generally considered to be largely autobiographical, gives a clue to the author's characterization of at least some of his heroes as probably eager but non-active participants in their relations with the heroines of his novels. Shrikant is seen to be an observant, sympathetic, sensitive, and reflective person but not as an initiator of any action. Even in his childhood, he acts largely in response to his friend Indra in all his night time exploits on the river Ganges. Later, in his life it is Pyari who takes the initiative and reminds him of their childhood fellowship and establishes a warm love relationship with him in which she accepts the limitations imposed on her as a 'fallen woman' but still regards him as the 'man' in her life. There are only two points where Shrikant acts decisively – once when he leaves Pyari in her village estate (where she builds a special house for him) and returns to Kolkata as Pyari gets more and more involved in her religious spiritual pursuits – and the second time when he decides to go to Burma to find his livelihood.

Sharadbabu's canvas is large and it provides scope for major themes to emerge and for all types of characters to function in major or minor roles. His novel *Shesh Prashna* (1931) raises important questions about the basic ethics of life and about conventional social morality. It projects a beautiful and brilliant woman, Kamala, who has been deceived by the man who claims to have married her. She has an indomitable spirit and a totally different view of conventional morality. She had been married to a local plantation worker who deserts her before she undergoes a make-belief marriage with Shivnath who brings her to Agra and then again abandons her when the opportunity for marrying the daughter of a rich retired man arises.

Kamala believes and propounds what could probably be described as the existentialist view of life. She is the daughter of a tea estate manager and a house servant. But, her father loves her and tutors her in history, philosophy and the basic skills of reading and writing.

When she arrives in Agra with her 'husband' Shivnath, the latter tries to conceal his marriage with her. Shivnath had been a professor at the local college but had been expelled from it for having been found drunk. He himself is now making a living by some minor trade. But, he is gifted with a sonorous voice and a musical ability. This is what brings him to the notice of an elderly retired and highly respected person of means, Ashubabu. Ashubabu is liberal minded and a lover of arts. He invites him for a musical evening at his house. It is at that musical evening that Shivnath is recognized by his former college colleagues and questioned and exposed as an 'immoral' and selfish person.

Kamala gets to know Ashubabu by an accident when during a torrential rain Shivnath and Kamala are seen taking shelter under a tree outside Ashubabu's bungalow. Ashubabu calls them in and is struck by her beauty, her bearing and her poise. She is about the age of his daughter Manorama and he instantly takes a liking to her. But, he gets to know her better when, on a holiday, Ashubabu, his daughter, Manorama, Ajit and the local college professors go to visit the Taj Mahal. Shivnath and Kamala also happen to visit the Taj on the same day. Shivnath wants to avoid meeting the group because he is not too keen to have Kamala meet the college professors, but Kamala persuades him to meet Ashubabu and his friends. It is at this meeting that Kamala shocks everybody by her views on the Taj. She accepts the fact that it is a beautiful monument, but rejects all the sentimentality surrounding it as a monument dedicated to love. She points out that the King had many queens and it is unlikely that he built the monument as a memorial of love for his dead queen. This disturbs everyone gathered there and particularly Ashubabu, who is a widower and has stayed unmarried out of his love for his dead wife. Yet, he is tolerant of Kamala's views and is impressed by what she has to say on the subject. Sharadbabu's skill as a novelist shows how a relationship of great warmth and affection and trust for each other develops between the elderly Ashubabu and the young Kamala. He later begins to look to her for advice and counsel especially when his daughter runs away with Shivnath. She refuses to support him when out of anger he tries to punish his daughter Manorama by depriving her of her hereditary rights and of financial support.

The novel *Shesh Prashna* has no hero to speak of. It has a heroine and a few young men out of whom she chooses the most eligible one as her consort. She refuses to go through any marriage ceremony and insists that their love for each other should sustain their relationship. If the relationship breaks she would still cherish the moments of that relationship as a one-time reality. When Shivnath deserts her to marry Manorama she does not complain about it and says that what he gave her when he was in love with her was still valid as love and something she still cherishes. But, she does not fool herself when Shivnath who is faking an illness tries to make up with her. The only person who really attracts her is the young revolutionary, Rajan, who works for the poor in the midst of an epidemic despite the constant threat of being taken in by the police.

Throughout the novel she argues about the futility of going after old ideals and values and insists that new values and new institutions have to be founded anew by each generation not on the basis of historical memory but existential reality. She refutes the idea of reviving the concept of an ashram school and tells Harenbabu that he would do much better to feed the children and send them to normal schools and colleges, than treat them as acolytes to grow up to be sadhus.

Vipradas (1935), is another of Sharadbabu's major novels. It begins as the story of life of a Zamindar's family but the novel does not discuss the Zamindari system. It deals with the life of the Mukherji family. The family consists of Vipradas who is the male head of the family, his widowed stepmother, Dayamayi, who has brought him up, Vipradas' younger brother, Dwijdas, Vipradas' wife Sati and their young son, Vasu.

Though Vipradas is the Zamindar it is really his stepmother who rules in the family. Vipradas is devoted to her and she has more trust in him than in her own son, Dwijdas, whom she regards as misguided because of his leftist leanings.

Vipradas has had no college education but he is a self-educated man and has a library big enough to require a separate room in the house. The novel gains its significance among the books written by Sharadbabu because of the epic size characters he has created in Vipradas and his stepmother Dayamayi. Even the other characters he has created in this novel are quite out of the ordinary – Dwijdas, Vandana, and the old house servant, Annada. None of them is small minded or selfish and yet a major tragedy develops in the family because of the very generous and trusting nature of Vipradas and Dayamayi's love for her daughter who has married a former friend of Vipradas who turns out to be a cad.

At another level is the relationship between Vipradas and Vandana. Vandana travels with Vipradas and her father from Balarampur to Kolkata. She had originally gone to Balarampur for a projected long stay because of the pressing invitation to her from Sati – her first cousin and Vipradas' wife. She feels offended by the fact that the orthodox Dayamayi seems to regard her father and her as 'outcastes' since the father has been to England and has not gone through the purification rites on his return. Vandana is keen to get back to Bombay immediately but finds that her father has business in Kolkata and has to accompany him to Kolkata. On the train from Balarampur she gets intrigued by Vipradas' physical and moral courage in dealing with the European crowd that has tried to take over their compartment and also by his social and philosophical opinions and his general bearing. She has gone to Kolkata to get away from Balarampur and the orthodox Mukherji family and wants to return to Bombay by the first available train. But, she has to stay on in Kolkata – first because of her father's illness and then because of Vipradas' illness.

During this period of almost a month she gains a new understanding of the traditional cultural values and familial relationships. She begins to respect and becomes almost devoted to Vipradas because despite his orthodox style of living and conformity to all the daily rituals of a Brahmin life he is tolerant, respectful and understanding of the values held by other people. His religious interests extend to the spiritual. He is truly philosophic in his life perspective. She comes to love him and he, in turn, admits his admiration for her but succeeds in showing her that their personal and social commitments lie elsewhere and must be respected. Vandana gains a new understanding of the traditional familial life and finds that it has more depth, is more family and community based and in that sense superior to the somewhat shallow, totally individualistic and self-oriented lifestyle of the westernized Brahmo upper middle class with which she and her father have come to be associated, though Vandana's father has never formally become a member of the Brahmo Samaj.

When Dayamayi decides on building a new water tank for the Balarampur village and the surrounding hamlets Vipradas is unable, because of his health, to go and supervise the preparatory work. The responsibility for the entire operation of preparing for the formal inauguration of the water tank falls on the young Dwijdas. Vipradas agrees to go to the inaugural ceremony and Dwijdas persuades Vandana also to join the ceremonies.

Everything in the Mukherji household has to be done on a grand scale. The whole village and the peasantry dependent on the Mukherji estate are invited to the ceremony. Dwijdas has worked hard to make all the preparations for the religious as well as social aspects of the function. Vipradas arrives with Vandana a day prior to the main ceremony. Among the invitees naturally are Dayamayi's daughter and her husband, Shashadhar.

On one occasion Vipradas finds his brother-in-law in his room and drags him out of the room with his own hands. This is when the bomb explodes. Shashadhar makes an issue of it and goes to his mother-in-law and says that he has been insulted in the house and he can no longer stay in it. Dayamayi asks what the matter is and he tells her that Vipradas has insulted him and unless he apologizes for it, he and his wife would immediately vacate the house.

Dayamayi does not know what has happened and sends for Vipradas. No one in the family knows why the enmity between Vipradas and Shashadhar has arisen. Vipradas refuses to apologize and now Dayamayi is caught in a difficult situation and finds that she has to choose between her dear son and her son-in-law who has come in response to an invitation. Vipradas makes it clear that if he leaves house it will be forever. Dayamayi is incensed and says her daughter and Shashadhar cannot be asked to leave the house. Vipradas declares that he will leave the house, the moment the formal ceremony of the opening of the tank is over.

The following day the Mukherji household breaks up. Sati also decides to accompany her husband with their son Vasu. Dayamayi locks herself in her room without food or water and refuses to open the door. Dwijdas knows that it is of no use trying to dissuade Vipradas from his resolve whatever the reason for it may be.

Dwijdas goes to the station with Vipradas to bid goodbye to his elder brother, his sister-in-law and Vasu. On his return he sits with the account books and finds that Vipradas has become a pauper and he suspects that Shashadhar has defrauded him. He makes up his mind to sue Shashadhar, something that Vipradas might not have done out of consideration for his sister.

The rest of the novel is devoted to the development of a close relationship between Dwijdas and Vandana who has stayed back at his request for a few days. She goes back to Bombay with a promise that she will return to Balarampur if he sends for her.

She does return after some months when Dwijdas sends her a telegram. Dayamayi has lost interest in life and is more and more involved in her poojas and fasts. Vipradas comes home after about a year. He has lost his wife after a brief illness during their wanderings. He has come home to perform the death rites. Dayamayi decides to go on a pilgrimage with him and thus the mother and her stepson come together again. But, they leave the house with the idea of not returning home. Vipradas has no money of his own and how he and his old mother are going to meet their expenses during the journey is not made clear, unless it is assumed that Dayamayi who is still the head of the family is going to depend on her own money. Before they leave on their pilgrimage Dwijdas asks Vandana to request Vipradas to leave Vasu behind. Vasu was closer to his uncle than to his father in any case. Vipradas agrees to the request.

Vipradas is the shortest of Sharadchandra's three major novels. It discusses no major social problem except contextually – the difference between the Brahmo high society and the traditional Hindu family. It stands out for its sharp characterization of each of the characters that appear in the novel including Annada, the domestic servant who has been with the family for many years and is devoted to it. The high-minded and principled Vipradas, the strong-willed Dayamayi who has looked after the estate while her children were still young and has ruled the family with love, and the delicately painted Sati who stays in the background and cements the family relationships through her affectionate handling of the young brother-in-law, who might otherwise have found himself alone in the family. The modern, well educated and intelligent Vandana struggles to find meaning in a totally different culture and succeeds in gaining a mature understanding of it. Each of these characters is thoughtful and reflective and achieves an individuality of its own.

Sharadchandra has several other shorter novels and short stories. I will discuss two of the shorter novels, and a few of the short stories in this paper.

The first of these is *Gaon-Ganga* (I do not know the Bengali title of the novelette since it is not given on the face sheet of the Marathi translation). I have loosely translated it as the *Village Ganges* (1916). The novel belongs to Sharadbabu's earlier phase as a writer. Unlike *Vipradas*, or *Shesh Prashna* or *Pather Dabi* which are all located and deal with urban life, *Gaon-Ganga* deals with rural life. This is a very small novel – hardly 130 pages – but a gem in its own way. It deals with village life and more particularly with the Zamindari system and the system of rival factions in a village. It has an identifiable hero, an identifiable villain and a possible heroin. Ramesh Ghoshal is the hero, his cousin brother Veni Ghoshal is the villain and Rama Mukherji could have been the conventional heroine, had she not been widowed in her childhood. Rama and Ramesh were great friends in their childhood but Ramesh Ghoshal had left the village for education and returns to it only to perform the death rites of his father. He has been away for several years and returns after obtaining a degree in engineering from the Roorkee Engineering College. The Mukherjies and the Ghoshals were great friends and had come to the village, Kumbapur, at about the same time and established large zamindaries over the years. But, during the years that Ramesh was away his father and his uncle separated into two households. Ramesh had no immediate relatives in the village except his cousin Veni and Veni's mother, and Ramesh's aunt, Vishweshwari.

In rural life, especially among the gentry, death rituals are a major event and who is invited to it or not invited is closely watched. Without being aware of these nuances, Ramesh decides to call all the Brahmin families in the village to the ritual function and to the feast thereafter.

This displeases Veni who is keen to keep his crowd together and does not like them going to a meal at Ramesh's house. Earlier when Ramesh had gone to him seeking his advice on whom to invite he was cold shouldered. Veni even refused to attend the meal because of the old family rivalry. Ramesh who had been away from the village for over ten or fifteen years is not aware of the groupings in the village. When he goes to Rama seeking her help in preparing for the event he is rebuffed by Rama's aunt who tells him never again to enter the house.

The fact is that Rama as a woman would have been unable to manage the zamindari by herself and has become dependent on Veni for most decisions relating to her own estate.

Since Veni refuses to attend the ritual in Ramesh's house she could not attend it either whatever her own inclinations were in the matter. Ramesh goes to seek the advice of his own aunt – Veni's mother – and she tells him that he better consult Veni. When Ramesh tells her that he has already been rebuffed by him she feels helpless though she knows her son is a bad and exploitative Zamindar.

Veni's effort is to make it difficult for Ramesh to live in the village. But, Ramesh is made of sterner stuff. He decides to go ahead and perform the rites for his father and also invites all the Brahmins in the village without any thought of who belongs to whose group. Not surprisingly all the invited Brahmins attend the meal. During the meal a lot of the village gossip is exchanged. Ramesh finds a very poor old Brahmin who has brought all his children to the meal as this was their only chance of having a square meal in a long time. Ramesh feels sympathy for him and accompanies him to his home after the feast is over. He comes to know about the details of the politics of the village and about all the persons who have attended the meal though some of them belong to Veni's camp. The old man tells Ramesh that everything that has happened and not happened at the meal will be reported to Veni by the evening.

An important development is that Ramesh's aunt – Veni's mother – Vishweshwari turns up at Ramesh's house and takes charge of the stores and supervises the servants as they serve the guests. This greatly encourages Ramesh and subdues the vociferous members of the gathering and shows that there is at least one senior member of the Ghoshal family who stands behind Ramesh.

Ramesh has spent a great fortune on the ritual, the meal and the presents of cloth that he gives to the poor who gather outside his house. Ramesh had employed professional cooks to prepare the meal and had ordered sweets from Kolkata.

Sharadbabu uses the occasion of the feast to bring out the kind of gossip that goes on in a village and the petty rivalries that exist between individuals and between factions in the village. There are arguments and fights among the guests which are based on their own relationships with each other and have nothing to do with Ramesh or with the function where they are guests.

At the end of the second day of feasting Ramesh goes to his aunt to thank her. She talks affectionately and encouragingly to him and urges him to stay on and do something for the peasantry that is dependent on him. She is seen as an unusually insightful woman and tells him that nothing worthwhile can happen in the country unless the conditions in which the peasantry works and lives are improved. One has to remember that this novel was written before Gandhiji had returned to India from Africa. There were not many who had the insight to see that rural India was the real India.

Ramesh visits his estate, meets the villagers and tries to understand their problems. He invites them to his house and makes out plans to improve their conditions. Two of the villages in his estate are Muslim villages. He finds that these villages are united and have capable leaders.

When these leaders mention that their children have no facility for education, he provides them with funds and other help to start schools where their children can learn the three R's (reading, writing and arithmetic) in their own language. They are grateful to him and become supportive of him, in his other reform measures as well. Despite his sympathy and kindness toward the villagers he is firm in the collection of legitimate dues from them.

All these activities contribute to increase the displeasure of Ramesh's cousin who sees a threat to his supremacy in the village. A development occurs during the rainy season which brings things to a boil. Heavy rains flood the fields and the crops are endangered in the fields of Ramesh's peasantry. The floods do not recede even after the rain has stopped because of a small dam that Veni and Rama have constructed to retain water in their own fields. Ramesh goes to Veni with a request to breach the dam and help the farmers. The request is turned down because of the loss it would cause to their crops. They have appointed strong men to protect the dam but looking at the total ruin that poor farmers would suffer Ramesh advises them to break the dam and personally joins them in breaking it down. Ramesh is able bodied and skilled in the use of the lathi. A regular fight occurs and Ramesh and his men succeed in effecting a breach in the dam. The fields of the peasants are saved. The strong men appointed by Veni suffer a defeat. They go to Veni to report on the event where they get scolded for their ineffectiveness. But, they praise Ramesh for his bravery and say that there is no one who can match him in the use of the stick. This makes Veni wild and he wants to punish his strong men for their failure. Rama who has listened to the conversation finds herself pleased though she had earlier turned down Ramesh's personal request for breaching the dam and allowing the water to flow. She had in fact suggested that Ramesh should pay for the damage caused to their field because of the breach.

Sharadbabu develops the whole sequence of the changing relationship between Ramesh and Rama with an uncommon artistry. From apparent indifference and indirect rudeness she comes to admire him as in the old days but dare not side with him against Veni. Rama happens to meet Ramesh near a holy place, Dughdapushkar, located at some distance from the village. Rama is in the practice of going to that temple on certain specific days of the year. Ramesh is not aware of it and is surprised to find her coming out wet after her bath in the river. He does not wish to embarrass her by showing that he has recognized her but she passes close enough to him and tells him to come to the house where she is staying in that location. After allowing her time to go and change into dry clothes Ramesh goes to her house and Rama finding that he has no other place to go to urges him to eat at her house and spend the night there … . She has a woman servant to help her, who would serve as a chaperon. But, Rama cooks the meal herself and serves it to Ramesh and derives great pleasure from it. Ramesh also eats a meal that has not been prepared by his servant for the first time since his return to the village. This is the first time that she has met Ramesh in a friendly fashion without being under the constant supervision of her aunt and the agents of Veni. After his meal is over Rama tells him to spend the night in the other room. The presence of the servant serves the purpose of providing them with an opportunity to speak freely to each other. Nothing much of consequence happens but this helps to remove a lot of misunderstanding on the part of Ramesh who in any case has both sensitivity and sympathy for her.

To prepare a meal for someone for whom one cares and to serve it to him personally and sit and wait on him is obviously an important facet of a close relationship between man and a woman in Bengali society. The motif repeats through nearly all of Sharadbabu's novels.

Ramesh has done a lot of good work in the village and in his zamindari villages. Apart from the two schools he has established, he undertakes health and education work and is helping the villagers to fight the menace of malaria. He also helps the local school by supplying them with new furniture and books and maps. Ramesh's aunt is very appreciative of all his work and urges him not to leave the village without completing the good work that he has begun. She points out to him that ignorance is the root cause of the misery of the peasants. Without education they cannot protect themselves against disease or against the high-handedness of the landlord and the police working in unison.

Veni is now waiting for an opportunity to discredit Ramesh and bring him down in the eyes of the villagers. He asks his strong men to file a police complaint against him for having caused them injury while they were doing their duty. But, they refuse to oblige him and say that they would never do such a thing against a truly brave man.

Another occasion occurs. One member of Veni's faction comes to Ramesh begging for a loan and pleading that he would go hungry without such a loan. Ramesh verifies the situation through his clerk and finds that Bhairav Acharya has lost his house due to the machinations of Veni and that unless Bhairav can remit a sum of some thousand rupees in the court he cannot get possession of it. Bhairav rolls on the ground begging for his help. Ramesh gives him the money as a loan and the Brahmin goes away blessing him.

Within that same month Ramesh happens to be passing the lane where Bhairav Acharya's house is located. He is surprised to find a great celebration going on in his house to which he has not even been invited. Bhairav has not yet returned his loan and still finds all this money to celebrate and hold a feast at his house. Ramesh gets angry and suddenly enters the house and asks for Bhairav. He goes up to where Bhairav is and takes his hand in his strong grip. Bhairav starts shouting and crying aloud. Ramesh could easily have hurt him in his anger but then Rama who happens to be on the scene quickly goes up and holds Ramesh's hand and tells him to let Bhairav's hand go. Ramesh relents and leaves the house. But, Rama has made a spectacle of herself in the eyes of the villagers. Reports of the event go round the village in no time and Veni also comes in to join in the commotion. Rama leaves the house. But, Veni has now got an opportunity to get Ramesh into police's clutches by making Bhairav accuse Ramesh of having caused him bodily injury. The case is heard in court. Rama is called as a witness and she is unable to give convincing evidence which would free Ramesh. She is also under the threat of Veni making this an excuse for lampooning Rama if she does not side with him in the case. Ramesh is found guilty and sentenced to six months of imprisonment.

Ramesh loses the case but gains the support of not only all his peasants but also all the villagers. When he is released from prison he is taken round the whole village in a triumphant procession in which Veni tries to cash in by riding with him. But, he knows that he has lost the leadership of the village. Rama has been compromised because she has been unable to give evidence in court which would have protected Ramesh and avoided his imprisonment. When Rama celebrates the Durga pooja at her house no one turns up except one poor Brahmin – the same one who had told Ramesh of all the rivalries in the village. He tells Rama that no one is likely to attend the pooja in her house because she had given evidence against Ramesh in the criminal case.

Rama is under great mental stress and falls ill. She sends her younger brother to call Ramesh to the house. When Ramesh goes to meet her she tells him to oblige her by taking up her property and treat it as held in trust for her younger brother and she also asks him to take her brother under his wings and make him a good man. She says that if she survives she will leave the village and go to Kashi on a final pilgrimage. Veni's mother, Vishweshwari also blesses Ramesh for benefiting the villagers and tells him to continue his work. She is also going to Kashi and takes Rama with her.

That is the substance of the story which is enriched by glimpses of village life, and of the rivalries among landlords and the inevitable factions into which the villagers are divided. It portrays the character of Vishweshwari as the only wise woman who knows where the interests of the villagers lie and how they can be best served. She advises and carefully watches as Ramesh is engaged in his service projects and comes out victorious in the eyes of the people if not in the eyes of the court. It portrays the scheming landowner and the helpless widow who cannot independently manage her own estate and is all the time under the watch of the villagers who are waiting for her to take the first wrong step.

I have given disproportionate space to a small novel but it is a complex book despite its small size.

The other short novel which I wish to deal with is not as small as the one I have just summarized. This is the novel Vijaya–Dutta (1917–19), not as well known as Sharadbabu's major novels but is very interesting. Here again there is an heiress to a large zamindari estate. She has no close elder relatives to advise her and is nearly held 'captive' by a friend of her father – Rasbihari – who manages her estate and intends to get her to marry his son and become the owner of the property to which Vijaya is heiress. Rasbihari is from the lower castes and has tried to free himself from the status barrier by becoming a member of the Brahmo Samaj. Vijaya is a Brahmin by caste but is also a member of the Brahmo Samaj. She is a major and can take her own decisions but having been brought up in the city she knows little about village life and land management.

The romantic strand to the story is provided by a penniless owner of another property owned by another friend of Vijaya's father. Vijaya's father had intended him to be his son-in-law and had helped him to get his education and even helped him go abroad to become a doctor. The name of this penniless doctor is Narendra and his father was also a close friend of Vijaya's father. This father had become indebted to Vijaya's father because of his drinking habits and wasteful ways.

The story revolves round Rasbihari's efforts to drive Narendra out of the village and get Vijaya to marry his only son, Vilas. The other strand in the story is about the differences in the Brahmo and the Hindu societies living in the village. The Brahmo Samaj – a reformist sect – was relatively well accepted in urban Bengal where the Brahmos could follow their distinct way of life characterized externally by a certain measure of westernization in clothes and by non-observance of Hindu ritualistic practices. In rural Bengal the Brahmo Samaj never found a secure footing. Initially Vijaya's father, Vanamali, and Rasbihari had both decided to live in the village but Vanamali – a Brahmin by caste before he accepted to be a Brahmo, found it difficult to make the adjustment and to meet the constant harassment by the Hindu community of a Brahmin who has lost caste … . So he leaves the village and returns to Kolkata. Rasbihari who came from the village and from a backward caste had no urban roots and he has no option but to stay on in the village. Jagadish who was the third member of the small group of college friends was also a Brahmin and had not become a Brahmo. He settles in a law practice in another small district town. He earns well and builds a house in the same village as the one from which Rasbihari and Vanamali originally came. Narendra is Jagadish's son. Jagadish wastes all his accumulated assets on drinking and finally mortgages his house in the village to Vanamali to be able to meet his day to day expenses. Finally he commits suicide.

But, during his days of prosperity Jagadish and Vijaya's father had exchanged correspondence hoping that their children would marry each other. But, then Jagadish dies a pauper and has become a debtor to Vijaya's father. The latter also dies without telling Vijaya about his friendship with Jagadish and his intention for her to marry Narendra.

So while Vijaya and Vilas are both Brahmo Samaj members, Narendra is a Hindu Brahmin. Vijaya and Narendra meet accidentally and are drawn to each other but Rasbihari and Vilas try to keep them as far from each other as possible. Since Narendra is without any money and his father's estate is mortgaged to Vijaya he is asked by Rasbihari to vacate the house in which he lived while in the village.

Despite this Narendra finds opportunities to visit the village and spend time in his old house which has now become a Brahmo Mandir. This becomes possible because the officiating priest has become fond of Narendra. Narendra successfully treats the priest's wife back to health when she is ill. He also treats Vijaya when she falls ill during a period when there were a few cases of smallpox in the village. Narendra tells her definitely that what she is suffering from is not smallpox but it might still require her to rest for a few days.

Basically *Vijaya* is a typical love story with the hero and heroine going through a difficult period of helpless separation but finally succeeding in marrying each other. The novel is of interest as a love story but also as it depicts village life and its intricacies. Apart from *Gaon-Ganga* (1916) and *Bhairavi* (1923), this is the third novel which brings out the great power that zamindars exercised over the life of the villagers in rural Bengal. Almost immediately after Vijaya moves to the village from Kolkata she is faced with a problem because her Brahmo manager has issued an order that no noisy pooja rituals would be allowed in the village. Vijaya has to meet a delegation in which Narendra – whom she has not yet met – comes to plead the case of his elderly uncle who wants to perform the pooja and tells her how harsh the regulation is. Much against the wishes of Vilas, who is then acting as her office secretary, she accedes to Narendra's request.

Rasbihari is a wily character and astute in making his moves. Vilas is efficient but often exceeds his brief and does not always see where his interests lie. His father is trying to promote his interests and under the garb of promoting the Brahmo faith he almost succeeds in getting Vijaya to marry

Vilas by declaring their engagement in a small gathering at the opening of the Brahmo Mandir. But, his own priest lets him down and marries Vijaya to Narendra by adopting the Hindu ritual which does not require a prior public notification.

As a novel *Vijaya* impresses because of the way the author depicts the miserable condition of a captive princess – both beautiful and wealthy – and the way she meets the manoeuvres of her captor who is also her guardian. There are a couple of situations when she angrily and boldly puts aside his instructions but he is patient and knows when to relax controls and when to impose them. If the princess manages to escape the captor it is solely due to the chance of a sympathetic, religious counselor who helps her in a somewhat clandestine way.

In this story there is no real prison and no real captor. The princess is free in theory but is bound by her knowledge that without an able male by her side she cannot function in the village. Despite her education and her religious faith she has to abide by village convention and cannot be bold in expressing her own wishes. There is also the fact that she does not know Narendra well enough to openly lean on him for support though she is attracted to him.

Vijaya cannot stand in the same company as Sharadbabu's other heroines. She is certainly no Kamala, nor Vandana with their definite opinions on most issues, or even the milder but yet clear-minded and committed Bharati. Yet, she is an attractive and talented woman who would make a good wife to her equally unassertive but sensitive and professionally able husband.

In Sharadbabu's writings there are not many ill-tempered or vicious women characters. I have found only two of them playing a somewhat leading role. One of them is the heroine of the story 'Sati – the Devoted Wife' and the other is Digambari the mother of Narayani in the short story 'Chhota Bhai' (*Ramer Sumati*, 1914). Another vile woman character is Swarnamanjari in the novelette *Arakshneeya* (1916).

From a consideration of the larger and smaller novels I would now like to turn to Sharadbabu's short stories. Being short they do not allow the same space for development of character or plot. Sharadchandra's short stories however are still stories. They are not just depictions of a mood or a single incident like the modern short stories which appear in current newspapers or magazines. Sharadchandra's stories have a beginning, middle and an end.

I will not discuss either 'Devdas' or 'Swami', which are all too well known and have been made into full length movies. I will take 'Nishkruti' which is one of the less known of Sharadbabu's stories. 'Nishkruti' means restitution of a right or an object. I like the story because of the vividness with which the characters emerge even in the space of about sixty to seventy pages. The main characters in the story are Girish and his wife Siddheshwari, Harish and his wife Nayantara, Ramesh and his wife Shailaja. Girish and Harish are real brothers born of the same mother. Ramesh is a distant cousin and is dependent on the family. Shailaja, wife of Ramesh, is the youngest woman in the family. She has two small children but she is really the one who is doing all the cooking for the family and managing the household accounts and also looking after all the children. She is short tempered but affectionate to all the children and ensures that they all do their studies and behave properly with respect to all the elders in the house. All the children in the family love her despite her strictness.

Siddheshwari – wife of Girish, a successful lawyer – is chronically ill with malaria and for many days of the week she is bedridden. She is very affectionate to all the children including Shailaja's two children who sleep with her in her bed as do all the other young children in the family

Everything goes smoothly until Harish and Nayantara, who originally used to live separately, in another town, join the household with their children. Their children are not particularly well disciplined and the eldest son is rude and a bad influence on the younger children.

It is clear that the reunion of the families of the two brothers Girish and Harish is going to be problematic. Girish is generous. He is a leading practitioner in town with a substantial income. Harish has a medium-sized practice and is calculative. His wife Nayantara is even more calculative and begins to find the presence and influence exercised by Shailaja disproportionate to her status as the youngest woman member of the family.

Nayantara and Harish have also lived in a larger city before they come to join the senior family. Nayantara has spoilt her eldest son by giving in to all his demands and spending a considerable amount of money on his clothing.

The first clash occurs not between the women members of the family but between Shailaja and Nayantara's elder son, Atul. One day when Shailaja is cooking in the kitchen Atul comes and stands on the threshold of the kitchen with his shoes on. Shailaja's instructions to the children are not to wear shoes inside the house and certainly not in the area of the kitchen. When Shailaja sees Atul standing in the doorway to the kitchen with his shoes on she tells him to go and remove his shoes. But, he does not obey her and continues to stand where he is. Shailaja is angry but says nothing and does not answer any of his questions. His rude behaviour is being watched by other children and they dislike his rudeness toward their strict but favourite aunt. Hari, the eldest of all the children, happens to be passing by and overhears Atul and asks Shailaja what the matter is. She points to the fact that Atul is wearing his shoes and standing in the doorway to the kitchen and would not move away from there. Hari gives a sharp slap to Atul and when he tries to hit back gives him a blow that makes him fall to the ground and get hurt.

This precipitates a major crisis. Nayantara complains to the elder sister-in-law who is fond of Shailaja and takes no notice of what Nayantara has to say. The other children stop talking to Atul because he has been rude to Shailaja, who despite her strong temper is a favourite with all the children. She is fair in her handling of all the children in the family and does not indulge her own small children either.

Siddheshwari is physically as well as psychologically a weak woman. Until Nayantara came to live in the house she was entirely dependent on Shailaja and treated her like her own daughter and allowed her to run the household But, Nayantara is a different kind of person – scheming and insidious. She insidiously works on her elder sister-in-law and poisons her mind about Shailaja. Shailaja tries to continue her close relationship with Siddheshwari but finds that she is now becoming cool in her responses to her and is probably also somewhat distrustful of her house management. Shailaja senses this and hands over the keys of the house including the keys to Siddheshwari's box back to her and stops talking to her unless she is directly addressed. Nayantara takes on a part of the responsibility for housekeeping.

Harish under the influence of his wife starts to needle Ramesh for doing nothing and for wasting his elder brother's money in loss making business enterprises. One day while the two brothers are eating their meal he insults Ramesh. Shailaja who is watching all this keeps quiet but probably motivates her husband to move out of the house and return to the ancestral village where there is still a house lying empty.

Ramesh appears one day before Girish and says that he and his wife would like to move out of the house and go to the village. Girish gives him the permission to do so. Harish and Nayantara are happy. Girish is probably not aware of what has led to this situation, but agrees to Ramesh's request hoping that this might make Ramesh do some real work and become independent.

As it turns out Ramesh is not good at anything. He tries agriculture and fails and then requests Girish for money again to do some business to which Girish does not respond.

One day by chance Girish has to go to the village home in order to attend the wedding ceremony at the home of some friend of his. When he reaches the village he also goes to the old house to look up Ramesh and his wife. He is greeted cheerfully by Ramesh's children and when he comes in and meets Shailaja he notices that she is without any of the usual ornaments befitting a housewife. He understands what has happened and decides then and there to make over all the land and the house in the name of Shailaja so that Ramesh can have no way of selling or mortgaging either the land or the house. He finishes the whole operation on the day of his visit, blesses Shailaja and returns home. This is his way of restituting the dignity of his young sister-in-law who has done so much for his own family.

The news of what Girish has done reaches Harish while he is at the local court and he feels crestfallen that his elder brother has done this despite all his own efforts to see that Ramesh is ruined.

When Girish returns home that evening his wife goes to her husband's room and bows down to him for the noble deed he has done.

The bald details of the story do not communicate the emotional content of all the human transactions with which the story is full. Sharadbabu's skill as a writer brings to life the events – small and big – of how a peaceful and warm household is disturbed by the small mindedness of the younger brother and his wife. It also shows how the elder brother who does not seem to have time for anything but his legal work is sensitive to all that his youngest sister-in-law has done for his family and it violates his sense of justice that her fortune should be left to her no good husband. There is also a suggestion in his action that Shailaja will now take control of things and her house to lead a modest but comfortable life.

The second short story that I will review briefly is 'Chhota Bhai' (*Ramer Sumati*,1914). It is again a story of about 68 pages. Shyamlal and Ram are two stepbrothers. Shyamlal is a clerk in the village Zamindar's office. But, he and his brother have a house of their own, a fish pond, some cattle and income from their family land. They can be considered to be comfortably placed. Ram is a young boy of 13 years of age and is full of mischief. He is not amenable to control by any one except his sister-in-law, Narayani, who has brought him up from the time his age was two and half years, when his mother died and handed him over to Narayani. Narayani is very fond of him and treats him as her own child and indulges his every whim. In course of time Narayani and Shyamlal have their own child but that makes no difference to the affection Narayani has for Ram who was then about six years old. Ram takes on the role of elder brother to his young nephew, Gopal, and takes him along on his exploits. Apart from the usual complaints from house servants and villagers about Ram's pranks there are no major problems.

The story opens when Narayani happens to fall ill and has fever for about four days. Ram is anxious and angry that the village doctor has not come in to check on his Bhabi's health. He goes to the doctor and in the presence of other patients threatens him that he will expose his dirty tricks of giving poor patients quinine mixed with chalk powder. The doctor is angry but comes to call on Narayani and gives her the medicine. Narayani's health improves but the doctor does not miss the opportunity of complaining to her about Ram's behaviour. This is only one of the many complaints that are coming to her almost everyday.

Ram attends school but otherwise he spends most of his time wandering about the village with his young friend-cum-servant Bhola. He engages in the usual pastimes of a young village boy, wanders around in the fields, climbs trees and eats whatever fruit is in season. Bhola is his companion in his exploits. Occasionally there are complaints but Ram does not have to go to other people's farms since his family has farms of its own.

Shyamlal is a peaceable soul and leaves the management of his brother to his wife.

The peaceful life of the family is disturbed when at Narayani's request her widowed mother who had been living with her brother comes to live with her daughter and son-in-law. Narayani's mother is mean and vicious and she does not like that her daughter should be so fond of her young brother-in-law Ram. Naturally Ram does not take kindly to her and teases her in many small ways until they become enemies of each other. Narayani has to play the peace-maker's role by scolding Ram and pleading with her mother. Matters come to a crisis when once Ram who is sitting on a guava tree is scolded by Narayani's mother for spoiling the raw guavas. He angrily throws one guava at her and happens to hit her on the face. This worsens the situation and the enmity between Digambari – Narayani's mother and Ram – goes on getting worse.

A number of other minor incidents take place and once Digambari calls a fisherman to catch two big fishes from the family pond. She does not know that the two fishes are favourites of Ram and he does not want them to be caught and eaten. All the servants are aware of it and caution Digambari but she goes ahead with her plan. One day when Ram is out on his exploits his faithful ally Bhola comes and tells him that his favourite fishes are no more. Ram cannot believe it and rushes home to see that the fishes are lying dead on the ground and Digambari is preparing to make a curry in celebration of some ritual occasion in the family.

Matters come to a head. The peaceful Shyamlal asks that the house be divided by erecting a central bamboo partition to separate one part from the other. Digambari feels victorious but Narayani goes off food and so does her young brother-in-law whose moods change from anger against Digambari and the whole household to a pitiable loneliness at being separated from his beloved sister-in-law. He also goes without food for a day, grumbles aloud and says he will eat raw rice. He also tries to cook a meal for himself, refuses to allow the house servant to secretly cook his meal for him. The only person who is gleeful is old Digambari who thinks that she has won a victory against the brat. She had been responsible for the separation by constantly complaining to her son-in-law about his stepbrother.

The problem is resolved only when Narayani in her own quiet way persuades her husband of the foolishness of the whole move and tells her mother to go back to her village. She promises to send her money regularly so that she will have enough to support herself but she does not want her to stay on in her house and break it up. Ram comes back to the house, is much more chastened but so long as he is with his dear sister-in-law nothing can curb his spirits.

The story is remarkable for the strong characterization of the young lovable brat, Ram, the vicious old woman who has not seen happiness in her own life and cannot bear to see it in her daughter's life either. She detests that her daughter Narayani loves her young adolescent brother-in-law as much as she loves her own son. Narayani knows that if Ram is to change it will only be through her affection for him and not through any coercion or punishment meted out to him. She knows also how to hold her family together. Shyamlal is out of the house during the day and is content to see his wife managing the house ably. He figures in the story only occasionally.

Sharadbabu's novels and stories focus primarily on family life except in *Savyasachi*, *Gaon-Ganga* and 'Shrikant'. There are a few harsh women in his novels. The heroine of 'Sati – the Devoted Wife' is one such character and probably Digambari in 'Chhota Bhai' (*Ramer Sumati*) is another. To some extent Sumitra in *Pather Dabi* is also harsh. But, most of his other women characters love and seek love. Most of the stories are about family life – its joyous moments as well as moments of sadness. Many of his novels are about women in which men appear as supporting characters. Even 'Shrikant' which is a story about its male hero, is really the story of Pyari or Rajlaxmi and then to an extent about Kamal Lata, the Vaishnavi whom Shrikant meets when he spends a few days in the Vaishnav Akhada. Sharadbabu analyses in-depth the emotional lives of these women. Even the snake charmer's wife whom Shrikant meets while still a young boy shows an exceptional courage when her husband dies and she has no one to support her. She reassures the young Shrikant and his friend, Vishnu, that she will find some way of coping with life.

The life conditions of women in Bengali society is a central theme in much of Sharadbabu's writing and it appears almost to be his prime motive for writing novels and stories. He only occasionally makes open references to their dependence on the males in society. He discusses it openly in *Shesh Prashna* as a central issue, but nearly every story or novel reflects his deep compassion for womanhood and his ability to delve the depth of their emotions. He has drawn vivid pictures of young unmarried women who are dependent on male protection even when they are well to do (Bharati) married women who have to live and cope with life's problems without any assistance from their husbands (Virajbahu), courageous women who chart their own life (*Shesh Prashna*), and women who live in misery and poverty in workers' huts and yet live under the thumbs of their husbands (*Savyasachi*).

His men characters also vary in their status and their station in life and in their characters. He has portrayed well to do noble men, poor humble men, crooks and schemers, elder men worried about the marriages of their young daughters, men who are brave and daring and men who are servile.

His canvas is broad and peopled by men and women of various statuses, projected in different moods and endowed with different temperaments. He does not idolize poverty or riches, he is trying to reveal their souls. Even when depicting poverty and suffering he does not pity the characters but shows them as people coping with their problems with dignity and faith. They are characters from everyday life – not pictures drawn to carry any message.

What stands out in his writing is the author's deep understanding of human life and his empathy with those who are struggling to cope. It could probably be said that he is more occupied with life's sufferings than with its celebrations, yet he is not a pessimist, nor a misanthrope. He loves human life and human beings. He can portray joy and success but his writing seems to be underlined largely by a kind of sympathy and compassion.

II

The contours of social life have changed a great deal since the days when Sharadbabu lived and wrote. The joint family and its ideals do not loom large over the middle classes – especially in the urban areas. The old sentiments of reverence and respect for the elderly may not be current coinage. The young probably accept their stage of dependence on their parents grudgingly and want to be free to make their own lives and decisions as soon as they can. Middle class women are shown more and more as being independent minded in popular films and stories. Feminists may find that Sharadbabu's women are housebound and have generally no role to play in social or public life outside the family. Do the problems that Sharadbabu wrote about still make sense? What is the proportion of the general readership that can empathize with the dilemmas that his characters face? How many bother to read him now? I do not know. I suspect that not as many from the middle class read him now with the same avid interest as they did in the 1930s. The translations into Marathi of his books went through three or four reprints within a three or four years period. I do not think that there have been any new reprints recently. Is Sharadbabu still relevant – whether in Bengal or in any of the other linguistic regions where he was read eagerly earlier?

But, if contemporary readership is to be the criterion, then all classics beginning with Shakespeare and Milton and the 17th and 18th century novelists should be considered to be irrelevant. Leo Lowenthal in his paper entitled 'On Sociology of Literature' points out how 'women like Fausts Gretchen, Madame Bovary, or Anna Karenina cannot be interpreted by analogy, their problems simply cannot be experienced today because the atmosphere out of which their conflicts grew has passed. The social data of the period in which they were created and the social analysis of the characters themselves are the very material from which the meaning and the function of the works of art can be understood. If our would-be psychologists were to be completely sincere, they would have to confess that everyone of these women, if alive today would be considered stupid, frustrated neurotics who ought to take a job or undergo psychiatric treatment to rid themselves of their obsessions and inhibitions' (*Literature and Mass Culture: Communication in Society*, Volume 1, Leo Lowenthal, Transaction Books, London, 1984).

But, the fact is that Madame Bovary and Anna Karenina are still considered worthy of being read and are considered classics in their own right. And so are Sharadbabu's novels today. I do not suggest that they are contemporary models but they are liked for their heroines in their particular context. And that is partly the reason why so many of Sharadbabu's stories have been made into films.

Sharadbabu as a novelist is as great as any. He stands out due to his broad and deep human sympathy, his depth of understanding of human life, human aspirations, and human failures. The subtlety of his understanding and his skill in delineating the most complex relationships are unrivalled.

Most of his heroines are strong characters with a will of their own and assert themselves in many subtle ways. In his later novels particularly in *Pather Dabi, Vipradas* and *Shesh Prashna* the women do not play second fiddle to men. Even Viraj in *Viraj Bahu* is a highly self-respecting person though she cherishes the ideal of a being a pativrata. By portraying such women in his fiction he was in a sense laying the groundwork for a change in perspective about the position of women in society.

Equally great is his skill in character portrayal and character development. I have referred earlier to some of the variety of characters that he has portrayed from the rich and the powerful to the middle class in urban areas and the middle class in rural areas, as also the poor urban workers and the poor rural peasants. These are not static characters as on a canvas, they are shown to be developing, as the stories move from one stage to another. The characters develop and so do the relationships between these characters. The relationship between Vipradas and Vandana, between Dwijdas and Vandana, even the relationship between Vandana and her father, Vandana and Vipradas' mother – each of these is shown to undergo change and a certain maturity. This is true of all his novels and stories. The characters are live and not static.

Sharadchandra remains an observer. His characters are active. They are good, bad, vicious, saintly, cruel and kind. Sharadbabu does not take moral stances. He has no philosophy to propagate. He describes the life of his characters as he saw them but does not blame or praise them. His philosophy is essentially humanist. His sense of morality is based on truthfulness of word and truthfulness in relationships. He has a clear understanding of the human situations and therefore also an understanding and acceptance of deviance from traditions and social norms. Even the heroine of *Charitraheen* sustains the sympathy of the author and the readers.

Burma is an important locale in some of Sharadbabu's novels – in *Pather Dabi* and in *Charitraheen*, for example. This is partly because Burma did in fact play an important role in the life of middle and working class Bengali families. It was a heaven for job seekers. But, Sharadbabu uses it also to portray the different lifestyles and the freedom that Burma conferred on women – both the Burmese women and even the Indian women who migrated to Burma. As the outpost of the British Empire and a part of the Indian subcontinent until the British formally separated it, it played an important role in Bengali life. But, apart from being a place of employment one suspects that Burma was also a psychological hideaway from the caste restricted and male dominated society of India. It was also a place where early Indian revolutionaries sought sanctuary.

III

I have not read all of Sharadbabu's novels and stories even in translation. And certainly I have not read his other prose writings. Even so I have read about fifteen of his major novels and collections of shorter and longer stories. The first thing that strikes one is that unlike many of the voluminous contemporary British and American writers he is not a formula writer – neither of the P.G. Woodhouse, or the Earle Stanley Gardener type where the main characters are common and only the plots and situations vary within a narrow band. Nor is he like one of the modern 'researched novel writers' where the focus is on the plot and not on the characters, as for example, in novels like *Airport*, or *Hotel* or the novels that revolve round a professional lawyer as in the case of John Grisham. All these books are highly readable and I have enjoyed reading them. But, they lack the creativity and social sensitivity of a great writer.

In each of Sharadchandra's novels the characters and the stories are distinct. They do not follow a type. The characters are realistic and none of the situations he has described or the characters he has described are entirely 'fictional'. Sharadchandra is supposed to have avowed that he has written nothing that he had not seen or experienced.

It is difficult to say in Sharadchandra's case whether his characters occurred to him first or the plots of his novels when he wrote them. It seems that the characters he has portrayed and the stories evolve together as he writes them. His characters are not static. They grow and change as the novel progresses. The relationships between the characters are also dynamic. Each of his characters is distinct. Most of his novels are about women, but his women heroines do not fall into a type.

Viraj in *Viraj Bahu*, Kamala in *Shesh Prashana*, Vandana in *Vipradas*, Bharati in *Pather Dabi*, Bhairavi in *Dena-Pavana*, or even the heroines of his short stories are each different from one another.

I will take the examples of some of these heroines and show how they grow as the story proceeds.

Viraj in *Viraj Bahu* (1914) is a beautiful, young woman of great self-esteem; she is dedicated to her husband, Neelamber, and her great life wish is to die as a *pativrata* at the feet of her husband. The husband and wife are both dedicated to each other though unlike Viraj who is aware of the demands of day to day living; Neelamber is shown as a person capable of great love and affection but unwise in the commitments that he makes. He is also a ganja addict. At the time of his younger sister's marriage he undertook the responsibility to pay for the medical education of the bridegroom. They were a comfortably placed family with lands and fruit gardens. But, this single act of agreeing to support the education of his sister's husband precipitates a crisis. It is a commitment beyond their resources. Inevitably the couple finds it difficult to meet their commitments and enter a debt trap where they cannot even meet the interest commitments on the loans that Neelamber has taken to support his brother-in-law's education.

The relationship between husband and wife gets soured though Viraj continues to be as devoted to her husband as she always was. The financial situation becomes so difficult that they find it difficult to have two square meals a day. And the relationship between them becomes difficult precipitating frequent disagreements. Viraj finds a source of income by secretly doing the work of preparing earthen moulds for a brass vessels factory. This is work normally done only by untouchable women, but she adapts to the reality and manages to eke out a living for the family. But, then the factory closes down and Viraj loses her source of livelihood. At one point the situation is so bad that Viraj has to borrow rice from her own untouchable house servant. In a fit induced by his dope addiction Neelamber hits his wife with his paan box and charges her of her having been unfaithful and asks her to leave the house.

Viraj leaves the house at dead of night and first thinks of committing suicide in the river close to the house. But, then an ominous thought comes to her of giving in to the temptation offered to her by the Zamindar's son. She gets on to his boat with the help of her former house servant. As the Zamindar comes close to her she is revolted by the idea and jumps into the river which is in a great monsoon flood.

She partially swims and is partially carried down by the current and finds herself downstream in Hooghly, where in an unconscious condition she is carried by a stranger to a local hospital.

She had been thrown out of her house by her husband on a baseless suspicion while he was under the influence of ganja. He had hit her with a metal box which leaves a wound on her forehead. She gets on to the boat of the Zamindar but is revolted by the idea of having any relationship with him and jumps into the river.

She is now a *kulata* in the eyes of the villagers. What is more is that she herself suffers from a deep sense of guilt because she had once entertained the thought of surrendering to the advances of the Zamindar. As a result, she feels the option of her returning home is closed to her. She has nowhere else to go. She has lost the use of one arm during the period that she is floating down the river.

She has to take to begging. Sharadbabu describes her physical and mental suffering and the changing of moods through which she goes over a period of nearly two years of begging along the streets and along the way to the temple near her native village.

On the other hand, Neelamber also recognizes his great error and feels guilt for his actions of that one night. He knows that in the eyes of the villagers his wife is a permanently blemished person. But, his love and respect for her are unshaken. He scolds his sister for talking slightingly of her sister-in-law.

But, both Viraj and Neelamber have become mellower personalities. The author describes the physical and psychological movement of the two characters with great sensitivity. The whole psychological journey from the time of their period of being debt-ridden, through their economic and psychological difficulties to the crisis precipitated by Neelamber's thoughtless action under the influence of dope, and the period of pining of both the husband and the wife for each other during the long separation. All this is described by the author with great economy of words and yet with great skill.

The novel ends with Neelamber and his sister accidentally finding Viraj on their way home, near the temple where Viraj is lying down waiting for death. Neelamber picks her up and brings her home and Viraj's great desire to die on the lap of her husband is fulfilled.

The basic story and the relationship between husband and wife belong to the early 20th century. In present day terms they may not make much meaning. But, if the reader recognizes the social context and the norms of the society of that period then the novel is emotionally moving and marked by great craftsmanship on the part of the author. The characters described are not static; they change and grow in maturity.

IV

The question of morality and immorality, of marital fidelity arise in many of Sharadbabu's novels. It arises in *Viraj Bahu* (1914); it arises in *Charitraheen*, (1912) and then again in his last novel *Shesher Parichaya* (1943). Sharadbabu expresses no view of his own. What he does is to show the character's own response to the situation and the associated sense of guilt or failure to be truthful. It also brings up the issue of the ideal of *pativrata* which is not an ideal applicable to both the sexes but only to the female sex. Men have had the freedom to indulge in their sexual appetite the way they pleased. They may be criticized or looked down upon by society but obviously no sin seems to be attached to the act as it does in the case of women. Sharadbabu explores various dimensions of this situation but at no place does he give his own opinion on it.

I am going to discuss this issue as it is handled in *Shesher Parichaya*. It must be pointed out here that Sharadbabu did not complete the novel himself; we do not even know how much of the novel had already been written by him when he died. What we do know is that Radharanidevi and her husband – both literary figures of some renown – had detailed discussions on the theme of the novel before Sharadbabu died. They probably knew how Sharadbabu expected to proceed with the story. Radharanidevi undertook to complete the novel at the request of Sharadbabu's publisher. Since the novel was first serialized it may be possible to ascertain at what point Sharadbabu had left the novel. But, I do not have the means to do this check at this point.

Despite these limitations I feel it might be worthwhile to discuss the main theme of the novel and the attitudes of the characters to some of the issues involved because surely they must have been broadly defined by the author when he conceived of the book.

Savita – variously called Mai or Bahu depending upon who is speaking to or about her – is the heroine of this novel. She is beautiful and young. She was married young but as the second wife of a widower, Vrajababu, who is both a big landowner and a businessman dealing in agricultural commodities. They live in a big house in a large village not far from Kolkata. At a young age Savita becomes the head of a large household which has some permanent relatives of the husband living in. These relatives – cousins, aunts, etc., are older than Savita but have to accept her position as the wife of the family head. Not everyone is happy with this position but they cannot fault her for anything. She attends to all her duties in the kitchen and the upkeep of the household and treats all elders with due respect. Apart from being her husband's consort she is also his advisor on many of his social and business affairs.

Her particular interest is in educating young boys who need support to be able to continue their education. Among many others is Raju, an orphaned boy from her own village.

So far as her married life is concerned she is the mother of a young girl – Renu, who is her only child. There is probably a large age-gap between her and her husband. Already her husband has started giving a substantial proportion of his time to prayer and to the worship of the family deity – Govind. Savita dutifully helps him in his religious observances and observes the necessary fasts as a good wife. But, it would appear that prayer and worship could not occupy the same central part of Savita's life as they did in the life of her husband.

In the big household there are several guests who come and go. But, one among them visits the home more frequently and stays for longer durations. His name is Ramanibabu. Young Savita and he are drawn to each other. One night a cousin of Vrajababu suspects that Savita is in Ramanibabu's room behind a locked door. He knocks the door and shouts out loud enough for the whole household to be aroused.

Savita opens the door and comes out holding the hand of Ramanibabu and tells the household not to create any incident saying that Ramanibabu and she are both leaving the house that very minute. Vrajababu, who is at the other end of the corridor, shouts out to her and reminds her, 'You are leaving your daughter motherless'. But, the two have already walked out of the house.

Savita leaves the house because she knows that in her husband's household she has now no place, not even as a servant in the family. Her act is forced on her by her own impetuosity. She holds her husband in great respect for the good man he is, but there is no way now she can go back to him.

There is a world of difference in Viraj's leaving her husband's house when under the influence of ganja her husband forces her out of the house and Savita leaving her house as result of her own impetuous action. Yet, both the women suffer and yearn to get back to their husbands. In Viraj's case it is the fulfillment of her religious and psychological need to die at her husband's feet as a *pativrata*.

It does not take long for Savita to realize the immensity of the difference between her life as Ramanibabu's keep and her earlier position as the female head of her husband's home. Yet, she suffers the agony of her fallen status for thirteen long years. Ramanibabu is an unrefined person incapable of genuine love, or kindness, or nobility of mind. He is calculative, suspicious, jealous and petty. He is possessive and likes to show off Savita's beauty to his friends. At the end of these thirteen years Savita finds it difficult to be by his side and to meet his every demand. Finally, on a day when she is unwell she refuses to come out and meet his valued friends. Savita has to tell him that she is no longer interested in living with him. He retorts that she will find herself on the road and she might actually have found herself on the road but for the fact that the rich friend, Vimalbabu, whom she has refused to come out to meet. He turns out to be a noble person who is capable of giving her true friendship. He buys the property in which Savita and a few of her tenants are living and gifts it to Savita. At long last both discover that they can find genuine sympathy and love for each other without entering into any sexual commitments. It takes time for Savita and Vimalbabu to know on what terms they can remain friends with each other, but they find that relationship.

Once before meeting Vimalbabu and before she had severed her connection with Ramanibabu, Savita had met Vrajababu in Raju's room by chance. Vrajababu behaved civilly with her and told her to come to Raju's room again so he might return to her the jewellery and the money she had invested in his business. Accordingly, Vrajababu gives back to her all her jewellery and also returns to her the money she had given him to invest in his business because, he says, his business has suffered and he is not sure whether it is safe for her to keep her money with him. Savita is overcome by Vrajababu's generosity even in his moment of adversity. But, when she asks him to say that he has forgiven her he declines to say the words and only asks, 'What will you do with my pardon?'. That remains as a deep wound in Savita's heart.

Soon after Vrajababu and Savita had this meeting, Vrajababu really suffers a great loss in his business and has to sell off his palatial house to pay off the creditors. He has no money left and tries to make both ends meet by moving to a smaller house and a simpler mode of living with only one servant. When Renu falls ill Raju helps out with his own meagre resources and pays the doctor. Later they decide to move to the original village home which Vrajababu has given away to his brothers and cousins. He finds he is not welcome in the village because he has an unmarried daughter born of a woman who has left her husband. Life becomes harder and harder, and finally, Vrajababu and his daughter move to Vrindaban and live as members of a Vaishnav group.

Vimalbabu and Savita go on a long trip visiting various places of pilgrimage and finally end up in Vrindaban where Savita meets Vrajababu and Renu who have been reduced by circumstances to live there as members of a Vaishnav community. When Savita meets them she finds that both of them have suffered in health. Her young daughter dies in her arms in an epidemic of the plague. Her husband escapes that disease but has otherwise grown really old and needs regular nursing. Savita decides to stay and serve him. She feels grateful that he agrees to be served by her. Vrajababu's third wife also comes to Vrindaban to take him back home. Savita, who is not recognized by the third wife, tells her that he needs to be nursed where he is and she can nurse him if she is willing to stay in the poverty of Vrindaban because Vrajababu is really not in a condition to be moved anywhere. The third wife decides to go back and leaves Vrajababu in the care of Savita.

This is where the novel ends. Savita serves her husband and nurses him. He accepts her service.

The novel is rich with stories of at least three other characters – Raju, Sharada and Tarak babu. Sharada is another 'fallen' woman. Her husband is dead and her lover has deserted her. She tries to commit suicide and is saved from death by Raju as at Savita behest he takes her to the hospital and stays all the days with her until she is out of danger. They are both in love with each other but they cannot marry each other.

Tarak is a friend of Raju but is more industrious and also more self-centred. He completes his education and becomes a lawyer. He is successful as a lawyer but proves an ungenerous friend both to Raju and to Savita. He rejects Raju's suggestion that he marry Savita's daughter – Renu – and makes a successful marriage with the niece of his senior. This ensures that he has a secure and successful life.

Before leaving Kolkata Savita had called Raju to her house and in the presence of Vimalbabu and Sharada entrusted to him all her jewellery and property and asks him to make good use of it in the service of other people. He suggests that she better entrust this responsibility to Tarak who is a good lawyer, but Savita rejects the suggestion and insists that he will do the job better.

In *Viraj Bahu*, in *Charitraheen*, in *Shesher Parichaya* and of course in *Shrikant* the theme of female chastity occurs prominently but in none of these novels does Sharadbabu take a moral posture. He merely depicts the conditions through which the women pass, their psychological suffering and the way they try to come to terms with themselves.

It is only in *Shesh Prashna* (1931) that he depicts a character – Kamala – who refuses to accept the social definition of what is moral or immoral. She rejects the social sanctity of marriage and insists that love between man and woman is all that matters. At the end of the novel she refuses to marry Ajit, the man she has chosen, and insists that they will live together only as long as they love each other and even assures him that if and when they both feel that they cannot live together she will teach him how to live without her. The novel *Shesher Parichaya* was written after *Shesh Prashna*. One wonders why he again conceived of a character like Savita who carries a great sense of guilt for her infidelity and finds peace only when she is finally reunited with her married husband though only to serve him in his last days before death.

V

Our discussion so far has focused on women characters in Sharadbabu's writings. This is natural because Sharadbabu's novels focus largely on women and their life in the early 20th century Bengal, but this does not mean that he has not created memorable male characters in his novels. He has created such characters but they are far fewer than women.

The ones that come to my mind easily are the characters of Savyasachi and Vipradas. Savyasachi is the early 20th century revolutionary who belongs to an international organization and operates nearly all over the East and the South Asian region. He has contacts in China, Burma, and India and occasionally mentions a few other countries particularly in the Far East. But, the novel depicts his life in Burma. One gets a glimpse of his importance in the revolutionary movement by the way other revolutionaries from the region accept him as their leader and by his decisive influence at the meeting of the group of revolutionaries when they try Apoorva for his treacherous disclosures to the police.

But, in the novel what stands out is Savyasachi's particular philosophy of revolution. It is a philosophy of political revolution rather than social or economic revolution. It would seem to be earlier than even the Bolshevik revolution and certainly is much more limited than the Maoist revolution in its scope. It does not appeal to a modern reader as a model for a national or international revolution, but those were days when revolutionaries focused on killing of representatives of the ruling political power at the individual level as a means of creating a false sense of pride, unrest and dissatisfaction among the lay population and strike some fear among the foreign rulers. The revolutionary group represented in Burma was primarily Indian, drawn from various parts of the country and from different occupational groups. Mr Talwalkar is a Maharashtrian; Mr Iyer is obviously from the Tamil region of the erstwhile Madras Presidency. There is a Sikh from Punjab and some particularly violent persons from the undefined eastern part of the country. Savyasachi himself is from Bengal. Sumitra is the President of an innocuous looking Committee which works among industrial labour and attempts partly to bring relief to them and partly to awaken them to their own condition. Even this is a secret activity not favoured by the government of the day in Burma. A rally to awaken workers to their condition is broken up by the police and Mr Talwalkar who makes the boldest speech on the occasion is arrested, beaten up and later killed by the government.

This compels the other revolutionaries to go into hiding for the time being and Savyasachi to leave Burma after arranging for Sumitra to go to Jakarta where she has a home.

Savyasachi stands out as a man of courage and conviction, who has thought out his own particular philosophy carefully and justifies it to Bharati who is the youngest recruit to his group and speaks out against violence altogether. Savyasachi has been in the movement for more than half his life and continues to adhere to his particular philosophy. His main role seems to be to keep the group together in Burma as well as in other parts of Asia. He treats Bharati as his younger sister and his relation with Sumitra remain distant though he has saved her more than once from brigands who are after her for her property. Sumitra herself is emotionally more involved with him than he seems to be involved with her. He treats her politely as the President of the local revolutionary group in Burma. But, after the break up of that group she has to leave Burma.

The finer aspects of Savyasachi's personality come out in his relations with Bharati, with the poet whom he advises to write revolutionary poems and with other members of the group who are not full time revolutionaries. He is particularly proud of Talwalkar's courage of conviction. And he is sorry when Talwalkar is killed by the government. He does not judge others harshly and is more accommodative than Sumitra. He even accepts the limitations of Apoorva and advises him to engage in activity more suited to his temperament. He accepts Bharati's love for Apoorva and blesses them both. During his stay in Burma he is content to let Sumitra play the role of the boss, himself remaining in the background. Once the Committee is broken up Savyasachi has to remain in a secret hideout in the jungles on the banks of the river. On one occasion he takes Bharati to that location. There is a tribal woman and her children who seem to supply him with the bare necessity of food and shelter. He has his own boat which he rows skillfully up and down the river. His most trusted colleague is a Punjabi who, working as a postman for the Burmese government in Rangoon, has a greater freedom of movement in the city.

Savyasachi is a man without a family and his only work is the work of organizing the revolutionary groups within the area allotted to him. He is a man of few words but can be loquacious when the occasion requires and ingenious in his ability to take on different garbs to keep himself from being recognized by the local police. At the beginning of the novel a high-level police official from Bengal has come to Rangoon especially to intercept and arrest him at the river jetty where the boat from Kolkata lands. He, along with a few other persons, is taken to the local police station but escapes from being identified despite careful scrutiny by the Indian police official and the local Burmese officials.

Another important male character created by Sharadbabu is Vipradas. Vipradas is a big Zamindar in a village located a few hours away by railway from Kolkata. He does not have much formal education but has educated himself by reading widely. He is upright in his dealings with all – members of the family, servants and peasants. He is strict but considerate. He knows his rights and when challenged assets them. Within the family he looks after all the work of the zamindari and also the marketing operations with a largish office in Kolkata. He is respected and feared by the villagers and his subordinates. But, they all have an implicit trust in his uprightness and fair dealing. He is religious by temperament and observes all the rituals expected of a Brahmin of his status. He observes rules of diet and fasts and daily prayers as required by his upbringing. He is physically and morally tall and strong. The only person who can order him to do something is his stepmother, Dayamayi, who has brought him up. He is married to Sati and has a son, Vasu. He has a younger brother, Dwijdas, who has had college education and has some incipient leftist leanings. His own mother distrusts him because of his leanings and will not entrust him with any responsibility. The person who guards his interests is his sister-in-law, Sati. She gives him money when he needs it and has full confidence in his integrity and ability. Vipradas has no prejudice against him and is certain that when the responsibility falls on him he will shoulder it with ability. He takes his younger brother's seemingly rebellious behaviour as a mark of his youth.

Apart from the fact that he is a good administrator and businessman he has a mature mind which has thought out carefully matters – religious and spiritual in so far as they concern his own life. While he is orthodox he does not look down upon people with different views or religious backgrounds ... . He lives his own way of life and respects the right of others to live by their conviction. But, he will not tolerate insult or injustice and is prepared to stand up for his rights even if it comes to a physical confrontation.

Sharadchandra has caste Vipradas in a classic mould and has attributed to him the qualities and moral judgment comparable to that of the epic hero, Shri Ram. As the novel proceeds and even at the end Vipradas remains true to that ideal. He succeeds in pointing out to Vandana her error in seeking to establish a closer relationship with him than would be justified by his commitment to his wife and the rest of the family.

Toward the end of the novel when a major disagreement develops between him and his stepmother he prefers to leave home with his wife and child than give in to her demand. At the very end, after his wife had died during the travel away from home, he comes home to perform the death rites for her. At the request of Vandana, who has now married Dwijdas, he agrees to leave Vasu at home with them and goes away again accompanied, this time, by his stepmother Dayamayi on a life of pilgrimage.

A third engaging and lovable male character created by Sharadchandra, but one which is on a much more modest scale, is the character of Ashubabu, the retired old man with his unmarried daughter, in *Shesh Prashna*.

Ashubabu is an elderly, affable, retired person who has spent several years in England and Europe and is a man of means. It is not quite clear what his profession was when he was still working but he is obviously well educated and well read. He loves to have educated younger people around him. He is a widower and has an educated, good looking daughter of marriageable age. When his wife died he was probably middle aged and could have married again. He chose to remain unmarried as a mark of his love for his dead wife. He comes and settles in Agra and soon becomes the centre of the educated Bengali middle class in Agra. He likes to have younger educated people – college professors, as it happens – around him and makes a special effort to collect such a group by inviting them to a musical evening at his house. His daughter looks after the house with the help of some servants and is particularly caring of her father.

At the point when he comes to Agra, his daughter, Manorama, is already engaged to be married to Ajay, an engineer who has just returned from England after obtaining higher qualifications in his field. Ajay and Manorama might have married before Ajay went to England had it not been for one of Ashubabu's relatives who prevents the marriage from taking place then on grounds of astrological predictions.

Ashubabu is a genuine liberal, with a broad view of life and tolerance for the values and foibles of other people. His liberal values and the catholicity of his outlook get tested in the relationship he develops with the various characters in the novel – particularly with Kamala, whom he gets to know as Shivnath's wife.

Shivnath is an educated man of dubious character. He had been a professor at the local college earlier but was dismissed because of his heavy drinking habits. He then takes to some kind of a business in partnership with an old friend. This friend dies and Shivnath takes over the ownership without paying any compensation to the family of his friend. He has a good musical voice and it is this that draws the attention of Ashubabu and his daughter Manorama whom he meets accidentally on a train. Ashubabu hears him humming a tune and then gets to know that Shivnath has some musical ability. The former invites him for a musical evening at his house and invites all their new friends to the music concert which is followed by dinner.

Shivnath does not bring his wife to the concert. In the course of the conversation that follows the concert his former college colleagues recognize and expose him for what he is. They make him admit that he had left his service in college in a compromising position, that he has married a girl without going through a proper marriage ceremony, that he has deceived the family of his friend while taking over the business of his friend and that generally he is not a man of probity. Ashubabu still treats him politely as his guest and continues to invite him for more concerts at his house. Shivnath manages to develop a close relationship with Manorama despite the fact that he is already married. Ashubabu is not aware of this development and continues to invite Shivnath to his house for musical concerts.

Ashubabu gets to know Kamala accidentally when he sees that Shivnath and a woman are standing under a tree outside his bungalow sheltering under a tree in very heavy rain. They are both drenched and Ashubabu asks his servant to call them in. He asks his daughter to help them to first have a bath and change into dry clothes. When they come in Ashubabu is struck by Kamala's exceptional beauty. He tells his friend Avinashbabu that she looks like the Goddess Laxmi. He is also impressed by her sophistication in speech and her dialogue with the housemaid in which she asks for a new soap because she does not like to use a soap which has been used by others.

As it happens, these are the very things that prejudice Manorama against Kamala. She thinks she is a lower class girl pretending to be of upper class. The fact that she is Shivanath's wife with whom she has become friendly may have contributed to her prejudice.

The next meeting between Ashubabu and Kamala is equally accidental. Ashubabu and his group of college teacher friends plan a visit to the Taj Mahal on an afternoon. Shivnath and Kamala also happen to be at the Taj at the same time. Shivnath is not keen for his wife to meet the highly educated group out of the fear that her social background might prejudice them all.

Kamala is the illegitimate child of a European tea estate manager and his maid. She is socially an outcaste and Shivnath has married her because of her beauty without going through a socially recognized Vedic marriage ceremony. Kamala has had no formal education but her father who was fond of her had given her a great deal of education in history, philosophy and developed in her a great sense of value for truthfulness, self-respect and personal independence. After her father's death her mother gets her married to another tea plant worker who runs away. The mother and daughter then work in Shivnath's village home and Shivnath goes through a marriage of convenience with Kamala. But, Kamala is not conscious of any sense of inferiority. She persuades Shivnath to go and meet Ashubabu and his group.

As the group sits down they discuss among other things the beauty of the Taj. Ashubabu regards it as a monument symbolizing the Emperor's love for his dead queen. Without any self-consciousness, Kamala questions this assumption. She says that the Emperor had many queens and it is difficult to assume that he had any particular love for one of them. It would be more appropriate to regard it more as an expression of the King's desire to create an object of beauty. Everyone is shocked – first because she has contradicted the elderly Ashubabu and secondly because of the views she expresses on love, the institution of marriage and the commitment to love that is attributed to the Emperor. This could have offended a tradition bound elderly person. But, Ashubabu responds by asking Kamala whether she does not accept that man's devotion and love to his wife might persist even after the death of his wife? Kamala considers that while love is important as an existential reality, such attachment after death is sentimental and of no significance in itself. Ashubabu is shocked and asks her whether his remaining unmarried even after the death of his wife does not show his loyalty and love for his dead wife. Kamala questions it and says that it only means that he did not feel the need for a partner after the death of his wife and that was probably related to his being an aged person. Ashubabu says he was not that old when his first wife died and could have married again but for his sense of bondage and loyalty to his dead wife. Kamala disputes that and says that while he might not have been biologically old at that time he must have been psychologically old. Shivnath and the other friends who are present feel shocked at her statement and are inclined to consider her impertinent. Ashubabu however becomes thoughtful and says this is something that needs to be thought about. Kamala's statement first goes against his grain because he had always regarded his remaining unmarried, despite the persuasion of many of his friends, to be an act of faithfulness to his wife's memory and a testament of his love for her. Ashubabu instead of being offended is impressed by her candour and her ability to speak out her mind.

Later Ashubabu and Kamala are drawn to each other, he begins to regard her as his niece and seeks her counsel in the difficult situations. When his daughter, Manorama, runs away with Shivnath, he is sufficiently angered and hurt to want to disinherit his daughter, but Kamala points out to him that by doing so he will be depriving her of any support when she might need it the most.

In the meanwhile, Ajit and Kamala are drawn together and toward the end of the novel, they decide to go away to Amritsar and live there in an unmarried alliance. Kamala believes that the sanctity of marriage lies in the love that two persons feel for each other and that a marriage ritual is no guarantee that it will sustain that love. Ashubabu blesses them both at the point of their departure.

Ashubabu is a retired old man. He is not to be compared with Vipradas or Ramesh. He is not a man of action but one who is capable of genuine affection for other human beings. He is traditional in his outlook and is flabbergasted when a middle aged widow who has taken shelter with him expresses love for him. She leaves Ashubabu's household and goes and lives in the Ashram conducted by her bachelor 'brother-in-law'. Ashubabu still has the resilience and the ability to recognize new perspectives as in the case of Kamala and Ajit and to meet the crisis in his own life when his daughter runs away with a man who has deserted his own wife.

VI

There had been a reference earlier to the fact that the motif of the 'fallen' woman occurs in several of Sharadbabu's novels. One of the letters written by Sharadbabu to his friend Prathambabu dwells on this point and gives an insight into his thinking on this issue.

On 17 April 1913, he wrote a letter to Prathambabu as follows:

> I am going to send you for your perusal as much of my novel *Charitraheen* as I have been able to rewrite. I will send it by the next post. Kindly return it after you have read it. The reason I am asking you to return it is that you may not like the approach I have adopted in this novel. I am doubtful whether you will appreciate it. I am therefore not asking you to publish it. 'Samajpati' (A veteran critic and editor) has written to me that he has read and liked the book immensely and has returned it to me. This is one of my 'wild' pieces of writings. Who will read it carefully and understand it in its true sense? And who is going to appreciate it? I may even consent to have it published in your magazine (*Bharatvarsh*) if you find it suitable. But I would not like you to publish it because I have written the book. I do not wish you to do it as a favour. I would not like that. I want your true opinion – and that is what is needed in all literary writings. Besides, I am not sure whether Dwijada (Dwijendranath Rai) will like it. If he feels that I should change some portion in it I would not be able to give my consent to it. I will not agree to change even a line in this book. Even so I would like to say one thing to you. Don't make up your mind by just reading the title or the initial part of the book. I am a student of ethics – a true student. I know ethics and don't think that I understand it less than anyone else. Whatever it is I would like you to read it and let me have your true opinion. But while giving your opinion try to understand my real motive in writing this book. This is not a book that should be published by just anyone. If you really think that it is worthy of publication please let me know. I will complete the rest of the book in a short time. I know what the end of the story is going to be. I do not write whatever comes to my mind at the time I am writing. I first decide what I want to say in a book and write the book with great deliberation. That is why the events in my novel cannot be changed. (Source: Preface written by B.V. Warekar to the Marathi translation of 'Charitraheen' published in 1949)

This same forthright attitude to moral issues, found in Sharadbabu's first major novel *Charitraheen*, is found again in Sharadbabu's later novels *Shesh Prashna* and *Shesher Parichaya*.

Sharadbabu was a serious thought-provoking writer who took his work seriously. He was conscious of his artistic ability and what he wanted his characters and stories to convey.

II
The Artist and His Times

Every creative artist is influenced by his times. This need not mean that all writers born in a particular milieu will respond to their environment in the same way. The influence of the times is mediated through the particular artist's life circumstances and by his personality. In Sharadbabu's writings, his particular life circumstances and his sensibilities proved very important.

Reading Vishnu Prabhakar's definitive biography of Sharadchandra Chattopadhyay, it is apparent that Sharad's father was a dreamer and did nothing to earn a livelihood and support his family. This meant that Sharad and the other younger siblings spent their early childhood as members of their maternal grandfather's big household. Sharad's parents also lived there as dependents. The mother worked hard in the house and tried to bring up her children with the right values and good work habits. Sharad was obviously an intelligent and sensitive child. He maintained a reasonably good record at his school but he was not regular in his studies and managed his examinations by working in the few days immediately before his examinations. Otherwise, he was a wanderer. Much of what he has written about Shrikant's early life seems to apply to him. He wandered about in the woods surrounding the house and often rowed down the river in a boat with his friend Raju. This wandering and the contacts he developed with the poorer, working classes during these wanderings left a deep impression on his mind. He was naturally sympathetic to the suffering of others – particularly women. In his turn, he drew their sympathy. They easily shared their life's worries with him and found a sympathetic and responsive listener. His sense of empathy is reflected in all his novels and stories. He seemed to prefer spending his time with the lower working class families than with the middle class.

Sharad and his siblings lived in the maternal grandfather's house for several years and then the grandfather seems to have asked his son-in-law to earn and support his own family.

In Rangoon, his own economic condition was poor and it was natural that he should live in poor quarters. But, it was not as though he had no contacts among the upper caste Bengali families in Rangoon. He was in fact warmly received when he first went to Rangoon in the family of ... but over time he developed a style of life and habits of drinking and addiction to opium that made him feel inferior and avoid relations with the well to do families. The people among whom he lived did not often have a settled family life and he came across women who had been cheated by the men who had brought them to Burma and had drifted in search of food and shelter. He befriended some of them. Among his neighbours were workers of the local mills, peons working in offices, or innkeepers and men of lower middle class families. Sharadchandra seemed to avoid the Bhadralok in Rangoon and later during his visits to Calcutta he avoided contact initially even with his uncles and friends.

15

Diversity, Diffusion and Social Transformation of Rabindra Sangeet under Globalization

Susmita Bhattacharyya

Globalization has brought enormous change to India's rich culture. Anthropologist Tulasi Srinivas describes globalization's impact as follows: 'Indians are familiar with the West and its cultural influences, and so the responses to cultural globalization in India take different forms, ranging from hybridized acceptance to total rejection' (in Berger and Huntington, eds., 2002). There is no question that western cultural values have entered India through capitalism and the media and that this market-oriented, media-driven influence has affected India in no small measure.

As an artistic composition music includes meaningful symbols. These symbols can be represented in various ways. Listening to music can be treated as an interaction. Undoubtedly music is a cultural construct of a particular society, and Rabindra Sangeet is no exception. Bengalees are highly sensitive about their cultural heritage. Rabindra Sangeet stands at the apex of the musical hierarchy of Bengal. So this genre is inseparably linked with Bengali ethos and culture. Initially, the listeners of Rabindra Sangeet were delimited with respect to some specificity (like economic background and even education). Critics think that Rabindra Sangeet represents 'high culture'[1] but this situation has dramatically changed during the last few years. Now people from all walks of life and of all strata are found to be interested in Rabindra Sangeet. This all-encompassing interest is reflected clearly in the music market of Bengal. Rabindra Sangeet is treated as a marketable object. It has a stable demand throughout the year. Initially, Rabindra Sangeet was confined to Shantiniketan belt and among some pocket listeners (family-based) in different corners of Bengal. But now the number of listeners is increasing day by day. Increasing popularity of Rabindra Sangeet is coincided with quantitative leap of demand. Consequently, Bengali music industry visualizes the phenomenal occurrence of transformation of Rabindra Sangeet.

The most important far-reaching effect of cultural globalization is the commercialization of culture. Production and consumption of cultural goods and services has been commodified, along with the essentials of social life (marriage and family life, religion, work and leisure) that are the crucibles of cultural creations. Culture, whether it is music, food, clothes, art, sports, images of age, youth, masculinity or femininity, has become a product, sold in the market place (Akande, 2002). This transformation can be analysed from different theoretical standpoints. In this article, the points of focus are listeners, marketization and theoretical approaches. I define culture for my purposes as values, attitudes, beliefs, mindsets, central tendencies, worldviews and orientations that are prevalent in a given society. It is emotionally held and long-lasting rather than instrumental short-term behaviour (Edgell, 2003).

Indians, especially Bengali, are very self-conscious of their cultural identity. The anxieties about the impact of globalization and marketization of economy, media and information systems, the leisure and style of life, etc., upon the symbolic contents and the foundations of the tradition have today generated considerable debate among the social scientists. The significance of locality and local culture and its relationship with the nation-state and the national culture has been widely recognized. This is manifested through the sociology and social history of communities and cultures in India and the trends in the methods of their study. Significance of 'locality' (e.g., Tagore's resident land Shantiniketan) and its role as the building block of Rabindric culture has been increasingly accepted.

Listeners

Music is the bridge of interaction between two inseparable groups – the creators (singers and composers) and the receivers, i.e., listeners. Rabindra Sangeet creates its own group of listeners. Listeners are the products of social context which includes the nature of socialization, interaction and self-conscious cultural identity. The act of listening is a response to a particular pattern of music. This trend is prevalent among the listeners of Rabindra Sangeet also. An act of listening is somewhat related to pyramid of communiqué, it can help analyse the ways of spreading music from individual to societal level (intrapersonal, interpersonalin, tra-group, inter-group, institution/organizations, societywide). The whole society is involved in the process of spreading music. At an echelon under the society, there are several kinds of musical network. One type involves the larger society at the regional level, city or town, another is presented by the organizational level. It should be related with multiple areas of operation. But those factors should be integrated within their own organizational boundaries. Another variety is represented by institution. Following this level there are varied types of communication level. This level is based on some shared features of daily life. Here, the key questions concerned are of attachment and identity, co-operation and norm formation. At the inter-group and interpersonal levels, attention is given on forms of conversation, pattern of interaction, influence, affiliation (i.e., degree of attachment) and normative control. At the interpersonal level, processing information deserves attention. The process of globalization makes communication easily accessible. So music as an object of communication is not limited to a specific region. The impact of globalization on local culture and the changing role of the nation-state can be examined by observing the particularities of the social and cultural patterns and their local, national and transnational manifestations in India. As Rabindra Sangeet crosses the national boundary, the cross-national peripheries, the members of listening group increase day by day. The listeners are no longer confined to West Bengal and Bangladesh; they now extend across the oceans towards the western countries. Anyone can now have access to Rabindra Sangeet in this era of global communication, i.e., an extension of cultural globalization.

The researcher has undertaken a small survey of the listeners of Rabindra Sangeet. An interview schedule was used for data collection. The age group starts from 18 years as the impact of Rabindra Sangeet cannot be studied properly before 18 years. People below this age generally like noisy songs. So they are not the target listeners of Rabindra Sangeet. Table 1 below depicts the age groups with respect to their opinion about listening to Rabindra Sangeet:

Table 1

Age Distribution of the Respondents on the Basis of Traditional and Fusion Rabindra Sangeet

Age group	*Traditional Rabindra Sangeet*	*Fusion Rabindra Sangeet*	*Total*
18–25 (young)	2	8	10
25–35 (young adult)	6	4	10
35–50 (adult)	7	3	10
50–60 (mature adult)	9	1	10
60 and above	10	0	10
Total	34	16	50

The data in the table shows that 80 per cent young listeners (i.e., 8 among 10) are attracted by fusion Rabindra Sangeet. They find the traditional pattern of Rabindra Sangeet very monotonous. About 60 per cent of the total respondents say that children are not interested in this genre. Rabindra Sangeet is too serious for their adaptation. A total of 80 per cent of the total respondents say that transformation has taken place in this type of music. According to them, the existence of new technology along with its application has changed the world of music. Rabindra Sangeet is also associated with that change. In case of this genre instrumentation and new arrangements are causative factors for this entire transformation. They agreed about the marketability of Rabindra Sangeet in music market. This is crystal clear from the survey that age factor acts as an important variable here for the determination of listening pattern. Generally, people are non-interested listeners of Rabindra Sangeet in earlier age. But, the situation has changed gradually. In fact, with the increase in age, the interest in Rabindra Sangeet comes to the surface. The data shows that attraction towards fusion Rabindra Sangeet decreases with increase in age. Modern technical adoption and fusion Rabindra Sangeet have indicated a clear change in the response pattern of this genre. This change of cultural environment has a positive impact on the spreading effect of this genre.

Listening to music, irrespective of its parent tradition (Western, Indian, etc.), is indeed an involved process, as complex as the discipline itself, with its well-codified tenets. Apart from knowing the 'rules of the game' audiences of Indian music have yet another role, in the sense that they are expected to participate actively in the performance with interjections and gestures communicating their positive responses. A knowledgeable audience knows how and when to appreciate, while the performer is expected to be receptive to the reaction of the audience and be inspired, and rise up to the expectations of the audience (Rao, 2002).

The quality of performance is dependent on the quality of the audience participation. It is definitely a two-way communication, where the performer and the audience share a symbiotic and mutually beneficial relationship. It is therefore obvious that the audience for Indian music has to be not only initiated, but also knowledgeable enough to inspire the performer by communicating their approval at appropriate junctures.

The emerging situation is also blurring the aesthetic criteria. We are aware that every music tradition has its own aesthetic criteria and the validity of the musical experience is to be judged by a different set of criteria. In Rabindra Sangeet the intention of a performer is to create aesthetically pleasing music. Today, influenced by the popular genres of music, audience of the same, however, seems to be nurturing 'holdall' criteria, wishing for instant sensory gratification, irrespective of the type of music (e.g., sensation that is created with bouts with percussion, speed, loudness, display of virtuosity, etc.). Concerns have been expressed about such expectations and the resultant response affecting the musical quality and variety in terms of repertoire (ibid.).

In craze for broad menu, audiences/listeners often demand for popular genres, to be included in the recital of Rabindra Sangeet. The 'new age' audience expects not only audio but also visual gratification from the performance, (e.g., fusion Rabindra Sangeet) which by its very nature has least appendages from the extra-musical world. In this manner, the former seems to vie with the popular and catchy genres, which essentially thrive on loud, booming and artificial sound effects. It is noteworthy that the audiences/listeners as well as musicians have accepted and adopted some new timbres that are electronically produced – drone machine, electric guitar, etc. (ibid.).

Marketization

The era of globalization is here and with it a new concept – global culture. For those of us who see our task as one to respond to this phenomenon of globalization, it is critical to unpack the meanings that surround the concept of a global culture. I understand globalization as a term used to describe the transformative activities characterizing contemporary politics, the current world economy and the peoples and cultures of the world. The new global culture is the expression of deterritorialization and a borderless world. Operating through the logic of late capitalism, it can be seen as the creation of powerful media empires and transnational companies with a culture of consumption or the capitalist agenda as one of the primary signifiers of the era of globalization (Rao, 1996).

In as much as 'the new global' culture owes its existence to powerful media empires and transnational companies promoting a culture of consumption that announces the arrival of the era of 'boundarylessness' as a global cultural signifier. In other words, global culture seen through a desire for the dissolution of boundaries in order that personal freedom and free trade be facilitated and at the very same moment articulates distinct cultural characteristics that are 'innate markers of difference' (ibid.).

Commercialization, as an aspect promoting the culture of consumption, is transforming Rabindra Sangeet from the local, the regional and the national to a free market arrangement. It is related with marketable commodities that can be correlated to competitive pursuit of larger markets. Advertisement is an added advantage of this. Advertising of commodities sold around the globe specializes in emphasizing boundaries, caters to a demand for difference and exploits 'otherness' through its attempt to resurrect universalism under the aegis of global consumption. Locked in the advertisement are the dichotomous discourses of tradition and modernity striving to reconcile dissonant identities. The advertisement is also representative of a popular orientalist tendency. Here, the relations are calculative and utilitarian. The commercial variant of a communicative relationship does not support ties of mutual attachment, but there is a threat. Commercial environment of media production provides a straitjacket that closes off possibilities for innovation and creativity. Music can be accepted as an institution by some sociologists. They focus on some specific features like training procedure, stylization, presentability, and so on.

There are some perfect institutional features of music. These characteristics help to recognize music as an industrial object. The emphasis is also on technical component. Technical system includes songs, musical instruments, voice, singing style, and so on. Technology actually revolutionizes the field of music in modern days. Each and every genre of music has its own technique. Today, music world is revolved around new musical instruments as well as arrangements. Singers of today have to coordinate the style of singing according to instrumentation. In Rabindra Sangeet this kind of technicality deserves attention. Hence, the singers of Rabindra Sangeet have to be technically sound enough to be successful in today's music trade. It can be said that the scenario of transformation of Rabindra Sangeet is associated with its institutional aspect as competence in Rabindra Sangeet comes from the technicality of singing style, that is, proper training is required from recognized organizations. Like any other market product Rabindra Sangeet too is associated with production, distribution and consumption-oriented activities. Production includes singers, musicians, recordists and studio owners. Distributional activity mainly includes selling of produced music in the form of compact disc and cassettes by the respective companies. TV channels and FM radio stations too wonderfully enter into this network to give a fillip to the spreading effect. Consumption is related to listeners. They are dispersed in all corners of the world and music market utilizes this situation.

Since World War II, commerce and industry have globalized. Transnational corporations (TNCs) are playing important role in global economy. National issues may be influenced by international scenario. In this era of internationalization, the field of music is going through complete transformation. In case of Rabindra Sangeet, this transformation is vividly observed. Informatization is a new trend of today's world (McQuail, 1994: 26). This is related with growth of information-based occupations. Initially, the task of making and distributing music was very costly, so people were not interested in this trade. But, with global market integration and opportunity emancipation, the cost has come down. Therefore, small and independent companies are trying to enter into the music market. Now companies are the agent and sole distributor of music and they are playing vital role in promotional activity too.

The division of labour operates perfectly in Bengali music industry also. In case of Rabindra Sangeet there is clear-cut division between desk job, marketing, promotional, and other departments. There is a selection committee for maintaining the quality of the product. It is only after the dissolution of copyrights on Rabindra Sangeet by the Vishwa Bharati that the genre came to be utilized for mercantile purpose with introduction of instruments, background music and fusion of any kind. Now, the industry is completely goal-oriented in its applicational aspect. Departmentalization in this industry is very common today. It indicates the presence of multiple power centres of control. This differentiation helps to increase the efficiency of the performance of the industry. So, the re-patterning of industrial aspect is a necessity now.

Rabindra Sangeet industry is associated with professionalism today. It brings a marked change in the sphere of Rabindra Sangeet. It can be said that we live in a music-producing world. Music turns to be an object of consumerism. In this consumerist society music industry is operating as a factory set-up, especially for utter professionalism. Professionalism occurs in career prospects of Rabindra Sangeet singers. Previously, Rabindra Sangeet was treated by singers as a specific and specialized genre. So, the singers of Rabindra Sangeet were not associated with other genre. But, in this modern world, Rabindra Sangeet has lost this kind of particularism.[2] Due to increasing popularity, by and large, Bengali singers are now interested in singing Rabindra Sangeet, though there are some particularistic singers of this music. So, there is simultaneous existence of particularistic and universalistic trends in this genre.

There are different types of listeners too for this music. The concept of selectivity is important here. Selectivity is related to the choice of the object of listening. On the basis of selectivity listeners of Rabindra Sangeet can be broadly divided into two groups – ritualized listeners and instrumental listeners. Ritualized listeners are those who are habituated with all kinds of Rabindra Sangeet. Instrumental listeners are associated with specific choice. In case of Rabindra Sangeet some listeners are fond of 'tappa'[3], while some people like songs of dance drama. They are instrumental singers of Rabindra Sangeet.

The role of media is noteworthy here. Channels are doing their job excellently, especially Tara Muzik is highly associated with the promotional activity of Rabindra Sangeet. Reality shows are arranged for Rabindra Sangeet separately. Various sources are available for listening to Rabindra Sangeet. These include FM radio, music channels and compact discs (CDs).

Another added factor is the gradual increase in reception possibilities as apparatuses have become cheaper. Decrease in cost of CD players, computers and mobile sets with musical players are the proof. Another change has been the rapid development of new ways of recording, storage and retrieval of sound. New technology attracts new generation. Rabindra Sangeet of Pankaj Kumar Mallick was completely rejected by the young generation. But, the same song of Kishore Kumar was accepted as a hit song. The innovation of CD players shifts the control of reception time from senders to receivers. As a result, homogeneity of the listeners declines due to individualization of behaviour and personalization of choice. Interactive use of various media also changes the domain of listening. One-way system of listening to music has now become multiple network oriented system. The significant interconnectedness of new technique underlines the logic of growth in the act of listening. There is internationalization of transmission and reception. Listeners are no longer confined to one place or within one set of cultural boundaries. In this age of cultural globalization the listeners have access to their favourite Rabindra Sangeet from different corners of the world. The revival of interest in Rabindra Sangeet was strengthened by the emergence of new educated middle class of urban area. Different music colleges, Rabindra Bharati University and Vishwa Bharati University are taking steps for promotion of Rabindra Sangeet. As stated earlier, Rabindra Sangeet is now associated with new types of arrangements and instrumentation. It should not be related with experimentation, is an issue of debate. But experimentation on this genre involves lots of new listeners in its fold. So, the importance of experimental Rabindra Sangeet cannot be overemphasized for the perspective of involving new group of listeners. Due to the popularity of this genre digital downloading is associated with it. Rabindra Sangeet can also be used as ringtones.

Fusion Rabindra Sangeet is completely a new entry in the field of Bengali music industry. '*Pagla haowar badol dine*' was a very popular Rabindra Sangeet. Some years ago, the same song was treated in a different way adding 'hulala'. This has a new kind of instrumentation also. This song attracts young generation in a marked way. It has also sparked off a debate among the listeners of this genre. Conservative listeners are completely disinterested in this kind of representation. Regular listeners are also in this group. But there are some new listeners who become interested in this genre due to the new mode of packaging. Now, the buzzword of music industry is 'seeing music', i.e., visualization of music in the form of DVD and VCD. Intervention of other medium also revitalizes the Rabindra Sangeet. In this age of individualism the choice of listening object depends on individual. Each person has his/her own choice. This choice-specific behaviour reflects in music market.

Social transformation of Rabindra Sangeet has positive as well as negative effects. Positive effects are many in number. Now, most of the famous singers of Bengali as well as other music industry are interested in singing Rabindra Sangeet due to the extension of market. Another striking feature is the involvement of Bangla band in this genre. The demand for this genre is increasing day by day. This encourages big corporate houses to invest in Rabindra Sangeet. Initially, only older people were associated with genre. Young generation thought it to be melancholic and monotonous. But, the situation has now changed with the introduction of fusion music and new kinds of instrumentation. So, the traditional age barrier breaks down. Hence, Rabindra Sangeet now cannot be treated as the property of older generation. The myth of generation gap centring Rabindra Sangeet has totally disappeared. Previously, only upper and upper-middle class educated people were associated with this genre. This class-based distinction is also totally obsolete today. People of all spheres of life are now listeners of Rabindra Sangeet. Rabindra Sangeet is also used in films and TV serials in a considerable amount, which has helped popularize it in a great manner. The market statistics show that Rabindra Sangeet faces least ups and downs in comparison to other musical products of Bengali music industry. Now, the industry of Rabindra Sangeet involves a lot of common people in its fold. There is only one negative effect of this transformation. Sometimes, the use of Rabindra Sangeet becomes unnecessary and forced. Actually, the directors think that their product will be the indicator of 'high culture' with the use of Rabindra Sangeet. But this is not always fruitful.

There can be multiple additions and alterations within the sphere of Rabindra Sangeet. Traditional Rabindra Sangeet was presented in a specific way. The role of background music was least important in Rabindra Sangeet until 1980s. But, the application of technology has revolutionized this genre. The new form gains popularity among flexible listeners. In today's world economic condition of the listeners determines the choice of listening to music. Listeners are now able to pay the price of CD on the basis of his/her pocket. Awareness about the choices available and the amount of information possessed play an important role in the formation of group of listeners. Active listeners can now plan the use of music accordingly. Besides, Listeners today are also very much interested in characteristics, personal and professional background, attitude, value and behaviour of the singers. Actually, modern listeners are influenced by inner and outward qualities of the singers. Consumerism becomes the key concept today. This attitudinal change is reflected in the market of Rabindra Sangeet also.

Theoretical Approaches

This transformation in the world of Rabindra Sangeet is theoretically well interpreted by the social structural approach (McQuail, 1994: 9). It gives attention to media system and organization and their relationship to society. Like other genres of music, Rabindra Sangeet has its own structure. It helps to maintain a stable self-regulating balance between demand and supply. The behavioural approach focuses on the behaviour of the individual in the context of listening (ibid.). Individuals can be classified according to relevant variables like social positions and behaviour. The cause of preference of music of listeners can be determined by this model.

Socio-cultural approach deals with the particular social context of the listeners. According to this, the musical preferences of the listeners depend upon the pattern of family and the process of socialization. The same also implies to Rabindra Sangeet. As a theory, functionalism explains social institutions in terms of the society and individuals. In case of music the needs are mainly associated with continuity, order, integration, motivation, etc.

Music as a form of entertainment provides individual reward, relaxation and reduction of tension. It helps people to cope with the problem of life. In this context, Parsonian[4] AGIL model works well (Turner, 1995: 69). Self-interested listeners are seeking utility when they are listening to music. The idea of utility varies according to different age structures. In the old age religious utility can be served by music. Old age lovers of Rabindra Sangeet like '*jibano jakhon shukaye jay*' (when life comes to an end), whereas young children like '*aamra sabae raja*' as a medium of serving their utility.

Music is a part of cultural industry. The Frankfurt School, in its extensive study of cultural industry, found that cultural industry implies the entertainment-oriented industry (ibid.: 84). They argue that the spread of culture industry undermines the capacity of individual for critical and independent thought. They opined that art disappears in this age of commercialization. Market becomes the determining force in the sphere of art. Postmodernism undermines the traditional concept of culture. Traditional notion of culture emphasizes on fixity. Postmodern culture opposes this kind of fixation. In Rabindra Sangeet there are various signs of postmodernism. '*Koto kalo robe bolo bharoto re*' or '*kali kali bolo re aaj*' can be regarded as examples of postmodern culture of Rabindra Sangeet. Actually, postmodernism refers to social, economic and technological development through the proliferation of media. Habermas analyses the importance of public sphere in this context. In public sphere various issues emerge. It is the birthplace of different debates and a place where individuals come together as equals. They form a forum for discussion. It can be said that the existence of public sphere is marked in Rabindra Sangeet. '*Bishwo bidya tirtho prangano*' is an example of this. Baudrillard related the spreading of media with the new reality, known as hyper reality (Ritzer, 2007: 482). Hyper reality is created and composed by the interaction of people and media image. '*Basanti he bhubano mohini*' is such a composition of Tagore. This is a splendid description of spring nature and the listeners feel a complete detachment from the reality whenever they are enjoying this type of song. Thus hyper reality is created by Rabindra Sangeet. Walter Benjamin, in his classic essay 'The Work of art in the Age of Mechanical Reproduction', draws a theory about the revolutionary qualities of media technologies. Rabindra Sangeet is no longer tied to the ritual of the concert hall, where tickets are costly. There is a transition from ritual to exhibition value. This is a transition from original use value to reproducible exhibition value. Raymond Williams argues that the history of communication follows the same pattern in different societies. According to him, various forms of information and entertainment communications caused by social and cultural demand emerge from there. In case of Rabindra Sangeet this is highly prevalent and it is able to create market and consumer demand, so this genre is now related to the entertainment industry.

Transformation in the sphere of Rabindra Sangeet is not a new phenomenon. The process has started from the period of contact with the Western world. In terms of sociology it can be said that the process of westernization is a stepping-stone towards the commercial voyage of Rabindra Sangeet. Bango Sanskriti Sammelon plays an important role as the initiator of cultural communication across national boundary.

The bureaucratic structure of Rabindra Sangeet is concentrated in rational application. Due to its industrial set-up rationality is viewed in business strategy also. There is a constant debate over the quantitative versus qualitative aspects of Rabindra Sangeet. Quantitative aspect deals with number of CDs or cassettes released in a particular period of time, amount of investment, profit, loss and so on. Qualitative aspect deals with the impact of Rabindra Sangeet on the listeners. This debate is never ending. But, the lovers of Rabindra Sangeet can never ignore the eternal ethos of this genre. This becomes the part and parcel of Bengali life.

Conclusion

One of the major reasons for the above change is linked to the paradigm shift that occurred with respect to patronage. By the end of 19th century, the British established sovereignty by annexing individual principalities, and with this the performing arts like music and dance that once enjoyed generous support from the native rulers became bereft of patronage. In the 20th century it was left to the masses to patronize the arts and the performance arena shifted from the royal courts to large halls. Patronage by public at large contributed to a much wider diffusion of art music, having far-reaching consequences on the life of music and musicians in India. The authority and control wielded by a single patron was diffused to common public, who now had to pay to listen to the performance. The audience-performer relation thus had an added dimension, wherein, having contributed monetarily the audience had a 'say' in the process and could dictate its way indirectly or directly. The performer too felt obliged to 'please' the crowd and perhaps play to the gallery instead of satisfying a single patron. The choice of repertoire, for instance, is influenced by the occasion and the profile of the audience. The audience often expected to be indulged and sought additional repertoire from the performer, especially at the end of the recital. Performer, knowing the 'power' of the audience to 'make' or 'mar' his career, resorted to oblige his 'new' patrons (Rao, 2002).

Although this trend continues to certain extent even today, the story of patronage seems to have come a full circle with the entry of a new player – the corporates and business houses – who are not patrons but sponsors. They are more concerned about the visibility to their brands rather than about the art they 'claim' to support, thus, bringing more commercial elements into the art world. Today, the audience has its own idea about what music should be. It seems that the technology has superseded almost all processes of conventional transmission and propagation in a qualitatively different mode. Availability of the technology to record and reproduce sound from the beginning of the 20th century has revolutionized the way music was produced and heard in India. This has led to the development of a virtual audience – an audience that could listen to music, without leaving home and Rabindra Sangeet is no exception. From a small percentage of the elite that initially had access to such technology, it soon reached the masses, having far-reaching effect on the extent and variety of music that was produced throughout the century.

In the last few decades, Rabindra Sangeet has received a further boost with the advent of electronic, especially digital, technology. The aspects of creation/performance, preservation and propagation of this kind of music have new meaning in the realm of digital technology, which offers yet another possibility that was hitherto unheard of – the ability to create a virtual space in which such music can be heard, exchanged, learned and taught.

Like any other technology, this too is a double-edged sword having both favourable and detrimental effects on the art of music. The ease and convenience with which a large amount of 'programmed' music is made available has affected both performers as well as listeners, bringing in a paradigm shift in the way this kind of music is created and appreciated, besides the fact that a considerable part of the audience now prefers to move away from the 'live' to 'virtual' situation (ibid.).

Notes

1. For Bourdieu taste in cultural goods functions as a marker of class and he seeks to map out the social field of different tastes in legitimated high cultural practices as well as taste in lifestyles and consumption preferences (1986: 128–29).
2. A culture centred on the promotion, sale and acquisition of consumer goods (Bilton et al., 1996: 656).
3. 'Tappa' is a form of Indian semi-classical vocal music. Its speciality is its rolling pace based on fast, subtle and knotty construction (*Wikipedia, Free Encyclopaedia*).
4. Parsons was probably the most dominant theorist of his time. His major work is *The Structure of Sociological Theory* (Turner, 1995: 57).

References

Akande, Wole (2002). 'The Drawbacks of Cultural Globalization', *Yellow Times*.

Berger, P. and F. Huntington (eds) (2002). *Many Globalizations, Cultural Diversities in the Contemporary World*. New York: Oxford University Press.

Bilton, T. et al. (1996). *Introductory Sociology*. Basingstoke: Palgrave.

Bourdieu, P. (1986). *Distinction: A Social Critique of Judgements of Taste*. London: Routledge.

Dasgupta, A. (ed.) (2007). *Music and Modernity*. Kolkata: Thema.

Edgell, Alvin G. (2003). 'Globalization and Cultural Encounters', *International Third World Studies Journal and Review*, 16.

Malinowski, B. (1961). *The Dynamics of Cultural Change*. New Haven, CT: Yale University Press.

McQuail, D. (1994). *Mass Communication Theory: An Introduction*, 3rd edition. London: Sage.

Rao, Sangeet (1996). 'Otherwise? The Selling of Global Cultural Difference', *Sanskriti* [a bimonthly publication].

Rao, Suvarnalata (2002). 'Indian Art, Music and Changing Audience World Wide', proceedings of the seminar on 'Globalization and Indian Music', edited by S. Rao, ITC - Sangeet Research Academy, NCPA and Music Forum, Mumbai.

Tagore, Rabindranath (1982). *Gitabitan*. Vishwabharati: Santiniketan.

Turner, J.H. (1995). *The Structure of Sociological Theory*, 4th edition. Jaipur: Rawat Publications.

16

From Site to Terrestrial Television

Television in Everyday Life in Rural Rajasthan

Biswajit Das

This paper offers a qualitative and descriptive analysis of the ways in which viewers lived a significant proportion, with wider ramifications, of their everyday life with television in rural Rajasthan. None of these viewers made names for themselves individually. As a social type, they represented a different breed in the Indian landscape distinct from their urban counterparts: urbane, educated and professionals. Although far from being the majority of the city's middle class, these men and women worked in the field, moved back and forth to the city for daily requirements.

Hardly, the rich in the villages could afford to sustain their tastes and spending in the city's department store culture and entertainment business. Visible in daily life as peasants, artisans and labourers, they bridged the vast social space separating the rural from urban Rajasthan.

Past research has shed much light on the impact of television on rural audience (their behavioural pattern, development, health and family welfare, agriculture, education and so on). Most of these scholarships carried out with an eye toward the dreams and actions that gripped the focused attention on rural existence in Indian society and its developmental ventures.

My goal is not only to draw attention to a little examined area (Television Studies) but also to suggest a different pattern in the relationship between viewers and the television in the countryside. As new types of television channels made inroads into the countryside with the advent of cable television through Terrestrial Satellite Revolution, they fostered a new style of life among the viewers, who felt the need to adjust themselves to the imperatives and routines of urban life. As these men moved between home and work, a type of existence evolved that was embedded in their respective material as well as social characteristics of the rural society.

My paper attempts to capture the above trajectories in rural Rajasthan through imagining a way of writing about objects that would attend to their peculiar and changeable life in the viewers' lives. It also provides a way of thinking through things rather than thinking them through. Equally, it is important to capture our relationship with the quasi-objects in our day to day interaction in everyday life as our everyday experience is embedded within cultural and institutional formations that are malleable but durable. It organizes social action in powerful ways and at the same time it is modified by it. The task of analysis requires to distinguish structural shifts from surface changes and to connect them to the vagaries of biography.

How do people relate themselves to the medium and the televised events in their day to day lives? In the sphere of everyday life, do people trust television? Do people believe what it says? And finally, do people believe what the people say in the television?

Television and Popular Memory

The introduction of television in the mid-1980s in rural Rajasthan can be viewed as a critical event in the medium's genealogy, providing insight into the way television acquired meaning as a cultural form. Today, the medium has almost received acceptability and is 'taken for grantedness' in everyday life in rural area. However, the initial years also provide interesting account about people's perception of technology and life surrounding it.

Memory of Television

During the interview, the questions relating to the respondents' first memory of television turned out to be very insightful for our research endeavour. Most of them were initially hard-faced and reluctant, however felt comfortable and opened up gradually. Some of the responses were:

> My first memory of Television is of days I was young ...
> Oh, those were the days ... things were very bad here ...
> Something like Television ... some people came ...
> They said our problems would be solved by watching it ...
> My distant memory, I don't know ...

I encouraged the respondents to narrate their childhood experiences: 'Well I am a Rajput by caste and we live in this village for more than hundred years ... this is our village ...

After few minutes of interview, I came upon the first memory of television:

> those were the days ...
> people were going out in search of jobs ...
> there was drought and famine ...
> somebody said that some outsiders came with a machine ...
> some people are inside the machine ...
> they advise you solutions for all kinds of calamities ...

While verifying this popular memory I came to know that the village was dominated by Rajputs. Television was introduced in this village when the region was afflicted with drought and famine. Television's role was viewed as a messiah to solve the calamities in the village. Each participant came up with a distinct memory of his/her own. One of the old women said:

> she wanted to see that machine ...
> she was not allowed to go in the evening ...

In a society where male and female relations are so distant and where women remain constantly under veil and never venture into a public place to share with the male folk. Be it in home or outside they have to maintain a distinct image for themselves otherwise they are ostracized by the community as well as the village society.

Memories of television increased in importance as the interview progressed through time, and the same events were quoted by the participants more and more often. Another old woman in the village mentioned that:

> During her childhood her neighbour said ...
> not only it speaks...
> seen through naked eyes ...
> so many things ... so many people can remain inside the box ...
> TV sets are made in foreign countries ...
> Only foreigners can do such wonders ...

Another young male respondent, while narrating his childhood experience of television said:

> This machine was meant for the upper caste people ...
> His father never went nor did he take him to the sight ...

By cross-checking, we were able to put a date to this memory. The official memory of the SITE experiment dates back to 1976. This experiment was introduced in Rajasthan for educational purpose. The experiment continued for some time and subsequently, the countrywide school education project was introduced through television. Experiments have been undertaken time and again with a pretext of reaching the rural audience. Further, a developing country cannot openly support such investment in television technology unless there is an element of 'rural' anxiety associated with it.

The popular memory of the villagers cannot recall these experiments in a chronological order. As some of the elderly men said that they did not get the chance of watching television in their tender years due to existing social deprivation within the rural society. Inter-caste hierarchized relations in rural society were the marker as well as the decisive factor in governing communicative relations. Television as a technology could not remain outside the purview of such hierarchy, neither could it bridge the gap between upper and lower caste in the village community. On the contrary, inter-caste relations governed the social relations of appropriation and acquisitions of TV technology in rural society.

Some of the upper caste members in the village provided interesting accounts relating to their memory of television. As an elder member highlighted: He was very young when the TV set came to the village and was installed in the school. The school was chosen because it was more spacious so that more people could watch it. Every evening he used to go with his father to see the programmes. There, he used to meet his friends and they used to sit in the front row to watch the programme. They used to scream when the image came on the screen. The images fascinated them because their curiosity was to know, 'how somebody could manage to remain inside the box'.

They visited the school the next morning and loitered near the TV room, which used to be locked during the day time. Whenever they had a chance to enter the room, they looked around the set and 'explored the hole through which the man entered inside the TV set'.

During evening they used to watch varieties of programme starting from agriculture, family planning, rural development and so on. Most of these programmes used to give advice using various types of seeds, manures, pesticides, small family norm, family planning programme, sanitation, cleanliness and health and hygiene.

Some of them used to go back home and discuss with their parents about 'following the instructions as advised by the man inside the box'. Their parents used to argue with them by saying that 'this man did not know anything about their village. Neither, did he have any ideas about the land and soil, water resources and the economic conditions of the household in the rural areas. Whatever he was prescribing was meant for rich households with good land resources. If we would follow his advice, we won't get any thing from the land, what we are getting now'. While verifying this statement, we realized that most of the messages telecast during SITE experiment in Rajasthan were developed in Delhi and were telecast from Delhi. Most of these messages were telecast for a uniform 'public' situated in diversified regions of Rajasthan. Since it did not take into account the diversity in the region, most of the messages could not have any impact on the rural viewers.

The children remained confused regarding the authenticity of the voice. They were not sure about whom to trust, whether, their parents, who had been struggling hard to produce a bumper crop in a desert area through their rich experience or an alien person coming through television and providing his sheer expertise and solution for each and every problem. In a desert area, where one encounters all kinds of problems starting from drought, lack of rain, water resources, lack of cash, hunger and poverty, lack of health infrastructure or any institutions to support, such messages were meaningless for them unless they were backed by concerned agencies to support.

Soon Chitrahaar (programme based on film songs twice a week) and Sunday feature film added glory to the television set. All of them regularly visited to watch Chitrahaar and the fascination for Sunday feature film was an extra incentive. They never had any exposure earlier about film songs or movies. They used to scream, laugh and enjoy when they used to see the heroes and heroines do love making on the garden, agricultural field, and in parks.

It is interesting to note that school in the village context was never an exciting place to visit. In a desert area, where people are constantly migrating outside the village for their survival, school was a luxury for such population. Further, the larger thinking prevailed in the village that 'school education would snatch away their children from them'.

However, the inauguration of television in the school premises made it more a site of fun and joy. Even though, most of the children did not visit in the daytime to attend the school, they made themselves available during evening for sheer pleasure and fun. Children, not attending the school have no distinction between play time and non-play time. They need to be engaged in such environment. Television provided them an opportunity to be engaged with. The school premises used to be crowded everyday during evening for viewing programmes. Occasionally, some of the members of the untouchable castes used to visit the site but left the premises early before any untoward incident took place.

The school received another TV for the countrywide educational project. The children attending the school were shown educational programme in the daytime. It was difficult for them to understand because of the language. The uses of teaching technologies were alien to their experience. In a rural school, where even a blackboard and chalk is a luxury, their sudden exposure to such teaching method through TV was quite astounding. But, evening was a great fascination.

Although school as an institution is introduced to bridge the gap between gender, caste and community, however this institution could not fulfill its mission, rather succumbed to the dictates of the upper caste members in the rural society. Neither the girl child nor the lower caste children could reach the threshold of the school. The girls were only allowed to continue their primary education. Most of these female children had undergone child marriage and now counted the days/years to join their husband and the in-laws' house. They stayed back at home and prepared themselves for the role of would be 'daughters-in-law' in distant places.

As one of the elders said: 'the more they go to the school, the more they have the power of reason, the more they have the power of reason, the more they argue. An argument in the in-laws family would create bad name for her as well as for her family'. Thus, the girl children were doubly oppressed both by the family as well as by the forces outside the family. Neither were they allowed to go to school nor even to visit their friends very often. They were the worst sufferers. As long as they were at home, they remained imprisoned. The moment they shifted their residence after marriage, they had a veiled existence.

During the mid-eighties, investing money on a TV set was an impractical proposition as the viewing hours were less, and the infrastructure for television software was not developed in India. Most of the programmes shown on TV set were based on development. Entertainment was the least priority. However, the early nineties saw a remarkable transformation in Indian landscape. Along with the 9th Asiad Games, the television programmes mushroomed, the viewing hours increased and a second channel came up in subsequent years that catered to the urban areas. But, the problem in rural areas remained as usual. The urban areas took the major share of Doordarshan, except, the other regions which were connected through network programme. Prior to the introduction of network programme, at least there was a focus on rural area. Along with the expansion of television, even the rural viewers and their programmes were marginalized.

On the contrary, the urban areas were filled with colour sets due to relaxation in export-import policies by the state, while the viewers in the rural areas still loved to retain their community viewing and chose the school premises as a site for spectatorial contract and gaze. This viewing could not continue longer due to withdrawal of experimental programme by the Central Government. Seduced and overpowered by television, the viewers now desperately looked for places to have a glimpse of the set. However, few privileged ones could afford a TV set in the village.

While interviewing these households, one gets an interesting account of television's penetration right from the public sphere to the domestic space. As one of the respondents reported: His family members vividly remember those days when TV arrived at their home. 'It immediately passed through word of mouth to everyone in the village. People flooded his home to see the TV set and praised him for his new acquisition at home so that later on they could visit and have a glimpse of it'. In the initial days they had a problem of locating the TV set within the house. This dilemma was not due to the members' preference for location of the TV set within the household but the army of villagers who swarmed into his house regularly. They used to keep the set in the lobby so that everyone could watch it. Others, who could not have an access to the images, were satisfied with the audio of the TV set. But, the craze was much more to have a glimpse of the visual which was quite alien to their society and culture. As he said, 'Now, almost everyone in the village has a TV set, even more than one set so nobody visits their home to watch TV these days'.

Gradually, the attention shifted from school to home. It was equally a shrinking of space from public to private. In a society where 'public' is maneuvered by the vested interests, such binary oppositions remain blurred and question the very term 'public'. The earlier rhetoric of broadcasting for 'education' and 'information' lost its potency along with a shift to consume TV programme like any other product. There was also a shift from community viewing to group viewing of TV.

Today, television has been consumed like any other domestic item in the rural household. While inquiring about the acquisitions of TV set in the households in the village, the responses were quite interesting to note. Broadly, there were two sets of responses: (a) television came to the household through marriage, and (b) television was bought when Ramayana and Mahabharata (mythological) serials were telecast.

In case of the former, the relationship between TV set and marriage is quite intriguing. TV set is added as an extra item to the dowry price for marriage. Earlier, radio and tape recorder were the usual items given for dowry in marriage. Today, television has replaced these items and established its superiority over these items as a symbol of status. The groom's family discuss with much pride about the items they received as brideprice from the bride's family. The bride's father is a double victim in this entire process. He insists to offer as well as gives dowry with a fear that his daughter would not be ill-treated. Both the acts are illegal. In some families, the case is completely different. They not only would like to show off the various items they are giving for their daughter's marriage, but it also becomes a point of discussion for sometime in the village. As some respondents said, 'they did not ask for it but when the bride's father insisted to accept, they could not deny'. While verifying this statement from others in the village, one receives horrendous accounts about the dowry system in the village and more specifically about the groom's family. As some of the younger lots said: TV has become such a common object that whether you ask or not you are likely to get a TV set during marriage from the bride's family. One comes across more than one TV set in the average houses. However, they use only one set for viewing and the rest remain packed and unused with a hope that it can be used for further marriage negotiations in the family. Since joint family is the norm of rural households, it is obvious that someone would marry from the family or would marry within few years. TV set is preserved for that purpose.

In case of the latter, most of the houses have acquired their TV sets within last seven/eight years. But, their memory of purchase is related with memory of television. Both the serials (Ramayana and Mahabharata) were telecast in early 90s through Doordarshan channel. Over the years these serials have been time and again repeated by various cable channels. Here popular memory of an event collapses with the technological memory. TV technology cannot only recreate memories through storing and retrieving the messages but can also dictate the rites of passage for the society.

The village houses today are linked to one another through wires and look like a wired cosmos. In most of the cases, the antennas are replaced by wires. Antenna, which remained a symbol of status in past years, has been replaced by wires. The location and size of antenna on the rooftop of the house became a marker of opulence and displayed power position in the rural social structure. As one young man belonging to untouchable caste said, 'he thought antenna was used for distracting birds in the village. Although he used to hear from friends regarding the programme coming through TV but his friends never expected him to visit their houses to watch TV program'. It clearly shows the distinction between people having and not having access to TV set in the village. Although, cable wires have no doubt attempted to homogenize the households through a common thread or wire, however, the privileged few still retain both to exercise their position in an inegalitarian set-up. In this context, it is worth noticing that the tendency toward the standardization of the products and homogenization of tastes responds to the market demand by continuously renewing designs of technology with a hope of proving differences. However, the rural society responds to such innovation through their internal logic of differences. So that difference becomes a visible substance.

One can overhear sound and noise from the houses while passing through these units. These sounds and noises are not because of conversation within the household but due to the discussion during group viewing and frictions over choice for channels.

Most of these households have indigenous, black and white sets which are manufactured by local companies. These local sets do not provide the facility of sufficient channels nor the technology is sophisticated enough to receive all the signals beamed by terrestrial satellites. People are happy with the sets they have, they do not aspire much. As one of the elders said, 'If I would have more money I would buy a stitching machine so that I can do more work and feed and clothe my children properly'. It shows that investing further in TV is not a priority amongst various members in the village.

The local cable operator provided interesting accounts of the rural society and the viewing pattern. Every day, the cable operator received loads of complaints regarding transmission fault, lack of visibility and lack of audio reception. But, the cable operator denies such allegations and highlights that in most of the cases these are pretexts for not paying the monthly rent for the cable operations. Further, the TV sets purchased by the villagers do not have sufficient facilities to receive or catch the cable transmission. When he reports to various households regarding these problems, he gets scolded by them and the villagers question his integrity. As one of the young respondent commented 'the TV set is perfectly ok. He does not know the mechanism of it

... he grumbles for more money ...'. While inquiring from the cable operator, he said ' most of these houses have more than one TV set, the members of the household make cross connection to these various sets. In few cases, some of the houses do not ask him formally for cable connection, but illegally avail the facilities in the night by making cross connection. It was difficult for him to make surveillance in the night. However, he knew about them through other sources. Neither can he ask them to stop this practice nor charge them for illegal acts. Because he does not possess license as a cable operator, further, any such awkward incident would jeopardize his business. Most of the villagers do not pay regularly, nor do they pay the full amount to him'. The question arises here what is an illegal act? When the villagers know very well about the illegal operation undertaken by the cable operators, they try to have an upper hand on him and engage themselves in such acts because cable operators cannot be the authority to control them.

Besides the TV set, there are other means of communication such as tape recorder and radio available in the average households. Newspaper is a distant dream due to lack of accessibility. Most of these gazettes are lying unused due to fascination to see images through TV, 'which is a combination of all' as one of the respondents reported during our fieldwork.

Invariably in most of the cases, the TV set is located in the bedroom of the houses. The TV set is yet to receive a distinct architectural space in the households. Neither, the village households can provide such luxury for television. The architectural space constitutes of two rooms in the house. One room is used for storing grains and other domestic accessories. The other room is used for sleeping purpose. TV is placed in this room. It is difficult to locate or assign any single room for any specific purpose. The same room is used for sleeping, eating, viewing television programmes and children study in the same room.

So many activities are undertaken simultaneously so that the room becomes a hub of activities. Earlier, their leisure time was spent in sleeping, listening to audio cassette recorder or radio songs. Now these activities are replaced by viewing television. Since TV has occupied a central position within the bedroom, it is a constant source of 'distraction for other activities' as reported by one of the respondents in the village. In fact, TV has a visible presence in the rural household.

Cultural Memory

Religious programmes receive a priority in the village. The serials based on mythology have a wider appeal cutting across caste and religion in the rural society. As one elder member of the untouchable caste said:

> They watch all the religious programs and have become more religious and perform rituals as prescribed in the Hindu social order. Since they were not allowed to read the religious texts, they get to know about the deities, god and goddesses and the rituals through television.

Besides, another elder person reported:

> being Muslim, they watch all kinds of Hindu religious program.

While asking about his interest in Hindu religious programme, he said that in the village:

> there is no such distinction between 'Hindu and Muslim'. Both of them live like a community member. Since childhood, they have been listening about various Hindu religious program be it in school, community, and media. Obviously they know about Hindu deities, mythologies and religion so much as the members of Hindu community. Their peer groups are mostly members from the Hindu community.

Few more respondents reported: they had read and knew the stories through their parents and grandparents in their childhood, the image was an additional attraction. Some of them said that they 'gained knowledge through it'.

While visiting several households, one notices that the walls of the room are decorated with calendars/posters of mythological figures and deities. Although it is difficult to correlate between watching TV and religiosity, now people are more aware about various mythologies and legends.

Earlier, the elders used to visit the temple or go for 'satsangh' to listen to religious discourses from the village priest, who used to tell them mythological stories in the evening. The whole village elders used to sit around him and listen to stories. Ever since the arrival of television in the household, such congregation thinned down. It is not that they question the authority or the veracity of the village priest, but the images through television has a gripping effect on them. Television provides them both with the stories as well as the images. Whenever they have doubts or require clarification they approach the priest and clarify their doubts. The priest himself watches such programmes to keep himself updated besides reading the texts.

Probably religion provides a smokescreen to hide the reality in rural society. People specially, women feel shy to speak boldly about any other programme except religious serials. Speaking about religion provides them moral sanctity as well as determines their position in rural community. Few more respondents had different responses to record: they were puzzled to see the actors and actresses portraying the mythological characters who were very much involved in campaigning and contesting in elections as well as acting in films. For them, both religious serials and Hindi movies are alike, except the religious programmes which have powerful messages but these cannot be followed and practised in the contemporary time. The religious serial does not come everyday, further, there is yet the need to have an exclusive religious channel through the cable network. In this context, their consistent reply to the researcher regarding preference for religious serial is subject to scrutiny. The shift from the tradition of oral narrative of mythologies to the televised serial implies a dramatic continuity without any fixed boundary and time. The villagers only know about its beginning but have no idea when it will end. Through the mechanism of recognition, there is an identification of the world of the story with the viewer. At every point of the story, the viewer is put in a dilemma of a given reality that may be accepted by him/her either passively or with a modification but can never be rejected. Such mythological serials provide the possibility of recognition whereby the hero no longer moves in the mystical or supernatural domain but in the space of the real and possible. This hero is the mediation factor between the myth and the serial. The relevance of this hero in the contemporary scenario is more pressing because his role is to undo injustice and fight for establishing moral truth.

Other programmes such as family drama and movies are equally liked by the villagers. The reception of television programmes has different implications on the viewers. One of the younger female respondents, who is counting her days to join her husband and in-laws family provided fascinating account regarding various programmes: She likes family-based serials and feels concerned about it. It helps her a lot to know about how to adjust in her in-laws house as well as about possible problems in future. These programmes have almost become role model in her life. She comes to know the time of programme from the television in advance. In case she misses any, she inquires from other family members as well as the neighbours. Sometimes, while sharing with others, she gets to know about these programmes. She does not like to miss any. She makes extra effort to know about the programme. She gets up early in the morning and switches on the TV set. She likes the advertisement very much. She is fascinated with the soaps, lipsticks and other consumer durable items advertised through television. Whenever her husband (due to child marriage practice in the village, most of the girl children are married in their early tender years but only shift to husband's residence after reaching puberty) visits her home, she asks him to buy these commodities for her during her next visit. Earlier, she used to visit her neighbour's house to watch television programmes. Sometimes she stayed there till late hours. Realizing her conspicuous absence at home, her father decided to buy one for home so that she can watch it as long as she is at home and will then take it along with her as dowry price. She finds it funny in the movies where hero escapes with the heroine and the parents fight between themselves.

Another female respondent reported: She likes family drama because it is like the real life. The working women shown in television fascinate her because 'they have more freedom and independence'. She is always fascinated with their lifestyle and laments that TV is for city life. However, the elder members constantly discourage her to watch TV and concentrate more on work. Her mother always coaxes her about her future and cautions her that she is not following the right path. Rather, she should learn varieties of work for which she will get praises in her in-laws home. Her mother pulls out the plug of television when she is watching excess of it.

Her sister-in-law, who is recently married, has interesting responses to make: She does not forget to put her veil on her head while watching TV because lot of men and women come in TV. She feels scared to lie down in the bedroom during daytime when her husband is away for work. Television's visible presence in the room has added to her fear. If she rests alone, somebody might come out from the TV set and hold her physically, which would be an embarrassment for her as well as to the family.

Since hierarchy governs the social relationships both within and outside the house, it is obvious that the daughter-in-law in the house has to use her veil while watching the television programmes because watching television is always a group occasion whereby the entire family members sit together to see the programme.

One of the elderly persons responded by saying that: he does not sit inside the room. His son and daughter-in-law sit in front of the television in the bedroom and he asks his son to put a chair near the door so that he can see the programme. In a society where the relationship between father-in-law/mother-in-law and the daughter-in-law are so distant that even television technology could not bring them together. Indeed, TV is selectively used and appropriated by the community members so that it cannot affect their relations in everyday life.

While interviewing one young mother of two children, we received interesting accounts of the internal dynamics of television viewing pattern in the house: She is not able to watch frequently television programme due to pressure of work. Although other members watch, she cannot sit with them and watch it because it will not be appreciated in the in-law's house. While lamenting over her miseries, she explained that she missed the serials and remembered them. While narrating various episodes, she showed her eagerness as well as enthusiasm to share with someone about the television programme which she missed badly in the in-law's house.

Earlier, she had no time for leisure. She devoted time for childcare because the children were small and dependent. Before her wedding, she used to play with her friends and watch TV in her village. She preferred to play with friends inside the home. However, during evenings she used to come back home. She used to like advertisements in TV and used to know about new detergents, soaps, toothpastes, cold drinks, etc. She found the serials better than the local programme. Initially, she used to get scared and run away from the TV room, thinking that the story was true.

The programmes have impact on the viewer's lives. As some of the male members in the village reported: By watching television programme 'you can see what happens when you do something wrong in your family. Through television, you can learn about life of different people. Even though the conflicts shown in the television programme are alien from my personal life, still I can relate to them'. According to them, 'these serials show the right path to follow'.

It is in this context important to note that TV is capable of creating a fascination for the exotic. It transforms the local/indigenous culture into an entertaining show whereby it combines both primitive and modern, ceremonies and costumes, with a constant reminder of the difference as well as the subordination of the primitive to the modern.

There are other respondents who view the programmes differently. As some of the respondents commented, 'Entertainment programme based on English language are not watched in the village. These programmes display nudity and naked bodies. They get scared of showing it to their female members and the young generation'. While the male members are scared of their families to watch such programme, they do not mind to derive their voyeuristic pleasure by watching a movie in the theatre hall. Some of the male respondents reported: they enjoy it there because the size of the images are bigger, more people watch at a time and the enjoyment is more and it is more fun. One of the respondents narrated his experience:

> I went to see once an English movie. I don't remember the title of the movie. The poster displayed outside the movie hall as well as the posters in the streets fascinated me to see the movie. But, my desire of watching sex and

> pornographic objects were fizzled out, once I was inside the hall. It is the deliberate strategy of the owner of the film hall to seduce the viewers to watch English movies by making such obscene posters so that more people will be attracted.

In a society where sex is a taboo, and closely confined to the private domains, the viewers are seduced to watch them in the hall. Now, he is happy and thanks the cable operator who provides enough of them. As he pointed out:

> now there is no need to go to a hall to watch English movies, one can see violence and sex in Hindi movies as well as through cable television.

Television has generated the demand to consume domestic items, kitchen appliances, etc., in the rural households. In this regard, the advertisers have succeeded in penetrating the rural hinterland which were otherwise isolated and unprofitable proposition from the market point of view. One of the male respondents reported: 'his wife asks him to buy several household items for domestic consumption such as pressure cooker, fan, fridge, etc. Since he knows that he cannot afford it, he keeps quiet and assures her that when they would have money he would buy it for her. His wife's grievances are combined through the television programmes and unleashed while watching the programmes in the night'.

However, there are villagers who are yet to get addicted to the TV screen. For instance, few respondents say that they do not like the noise of it. Some of them have radio sets and like to listen to radio programmes. For them the maintenance of radio is cheaper than television.

One of the female respondents in the village reported:

> I watch it only with girls not with men. What comes through TV only happens in cities not in the rural area. TV is such a funny medium where people talk among themselves but hardly they talk to us.

She has an apprehension that the more the girls watch TV programmes, there is a possibility that they might elope away with the boys creating humiliation for their family in the village.

Most of the villagers are worried about the children in the village. As some parents reported: 'television breeds the distinction between "us" and "them" in the child's mind. Most of these programmes are located in urban context in a nuclear family set-up. Since we live in a joint family set-up, we constantly encounter uncomfortable questions from the children regarding "mine" and "yours". Nothing in a joint family set-up is personal, everything is collectively owned. It has a dangerous repercussion for the future'.

The children have a better sense of memory of the programme than their parents. They not only watch the programmes with their parents in the evening but watch the repeat of the same programme with their friends in the daytime. They inform the parents about the forthcoming programmes so that they manage to make them watch and join them while watching the programme. The children provide the connecting link between the past and the present episode of the programme.

Political Memory

The villagers seem to be well informed about 'politics' and ongoing political events.

Irrespective of owning/not owning a television set, the villagers have shown their ability to discuss politics at great length. However, television cannot be made responsible for their knowledge and information. Although, in recent years, the other sources of information are declining as television has taken centre stage in the village. Most of the interpersonal occasions are also at stake as television arrests their attention and demands more time from them. Hardly, they can socialize and interact after day's hard work. Occasionally, the failure of electricity brings them together to their meeting places which used to be the centre of discussion earlier. These centres still continue but have lost their vigour and vitality. During interview, visiting some of these centres and discussing with villagers in the evening provided interesting clue to their political memory and role of television in providing that memory.

Television is not even spared by the villagers. As a source of information and news, it is still under scrutiny in the village. But, suspicion with regard to television has a very long history, which might extend beyond politics in the village.

As in 1976, a programme in the television highlighted the agencies where the farmers can apply for loans to purchase hybrid seeds and manures for agriculture. This policy was cited by many of those who were at school at the time, with no date or political context, still in their memory as a milestone of their school and family life.

Many people remembered, particularly in these terms:

> My first memory goes back a long way ...
> When I was at primary school ... mentioned to me about a news item
> Which mentioned about the means to get ...
> Still in my memory.

This incident remained in their mind during their childhood. They still remember this event because somebody discussed about their well-being and better future. Although their parents visited the concerned agencies and returned with a sense of frustration, however, the very idea of providing information for their well-being struck in their mind.

Some of the respondents remarked: Look at television there is scandal, communal tension, bribery ... they pick up somebody who is not the actual culprit ... I think when they want to trap somebody they can ... the real culprit escapes ...

Here criticism is aimed at both fronts: If the television is silent, it omits; if it speaks, it admits. But, it never informs. Suspicion felt by individuals can be accentuated if they are part of a group. The pressure and the absence of an image provokes criticism. Images represented from one edition of TV news to another are criticized as manipulative by three people and as excessive by another, as if television has mirrored its own worries. This mistrust is a result of people's dependence on television. For television is what remains when there is no other means of information available or when people give up using the other means of communication.

The villagers verify television's version of the facts with reference to another version which is supposed to be more reliable and authentic. Although they cannot negate completely television as a source of information, neither would they be interested to bank upon television. These uncertainties 'no ... but ... yes' reveal another dimension of the villagers. Most of the villagers while interviewing rarely expressed their attachment to television and to the medium. They cannot be completely 'impartial', neither do they disclose everything. One must be prepared that they also hide things ... as during the interview, it was noticed that all of them as a principle, critique the various items in the news but while filling the questionnaires, they say something else.

Some of the dramaturgic aspects of political events need to be highlighted in this context. The events portrayed through television can give rise to joy or sorrow. Rejoicing cuts across social political divides. Enemies are reconciled or they enter into dialogue. Death becomes very painful if it is unpredicted. Sudden disappearances cause more suffering and are remembered more vividly. Finally, betrayals reveal the darker side of the character.

The Babri Masjid issue was cited by four people as a moment of clear-cut social reconciliation which took place during demonstrations as well the coverage provided by television. It is often television which can give us this image of reconciliation. Two respondents, former school teachers, who were very critical of television, retained one strong memory of the Babri Masjid issue:

> I watched the events being broadcast because I didn't have anything else to do. But I was not very interested neither happy ... there was, however, something which stuck in my memory ... some of the chat shows where leaders from two different political parties ... both were hypocrites ... one was defying religion and the other was forwarding religion ... how can you defy religion ... the person who was favouring religion seemed to be more logical ...

A more intense form of reconciliation takes place where it involves two warring nations, represented from a biased standpoint by their heads of state. Here war is no longer a mere metaphor but politics itself. The recent terrorist strike in the USA was cited spontaneously by several people during the interview: the speech by President Bush and Rumsfeld telecast through Star News, made the people happy who were not politicized. One of them said: 'I was happy about that and I sat there all evening watching the programme'. Even people who feel excluded from politics, can make pronouncements on events which are not formulated in strictly political terms. They approve of reconciliation between two historical enemies but would doubtless have nothing to say about the future consequences of the Afghanistan peace process.

The memory of death of political leaders was retained particularly among people with low political awareness. They cited them so often that their frequency was established.

The reassuring versus worrying contrast is essential in the construction of a leader's image: 'Mrs Indira Gandhi was intelligent, I think she was reassuring, she managed to get peace and stability for the nation ...'.

Leaders who take part in a form of reconciliation or of change are opposed to those who are sources of instability, they are a part of a new category of memorable events.

Betrayal is mentioned primarily in terms, which are very common to political satire: 'Politicians break promises' was quoted by most respondents. Another type of event, also a common target of satire, is political scandal. Scandal tarnishes people's images. The most striking example arose from the recent defense scandal, corruption in high offices and bribery. In the case of people with a low degree of political awareness, it is impossible to deduce, at least directly the political position of all these memories, even if they are a contributing factor towards tarnishing or embellishing a political leader's image. In fact, they reflect an outlook which is non-political.

The metaphorical schema discussed above is not incompatible with. On the one hand, certain events (betrayals, alliances) can be associated with several metaphorical systems at the same time. On the other hand, they can be applied to relations between people, to relations between camps and to relations between nations.

One of the few facts cited by all the participants was September 11 tragedy, the interviewers then returned to domestic events. Alongside September 11, various events were linked like India's preparation for war with Pakistan and other domestic events with much condensing of time. People remembered how events unfolded: The assassination of Indira Gandhi, Rajiv Gandhi, and Kargil war and the bombing of WTC, etc. People of a different generation, however compressed the time-scale considerably. They recounted the events as if the temporary absence of Indira Gandhi during the crisis preceded her definitive departure and her death has one thing in common; the prime minister vanished from the screen. As she withdrew from the world, she also withdrew from the media and from the public. These two departures were indistinguishable.

The memory of Mrs Indira Gandhi, who was in power for several years, was cited by everyone, either spontaneously or when prompted. Even some of them still think that she is alive and is the prime minister (specially, those who have not seen TV images or listened to the radio messages) of the country. Some of them admired her as a leader, as a mother, and as someone who was killed because the Sikhs did not like her. Although, television played a very dubious role in narrating the events, however, in time, it is the people and images which remain, rather than opinions and problems. Repeated broadcasts and retrospective programmes fix certain representations in people's minds at the expense of others. This is what occurred in the case of Mrs Gandhi; the cause of the death was disguised at that time, but because a public event a posteriori. In more general terms, images which are frequently shown, were associated.

Our research contradicts the image of a one-way influence, in the historical as well as in other domain. The viewers do not accept everything offered to them by the television, even if it is offered repeatedly, and is perceived to be a contradiction with what is learnt from other sources. The television can thus consolidate an image contrary to the one they wish to promote thus becoming counter sources of history. Three people, two of whom had direct experience of the war, thus contrasted the given image of the Kargil war with the reality they knew.

Conclusion

Television in everyday life, such as the sort that has been described above, does not necessarily occur everyday. It is rather, that eruption into the quotidian of an unlikely possibility that defines the shape of practice for everyday to come. The biographical detail I have been seeking to anatomize here tends to take the form of quotidian eruptions, serving to remind us of the shape of power structures underlying everyday life, creating a framework within which relations between all parties are supposed to be conducted. One of the reasons why television can be so effective in shaping everyday life, I would suggest, is because it exposes, and sometimes dramatically changes, the presumptions and presuppositions underpinning the underwritten, and mostly unspoken rules shaping the ways in which life is lived. Thus, it is in this world of hierarchized relations through caste, gender and religion, where the penetration of TV technology can shatter the presumptions of existing modes of communication and establish a rule for all to follow. And it is through the telling of stories about the events and consequences of television viewing that these rules become established. On the other hand, television viewing pattern can also serve to reveal the bankruptcy of established norms and rules governing everyday life.

This paper does not claim that this is the only possible way of perceiving the memory and biography concerning television. But, within the scope of this study, at least, the symbolic dimension of everyday life seems to involve everyone, whether or not they are conceptually prepared to analyse television in strictly analytical terms and play a part in them. Two aspects which are essential for the present study are the truth and the metaphor. The present study attempts to bring the metaphor to the forefront because it stands out in our transcript. While reading the interview material, other mechanisms, which can be called symbolic, are apparent. The respondents sheltered behind the same collective concept when it was a question of belief in various events, or in the truth as presented by television. The mechanism of projection, which ascribes to others the result of received information, allows people to gather information at a very low cost, and even at a very low risk. There is a twin risk here: that of confronting the consequences of an event alone, and that of having to make a personal statement as a response in an interview situation. In several cases, as the interviews progressed, generally at times when the respondents were emotionally involved, they oscillated between 'I' and 'they'. Their statement normally fitted in fairly standard pattern along the lines of 'think the people have liked it because there are no other means ...'.

This mechanism of projection also allows people to put aside the question of whether the fact mentioned is true since their statement takes recourse to collective opinion or to people allow a confrontation and interpretation of reality without any personal responsibility.

Thus, this paper offers a series of reflections on the study, addressing some of the general theoretical issues that underpin the project and identifying particular themes which have emerged in the course of the fieldwork. I must inform the readers that I am interested here in examining only the memory associated with television and would insist that what follows should not be interpreted as representing the totality of experience in that place. Rather, think of this, based as it is upon my own partial and particular experience over past few years in rural Rajasthan, as an exploration of some of the memories and biographical remarks associated with television. From my perspective, the contours of these biographical remarks come into focus through lenses ground in the experience of also living life elsewhere, to wit: other parts of the country. There are, of course, other ways of looking at these things ...

References

Agarwal, Binod C. (1976). *Media Anthropology and Rural Development: Some Observation on SITE*. Ahmedabad: Space Application Centre, ISRO.

—— (1977). *Social Impact of SITE on Adults*. Ahmedabad: Space Application Centre, ISRO.

—— (1981). *SITE Social Evaluation: Results, Experiences and Implications*. Ahmedabad: Space Application Centre.

—— (1989). 'Dual Ethics in Indian Communication: A Cultural Crisis', in T.W. Cooper (ed.), *Communication Ethics and Global Change*, White Plains, NY: Longham, pp. 147–359.

—— (1989). *Communication Revolution: A Study of Video Penetration in India*. Ahmedabad: Development and Educational Unit, ISRO.

Agarwal, Binod C. et al. (eds) (1986). *SITE to INSAT: Challenges of Production and Research for Women and Children*. New Delhi: Concept.

Atal, Yogesh (1977). 'Communication', in S.C. Dube (ed.), *India since Independence: Social Report on India, 1947–72*, New Delhi: Vikas.

Bhattacharya, Vivek Ranjan (1976). *Communication in a Global Village*. New Delhi: Chetana.

Damle, Y.B. (1957). 'Communication of Modern Ideas: Knowledge in Indian Villages', *Public Opinion Quarterly*, 20.

Desai, M.V. (1977). *Communication Policies in India*. Paris: UNESCO.

Dube, S.C. (1967). 'Communication, Innovation and Planned Change in India', in D. Lerner and W. Schramm (eds), *Communication and Change in Developing Countries*, Honolulu, Hawaii: East-West Centre Press.

Gupta, Surendra K. (1985). 'Sociology of Communication', in *Survey of Research in Sociology and Social Anthropology, 1969–79*, Vol. II, Delhi: ICSSR and Satvahana Publications, pp. 151–67.

Hartman, Paul, B.R. Patil and Anita Dighe (1989). *The Mass Media and Village Life*. New Delhi: Sage.

His, Alain (ed.) (1996). *Communication and Multimedia for People: Moving into Social Empowerment over the Information Highway*. Paris: Fondation Léopold Mayer pour le Progrès de l'Homme.

Joshi, P.C. (1989). *Culture, Communication and Social Change*. New Delhi: Vikas.

Melkote, Srinivas R., Peter Shields and Binod Agarwal (eds) (1998). *International Satellite Broadcasting in South Asia*. New York: University Press of America.

Mitra, Ananda (1993). *Television and Popular Culture in India: A Study of the Mahabharat*. New Delhi: Sage.

Nair, Sadananda K. and Shirley A. White (eds) (1996). *Perspectives on Development Communication*. New Delhi: Sage.

Patankar, P. and De Lillian (1973). *Social Communication in Family Planning: A Case Book*. New Delhi: Orient Longman.

Prabha, Krishnan and Anita Dighe (1990). *Affirmation and Denial: Construction of Femininity on Indian Television*. New Delhi: Sage.

Prasad, Nandini (1994). *A Vision Unveiled: Women on Television*. New Delhi: Har Anand Publications.

Raghavan, G.N.S. (1992). *Development and Communication in India*. New Delhi: Gyan Books.

Rao, Lakshmana Y.V. (1966). *Communication and Development: A Study of Two Indian Villages*. Minneapolis: University of Minnesota Press.

Ray, Samirendra N. (1995). *Communication in Rural Development: A Public Policy Perspective*. Shimla: IIAS.

Reddi, Usha (1989). 'Media and Culture in Indian Society: Conflict or Cooperation?', *Media, Culture and Society*, 11 (4): 395–414.

Roy, P. et al. (1969). *Impact of Communication on Rural Development: An Investigation in Costa Rica and India*. Hyderabad: National Institute of Community Development.

Saksena, G. (1996). *Television in India: Changes and Challenges*. New Delhi: Vikas.

Singhal, Arvind and Everette Rogers (1989). *India's Information Revolution*. New Delhi: Sage.

Sondhi, Krishan (1985). *Communication and Values*. Bombay: Somaiya.

Thomas, T.K. (ed.) (1990). *Autonomy for the Electronic Media: A National Debate on the Prasar Bharati Bill, 1989*. New Delhi: Konark Publications.

Tomlinson, J. (1991). *Cultural Imperialism*. London: Printer Publishers.

Vilanilam, J.V. (1993). *Science, Communication and Development*. New Delhi: Sage.

White, Shirley A., K. Sadanandan Nair and Joseph Ascroft (eds) (1996). *Participatory Communication: Working for Change and Development*. New Delhi: Sage.

17

Touristifying Himalayan Sikkim

Is the Commodification of its Nature and Culture Sustainable?

Vibha Arora

The term 'tourism' connotes a deeply sensuous relationship between bodies and landscapes, mediated through travel and motivated by our desire for leisure, pleasure, relaxation, to gain spiritual contentment or to seek a challenge, and above all to take a break from everyday routine. There is nothing new about travel and it has been traditional for us to travel for business and social visits, political, and religious reasons and above all in order to socialize and learn about other cultures and partake of the natural and cultural diversity. However, with improvements in modern means of transportation and communication, economic growth and changes in lifestyle, the numbers of those who travel for pleasure and recreation has become huge and fuelled the tourist sector both locally and globally.[1] With globalization and spread of tourism, the world has been effectively converted into an exhibition for our aesthetic consumption (Urry, 2002).

Tourism is recognized to be one of the fastest growing sectors in the services sector accounting for nearly 11 per cent of the global economy and India is not immune to its revenue generating potential. According to statistics provided by the World Travel and Tourism Council, tourism is poised to grow at a rate of more than 9 per cent in India (cf. Narayanan, 2006: 106). There has been global concern about the impact of tourism on local culture and environment. In December 2001, the United Nations General Assembly officially adopted a Global Code of Ethics for Tourism by passing resolution A/RES/56/212. With international tourism forecast to nearly triple in volume over the next 20 years, members of the World Tourism Organization believe that the Global Code of Ethics for Tourism is needed to help minimize the negative impacts of tourism on the environment and on cultural heritage while maximizing the benefits for residents of tourism destinations.[2] The Code of Ethics includes nine articles outlining the 'rules of the game' for destinations, governments, tour operators, developers, travel agents, workers, and travellers themselves. The tenth article involves the redressal of grievances and marks the first time that a code of this type will have a mechanism for enforcement. According to Article 4 of this code, a tourist is an integral user of the cultural heritage of mankind and contributor to its enhancement.[3]

Tourism is an image-rich, experience-based, social-commercial undertaking, evocatively aided by technologies of transportation, communication, and representation to distribute narratable experiences.[4] Images, impressions, representations, and dissemination of these in mass media (print, TV, internet) and in promotional material circulated by government and private developers invite and propel travel. These play a critical role in selection of a tourist destination. We cannot reduce tourism to a mere commercial activity, since it involves an ideological framing of history, the landscape, culture, and social experiences. The tourist gaze is constructed and sustained by a variety of non-tourist practices, such as TV, literature, magazines, and videos (Urry, 2002: 3). A tourist gaze is constructed through the signs collected and rejected and range from a romantic gaze (semi-spiritual relationship of affinity) to a referential gaze (linking names and places to institutional roles) and the anthropological gaze involving ethnographic impressions.

Touristic images emerge and evolve as hybrid forms, fusions of historical, local, and visitor imagery (Adams, 2004: 129). Cultural media play a critical role in cultivating an imagination about a place and disseminating this representation to others who in turn visit places in turn expecting representations to be realized as experiences. In this cycle, representations and realities merge and recreate places. This is an important component of the playfulness of places! Yogendra Singh is highly critical of the transformation of culture into a commodity under market capitalism and with globalization, and he underscores the shift from content to 'packaging' of culture (2000: 34). Very often heritage is mobilized and traditions are invented to stage spectacles and to seduce tourists. The historic past and living culture (un)knowingly become commodities with the locals actively performing for expectant tourists. The transformation of cultural ideas, objects, and performances into commodities for mass consumption can undermine local and smaller cultural identities (Singh, 2000: 35). Scholars argue that due to tourism, local culture is altered and often made meaningless to people (Greenwood, 1989). Singh appreciates the commercial potential of exploiting cultural goods (2000: 94), but simultaneously warns us against possibilities of the decontextualization and the displacement of meanings and values of cultural objects (2000: 35).

In many ways, tradition and modernity are creatively conjoined as places remake, recreate, and modify history, memory, and geography to cater to desires and interests of national and international tourists. To what extent are locals participating in this process of commodification of their culture and nature in Sikkim? Is it a mere top-down activity propelled by global capitalism or can there equally be a local and regional economic strategy to profitably use the revenue-generating potential of leisure culture? *Sikkim: The People's Vision* (Lahiri et al., 2001: 18) underscores the revenue potential of tourism for propelling growth in this resource-poor Himalayan state. Tourism has been identified as the engine of Sikkim's human development, economic growth, employment generation and poverty alleviation. The local voices in Sikkim are divided while the state government is proactively promoting nature and cultural tourism as part of its development strategy. This forms the central concern of this paper.

The growth of travel and tourism industry has been complemented by growth of 'tourist reflexivity'.[5] Places are not simply encountered, but are inextricably intertwined in complex performances involving residents/hosts and guests/pilgrims/tourists. Culture is not static and cultural forms and cultural goods continually evolve, enter, and exit from circulation in this interactive context of native-tourist encounter.[6] In their introduction to *Tourism Mobilities*, the editors Sheller and Urry emphasize that places are performed and are always in play and therefore 'on the move', they are constantly being made and remade by the mobilities of the tourists and workers. I will add here the vision and plans engendered and implemented by government agencies. Not only is tourism a form of mobility (pleasure of travel and urge to explore other environments) but many different kinds of mobilities of objects and people inform and shape tourism, make and unmake destinations, efface and recreate performances, memories and histories, not only realities but also realize our fantasies (Sheller and Urry, 2004: 1). Thus places to play (opposite of work and residence) are also places in play (fluid, in the making). Tourism is transforming the materiality of many 'real' places.

Promotional images bedazzle tourists but the tourist is certainly not a cultural dope who is gazing and glancing; contrarily they actively constitute any tourist locale. Tourists are enacting and inscribing places with stories – they are not mere spectators 'they step into the landscape picture and engage bodily sensuously, and expressively with their materiality' (MacCannell, 1999: 422). Simon Coleman and Mike Craig (2002: 9) assert in their Introduction, 'we see tourists fashioning stories about their travels – not in an academic fashion, but through the collection, editing, sorting of photographs, travel diaries, and memorabilia.' The proliferation of blogs available on the internet by travellers and tourists visiting Sikkim is a reflection of their engagement.[7] Nonetheless, it is the differing responses of various stakeholders living in Sikkim that form the core of this paper and this is what I will discuss at length here.

Sustainable Development and Cultural Continuity through Tourism

The tremendous growth of tourism in north-east India and Sikkim in particular are a consequence of the practical possibilities afforded by modern infrastructural development in transport and communications, technological innovations in the tourism and hospitality industry, economic growth after the marketization of the economy and its integration with the world market, changes in people's consumption patterns and lifestyles, which complement a heightened desire of a global citizen yearning to experience specificity and cultural distinctiveness. The Himalayan state of Sikkim lies in the shadow of Mt Kanchenjunga (28,216 feet), the third highest mountain of the world in north-east India. The towering majestic presence of Mt Kanchenjunga with its snow-capped peaks dominates the land and the imagination of the people of Sikkim and the tourists that come here. For the indigenous Lepchas and Bhutias of Sikkim, Mt Kanchenjunga is not a mere mountain, since it is regarded the residence of their guardian deity. This mountain is venerated in all prayers and especially worshipped annually in the masked dances performed on *dpang lha-gsol*, which during the monarchic rule of the Namgyal dynasty was celebrated as the national day of the kingdom. Recently many rituals and cultural performances that had been discontinued due to their nationalist associations have been revived and are being performed at a grander scale for attracting tourists.

Ideas about tourism can and do influence local politics, flavour discussions of ethnic identity, and channel local actions (Adams, 2004: 118). Demographically, nearly three-quarters of Sikkim's population is classified as being Hindu and Nepali with around twenty per cent being Buddhist. However, most tourist brochures and picture postcards incisively frame Sikkim as a Buddhist landscape by selectively framing Buddhist mantras, sacred texts, figures, murals, religious sites, and rituals. The commercial logic operating here is that the Buddhist heritage of Sikkim is eminently marketable and a global draw.

Even the official website of Sikkim has a separate section termed 'Buddhist circuit' wherein the major places and events connected with Padmasambhava (a reincarnate of Lord Buddha), Buddhist monasteries, and festivals celebrated by the main Buddhist communities of Sikkim are listed. The website declares that Buddhism continues to flourish in contemporary Sikkim in its 200 monasteries and *lha-khang* (temples in Tibetan language) and in the minds of the locals. It is visibly evident in the numerous stupas, fluttering prayer flags, the images and symbols of Buddhism that dot its landscape.[8] This logic explains the government of Sikkim's decision to construct religious sites and icons such as the 135 feet tall statue of Padmasambhava at Samdruptse in South Sikkim (inaugurated in 2005); the photograph of this statue has become one of the best selling picture postcards! Do the ethnically Nepali groups feel culturally marginalized by this representation? Yes, they do and many recent government brochures have started highlighting aspects of Nepali culture that they feel may attract the tourists. The funding of a 108 feet tall statue of Lord Shiva in 2006,[9] and the construction of religious centres at Solophok in South Sikkim and Indrakeel Dham in East Sikkim in 2005–07 are conscious endeavours in responding to the tourist influx and promoting Buddhist and Hindu pilgrimage tourism in Sikkim. As agencies and tourist operators shared, Nepali culture is not as marketable and as culturally authentic in Sikkim where they are still perceived as migrants. Most tourists prefer visiting Nepal to sample Nepali culture rather than experience it in Sikkim.

The Sikkim government vision documents harp on tourism as a development strategy and a potential that needs to be realized (Lama, 2001; PC, 2008: 28). There is great scope of promoting employment through tourism which is a human resource intense activity (Lahiri et al., 2001: 78). Developer planners emphasize the multiplier effect of tourism on an economy (PC, 2008: 145–46). Planners argue that tourism can facilitate and offset regional imbalances between different districts in so far as a sound environmental impact analysis guides the development of necessary physical infrastructure and services (information booths, hotels and resorts, good roads, rapid transportation facilities, water availability, maintenance of tourist attractions, the opening of restaurants offering gourmet and local cuisine, shopping complexes, and entertainment centres, guided tours and development of trekking trails) by the government and private agencies (Lahiri et al., 2001: 78–79).

In colourfully illustrated 'carefully' scripted pages of tourist brochures, booklets and books, and in periodically staged performances at various locales, the commercialization of nature and culture and the development transition of Sikkim is much evident. The debate on balancing quality tourism with quantity of visitors has somewhat been restricted to few policy circles such as of INTACH and those involved in the departments of culture. Tourism in Sikkim can be classified into three kinds of experiences: cultural tourism (Buddhist pilgrimage centres and monasteries, cultural festivals, scenic rural settings); nature tourism (sanctuaries, scenic Himalayas vistas, beautiful lakes and springs, forested areas); and adventure tourism (boating, river rafting, mountain climbing, rock climbing, mountain biking, paragliding, yak safari, mountaineering, hill trekking, nature trails, outdoor camping).

Nature and cultural tourism involves a decision of what to promote or commodify, and what to preserve as sacred (thereby not open to tourism) and keep sacrosanct or what to construct and reconstruct.[10] Conservation of nature and preservation of culture are important, and some caution is needed against sacrificing both at the altar of revenue-generating tourism. Synergies have to be established between them in order to have sustainable nature and cultural tourism in India's north-eastern region (Mishra, 2006: iii-vii). There are divided voices within the government and much confusion on how to effectively integrate development priorities with cultural sustenance.

Both planners and those whose livelihood are integrally tied with tourism are making varied efforts to evolve a unique selling point and formulate a brand identity for Sikkim. Elsewhere I have already discussed the cultural representation of Sikkim as a Shangri-la for global consumption in mass media (Arora, 2009), while government policies of hydropower development are perceived as threats to culture and heritage of the indigenous communities (Arora, 2010). The local Sikkimese may or may not subscribe to the idea of Sikkim being a Shangri-la but some sections of Sikkim *do* make an effort to cater to this tourist imagination *by* appropriating Sikkim's Tibetan Buddhist heritage and cultural history. The government of Sikkim on its part is trying to showcase the beauty of its landscape and its ethnic diversity by formulating a Sikkim Tourism Calendar.[11]

The rich natural heritage and the question of preserving the living cultural traditions of the diverse communities which live here attract tourists while concurrently they are perceived as necessary costs that may have to be sacrificed in efforts to modernize and develop. If we glance at figures of tourism in Sikkim, they are not as impressive or comparable to those available for other parts of India. One of the biggest reasons lies in the time taken to travel to Sikkim and poor connectivity by rail, roads, and air. The nearest railheads are Siliguri and New Jalpaiguri (about 110–25 kms away) and the closest airport is Bagadogra (about 124 kms away from Gangtok) with the roads connecting them with Sikkim being frequently blocked by landslides,[12] and more recently by the agitating activists of the Gorkhaland movement. Sikkim still lacks world-class infrastructure in facilities, accommodation, and services and there has been insufficient planning and marketing of Sikkim as a tourist destination. Partly these are accounted by poor leadership and ineffective public-private partnership which make investments in construction of good hotels and other infrastructure very difficult and extremely bureaucratic. There is a lack of trained human resources for significant growth in this industry.

According to government sources (PC, 2008: 149), there has not been much increase in volume of domestic and international tourists between 1997 and 2002 even though permit regulations were altered making it easier to travel to Sikkim. In 1997 only about 8,812 foreign tourists visited Sikkim while approximately 140,821 Indians travelled to Sikkim as tourists. In 2002, the statistics recorded are 7,726 for foreigners and 136,506 for domestic tourists. The website of Sikkim Tourism mentions that number of foreign visitors in 2003 were about 11,966 but increased to 23,000 in 2008. In contrast domestic tourists increased to 500,000 persons in 2008.[13] All foreigners are required to obtain Inner Line Permits (ILP) prior to entry into Sikkim, which cannot be extended here beyond 30 days and in many parts they can only visit as members of a group and through a registered tourist agency. There are many who even contest that these figures point towards anomalies in recording of statistics, but I will sidestep these issues here and focus broadly on the process and trajectory of capturing and 'touristifying' Sikkim.

The 'official' traveller's companion circulated by the Government of Sikkim invites readers to explore and experience Himalayan Sikkim by declaring it to be a '*Land of Peace and Tranquility*'. The cover-jacket of the traveller's companion *Sikkim: Small and Beautiful* authored by Alok K. Shrivastava[14] in 2006 declares, 'Holy, holistic and hospitality is the mantra and way of living of the Sikkimese. One comes to this blessed land as a guest and parts as a friend forever.' A scenic landscape of blue skies, snow-capped mountains, conifer trees, and scrub forests foreground this epithet and the author declares Sikkim to be a new destination of the current millennium (Shrivastava, 2006: 7). The opening paragraph states, 'nestled in the lap of the Himalayas, bounded by some of the highest mountain peaks, amidst spectacular terrain, pristine lakes, luxuriant forests, roaring rivers and gentle streams, Sikkim is a veritable paradise and a destination for all seasons (ibid.).' The naturally rich topography is evident in the varying altitude (440 to 8,540 metres), the presence of 21 glaciers, 28 mountain peaks, 104 rivers and streams, and 227 wetlands and lakes in a small area of 7,096 sq kms. A hilly terrain having 46 per cent of its area under diverse types of forests, Sikkim houses a spectacular diversity of flora and fauna; it is a biodiversity hotspot.

This book begins by narrating a brief history of kingdom of Sikkim, mentioning the turning points of its history and the process of its integration into India in 1975. Then there is a brief description of its ethnic population, the main places of worship (monasteries, temples, cultural festivals), cultural aspects such as the distinctive music, dance, cuisine, handicrafts of the different communities, the natural landscapes (lakes, mountains, waterfalls) with their rich flora and fauna (4,500 species of flowering plants and 362 species of ferns, 552 species of birds, 690 species of butterflies and moths, 150 species of mammals, 33 species of reptiles and so on) that can enthral any tourist. One of the advertising points of this narrative is peace and the negligible crime rate of this state! The ethnic diversity of Sikkim, the many Buddhist monasteries and sacred sites, cultural festivals that are celebrated in this land are cited as a great tourist attraction. Pictorially well-illustrated, this book is factually incorrect in many places[15] and not as well-written as another glossy book entitled *Sikkim: The Land of Mystique* guidebook that was produced by Eicher Good Earth Publication with the support of Sikkim Tourism and the Department of Tourism, Government of India in 2002. As a tourist destination, Sikkim emerges as a playful destination and a place in play.[16]

The year 2010 was declared as the year of tourism by the Sikkim government and a global destination of eco-tourism. The government is furthering private initiative and has realized that it needs to have sustainable and responsible tourism and minimize the ecological footprints of tourism by strictly regulating exposure and resource consumption by travellers.[17] A policy document entitled *Tourism Touches Everyone* was also circulated on the official website of Sikkim.[18] It is too early to comment if government policies of responsible tourism in Sikkim will bear fruit and prevent cultural dislocation.

How is tourism impacting Sikkim's natural and religious heritage? There are very few critical voices who are questioning this spectacular transition of Sikkim into a hub of tourism and tourism as a development necessity for infrastructural growth and generating critical employment and revenue. I have documented a mixed experience and local people have differing positions depending on their community, the how, where, and when aspects of their interaction with tourists. Sections with vested commercial interests imagine Sikkim in a particular manner. For those whose livelihood is critically dependent on tourists, tourism is a necessity and customer satisfaction is paramount. Picard (1995) has documented how tourist-oriented images and representations have been incorporated into Balinese conceptions of themselves. I have documented a similar process in Himalayan Sikkim.

For others who need to compete with tourists higher paying economic power, the rising prices of transport, local accommodation, and cultural items are profoundly altering their everyday life. Many Sikkimese are unhappy at the rapid unchecked commercialization of their landscape with national and international tourism, as this has widened income disparities along certain tourist routes and led to uneven regional development. Many Sikkimese drew my attention to traffic jams, landslides that regularly block roads, crop failure, the lack of employment opportunities, endemic corruption and negligible human rights, the conflict over natural resources especially the changing environmental landscape with the rapid disappearance of forests that contradict any imaginations of a Himalayan paradise.

Earnings from cultural tourism can and do revive local culture, reinvent traditions, reinstate cultural performances thereby strengthening local cultures and affirming identities (Shepherd, 2002). Any development achieved or spurred with tourism revenue and revival of cultural traditions is at a cost. Locals start performing for a culturally consuming (tourist) audience, which erodes 'authentic' traditions and distorts cultural representations. This erosion of cultural form is not unique to Sikkim, but has been widely reported (Greenwood, 1989: 173–78; Shepherd, 2002: 187). Yogendra Singh's analysis in *Cultural Change in India* overlooks the dialogic process that while culture is consumed and produced as a commodity, it is simultaneously sustained and preserved from extinction. His analysis overlooks those situations where the vanishing traditions and indigenous culture are given a fresh lease and recreated while nature is conserved because of tourism and critical employment and economic resources are directly and indirectly generated with tourism such as the revival of traditional crafts that are often purchased as souvenirs. In their present reinvented cultural form, many ethnic-nationalist rituals of kingdom of Sikkim such as *dpang lha gsol* are currently being performed as religious festivals for locals and tourists. Yes, we need to nurture local culture, while recognizing that this local culture is an evolving one and notions of authenticity are continually changing. Some aspects of culture get greater recognition and acceptability over others while others get elided and displaced; this is a selective process while everything about 'tradition' is not good either.

Tourism is increasingly becoming the catalyst for this evolutionary selection and the framing of local culture in Himalayan Sikkim. The Tibetanization of Sikkim is neither simplistic nor impervious to a corollary process of macdonalidization of culture (see Ritzer, 2000) or what I term the *samosization* of Sikkim's landscape. In my recent fieldwork in Sikkim in 2006–07, many people were vociferously voicing reservations. Some of them had commented that food could become an arena for contention:

> as more and more Indian tourists come to Sikkim henceforth our beef-eating habits are getting derided and restaurants are dropping beef and pork from their menus so as not to offend other Indian especially upper caste Hindu sensibilities. Why should I be uncomfortable eating beef and pork *momos* in my homeland? Why is the *samosa* replacing *momos* and *thukpa* (dumplings in soup) in the menu?

While the *samosa* has gained popularity in Sikkim and Darjeeling, (vegetable, chicken, beef and pork) *momos* have evolved into a popular, widely consumed snack in Delhi. These are definite cultural encounters and singling one trope of discourse would be erroneous; the dominance of a trope among circulating discourses indicates the negotiations over imaginations and tourist expectations.

Tourism can make cultural diversity and mainstream local cultural traditions more acceptable by reducing distance between them and what is nationally mainstreamed, this is particularly evident for India's north-east. It is now a common place to eat dumplings and *momos*, wear colourful shawls and use the carpets manufactured in north-east India, and listen to Nepali rock today after Prakash Tamang became an Indian idol, and all this is because of tourism and mass media.

I agree that tradition is a constructed past and can never constitute the ultimate benchmark of 'authenticity', however if the local people are concerned about distortions seeping in, then I am inclined to respect their views. For those who are concerned about vanishing cultural traditions, insensitive dilution and commercialization of culture to suit potential tourist tastes, mass tourism is not desirable. The most cited observation was, although tourism is good for Sikkim's economy and sometimes culture since many ritual practices that had been discontinued earlier have been revived as spectacles and performances for tourist packages, nonetheless insensitive cultural tourism has violated and undermined the spiritual and religious character of many events, festivals, sometimes even transformed places while promoting construction of new sacred sites and invention of traditions. Revenue earnings from tourism are not sufficient to level out local resentment at the spectacular proliferation and 'adulteration' of religious dances and sombre rituals and their transformation into staged festivities or the unchecked commodification of religious artefacts.

Planning and heritage preservation become critical here. As locales and sites enter the tourist imagination, the circulating traffic of consumptive goods (mineral water, soft drinks, food), people (locals employed, immigrant casual labour, and the visiting tourists), and ideas (cultural exchanges) need to be regulated and managed. Prayer-flags, prayer-wheels, religious paintings (*Thang-ka* in the Tibetan language) of Buddha and other Gods of the Buddhist pantheon, brass and clay figurines of the Buddha, and the ubiquitous silk scarves (*ka-btags* in the Tibetan language) are stacked by nearly all souvenir shops and constitute common tourist souvenir purchases. As a local explained:

> I am troubled by this recent transformation of our Buddhist prayer-flags into a decorative consumptive tourist souvenir. We have henceforth convinced and induced many of these local souvenir shops into giving a complementary one-page handout explaining the religious meaning and significance of these prayer-flags. However, this cannot ensure and enforce religious respect for our religious artefacts.

Have any decisions about public and private sanctity been made in Sikkim? During many discussions, both lamas and laity belonging to diverse ethnic groups communicated the urgency of establishing some boundaries, as the sanctity of Sikkim, a *gnas* (pilgrimage centre in the Tibetan language) could not be undermined or compromised at any cost. Tourists visiting sacred places including monasteries are strictly instructed to remove their shoes, not take any pictures, not to speak loudly, smoke and drink, urinate or engage in other body functions and even disturb the vegetation. Sometimes these instructions are posted on signboards while in other places the tourist guide is expected to repeat them to the visitors. The violation of these injunctions deeply disturb all equally. During fieldwork in the last six years, I have noted that violators of photographic censorship were deprived of their camera films, transgressors capturing wildlife and felling trees were dealt with severely and fined, although any serious acts of vandalism have not occurred as yet.

Some critical voices are questioning this spectacular transition of Sikkim into a tourist locale and tourism as a development necessity. Are there no other possible routes to development available for the people of Sikkim? The increase in air and noise pollution, the garbage, the environmental stress on natural habitats, the construction of multi-storeyed buildings as hotels and accommodation for tourists, and development of other necessary facilities for catering to tourists are being disproved of by many locals especially those based at Gangtok and Pelling. Some concerned citizens are pointing towards the need to adopt a trajectory followed by Bhutan's restricted/elite tourism that is not undermining its authentic Buddhist culture and natural heritage while sustaining it by high-priced quality tourism. The numbers of visitors are quite restricted in Bhutan, and many are arguing on a similar need for Sikkim.

Some recognition of critical stance towards tourism has been documented in recent government reports that mention the adverse impact of tourist traffic on the environment, and *now* these stress that mass-based tourism would not be feasible for Sikkim. Hence, official discourse is now pointing towards eco-tourism, village-based tourism, and adventure tourism that transform the government into facilitator while strongly integrating local communities in managing tourism and making them into strategic partners (PC, 2008: 150).

Eco-tourism and eco-tourists are routinely portrayed as benign – environmentally, culturally and economically (West and Carrier, 2004). Eco-tourists appreciate and protect nature and local communities benefit from this interaction. This explains why eco-tourism has become the cornerstone of Sikkim's official policy to earn revenue and conserve the natural and associated cultural landscapes. For instance, Sikkim Ecotourism and Conservation Federation, has identified various Himalayan treks that offer a tourist a rich exposure to serene nature and the ethnic diversity of Sikkim. Some admitted that trainings on eco-tourism are being organized and cultural conservation and nature preservation would be relevant in that context. Finally, eco-tourism works through partnership with local people, alleviates poverty, creates new skills and promotes local handicrafts, promotes conservation, and ensures that local communities are the ultimate beneficiaries. This explains why NGOs and local communities are being motivated to benefit and adopt village tourism and eco-cultural tourism[19] as part of their development strategies and without undue damage to ecology and loss of culture. The Mountain Institute has also been involved in developing and facilitating eco-tourism in western and northern districts of Sikkim.[20]

Eco-tourism and village/rural tourism can preserve rural culture, heritage, generate employment and economically develop the hills and valleys without causing undue pressure on the ecosystem and environment. This is precisely why home-stays are being developed as an alternative source of income and travellers are offered a chance to sample Himalayan Sikkim without the commercialization of culture and nature. Some of the villages of Sikkim like Kewzing, Kabi, Hee-Bermoik, Yoksum, Lachen, Lunchok, Tinchim, Damthang, Rong, Darap and others in Dzongu have developed home-stay facilities to effectively attract tourists to their natural scenic beauty, organize trek and take natural walks, facilitate visits to heritage sites, and offer a non-commercialized flavour of the local culture. It is too early to say how far these experiments will be sustainable and predict their impact.

Conclusion

The subjugation of local culture to the demands of tourism industry and the homogenization of local cultures with mass consumerism are not as inevitable as portended. Tourism can engender change and mutual respect between different groups and not merely obliterate local and regional cultures. Inter-cultural dialogue rather than objectification of culture of the indigenous people are critical for Sikkim's effective integration into the global tourist economy and sustaining its local culture. Both globalization and tourism can refashion and invigorate local and regional cultures, and more so when they get conjoined in cultural tourism. This is precisely why eco-tourism and pilgrimage tourism are being perceived as the growth engines for Sikkim's modernization and human development. Government policies are recognizing that responsible eco-tourism and cultural tourism can integrate sustainability with economic development in Himalayan Sikkim and in north-east India. It is heartening to note that the Sikkim government is increasingly moving away from the mass-tourism model after realizing the adverse consequences on the environment and the indigenous culture, and is learning from other locales whose economies are heavily dependent on tourism.

I duly acknowledge here that eco-cultural tourism can empower local communities, counter cultural dislocation, and give them a strong mechanism to control and shape their social futures. This does necessitate cooperation between local people, NGOs, government departments, industry, the managers of tourist and other cultural facilities, and other 'specialists' (such as priests, lamas, historians, anthropologists and ecologists). Sustainable tourism (especially eco-cultural tourism) requires a multi-stakeholder approach that integrates different sections of the economy and members of diverse groups living in a multi-ethnic setting and elicits high levels of community participation, which unfortunately is not evident in contemporary Sikkim. Even though the government has identified these issues and processes in theory and documented them on paper, yet what we can see are interesting 'isolated' experiments in some villages of Sikkim. It is too early to say whether these social experiments will provide us with the necessary solutions to Sikkim's under-development and preserve its fragile cultural and natural heritage.

Acknowledgements

Fieldwork for this paper was done in 2001, 2005, and 2006–07. I benefited from long discussions with numerous lamas based at Gangtok and the premier monasteries of Sikkim, owners of various tourist agencies, and especially thank

Tashi Densapa (who was earlier the Secretary of Tourism and now is the Director of Namgyal Institute of Tibetology) and Ms Nima Ithenpa of the Department of Tourism for sharing their insights and experiences. The usual disclaimers apply.

Notes

1. As Singh (2000: 237) contends, the dichotomy that we need to concentrate is not of leisure and work, but as one between 'leisure as consumerism' and 'leisure as communication' that promotes participatory socializing and expression.
2. Discussion about these is evident in the World Tourist Organization (WTO) website. http://www.unwto.org/code_ethics/eng/global.htm. The full text is available at http://www.unwto.org/code_ethics/pdf/languages/Codigo%20 Etico%20Ing.pdf accessed on 20 May 2007.
3. The UNWTO Resolution A/RES/506(XVI) adopted at Dakar, Senegal in December 2005, outlines the responsibilities of a responsible tourist and traveller. During my interviews in Delhi and Sikkim, both the tourist agencies and government officials did not display much knowledge about the code of ethics.
4. In a global market where tourists have a wide choice, both the government and the travel and tourism industry need to make a distinctive pitch.
5. Sheller and Urry (2004: 3) refer to the institutional process by which networks systematically monitor, identify, evaluate the actual locales and augment their tourist potential, identify, modify, and recreate elements of culture, geography, and heritage that can be globally disseminated as semiotic content.
6. The Incredible India campaign highlights this cogently.
7. This cannot be discussed at length here due to space constraints.
8. See http://sikkimtourism.travel/webforms/general/sikkimataglance/Buddhism_Sikkim.htm accessed on 3 March 2011.
9. The construction of Hindu pilgrimage sites is necessitated by the predominantly Hindu profile of both other Indians and the numerically preponderant Nepali Hindus residing in Sikkim.
10. Nature and culture are social constructions and these differ from place to place. However, it is not possible to expand on the generic conceptions of nature and culture that tourism is constructing and perpetuating here.
11. See http://sikkimtourism.travel/webforms/general/pdf/sikkim_tourism_calendar.pdf accessed on 3 March 2011.
12. The Pakyong airport in east Sikkim is still under construction.
13. See http://sikkimtourism.travel/webforms/general/pdf/sikkim_tourism_policy_10.pdf accessed on 3 March 2011.
14. He was then the Commissioner and Secretary, Department of Tourism, Government of Sikkim.
15. For instance, he states that the blood-brotherhood treaty was enacted in 1641 (Shrivastava, 2006: 13), which is not the case. In another place he writes, non-Lepchas are barred from settling in Dzongu (ibid.: 18), which is again

incorrect since even other Lepchas of Sikkim are barred from settling in Dzongu. The sweeping 'un-sociological' generalizations given here about various ethnic communities are discomfiting (ibid.: 17–20).

16. Arora (2009) focuses on the representation of Sikkim in tourist brochures.
17. See http://sikkimtourism.travel/webforms/general/pdf/sikkim_tourism_policy_10.pdf accessed on 3 March 2011.
18. Ibid.
19. Here ecological and cultural aspects of a landscape are combined to create a site for tourists.
20. Personal communications and information circulated on the Mountain Institute website.

References

Adams, K.M. (2004). 'The Genesis of Touristic Imagery: Politics and Poetics in the Creation of a Remote Indonesian Island Destination', *Tourist Studies*, 4 (2): 115–35.

Arora, V. (2009). 'Framing the Image of Sikkim', *Visual Studies*, 24 (1): 54–64.

—— (2010). 'Walking the 'Shangri-la' Sikkim Trail', in Debal K. Singha Roy (ed.), *Globalization, Marginalization, and the Marginalized: The Emerging Context*. Delhi: Manohar.

Coleman, S. and M. Craig (2002). 'Grounded Tourists, Travelling Theory', in Coleman and Craig (eds), *Tourism: Between Place and Performance*. New York: Berghahn.

Greenwood, D. (1989). 'Culture by the Pound: An Anthropological Perspective on Tourism as Cultural Commoditization', in V. Smith (ed.), *Hosts and Guests: The Anthropology of Tourism*. Philadelphia: University of Pennsylvania.

Lahiri, A. et al. (2001). *Sikkim: The People's Vision*. New Delhi: Indus Publishing Company and Gangtok: Government of Sikkim.

Lama, M.P. (2001). *Sikkim: Human Development Report 2001*. Delhi: Social Science Press and Gangtok: Government of Sikkim.

MacCannell, D. 1999 (1976). *The Tourist: A New Theory of Leisure Class*. Berkeley: University of California Press.

Mishra, S.K. (2006). 'Welcome Address', in R. Tandon (ed.), *Cultural Tourism and the Crafts and Textiles of the North-east*. Delhi: INTACH.

Narayanan, M. (2006). 'Building up Infrastructure for Tourism', in R. Tandon (ed.), *Cultural Tourism and the Crafts and Textiles of the North-east*. Delhi: INTACH.

PC (2008). *Sikkim Development Report*. Delhi: Academic Foundation and Planning Commission, Government of India.

Picard, M. (1995). 'Cultural Heritage and Tourist Capital: Cultural Tourism in Bali', in M.F. Lanfant, J.B. Allcock and E. Bruner (eds), *International Tourism: Identity and Change*. London: Sage.

Ritzer, G. (2000). *The McDonaldization of Society: An Investigation into the Changing Character of Contemporary Social Life*. Thousand Oaks, CA: Pine Forge Press.

Selwyn, T. (ed.) (1996). *The Tourist Image: Myths and Myth Making in Tourism*. London: Wiley.

Sheller, Mimi and John Urry (eds) (2004). *Tourism Mobilities: Places to Play, Places in Play*. London and New York: Routledge.

Shepherd, R. (2002). 'Commodification, Culture and Tourism', *Tourist Studies*, 4 (2): 183–201.

Shrivastava, A.K. (2006). *Sikkim: Small and Beautiful*. Gangtok: Government of Sikkim.

Singh, Yogendra (2000). *Culture Change in India: Identity and Globalization*. Jaipur: Rawat Publications.

Urry, J. (2002). *The Tourist Gaze: Leisure and Travel in Contemporary Societies*. London: Sage.

Wallace, G. and A. Russell (2004). 'Eco-cultural Tourism as a Means for the Sustainable Development of Culturally Marginal and Environmentally Sensitive Regions', *Tourist Studies*, 4 (3): 235–54.

West, P. and J. Carrier (2004). 'Ecotourism and Authenticity', *Current Anthropology*, 45 (4): 483–98.

18

Tourism in the Era of Globalization

Neha Kala

Globalization, thes buzzword of the 1990s, continues to be the dominant theme in almost all the contemporary discourses. Though globalization is a centuries old phenomenon its pace has dramatically accelerated in last few decades. As an academic concept it gained currency only in the late 80s. This most frequently employed term conjures up diverse connotations, associations and repercussions. Having its origin in economics, it was widely used in the context of world economies for long but it was soon recognized that it has severe impacts on virtually all dimensions of society. Smeral (1998) aptly contends that globalization is an umbrella word covering various trends in political, sociological, environmental and economic worlds. This never-ending process 'detaches economic life from the constraints of geography – physical, cultural and political' (Wood, 2000). As the world shifts towards a global economy, borders are becoming increasingly difficult to define. Scholars assert that globalization goes beyond the idea of permeating boundaries between nations but also crosses the traditional borders of time, space, scope, geography, functions, thought and cultural assumptions (Ashkenas et al., 1995, Boudreau et al., 1998). Robertson (1992) states that globalization as a concept refers both to the compression of the world and the intensification of consciousness of the world as a whole. Characterized by economic liberalization, privatization and proliferation of new information and communication technologies, this process of converting universe into a 'global village' covers a wide range of economic, political and cultural trends.

Globalization is a social construct (Rees, 2000) that is shifting the way we view the world – from one with multiple economies and diverse societies to a 'one-world' economy and homogenized society. It is a constitutive feature of the modern world, and modern history includes many examples of globalization (Giddens, 1990). Nonetheless, some of its antecedents can be traced in the intellectual discourses of 19th and 20th century scholars. Karl Marx (1979), a prominent social thinker viewed territorial compression as a consequence of capitalist production which drove the bourgeoisie to 'settle everywhere, and establish connections everywhere'. Industrialization and its associated technologies paved way for 'intercourse in every direction and interdependence of nations' resulting in annihilation of space. American literary figure Henry Adams diagnosed the existence of a 'law of acceleration,' as the main source behind the rapidly changing spatial and temporal contours of human activity. In order to have proper understanding of modern society, Adams stressed on giving a central place to seemingly irrepressible acceleration of basic technological and social processes in social and historical analysis (Adams, 1931). In his analysis of new media technologies in 1960s, the Canadian cultural critic Marshall McLuhan discussed the theme of a technologically based 'global village', generated by social 'acceleration at all levels of human organization' (McLuhan, 1964). But, it was probably the German philosopher Martin Heidegger who accurately prophesied that new communication and information technologies would soon spawn novel possibilities for dramatically extending the scope of *virtual reality*. Heidegger not only described the 'abolition of distance' as a constitutive feature of our contemporary condition, but he also linked recent shifts in spatial experience to no less fundamental alterations in the temporality of human activity: 'All distances in time and space are shrinking. Man now reaches overnight, by places, places which formerly took weeks and months of travel' (Heidegger, 1971). Although sharp differences continue to separate participants in the ongoing debate, most contemporary social theorists endorse the view that globalization refers to fundamental changes in the spatial and temporal contours of social existence. Globalization has taken a particularly intense form in recent decades, as innovations in communication, transportation, and information technologies (for example, computerization) have generated stunning new possibilities for simultaneity and instantaneousness (Harvey, 1989). As a consequence, globalization deserves to be recognized as a key idea in the context to understanding social change in the human societies in the contemporary times (Giddens, 1990; Waters, 1995).

In recent times the world has made significant progress over the immediate past century in the quality of life of its inhabitants. Further exploration for greater mental and physical satisfaction is, undoubtedly, the next logical search. Tourism provides in ample quantity, both these stimulations of the soul and senses to the human societies in the contemporary times (ibid.). With the ongoing continuous improvement in the quality of living standard, income as well as leisure, the quest for tourism is on the increase. According to Cohen (1974), tourism as a cultural phenomenon becomes possible only when man develops a generalized interest in things beyond his particular habitat, when contact and appreciation and enjoyment of strangeness and novelty are valued for their own sake. So long as man remains largely ignorant of the existence of other societies, other cultures, he regards his own small world as the cosmos. Primitive and traditional man used to leave his habitat only when forced to do so by extreme circumstances, whereas modern man is more loosely attached to his environment, much more willing to change it, especially temporarily and is remarkably able to adapt to new environments. The new information and communication technologies have made qualitative difference in the nature and pace of human interaction across the world as well as in their own cultural zones and localities. Nothing remains impervious. Media and computer technology are but one agent of this trend as they provide instant news and information to any corner of the globe. Similarly, advances in transportation networks contribute by providing access to destinations around the world with hardly more than a day's journey. A tangible manifestation of this increase in global accessibility and interconnectedness is the tourism industry. Tourism has been a central dimension of globalization, and it offers a useful lens on many key issues pertaining to development, identity, culture, commoditization, authenticity and ownership, inequality, environmental sustainability, and more. Before discussing these issues, it is important to have a better understanding of the relationship between globalization and tourism.

Tourism and Globalization: An Interface

Today, the desire to travel and to be a tourist is practically universal, and touristic practices pervade many areas of social life. However, leisure time accompanied by surplus income is essential in order to produce a tourist. Even as recently as the early 19th century only the aristocracy could afford the necessary expenditure in money and time. Technological achievements of the past two centuries, increasingly effective means of communication and transportation and the creation and growth of a moneyed middle class in many societies made traveling for pleasure a possibility for a large number of people. Globalization further accelerated the trend. Tourism and globalization share a complex relationship. Tourism, indeed, is a global trend. At the same time, it is part of the globalization process also. Peter Keller, the President of Association of Scientific Experts in Tourism exclaimed in his speech on September 1996 that 'globalization was changing the very nature of international tourism, with new destinations, and other forces which would make tourism the most important economic sector on a world scale' (Ryan, 1997). Scholars identify four major factors responsible for globalization of tourism:

(a) Geographical – many places on globe have become easily accessible than ever before.
(b) Cultural – the convergence of world tastes, product preferences and life styles.
(c) Commercial – internationally recognizable business practices.
(d) Economic – economic convergence resulting in lower air fares, favourable exchange rates, etc.

While tourism is sometimes the outcome of the globalization movement, the interaction between tourists and hosts, the inflow of capital and technology, caused by development of tourism and the initiatives for developing tourism transform it into a catalyst for the process of communication and globalization. Tourism, a phenomenon based on travel patterns of people, technology and cultural values, is a major mechanism in effecting the globalization process. On one hand, tourism is promoted by globalization through deterritorialization. On the other hand, tourism is promoting cross-border integration and interaction, which facilitates and promotes globalization. Appadurai (1996) recognizes tourism as an aspect of globalization. While describing globalization in terms of flow, he identifies five dimensions of global flows namely: ethnoscapes (the flow of people); mediascapes (the distribution of channels of information and images which flow from them); financescapes (the flow of capital); technoscapes (the flow of technology) and ideascapes (the flow of political ideologies, often of enlightenment or Western world view). All these global flows are embedded in tourism. Tourism depends on movement of people across national borders and is supported by a global media campaign. It creates financial markets and involves capital flow across international borders. Tourism relies on vast technological networks as is seen in flight and hotel reservation systems. And, finally, tourism facilitates the transfer of ideologies among culturally different people. Thus, each of these flows can be seen occurring within tourism (Macleod, 1999).

Tourism, now a universal practice, is flourishing rapidly to become one of the leading industries in the world today. It is established that tourism is a global activity and as such is part of much wider process of globalization. Globalization has direct impacts on deterritorialization of tourism destinations. First of all globalization of technology and the formalization of bilateral and multilateral relationship brought our world closer and facilitated tourism development. The geographical barriers were either lifted or became symbolical. Globalization actually led to what is also referred as the 'globalization of destination'. Shaw and Williams (2004) have discussed certain dimensions of globalization in tourism. Globalization of media promotes tourism by presenting images by satellite TV and internet to global audiences. Tourist destinations are advertised by tourism agencies especially via internet. Similarly tour operators promote travel within and outside the country. Global investment flows are creating global forms of tourism business like hotel chains, restaurant chains and integrated tourism companies. Another important dimension is the globalization of migration which recognizes the linkage between homeland and new areas of settlement boosting social tourism. Globalization in tourism implies that tourism businesses have ability to operate globally and many opted for a competitive strategy of internationalization. Global enterprises establish both global strategies and global market presence. Wood (2000) in his study of the Caribbean cruise tourism offers his view that it is the global economic restructuring that promotes new forms of the deterritorialization of capital, labour and touristic places. Wood also argued that globalization leads to increased internationalization of ownership and would steadily shake out and reduce the number of players in the industry. Of course, whilst tourism is affected by globalization, so too it enhances and sustains the process of globalization in terms of its own responses to the phenomenon (Wahab and Cooper, 2001). Changing business practices in response to the drivers of globalization in turn, sustain, extend and facilitate the process of globalization, and reshape the very boundaries that previously constrained them.

Globalization and Tourism: Implications

Modern globalization, a concept associated with late capitalism and built on a hegemony promoting neo-liberalism policies, is radically altering world economies and societies. The processes of deterritorialization, social interconnectedness, and acceleration are the significant features of globalization. These characteristics manifest themselves in all important domains of social activity including tourism. Although each facet of globalization is linked to the core components of globalization described above, each consists of a complex and relatively autonomous series of empirical developments, requiring careful examination in order to disclose the causal mechanisms specific to it (Held et al., 1999). Each manifestation of globalization also generates distinct conflicts and dislocations. Tourism is no exception to this. And that implies that globalization is a trend which tourism cannot get away from. Like globalization, tourism also depends on the movement of products, information and people around the globe. Tourism is distinct in the sense that it moves people to the 'product' rather than transporting a product to people. In the past one or two decades, a stable increase has been witnessed in international tourist flows, inter-regional and inter-organizational alliances, and foreign direct investment. These trends are especially prevalent in the developing world, largely because of their pristine nature, diverse culture, inexpensive goods and services, cheap labours, and other resources. Looking at the tremendous potential that tourism industry offers in the field of employment generation and foreign earning capacity, it has been identified by developing countries as their catalyst for economic development. In peripheral regions where alternative opportunities for development are limited, tourism provides a significant source of economic growth. Tourism is often seen as a tool for economic regeneration of depressed regions and also as an engine of development. The dynamics and highly differentiated expansion of tourism in developing countries over the last few years is reflected in changes in the ranking of developing countries in terms of tourist receipts and arrivals. All main tourism sources like WTO, WTTC, PATA have shown that the new global order offered has increased opportunity for many more less developed countries. Global tourism provides diverse experiences to postmodern tourists in quest for authentic and unique through contact with different cultures and original exotic environs. Long-.haul travel is increasingly bringing people from different cultural backgrounds in contact with each other and thus contributes to cultural revitalization. As a mechanism in the globalizing process, tourism creates new spaces for new cultural encounters and alliances. Therefore, international tourism is being extolled as a major force in bringing peace and understanding among nations. It is true that globalization plays a significant role in strengthening the economic benefits of tourism. In order to meet tourists' demand for newness, virgin areas are being brought under the tourism net much more easily than ever before. As a consequence, opportunities for local entrepreneurship and empowerment are created. With the increase in demand for heritage tourism and eco-tourism by the global age tourists, the conservation and preservation perspective becomes quite dominant. The focus of tourism agenda is shifted towards the revival, preservation and maintenance of cultural and natural tourist products.

Here one must not forget that tourism is not all positive, it incurs certain negative impacts too. Researches are replete with evidences where tourism has negatively affected the social, cultural and natural environment of the destination. It is already an established fact that tourism had brought pernicious and long-term damaging effects on indigenous peoples even prior to globalization. The present economic order further exacerbates and hastens these impacts. Before reposing all faith in the virtues of global tourism it becomes pertinent to understand the linkages between the flow of resources, capitals and tourism development. Various studies suggest that globalization is an uneven process where the affluent people have more access to the global flows. In other words, direction of these flows, be it capital, people or ideologies, is primarily from the developed world to the underdeveloped world. Tourism is inherently linked to this trend of globalization as international tourism; an expensive leisure pursuit which is largely a privilege of western world. Tourism is deeply rooted in history of colonization and unequal relations between people and regions. Not surprisingly, nearly all international tourists originate in the western world. In the light of this, tourism's flows are not equal. Tourism is, above all, the playground of unequal political and cultural forces that accompany the domination of the North over the South. The concept of 'the right to a vacation' in industrialized countries provides anyone with leisure time and the money to travel, an opportunity to experience another culture or part of nature. This creates numerous and serious repercussions for host destinations and their environments.

Globalization has at least two impacts on tourism development. First, the globalization of destination and touristic product and second, the tourism industry in the short and medium term will be mostly dominated by foreign players. Williams and Shaw (1998) suggest that the globalization of destination has been underway since the 1980s. This process was activated by two different forces. First, the foreign investment and inflow of labourers, who normally work as managers of tourist establishments, brought into the destination foreign practices. These practices affected not only the design of products but also the development and management of attractions. Second, in view of attracting foreign tourists, attractions and touristic products will be designed in the way foreign tourists would like to experience them. Authenticity would have to be compromised. In order to conform to tourist expectations, 'commodification' of cultural traits is done resulting in 'reconstructed ethnicity'. Religious rites and rituals, festivals, folk dances, local costumes, indigenous artifacts are reduced to just another product to be traded. Tourism is one globalizing influence that can initiate dramatic and irreversible changes within the cultures of host communities (Robinson, 1999). The tendency of large-scale tourism to dominate a whole regional economic base not only threatens but in many cases has also attacked the foundations of local self-reliance by destroying the traditional means of livelihood of local people. Johnston (2000) argues that tourism is the prime threat to indigenous homelands and cultures through its exploitation, dislocation and desecration. Unsustainable tourism has often had negative impacts on indigenous peoples and other local communities and ecosystems of which they are a part. In the globalized economy, many natural areas are targeted for eco-tourism. Eco-tourism promotes locally-owned enterprises, but with globalization and free trade, weak national capital often cannot compete with strong foreign companies. The lowering of trade barriers and facilitating unfettered foreign investment is time and again undermining the sustainability of smaller, locally-owned eco-tourism ventures in developing countries. According to

Anita Pleumarom (1999), 'Most of the profits are made by foreign airlines, tourist operators, and developers who repatriate them to their own economically more advanced countries. With increasing privatization and deregulation of the global economy, there are now great and justifiable concerns that Southern countries will lose out even more. More liberalization will lead to more foreign-owned tourist facilities and tour operations, and as a result, less income from tourism will remain in the local economy'. In the garb of eco-tourism, the environment is damaged and indigenous peoples' and local communities' human rights and rights of access and ownership to land and natural resources essential to food security, self-sufficiency and cultural identity are violated. The pervasive effects of globalized tourism can be seen in the way it has affected many indigenous peoples all over the world like the Masai tribe in Kenya. Besides loss of biodiversity, another threat that the expanding global tourism industry brings to indigenous communities is biopiracy, which often happens under the guise of eco-tourism.

Tourism is a globalizing process which assimilates the hosts and the visiting tourists. However, Robinson (1999) notes that there has been little evidence that tourism brings the world together. He further notes that source of conflict is often between persuasive and economically powerful developers and operators of the international tourist industry and the host country. The fundamental difference in goal of tourists and hosts, who are engaged in leisure and work respectively, engenders conflict between them. An even larger contradiction and potential threat, the demise of cultural diversity on a global scale due to acculturation, is emanating from global tourism and other global economic activity. Tourist-host interactions lead to acculturation process, which is more often an asymmetrical process resulting in absorption of host culture into the powerful tourist culture, thus fulfilling the central objective of globalization which is aimed at producing 'one homogenized world' with common standards and economic uniformity. The dissemination of Western products and lifestyle has been one result of tourism and is actively promoted by the WTO. There are apprehensions that if entertainment and communication industries prevail, then more fabricated culture, i.e., Hollywood and Disneyland will be forced on other countries and cultures while their rights to protect their own cultures will erode. The inclusion of cultural products in the elimination of barriers to trade and the increase in tourism will facilitate the growth of a tourist monoculture around the world. In a nutshell, one can agree with Ryan (1997) that globalization is a series of paradoxes in the tourism arena, which includes the paradox of micro-products competing in global market; standardization and uniqueness; and localization versus affiliation to international standards. These issues ultimately produce major challenges to many communities and regions that have undertaken tourism as a development strategy.

Conclusion

The whole dynamics of the present era can be summed up in one word that is globalization which is characterized by the escalating mobility of capital, people, ideas and information on a universal scale. Tourism and its associated economic activities are evidently not immune to such a wider context of the world economy. It is evident while analysing the interplay between tourism and globalization that both the phenomena are increasing the interconnectedness of the world. Tourism fits well within the context and scope of globalization. It advances the goals of globalization and it can be said that when tourism and globalization intersect, a compatible and positive relationship appears. However, the relationship becomes incompatible when the issue of sustainability is to be addressed. From a general standpoint, Trevor H.B. Sofield offers a vivid reminder that globalization has, at least, two divergent meanings, that of a process whereby some dominant culture will pervade every corner of the world and that of contact and juxtaposition among cultures formerly held apart, that seems to be supported by factual evolution. We need to wake up to this fear that if globalization will follow the first template, tourism itself would become implausible, for it thrives on its ability to offer diverse and unique attractions and experiences. The debate on uniformity versus diversity becomes more profound where tourism and culture are perceived as a means to achieve goals of both globalization and sustainability. Since tourism flourishes on localism, difference and continual negotiations of heritage, traditions and identities it has to strategically face the challenge of globalization which defies local differences and calls for homogenization.

Globalization is always a matter of degree and the velocity or speed of flows, movements, and interchanges across borders can vary in their magnitude, impact, or regularity. While cultural integration processes are taking place on the global level, there are increasingly pluralistic or polytheistic manifestations. Researches on these issues that have mainly stemmed from developing countries and regions suggest that various societies respond differently to the demands of global tourism. Examples are available where tourism has been instrumental in eradicating local traditions and bringing standardization of culture. Whereas, in some cases, tourism enhances place distinctiveness and is recognized as a force of heterogeneity. Many scholarly articles illustrate how small communities like Bali, with the help of local authorities while promoting tourism have simultaneously attempted to consolidate their cultural identity. A case study of the Mardi Gras celebration in New Orleans shows the resistance of local groups and individuals against the homogenizing effects of globalized tourism. It is interesting to note that at the same time, tourism is being used in keeping the core cultural trait intact. Such local efforts need to be multiplied manifold times to protect themselves from the perils of tourism.

As the dynamics of tourism and globalization extend to local rural areas, the role of communities, governments and voluntary agencies become significant. It should be acknowledged that nations, regions and people have rights to preserve their cultures from erosion by the dominant consumer culture. The state should determine the degree and magnitude of globalization with respect to tourism, keeping in mind the benefits of local residents. Well-organized and effective planning, administration, legislation and enforcement system is critical for any success in tourism. The impacts that globalization and tourism might have on various stakeholders need to be thoroughly assessed. To address pending challenges, researchers and planners for community tourism development need to build new theoretical frameworks and formulate proactive planning approaches that can mitigate the negative consequences while, at the same time, optimize the benefits that can result from the interaction between globalization and tourism. Tourism can be a force of globalization as well as localization only when 'tourism from below', which regards local people as the prime decision-makers, which respects local identities and which gives local people the right to accept as well as reject tourism, shall be considered seriously by all. Tourism based on consensus, participation and social equity can play a major role in realizing its promise of development and in effecting 'globalization from below'.

References

Adams, Henry (1931). *The Education of Henry Adams*. New York: Modern Library.

Appadurai, A. (1996). *Modernity at Large: Cultural Dimensions of Globalization*. Minneapolis, MN: University of Minnesota Press.

Ashkenas, R. Ulrich, T.D. Jick and S. Kerr (1995). *The Boundaryless Organisation*. San Francisco: Joosey Bass.

Boudreau, M.C., K.D. Loch, D. Robey and D. Straub (1998). 'Going Global', *Academy of Management Executive*, 12 (4): 120–28.

Cohen, Erik (1974). 'Who is Tourist?: A Conceptual Clarification', *Sociological Review*, 22 (4): 527–55.

Cooper, Chris and Stephen Wanhill (1998). *Tourism Development: Environmental and Community Issues*. New York: John Wiley and Sons.

Eriksen, Thomas Hylland (2001). *Tyranny of the Moment: Fast and Slow Time in the Information Age*. London: Pluto Press.

Falk, Richard (1999). *Predatory Globalization*. Cambridge, UK: Polity Press.

Giddens, Anthony (1990). *The Consequences of Modernity*. Stanford: Stanford University Press.

Harvey, David (1989). *The Condition of Postmodernity*. Oxford: Blackwell.

—— (1996). *Justice, Nature and the Geography of Difference*. Oxford: Blackwell.

Heidegger, Martin (1971). 'The Thing', in *Poetry, Language, Thought*. New York: Harper and Row.

Held, David, Anthony McGrew, David Goldblatt and Jonathan Perraton (1999). *Global Transformations: Politics, Economics and Culture*. Stanford: Stanford University Press.

Honey, M. (1999). *Ecotourism and Sustainable Development: Who Owns Paradise?* Washington, DC: Island Press.

Ingles, P. (2001). 'Performing Traditional Dances for Modern Tourists in the Amazon', in G. Santana (ed.), *Tourism in South America*. New York: Haworth Hospitality Press.

Johnston, A. (2000). 'Indigenous Knowledge and Rights into the Sustainability Equation', *Tourism Recreation Research*, 25 (2): 89–96.

Leung, P. (2002). 'Tourism and Economic Development of Less Developed Countries: The Case of Cambodia', *Tourism Recreation Research*, 27 (1): 91–102.

MacIntosh, A.J., T. Hinch and T. Ingram (2002). 'Cultural Identity and Tourism', *International Journal of Arts Management*, 4 (2).

Macleod, D.V.L. (1999). 'Tourism and the Globalization of a Canary Island', *Journal of the Royal Anthropological Institute*, 5 (3): 443–57.

Marx, Karl (1979). 'Communist Manifesto', in Robert Tucker (ed.), *The Marx–Engels Reader*. New York: Norton.

McLuhan, Marshall (1964). *Understanding Media: The Extensions of Man*. New York: McGraw Hill.

Pleumarom, A. (1999). *Ecotourism: An Ecological and Economic Trap for Third World Countries*. Penang: Third World Network.

Rees, William (2000). 'The Dark Side of the Force of Globalization', Parklands Institute Conference Paper, Vancouver: University of British Columbia.

Robinson, M. (1999). 'Cultural Conflicts in Tourism: Inevitability and Inequality', in M.D. Robinson, M. Robinson and P. Boniface (eds). *Tourism and Cultural Conflicts*. UK: CABI Publishers.

Robertson, R. (1992). *Globalization: Social Theory and Global Culture*. London: Sage.

—— (1995). 'Glocalization', in M. Featherstone, S. Lash and R. Robertson (eds), *Global Modernities*. London: Sage.

Ryan, C. (1997). Limits of Globalization: A Review of 'Globalization and Tourism' – The 46th Congress of the International Association of Scientific Experts in Tourism (AIEST), Rotorua, New Zealand, *Tourism Management*, September, 18 (3): 184–86.

Scheuerman, William E. (2004). *Liberal Democracy and the Social Acceleration of Time*. Baltimore: The Johns Hopkins University Press.

Shaw, G. and A. Williams (1994). *Critical Issues in Tourism: A Geographical Perspective*. Oxford: Blackwell, p. 143.

—— (2004). *Tourism and Tourism Spaces*. London: Sage.

Smeral, E. (1998). 'The Impact of Globalization on Small and Medium Enterprises: New Challenges for Tourism Policies in European Countries', *Tourism Management*, 19 (4): 371–80.

Sofield, Trevor H.B. (2001). 'Globalization, Tourism and Culture in Southeast Asia', in Peggy Teo, T.C. Chang and K.G. Ho (eds), *Interconnected Worlds: Tourism in Southeast Asia*. New York: Pergamon.

Wahab, S. and C. Cooper (2001). *Tourism in the Age of Globalization*. London: Routledge.

Waters, M. (1995). *Globalization*. London: Routledge.

Williams, A.M. and G. Shaw (1998). *Tourism and Economic Development*. England: John Wiley and Sons.

Wood, R.E. (2000). 'Caribbean Cruise Tourism: Globalization at Sea', *Annals of Tourism Research*, 27 (2): 345–70.

Index

Abraham, L., 72, 76
academic market place, 63
academic slums, 31
Adams, Henry, 305
Adams, K.M., 291, 293
adolescent family life education, 80
Ahir, D.C., 125
Akande, Wole, 262
Alexander, S.J., 83, 84
Aloysius, G., 115
Anandhi, S., 82
Appadurai, A., 306
Arora, V., 294
Ashby, E. and M. Anderson, 24
Ashkenas, R. Ulrich, T.D. Jick and S. Kerr, 304
author(s)
  as transformative intellectuals, 58
  composite skill of an, 53, 155

Babb, L.A., 115
Baber, Z., 115
Bang, R.A. et al., 76
Basham, Ardythe, 119
Bauman, Zygmunt, 143
Beckford, James, 114
Beltz, Johannes, 115
Berger, P. and F. Huntington, 261
Berger, Peter L., 18
Beteille, Andre, 13, 23, 24, 32, 33, 34, 35
Bhasin, S.K. and O.P. Aggarwal, 83
Bhattacharya, Sabyasachi, 13
Bhoite, Uttam and Anuradha Bhoite, 128
Bienen, Henry, 98
Binnie, Jon et al., 161
Bohra, N.N., 98
Boltanski, Luc and Eve Chapello, 6
book(s), 52, 66
  aims of, 53–54
  concept of, 54
  information-knowledge interface in, 53
  types of, 53, 54
Bose, Sumantra, 115
Bott, S. and S. Jejeebhoy, 76
Bottomore, T.B., 18
Boudreau, M.C., K.D. Loch, D. Robey and D. Straub, 304
Bourdieu, Pierre, 158
Brahminical theodicy, 184
Brahminism, 184, 185, 189
Brimnes, Niels, 150
Buber, Martin, 193
Buddhism, 124
Buddhist Society of India, 128

CARRHE, 10, 11
Casanova, José, 114
Chatterjee, Partha, 16, 17
Chaudhuri, Maitrayee, 3, 10, 11
Chauhan, C., 82
Chauhan, S.K. and S.L. Barua, 115
Choudaha, Rahul, 6
civil-military relations, 97
  in Asia, 99
  studies on, 98–99
Cohen, Erik, 305
Cohen, Stephen P., 98, 118
Coleman, S. and M. Craig, 292
commercialization of culture, 262, 291
compressed age
  concept of, 58
Connell, R.W., 73, 74
contemporary academic world, 14
contemporary global capitalism
  higher education in, 4
creativity
  and deviance, 218–19
  in Folk literature, 210–13
  in physical sciences, 216–17
  notion/concept of, 209, in the West, 209; in the Indian culture, 209–10
  time lags, 219–22
cultural globalization
  effect of, 262
cultural industry, 269
cultural lag
  concept of, 219
culture of intolerance, 61
culture
  notion of, 262

D'Souza, A.A., 80, 81, 83
Dadhich, N., 29
Daniel, Valentine E., 151
Das, B., 46, 123
Das, Chittaranjan, 195, 197, 198
Dattagupta, S., 29
Deb, Kushal, 18
democratization of education, 46
Devi, G., N.V. Reddy and M. Laxmanna, 83, 84
Dhiman, A., 82
Dirks, Nicholas B., 147
Dodge, Martin, Rob Kitchin and Chris Perkins, 158
Drene, Steve, 115
Dua, Vina, 115
Dube, Saurabh, 114, 115
Dussel, Enrique, 198

Edgell, Alvin G., 262
educational establishments
  in modern societies, objectives of, 53
educational policies
  in India, impact of globalization on, 47–49
educational towns, 32
Eldersveld, Samuel J., V. Jagannadham and A.P. Barnabas, 139
elite schools, 62

family life education, 80
  in schools, 82
  objectives of, 81
  perception of, unmarried men/women/youths regarding, 86–93
Forbes, G.S., 81, 84
Foucault, M., 71–72, 73

Ganatra, B., 76
Gelles, R.J. and M.A. Straus, 72
Giddens, Anthony, 77, 304, 305
Giri, Ananta Kumar, 194, 195
Global code of Ethics for Tourism, 290
global culture
  concept of, 264
global India
  higher education in, 4
globalization of tourism
  factors responsible for, 306

globalization
  and educational policies in India, 47–49
  and its implications for higher education in India, 44–47
  impact of, 216; on students, 62; on cultural and social identity of people, 164; on tourism development, 309–10
  phenomenon of, 304–6, 307
  tourism and an interface between, 306–7; implications of, 307–10
Gore, M.S., 122
Greenwood, D., 291, 297
Grewal, J.S., 115
Gupta, Dipankar, 115
Guru, Gopal and Anuradha Chakravarty, 115

Habermas, Jurgen, 8, 195, 196, 198
Hannon, Elliot, 4
Hansen, T.B., 115
Hardgrave, Robert, 114
Harvey, David, 305
Haynes, Jeff, 114
Heidegger, Martin, 198, 305
Held, David, Anthony McGrew, David Goldblatt and Jonathan Perraton, 308
higher education
  importance of, in the 21st century, 45–46
  in India, 4, 41, 44–45; in post-independence era, 31; quality deterioration in, 31–32; evolution of, 42–44; impact of globalization on, 44–47; changing trends in, 43
Hinduism, 184, 186
Hines, D.A. and K.J. Saudino, 72
Hohendahl, Peter Uwe, 8, 9
Hunter, James Davison and Joshua Yates, 7

Ignatieff, Michael, 143
India
  geographical profile of, 97–98
Indian Constitution, 42
  education in, 42
Indian society, 165, 221
  temples/sacred places in, 165
India-Pakistan relationship, 100
International Institute for Population Sciences (IIPS), 84, 85, 87, 88, 89, 92, 93
Irschick, Eugene F., 145
Islamic fundamentalism, 99
Israel, S., 84

Jaffrelot, Christophe, 47, 115, 118, 121, 123, 124
Jagannath Temple (Puri), 166
  cultural dynamics of, 169–81
Jammu & Kashmir, 101
  history of, 102
Janowitz, Morris, 98
Jayaram, N., 12, 34
Jejeebhoy, S.J., 76, 83
'jihad' movement, 99
John, M., 77
Johnston, A., 309
Jones, Kenneth W., 115
Joshi, Barbara R., 115
Joshi, P.C., 13
Juergensmeyer, M., 114, 115
Juma, Calestous, 9

Kabir, Humayun, 8
Kakar, S., 74
Kanungo, Pralay, 115
Karim, Afsir, 99
Karnik, 9, 10
Kaspersen, L.B., 74
Katju, Manjari, 115
Keer, D., 120, 124
knowledge society, 52
Kothari, Rajni, 14, 15, 19
Krishnan, K.V., 141, 142
Krishnaraj, Maithreyi, 14
Kulrija, Veena, 99
Kumar, Krishna, 100

Lahiri, A. et al., 291, 294
Lama, M.P., 293
Lauder, H. et al., 18
liberal education
  and sociology, links with, 17–19
  concept of, 4, 8
  importance of, 7
literature, 196
  and society, 196, relationship between, 193
Luckham, A.R., 98
Ludden, David, 115
Lynd, Robert S., 18

MacCannell, D., 292
Macionis, J., 72
Macleod, D.V.L., 307
Maffesoli, Michel, 157
Mahana, P.P., 116
Mahar movement, 119
  role of Ambedkar in, 119–24
Maharashtra, 116
  Buddhists in, 116
  Mahars of, 117–19
  neo-Buddhist Mahars of, 116–17
market-driven education industry, 4
market-ideology, 3
Marsman, J.C. and E.S. Harold, 84
Martin, Michel L., 98
Marx, Karl, 304
McLuhan, Marshall, 305
McQuail, D., 265, 268
Mead, G.H., 193, 196
military professionalism
  concept of, 98
Miller, Alice, 76
Mines, Diane P. and Nicolas Yazgi, 158
Mishra, S.K., 294
Misra, G. and R. Chandiramani, 74
Moscos, Charles C., 102
Moses, S. and C. Praveena, 84
Motihar, R., 82

Naik, J.P., 28, 29, 35
Nandy, Ashis, 14
Narayanan, M., 290
Narlikar, J.V., 29
Nash, R., 57
National Knowledge Commission (NKC), 35, 49–50
neo-Buddhism, 124
New Education Policy (1986), 35, 47
Nolte, J., 81
Nussbaum, Martha C., 8

Oberoi, H., 115
Oddie, G.A., 115
Olson, David R. and Nancy Torrance, 59
Omvedt, Gail, 115, 124, 133
Oommen, T.K. and Partha Mukherjee, 12
Oommen, T.K., 12
organized anarchy, 64
originality
  nature of, 216

Pandian, M.S.S., 115
Panikkar, Raimon, 193
Parhar, M., 33
Patwardhan, Sunanda, 116, 133
Perlmutter, Amos, 98
Picard, M., 296
Pleumarom, A., 310
postmodern culture, 269
postmodernism, 269
public institutions, 23
  in India, 23

Rabindra Sangeet industry, 266
Rabindra Sangeet, 261
  commercialization of, 264–68
  impact of globalization on, listeners, 262–64
  social transformation of, 267, 269
    effects of, 267–68; theoretical approaches to, 268–69
Raghavan, G.N.S., 25, 27

Raheja, G. and A. Gold, 74
Rajan, I.S., 75
Ramasubban, Radhika and B. Rishyasringa, 76
Rao, M.P., 84
Rao, Narayana, Sanjay Subramanium and David Shulman, 160
Rao, Sangeet, 264, 265
Rao, Suvarnalata, 264, 270
Raza, M. et al., 25
Rees, William, 304
religion, 113
  and reform movements, 114–15
  concept of, 113–14
  in India, 114, 168
  mobilization of, for dignity and development, 124–33
Ritzer, G., 269, 297
Robertson, R., 304
Robinson, M., 309, 310
Ryan, C., 306, 310

Saberwal, Satish, 12, 13, 150
Sakshi, 73
Sambaiah, Gundimeda, 151
Sarkar, Tanika, 115
Schelling, F.W.J., 8
security
  notion of, 97
Sen, Sudipta, 74
sex education, 80
  in India, 82, studies on, 83–84
  objectives of, 81
sexuality, 71
  in India, 72, studies on, 73–77
  meaning of, 71–72
Shaw, G. and A. Williams, 307
Sheller, Mimi and John Urry, 292
Shepherd, R., 297
Shrivastava, A.K., 295
Sikkim (a Himalayan state), 291, 292
  sustainable development and cultural continuity through tourism in, 292
Singh, Gurharpal, 115
Singh, Yogendra, 7, 12, 70, 164, 291
Sinha, S.K., 100, 102
Smeral, E., 304
Smith, Christian, 113, 114
social education
  role of textbooks in, 66
social exclusion
  in India, 46, impact of globalization on, 47
social science(s)
  role of, in India, 12
society, 196
  concept of, 196
sociology of textbooks, 52, 55, 60, 62, 67, 68
sociology
  and liberal education, 17–19
Sodhi, G. and M. Verma, 76
sponsored research, 16
Srivastava, S., 73, 74
Stella, A. and A. Gnanam, 32
Stobdan, P., 100
Straus, M. et al., 76
Strydom, Piet, 197
Sunder Rajan, R., 196

Tagore, Rabindranath, 43
technical education
  in contemporary India, 45
temple tradition
  study of, need for, 166–69
terrorist groups
  in South Asia, 99
textbook(s), 52, 53, 54, 60, 67
  consciousness produced by, 68
  in sociological sense, 54, 61
  stages in preparation of, 64–65
textual institutions, 59
Thakor, H.G. and P. Kumar, 83
Thapan, Meenakshi, 72
Thomas, Prince Mathews and Deepak Tiwari, 26
Tickoo, C., 24

time
  notion/concept of, 208, in the traditional Hindu culture, 214–16
Touraine, Alain, 196
tourism sector/industry
  in India, 290
tourism, 290, 291, 310
  and globalization, 306–10
  sustainable development and cultural continuity through, 292–300
tourist reflexivity, 292
touristic images, 291
transformative intellectuals, 58
transmodernity, 198
Turner, J.H., 268, 269
TV
  in rural Rajasthan, memories of, 273–88

Uberoi, J.P.S., 195
Uberoi, Patricia, 12, 13
UGC, 30, 32
university system
  in India, 25, 35, 44–45
university(ies), 4, 10
  as a public institution, 25–26
  changing profile of, 4
  in India, historical background of, 24–25; in research orientation, 26–31
  spatial aspects of, 32–35
Unni, J.C., 83
Urry, J., 290, 291
'useful' social science
  need for, 15

Vance, C.S., 71
Vatsayan, Kapila, 193
Vella, S., 75
Venkatachalapathy, A.R., 140
Vijayakumar, B., 27
Visvanathan, Susan, 159

Wahab, S. and C. Cooper, 307
Wakhlu, Somnath, 109
Waters, M., 305
Weeks, J., 71, 72, 73
West, P. and J. Carrier, 299
Wilkinson, T.S. and M.M. Thomas, 115
Williams, A.M. and G. Shaw, 309
Wood, R.E., 304, 307

Yashwantha, C.P., 83
youth sexuality, 70
  contextualizing the issue with emerging global changes, 71

Zavos, John, 115
Zelliot, Eleanor, 115, 118, 119, 126
Zimmermann, Ekkart, 98